THE SHOTGUN:
A SHOOTING INSTRUCTOR'S HANDBOOK

Gunfitting: The Quest for Perfection

The Shotgun

A Shooting Instructor's Handbook

MICHAEL YARDLEY

Foreword by Chris Cradock

• THE •
SPORTSMAN'S
PRESS

IN MEMORIAM
Chris Cradock
1911 – 1999

First published in the UK in 2001
by The Sportsman's Press, an imprint of Quiller Publishing Ltd

Second impression 2005

British Library Cataloguing-in-Publication Data

A catalogue record for this book
is available from the British Library

ISBN 0 948253 71 1

Printed in England by The Bath Press Ltd

The Sportsman's Press

An imprint of Quiller Publishing Ltd
Wykey House, Wykey, Shrewsbury, SY4 1JA
Tel: 01939 261616 Fax: 01939 261606
E-mail: info@quillerbooks.com
Website: www.swanhillbooks.com

Contents

List of Plates

1 *(top)* One must get into the habit of automatically extending the trigger finger along the trigger guard when handling guns.
(bottom) Taking a gun from the rack.

2 *(top)* An instructor must become familiar with proof marks.
(bottom) Old guns may have very thick barrel walls or weak spots created by water penetrating the rib.

3 *(top)* Shooting instructors must continually emphasise the importance of sustaining visual contact with the target.
(bottom) This young lady's corrected vision has been no barrier to shooting success.

4 *(top)* You can just make out the shot string on the way to the target in this picture.
(bottom) A nice style – 'relaxed concentration'.

5 *(top)* I like the whole demeanour of this skeet shot.
(bottom) I recommend left-handed pistol shooting as cross training for clay shooting.

6 *(top)* I favour using the pad of the finger on the trigger rather than the first joint as is sometimes recommended.
(bottom) This is my completed mount.

7 *(top)* Take pride in all your own shooting.
(bottom) Taking a high bird off the rear foot in the Churchill style.

8 *(top)* Group instruction is always a challenge.
(bottom) Ian Cawthorne instructing a game shot.

9 *(top)* Although this skeet shooter's stance is very wide, he looks in balance, well focused and as if he had found his rhythm.
(bottom) Double gunning requires balance and rhythm, not to mention an empathy with one's loader.

10 *(top)* Note my position here. We are both concentrating.
(bottom) A good professional in action.

11 *(top)* Trap shooting requires that one learns a cycle of concentration and relaxation.
(bottom) Clay shooting can be a great sport for the disabled.

12 *(top)* A student instructor watched by Alan Rose.
(bottom) Good shooting technique should combine disciplined preparation, economy of movement and relaxation.

13 *(top)* Arnie Palmer, after winning the White Gold Cup.
(bottom) A student instructor demonstrates foot position.

14 *(top)* A study in concentration.
(bottom) Never forget that the purpose of recreational sport – shooting or any other – is to have fun.

15 *(top)* The circle test.
(bottom) Frontal view of the completed mount.

16 *(top)* Jamie, then aged 11, under instruction from David Etherington.
(bottom) Air-rifle shooting under proper supervision is the ideal way to introduce a young person to shooting.

17 Alan Rose in two guises with the same client – gentle guide and serjeant major.

18 *(top)* Classic cross-firing.
(bottom) Many young shots and many women arrive for lessons with guns which are too low in the comb.

19 *(top)* All guns should be tested at a pattern plate for point of impact.
(bottom) Cartridge cases on top of the trap house indicate holding points for the common five-point system.

20 *(top)* The instructor's hand plays a crucial role.
(bottom) Chris Cradock instructing a left-hander.

21 *(top)* The Beretta 682 used by Chris Cradock for instruction.
(centre) A Beretta 303.
(bottom) Gunfitting in the Kemen factory in the Basque country of Spain.

22 *(top)* The Webley .410 bolt-action gun.
(bottom) The Kennedy Competition, typical of a new generation of competition guns.

23 *(top)* One of Alan Rhone's excellent Vari-Combs.
(bottom) This stock has been altered for a female shot.

24 *(top)* The instructor has come down to the boy's level.
(bottom) The instructor has clearly achieved a bridge of communication with this young shot.

Acknowledgements

Writing any book is a prolonged task which requires the forbearance of family and friends. If one is putting time into a book, one is probably failing to put it in somewhere else. In the case of this project, the losers have been my children. I take this opportunity to apologise to them for my frequent absences in the office and in the field. Perhaps one day they will read this and smile. I shall now proceed more conventionally.

This work has required a great deal of research – several years more than originally envisaged – and has led me to seek assistance from many quarters. In particular, I owe very special thanks to the late Chris Cradock, who died before he could see this book in published form. Apart from the generous preface which he contributed, Chris encouraged and advised me throughout the project. Nothing was too much trouble for him; he was quite extraordinarily generous with his time and effort. Chris was one of the great authorities of the shooting world, and the work I present here may accurately be described as 'after Cradock'.

I must also offer special thanks to all those who kindly read the manuscript (or parts of it) and offered their expert comments: Paul Roberts, Alan Rhone, Peter Croft, Piers Crump, David Becker, John Kenny, Richard Rawlingson, Trevor Scott, Ian Charlton, Phil Thomson, Bill Harding, Chris Potter, Ken Davies, Richard Law, Phil Boakes, Graham Morris, Willy Cole, Nigel Teague, Stuart Clarke, Dave Allen, Chris Symonds, Jack Montgomery, John Resteghini, Bernard Cole, Russell Wilkin, and, not least, Jan Stevenson (who, as ever, rescued me at a critical moment) and Andy Riva (who was responsible for many of the illustrations).

Graeme Rimer and Frederick Wilkinson at the Royal Armouries have supplied definitive answers to historical questions. Bob Pitcher of the London Proof House, and Roger Hancox of the Birmingham Proof House have provided invaluable and most friendly assistance, as has have Lieutenant Colonel J. B. Gunson and Dr David Leeming of the Royal Military College of Science, Shrivenham, David Penn and Paul Cornish of the Imperial War Museum, Dr Roger Giblin of University College, London, and Professor Mike Cooley of Cogswell and Harrison.

My role of honour within the gun and allied trades also includes: Dick Ward, Adrian Weller, Gordon Swatton, Jim Spalding, David Peel, Vere Richardson, David Marx, Carl Bloxham, Hugh Donnelly, Alan Rose, Michael Rose, John Bidwell, Chris Austyn, Chris Miles, Kevin Gill, John Batley, Alan Crewe, Andy Castle, Garry Kindley, Tobias Howard-Willis, Barry Simpson, Ian Bradbury, Tony Kennedy, Mark Schimchick, Joel Etchen, Leo and Joan Cerar, Frank Wyant, Fred Buller, Robert Nash, Luke Nash, Peter Blaine, David Maynard, Robert Frampton, George Wallace, Pat Lynch, Roger Horsnell, Ron King, D. R. Maynard, Muntaz Al-Daftary, Brian Jackson, Steve Denny, David Palmer, Mike Ross, Tim Emmenegger, Randy Mitchell, Ken Gagnon, Karl Bueggeln,

John Carlin, Tracey Dines, Roger Bryan, Litt's of Newport, Norman Cooper, Roy and Sally Sisler, Morris Bueneman, James Booth and David Bontoft. I would also like to thank Peter Page, former director of the CPSA, and John Roll-Pickering, former secretary of the BFSS.

Ian Paddon of the Environmental Health and Community Services Division of Colchester Borough Council has supplied important information on noise as it relates to shooting. Vision is crucial to shooting, and my knowledge in this area was considerably advanced by Dr Bruce Evans of the Institute of Optomentry; Dr Imran Akram of Colchester General Hospital; Simon Goldsmith, FBCO; Dr. Charles Gilchrist, Sam Cherry, Susan Decot and Mrs. Gemma Best, BSc, FCOptom. The nutrition, sleep and exercise chapter has benefitted from the input of Dr Phillip Letton, BM, MRCGP and Fiona Gosling, SRP. In the world of sporting journalism, I extend my thanks to Pat Farey, James Marchington, Mike Barnes, Julian Murray Evans and Graham Downing.

Mark Dolman and Ian Macgregor provided the opportunity to shoot far more game than I normally would in a season; because of this kindness, a variety of points connected with live quarry shooting could be verified in the field. Morlin and Harry Yardley made a splendid job of the bibliography. My editor, Sue Coley, has, once again, been a model of patient and thorough professionalism. Without all their support I should never have completed this project.

Finally, whilst taking full responsibility for what is written here, I want to acknowledge the particular influence upon my work of certain living authors: Bob Brister, Geoffrey Boothroyd, Michael McIntosh, David Butler, Ian Crudgington and David Baker all come to mind, and also to note my debt to some of the greats who have passed on: Colonel Peter Hawker, Dr. J. H. Walsh, Elmer Keith, John Nigel George, Percy Stanbury, Gordon Carlisle, Fred Etchen, Major Sir Gerald Burrard, Jack O'Connor, Macdonald Hastings, Frank Little, John Brindle, Don Lutz, Major Hugh Pollard, W. W. Greener, Robert Churchill, G. T. Garwood (Gough Thomas) and Ed Scherer. They live on in print, and in the new work they inspire.

Foreword by Chris Cradock

Mike Yardley's name must be familiar to many sportsmen. He is well known as a shooting instructor and as a writer and broadcaster. Educated both in this country and the U.S.A., he has a London University psychology degree and is also a graduate of the Royal Military Academy, Sandhurst. The author of seven books, he has been a regular contributor to *Shooting Times* and many other magazines, has formal qualifications in shooting instruction from the CPSA, NRA, NSRA, BFSS and is a Fellow of the Association of Professional Shooting Instructors.

I have read this new book of his with much interest. I am much impressed, not only with the comprehensiveness of its subject matter, but with the manner in which the safe shooting knowledge of its author is marshalled and presented so succinctly. I have shot with Yardley at various clay clubs whilst testing guns and I have found that he preaches safe gun handling at all times. His advice is impressive. His injunction on safety should be followed at all times by users of the shotgun: *If you do not wish to destroy it, don't point your gun at it.* Words of wisdom indeed! Many years ago, R. Payne Gallwey wrote on similar lines, 'If guns are pointed safely at all times, there can be no accidents...' We all must ensure our guns are always pointed safely. Then if such a gun *is* fired accidentally, the shot charge can injure no one. This precept is similar to the advice contained in Beaufoy's famous poem, 'Never never let your gun, pointed be at any one.'

Yardley takes his subject, guns and the better teaching of safe, accurate shooting very seriously. He covers in depth most aspects of guns and their safe handling. This is a vast subject and it speaks well of Yardley's wide practical experience that he can and does cover his subject both succinctly and well. Yet never is he in any way boring. The book is worth reading by any shooter, regardless of whether he shoots a lot or a little. It is a quarry worth mining; the answers to many shotgun shooting problems are to be found in its pages. The photos and diagrams are wide ranging and clear. There is much that will be of interest to any up-and-coming instructor. Indeed, I can wholeheartedly recommend its purchase to anyone interested in developing better, safer shotgun handling and shooting technique.

Introduction

Shooting instruction, like shooting, is a skill which must be learned. At least two shooting organisations and two other groups in Britain now run courses for would-be shotgunning instructors. The situation in the United States is much the same: more people than ever before want to qualify as instructors. In spite of the increasing interest in the subject, no basic text has been available for those attending courses, or indeed for anyone with an interest in becoming a shooting instructor, amateur or professional. The plethora of books on shooting is no substitute: most fail to consider shooting from the instructor's perspective. This volume is therefore designed to fill a specific gap, having noted that, I hope it may be useful to anyone who wants to consider his or her own shooting in more depth.

This is, necessarily, a work of synthesis. It brings together my own experiences as a shooting instructor, competitive shot and sporting writer, with those of many others. It has been written from a personal perspective but I have made the greatest efforts to be as objective as possible. Where differences of opinion exist, they are clearly stated in the text and various schools of thought presented (for example, all the major shooting methods are considered in the sections on shooting technique).

The contents should present few surprises to the experienced. As one might expect, there are chapters here on safety, on teaching method, on shooting technique, on gunfitting and other topics of interest to existing or potential shooting instructors (it is my intention that a companion volume will consider the technical development and history of shotguns and their ammunition). Readers may be surprised at the space devoted to some subjects, but I would note that a shooting instructor requires a depth of knowledge beyond that of the average sporting shot.

There may be opposition to this book in certain quarters. It could be said by some (and with good reason) that there are too many new instructors of mediocre or poor ability intruding on what is, commercially, a limited market. Hence, it might be suggested that a text book of instruction will aggravate the problem by giving away too many 'trade secrets'. I would counter such potential criticism by noting that a secretive attitude to instructional method, or indeed, shooting, serves no useful purpose and hinders the development of a scientifically based profession and sport. Does a textbook of surgery turn the possessor into a surgeon? Of course not. No more does a book on shooting instruction turn the reader into a shooting instructor. My intention is not to create a book of absolute answers but to get the reader thinking about shooting – their own and other people's – more analytically.

There is so much confusion concerning the status and training of amateur and professional instructors that is worth trying to dispel some of it before proceeding further. Those who may legitimately call themselves instructors fall into several, very different, categories of competence. A simple classification system might recognise at least three:

1. The (clay) club instructor – (often called a coach) is a part-timer who has sufficient ability and knowledge to set beginners off on the right, safe track. He or she will also be able to clear up many basic problems among more experienced shooters. The club instructor will have reasonable knowledge, infectious enthusiasm, a friendly-but-firm manner, and enough shooting ability to demonstrate basic technique well. He or she may have attended a formal coaching course, but not necessarily, and may also, but not necessarily, be an experienced competitor. A good club instructor will be well aware of his or her own limitations. (Note that there is an important distinction between the *coach* and the *instructor* although the words may sometimes be used as if they were synonymous. The instructor is responsible for the primary teaching of technique - safety, how to stand, how to apply forward allowance etc. The coach's role is to refine technique, to push the individual to his limits and to improve self-discipline and psychology. The two roles may be combined in the same person. Although the word coach is applied to club level qualifications, in precise terms the office of coach is usually a more advanced one than that of instructor; to be an effective coach one must have taken on the skills of the instructor first.)

2. The intermediate level instructor is usually an amateur, but may also work professionally (for example, on so-called 'Company Days'). He or she will have considerable instructional experience of clay shooting, broad knowledge and shooting skills sufficient to demonstrate all or nearly all types of shot *well*. The intermediate level instructor will be able to undertake most instructional tasks with most shooters. He may well have attended one or more formal courses of instruction and is probably an experienced clay competitor and live quarry shot.

3. The instructor-gunfitter is almost always a full-time professional (few others would have the opportunity to gain the requisite experience). The instructor gunfitter has a storehouse of knowledge based on at least five years of teaching experience. He will have learnt how to deal with almost any sort of person (including the chronically awkward and the advanced competitor), and will be able to demonstrate any sort of shot (most from either shoulder). The instructor gunfitter will be able to 'see the shot' on nearly all occasions and must be able to undertake just about any instructional task relating to clay or live quarry shooting. In particular, he or she will be a Master Gunfitter capable of dealing with all the anomalies of individual technique, physique and vision. The routes to becoming an instructor-gunfitter are various; most would involve something akin to apprenticeship under an acknowledged master. There can be no substitute for practical experience.

Within each of the above categories, one might also note sub-categories and variations in individual skill and interest. One instructor will specialise in game shooting, another will be more oriented towards trap shooting, a third will be devoted to skeet, and another will focus on sporting. This is to be expected, especially at the advanced level. However, I would also make the point that all good instructors should have a sound general knowledge of shooting and its various disciplines.

The scope of this volume is, necessarily, broad. The reader will find here the knowledge which I wish someone had given me when I began my instructing career. Gaining experience is the Catch 22 of shooting instruction. There is no full-time degree or HND course for the potential shooting instructor: all the courses currently offered are short and designed to be supported by experience in the field. This may depress some, but the aspirant instructor should never forget that having the motivation to acquire this experience is part of the rite of passage to becoming an instructor. And, happily, there are ways around the problem of gaining experience if you are determined enough. You can act as an assistant or 'button presser' to an experienced teacher, or make yourself useful to him in other ways such as trapping (indeed, many of the most respected professional instructors began as trappers). You can attend courses (not just in shooting and shooting instruction – from which there are many to choose – but in first aid, teaching practice and sports science and psychology). Generally, you can make an effort to consider your own shooting and that of others from a more analytical point of view; and you can take the opportunity to increase your knowledge whenever, and however, it arises: by reading, by visiting gunsmiths, by learning new shooting disciplines and by going to competitions (or indeed any shoot) to spectate. The good instructor, like the good shot, is skilled at watching.

This book is written for people who want to explore and teach shooting because they love the sport and enjoy the teaching process. It is for people who acknowledge that they do not know everything yet and who enjoy learning (Chris Cradock noted on the manuscript of this book, 'Those who are satisfied with their knowledge as is are brain dead!'. He made that comment after more than seventy years of shooting experience). One of the great pleasures of instruction is the revelatory moment: 'I've never noticed that before'. I have lost count how many times I have had that thought when watching someone shoot. It always indicates to me how much more there is to discover.

Just as an instructor must acknowledge that there is always something more to learn, he (or she) must also maintain a flexible, non-dogmatic, approach. Part of this is the ability to teach more than one method or style of shooting. Too many otherwise good instructors attach themselves to one system alone and refer to anything else as if it were a religious heresy. Although some methods are more generally applicable than others, no method suits absolutely everyone for all their shooting. To stick to one method alone is, ultimately, lazy. It ensures that some clients will not be well served.

If we are honest, we all have a favourite method or methods – I have written another book, *Positive Shooting,* on my favourite style for sporting clays (and it is mentioned here too) – but all the well known methods, my own included, are nothing more than a starting point for developing individual style. Moreover, many experienced shots use a variety of methods, consciously or unconsciously, when tackling different targets. One needs to learn which methods suit which people under which circumstances. One also needs the knowledge and confidence to combine aspects of different methods or to create new ones to suit the client.

Precision and economy in communication are fundamentals of good instruction. One needs a straightforward approach and a plan of instruction which will ensure nothing essential is missed. Clients must be given clear principles which they can take away and apply for themselves. To formulate these requires a thorough understanding of the ideas and skills which are being taught, and a most careful consideration of the individual client's needs. Everything that is not to the point must be eliminated. The best instructors use few words, but those words are well chosen and effective.

Does one need to be a good shot to teach shooting? There is no guarantee that the crack shot will be a good teacher. Nevertheless, is important for a would-be shooting instructor to be able to shoot with confidence and competence. The shooting ability required to instruct will depend on the instructional situation, but the crucial point is that the instructor must be able to demonstrate to a standard significantly above the ability level of the student (though he may use this skill but rarely). Nothing is guaranteed to lose the confidence of a client faster than a hashed demonstration by his instructor. As far as top level competitive coaching is concerned, first class shooting skills will obviously be of benefit, not least because they will allow for the instructor to fully understand the pressure his charge is under. One of the first duties of a potential instructor, therefore (before even considering any formal training), is to improve his or her own shooting. Too many would-be instructors arrive on training courses with wholly inadequate basic skills. Moreover, all student instructors should re-learn to shoot off the wrong shoulder. This will help them to demonstrate (but not to show off) in the future and, as importantly, will give them the knowledge of what it feels like to be a beginner again.

Finally, some say that shooting instructors are born rather than made. It us true that some instructors have more natural ability than others – some people are naturally better at communicating and getting on with others, some have less difficulty in diagnosing faults. Nevertheless, I believe that almost anyone with reasonable shooting experience, a love of the sport and dedication can be turned into a competent shooting instructor (just as 95 per cent of people can be turned into competent shots). There is no great mystery; what really counts is practical experience, sound theoretical knowledge and a great deal of hard work.

MICHAEL YARDLEY
Colchester
January 2001

CHAPTER 1

Clay Shooting Safety

The first aim of a shooting instructor is to produce a safe shot. The second is to produce a competent marksman or woman. Although both are related, the first aim is much more important than the second. The same discipline and control that promote safe gun handling also promote better shooting. The importance of safety training can hardly be overstressed. The habits you instil in your students will stay with them for life. Teach them well and they will be a credit to you and our sport; be sloppy or relaxed in your approach and you will be sowing the seeds for future tragedy.

As a shooting instructor, your immense moral and legal responsibilities do not end with your clients. You are also responsible for the safety of trappers, groundsmen, spectators and other members of the public. Moreover, your own life and well-being are dependent upon the practices you adopt. If you make a mistake, you can die, go to prison or live with someone else's death or wounding on your conscience. As one famous instructor put it, 'You cannot afford to make the same mistake once'.

Your first priority is to develop the right attitude, I call it the Safe Mind Set. It begins with the acceptance of two related thoughts:

An accident can happen to me.

I must always be active in preventing it.

Having accepted personal fallibility (which does not come easily to some men) and having contracted with oneself to be ever-vigilant, we may note that the Safe Mind Set also requires: knowledge (good motivation and vigilance are not enough by themselves), training (so that knowledge leads to effective action) and specific rules (which are a constant reminder of what we ought to do).

Two of the most important rules in shooting are:

1 **Assume all guns are loaded: if you do not wish to destroy it, do not point your gun at it.**
2 **Always check or 'prove' a gun unloaded: when it is passed to you, when you pick it up, when you put it down or when you pass it to someone else.**

Let us call these Golden Rules 1 and 2. Live by them (or die by ignoring them). If you are reading this as a potential instructor or as an experienced shot, they should already be second nature. They should, of course, be drummed into the heads and hands of your students at every available opportunity. It is good practice to say 'empty' or 'clear' whenever you prove a gun unloaded because it ensures your care will be noticed.

Never let an infringement of these rules slip by unnoticed or, indeed, any other infringement of basic safety procedure. Be aware too that most people who shoot would claim to follow the Golden Rules meticulous but in practice many, indeed most, do not. The problem is that many shots are insufficiently aware of their actions. They break these rules, and others, without even realising it. Why? In simple terms, because they are sloppy. If we go a bit deeper we might note that:

- **They have not accepted their capability to cause or suffer an accident.**
- **They have an unrealistically high opinion of their skills.**
- **They arc not as aware or as in control as they think.**
- **Their knowledge is incomplete and poorly integrated with their actions.**
- **Their motivation is inadequate.**
- **They have not bothered to train.**

Bluntly put, they are accidents waiting to happen. When knowledge and action are part of the same whole – as they will inevitably become when you accept your fallibility and determine to improve your knowledge and discipline through study and training – you approach a safer condition (you can never be absolutely safe). Safety will become an unconscious as well as a conscious activity. Moreover, the special situations with which the instructor must sometimes deal, may more easily and more confidently be confronted. Even Golden Rules can have exceptions.

In gunfitting and master eye diagnosis, for example, it may be permissible for a student to point a proven empty gun at the instructor, breaking Rule 1 (just about the worst sin in shooting in any other circumstance). However, this action must be at the instructor's stated request and after both instructor and student have proven the weapon unloaded together. (There has been some debate about this practice. After considering all the issues, I feel that there is no practical alternative to the procedure, although mirrors and closed circuit television have been suggested. Direct gun pointing tells the instructor a great deal about eye/rib relationship and is acceptable provided the obvious dangers are respected. Any alternative would require equipment which is not always to hand.)

As far as Rule 2 is concerned, it may legitimately be breached when an instructor is dealing with a beginner and places the butt of a gun in the student's shoulder as an aid to good gunmounting. The rule must also be broken when the instructor or anyone else is forced to take charge of a loaded gun in an emergency: for example, when a misfire or mechanism failure occurs (Golden Rule 1 being applied throughout of course).

In such cases, the instructor remains in control, is still committed to safety and is thus conscious of the weapon's potential throughout. The breach of one or other Golden Rule is specific and deliberate. A layered system of safety is still in place (see below). I have noted these exceptions, not to diminish the importance of the Golden Rules – their application is critical – but to show that one's attitude to safety is more important than any specific injunction. Rules alone will not protect you, nor can rules be devised to cover every situation.

Safety must become part of you. Common sense always applies.

The layer principle

A layer approach to safety may be described as a series of checks and procedures which have evolved to detect an unsafe situation, even if there has been
a failure at an earlier level, or if a layer has been deliberately breached. The first
and most important level of safety is one's general mental attitude, as already
described: contracting to be safe, putting real effort into vigilance and accepting human and, most especially, personal fallibility. Next, we might note
Golden Rule 1: keep the gun pointing in a safe direction at all times. If everything else fails, an accidentally discharged gun will not cause injury if you
adhere to that all important principle. (The muzzles of an aware shot's gun
seem to behave magnetically: they are always controlled in a safe direction no
matter how the gun is otherwise being manoeuvred.)

Supporting Golden Rule 1 is the practice of keeping one's fingers away from
the trigger at all times when one is not shooting or dry-firing in a known safe
and permissible direction. Golden Rule 2 also supports Golden Rule 1. Its
basic action, checking the chambers, may be repeated whenever the person
holding the gun thinks appropriate as well as in those circumstances when it is
an obligatory action as defined in the rule (i.e. when it is passed to you, when
you pick it up, when you put it down or when you pass it to someone else).

Shaping behaviour

You must maintain the right attitude and adhere to the Golden Rules all the
time, especially when you know a gun is unloaded and when no-one is watching you. If you apply safe gun handling rules habitually, you will be programming yourself to be safe: an inner red light will be switched on, if you ever
breach a rule unintentionally. In the context of conditioning – learning – psychologists speak of *shaping* behaviour. You must shape your own and that of
your students by constant repetition of safe practice, positive reinforcement of
safe gun handling and immediate negative reinforcement of any suspect, or
overtly dangerous behaviour. It will come to the point when anything other
than safe behaviour feels wrong. Internalising safety, making it an unconscious
activity as well as a conscious one, is one of the great goals of safety training.

Much the same may be said of other basic gun handling rules: they must be
a habit if you are to evolve into a safer gun handler and the motivation to apply
them must, primarily, be internal. What are these basic rules? We might summarise (and the list is not intended to be exhaustive):

- Be careful.
- Keep the finger off the trigger unless firing.
- Keep the gun unloaded.
- Keep it open.
- Check for obstructions whenever you prove a gun empty and again before
  loading.
- Be certain of your target before firing.
- If in doubt, stop! and think.

The safe shot will always try to build up as many safety layers as possible. All but one of the rules above are towards the same end: avoiding someone being shot by an accidentally loaded gun. Rules and layers are not quite synonymous, it should be noted. One rule may cause you to repeat the same action many times, and thus create more than one layer of safety.

The application of the layer system should become part of your normal behaviour. We may not always be able to have as many layers as we would like, but it is always possible to achieve multi-level safety. Thus when someone needs to point a gun at me for gunfitting purposes or master eye diagnosis as mentioned earlier – clearly a less than ideal situation from the safety standpoint – I always make sure that the client and I have proven the gun empty together (two pairs of eyes are better than one), that I have inserted my fingers into the chambers, and that the gun is closed and the safety applied immediately there-after. If I know the action of the gun will not be damaged by dry firing without snap caps, I also will 'fire' it into the ground before applying the safety. (I never introduce snap caps into the procedure because of the potential danger of con-fusion.) My working principle is to reduce the risk whenever possible by increasing the layers.

Never short-cut safety. Do not be afraid of double-checking. *Never assume.* All this is easily said, but to remain vigilant all the time, every day, all day, at the end of the day, when you are tired, when you feel unwell, when you are cold and wet, requires the greatest effort and discipline. However, the hard fact remains that the alternative to constant vigilance may well be terminal. Shooting accidents do happen. In my experience, anyone who is working with guns long enough will one day experience an accidental or, as they call it in the Army, negligent discharge.[1] If you have practised good safety habits until they are second nature, the probability is very high that the day your gun goes off unexpectedly, it will be pointing in a safe direction.

Beware the phantom cartridge

As one very experienced instructor once told me, 'Guns grow cartridges'. He was involved in a case where a semi-automatic shotgun was left, action-open, on the grass by its owner. Another person bent over it to have a look and, unwittingly, allowed a cartridge to tumble from his breast pocket into the open chamber. Luckily another instructor saw this and, when the observer left, replaced the live cartridge with a snap cap just to see what would happen. The owner returned, picked the gun up and failed to observe Golden Rule 2. His potentially fatal assumption was that no-one had interfered with his gun in his absence. When the instructor intervened and pointed out that the gun was loaded, the owner was profoundly shocked. The moral, of course, is never to assume (we might also note that the gun should not have been left unattended and it would also have been prudent if a breech plug or handkerchief had been inserted into the chamber).

It is interesting to note that in the sports of Practical Pistol shooting (history in the UK, since the handgun bans of the late 1990s), Practical Rifle shooting and Practical Shotgun shooting – the so-called 'action disciplines' – there has

never been a fatal accident. Safe gun handling, and specifically muzzle awareness, are the focus of much more attention in these activities than in the conventional shotgunning disciplines. The practical sports appear more dangerous
(and have attracted some unkind comments from those unfamiliar with them),
but are statistically safer because everyone concerned is so aware of the potential for accident. In shotgun shooting by contrast, people are frequently far too
relaxed in their attitude to safety (although they may believe otherwise).
Consequently, people get killed and maimed with sporting shotguns every year.
The danger is underestimated, I believe, because most non-fatal cases receive
no publicity. This is good for the reputation of the sport, but not so good for
the safety awareness of participants who might otherwise be motivated to take
even greater care. The idea of an accident is still far too remote to most shotgun users.

Statistically, we are still safer than many (indeed, the great majority) of sports
– fishing and football are significantly more dangerous. But safety in sporting
shotgun shooting could be improved. My work as a shooting consultant to the
legal profession often requires me to comment on shotgun accidents which
occurred because common sense and the most basic rules were breached. I
have yet to be asked to comment on an accident which could not have been
prevented by observance of Rule 1. The average, untrained shot points his or
her gun at other human beings far more often than one might expect. If you
doubt this, spend some time in a gun shop or in the car park of a game or clay
shoot.

Instructional safety and control
The first thing to be said here is, 'Brief your clients about safety before you let
them touch a gun'. Be firm, but do not be aggressive or arrogant of manner.
Show students why they need to be concerned about the subject. When
explaining, do it clearly and concisely, starting with the two golden rules.
Demonstrate the power of the shotgun (shooting a plastic container full of
water as part of a beginner's first lesson can be dramatic and effective way of
doing this). Explain that a closed gun is always considered loaded. Keep up
safety training and reinforcement of good gun-handling practice throughout
your relationship with the client. It is not a separate subject but a constant factor in all instruction.

Physical control
When dealing with beginners and others who have insufficient control of their
guns and minds, you must always be in a position *physically* to stop them
should they begin to point the muzzles in a dangerous direction. The instructor should stand on the same side of the client as the gun is mounted and (ideally) keep both hands free. How does the instructor operate the trap and still
keep his hands free? There are various options:

- Make use of a manual trap and trapper who can hear your word of command or whistle.

- Place the release button of an auto trap in your pocket and operate it through the cloth.
- Use a foot or acoustic release.
- Appoint a button presser (my favourite when using auto traps).

You will usually stand considerably closer to a beginner than to an experienced shot: physical intervention may be required at any moment. With children, it may be appropriate to kneel or crouch down beside them to maintain effective physical control and to make them more psychologically comfortable with your presence.

Never turn your back on a beginner with a gun. Always keep control of the cartridges. The gun should only be loaded just before the shot is taken. If there is any delay, for example because you want to explain a point, break the gun and unload. Whatever the standard of competence of the shooter, you must constantly be on the lookout for potential danger, and take action *before* it develops. You will develop a feel for this, but it is always hard work and requires great concentration.

If you 'switch off' while instructing, even momentarily, you are courting disaster. Part of the responsibility of being a shooting instructor is to accept the need for constant vigilance. This places you under considerable stress. It goes with the job. When working with guns, **you must continually guard against familiarity breeding contempt**. This requires an active approach to safety: constant alertness to potential danger and the conscious acceptance of, and guarding against, your own fallibility. I realise that I am repeating myself here. Good instruction often requires the repetition of important points. Do not be afraid to do it.

Setting a good example

Not only must an instructor be able to anticipate his students' actions and block them if necessary, he must always set a good example. You are the role model for your students. If your own gun-handling is suspect, how can you expect them to develop safe habits? It may hurt your pride, but I am willing to guarantee that your gun-handling could be improved. Very few of us are as safe as we should like to think: the safer shooter – instructor or not – is the one who knows it *can* happen to him (or her) and guards against it.

When students see an instructor handling a gun, they should be able to discern special care and respect. The instructor's movements should be precise, perhaps even a little theatrical. There must be an aura of control. Muzzle control, in particular, must be perfect. If the instructor's special care is noticed, it is likely to affect the behaviour of the client. Gun safety is infectious (as is lazy gun-handling).

Summary: basic instructional safety.

1   Brief clients first.
2   Be close enough to intervene.
3   Never turn your back on a beginner with a gun.

4   Keep possession of the cartridges
5   Set a good example.

PROCEDURES WHICH YOU SHOULD TEACH

Muzzle awareness
Constant awareness of where the gun is pointing is a foundation of all safe gun handling. Pass it on to your students by example and by specific instruction. Do not feel foolish about labouring the point. Impress on them the importance of controlling the muzzles with the greatest care at all times. Make them precisely aware of what they might be pointing the gun at. For example: draw to their attention the fact that a partition wall would not stop the charge from a shotgun, and is therefore to be considered a danger zone – a person might be standing behind it.

General handling: a closed gun is a loaded gun
Never pull a closed gun towards you by the muzzles (a number of people have been killed by taking guns from vehicles in this manner). Never lay guns down unless the action is open (unless putting a proven empty gun in the rack). Never leave guns propped up against walls or trees. Never handle someone's gun without asking. Never horseplay with guns. All these things may seem obvious but it is remarkable how often such basic rules are ignored. People are killed every year with sporting or military firearms which someone thought were unloaded.

Removing guns from slips
Break-action guns should be partially opened before being fully withdrawn from a slip. This is an easy process. The slip is opened with the muzzle end pointing in a safe direction. The weak (non-writing) hand grabs the barrels

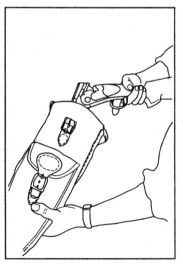

from outside through the material of the slip. The strong hand holds the butt sole and pulls the stock out a few inches, to allow the same hand access to the slip so it can take a more secure hold of the gun at the grip. During this procedure the trigger finger should be extended along the trigger guard, or placed flat along the head of the stock.

Once the action of the gun is visible, the thumb activates the top lever. The gun is broken, the chambers are checked unloaded and the gun may now be taken from the slip. The trigger must not be touched at any time. The

When taking a gun from a slip, **control the muzzles**. Keep them pointing safely down and break the gun before removing it. Keep the trigger finger off the trigger.

muzzles must be controlled throughout and, once the gun is free of the slip, the chambers should be checked again and the barrels proved for obstructions.

Taking guns from racks

When you take a gun from a rack, do not, as many do, sweep the muzzles past the bodies of other shooters before opening the action and proving the gun clear. It is an obvious and common breech of the 1st Golden Rule. Instead, get in the habit of opening the action of break-action guns with the muzzles still pointing skywards.

Loading

The proper procedure for loading a break-action gun is to look down the barrels first: to check for obstructions such as mud or snow blocking the muzzles, or a smaller gauge cartridge which might have fallen down the barrels. This cannot easily be done with repeaters. In this case, it is advisable to check that a gun is unobstructed at the beginning and end of any shooting session. This may be done by removing the barrel (impractical); by proving the action and magazine unloaded, locking the action back and looking down from the muzzles (acceptable, although it is another exception to Golden Rule 1); or, by the 'Cradock method': allowing a small, heavy object, inserted into the chamber, to fall through the barrels into a waiting hand. Chris had a small silver penknife which he kept for the purpose, although a couple of inches of ¼ in. diameter brass rod or a torpedo-shaped fishing weight would do just as well.

Confusing cartridges

It is well-known that a 20-bore cartridge may be inadvertently loaded in a 12-bore barrel and a 12-bore cartridge then loaded on top. It the gun is fired the 20-bore cartridge creates a major obstruction and, because of the massive increase in pressures, an explosive situation is created which may well lead to a barrel burst near the chambers. This is, of course, extremely dangerous. Serious injury to hands and/or face may occur. A similar accident is possible with a 28-bore cartridge in a 16- or 20-bore and there are other possibilities too. Guard against them. Keep separate cartridge bags for twelves, twenties and anything else you use regularly. As an added precaution, always check your pockets thoroughly after using a small-gauge shotgun.

Gun closure

Closing a gun, like loading cartridges into the chamber, may seem simple, but to perform the action properly requires specific tuition and some thought. The first point to make is that when you close a drop or break-action gun, or bring the working parts forward on a repeater, you must make sure that your finger is off the trigger and the muzzles are pointing in a safe direction. If the gun should go off accidentally, as can happen due to a faulty mechanism or because one has inadvertently left one's finger on the trigger, no great damage will be done.

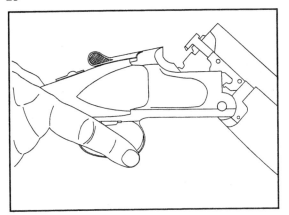

Always keep your finger off the trigger when handling guns.

Never slam guns shut

The action of closing the gun should always be done with control. *Never* slam a break-action gun shut. If the mechanism is faulty (and it should go without saying that one should not be using a gun, if one knows that it is), a violent action is much more likely to bring about an accidental discharge, especially in guns with light trigger pulls. Moreover, abrupt gun closure accelerates wear of mechnical parts and is also a common cause of broken stocks. Although the closure of a break–action gun should be a controlled movement, the top lever should not usually be touched as the gun is closed. The gun is designed to snap shut (and bolt) automatically as the face of the action meets the barrels. If the top lever is controlled during closure, full bolting may be impeded. Some guns which have been re-jointed may need to have 50-100 cartridges fired through them to allow everything to bed in. Until this occurs, it may be prudent to push the top lever towards centre *after closure* to ensure that the bite is properly engaged.

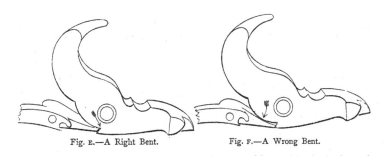

Fig. E.—A Right Bent.   Fig. F.—A Wrong Bent.

The way the bent engages with the sear will have a profound effect on the quality of trigger pulls and on the safety of the lock (from *The Gun and Its Development* by W.W.Greener). If for any reason the sear and bent do not engage perfectly a gun may become prone to accidental firing. This may occasionally happen even if sear and bent are properly fitted.

Keep the barrels pointing down if possible

Usually, the barrels should be controlled to point at about 45 degrees towards the ground (and in a designated safe zone) as the gun is closed. This method of closure maximises control and reduces risk to trappers and other third parties from accidental discharge. There are exceptions, however. In some circumstances, 45 degree down closure may be awkward or even dangerous. When shooting from a cage with a cross bar, the rule should always be to take a position well forward in the cage and to close the gun with the barrels positioned over the bar. If the bar is positioned high, 45–degree down closure may be difficult. If this is the case, do not worry, but make sure the gun is kept pointing in a safe direction and closed with control. Never load and close the gun with muzzles pointing down inside the cage and then manoeuvre the barrels up and over the cross piece. This is a dangerous practice (and something to be immediately corrected if seen).

When trapshooting, most participants close their guns by bringing the barrels up so that they end up more or less parallel to the ground and out and above the trap. This may be considered acceptable for these disciplines. Similarly, if there is an obvious ricochet hazard to one's front, 45-degree down gun closure may be inappropriate. As always, common sense applies. One cannot create perfect rules for every eventuality. In most circumstances 45-degree-down gun closure makes sense. It is an excellent habit to acquire for anyone who is going to shoot clays *and* game. Closing guns with barrels pointing towards the horizon is certainly something to be avoided at all costs when shooting live quarry (and may explain why the old dictum of bringing wood to metal evolved). Its danger to approaching beaters, companions concealed by tree or bush, mushroom hunters or romantically inclined couples rolling in the bracken should be immediately obvious.

Gun closure specific instruction
I teach closure of the break or drop-action gun to novices as a set-piece drill with three movements:

Having made sure that the gun is pointing in a safe direction and that the barrels are not obstructed:

1 Hold the stock of the open gun gently wedged between forearm and rib cage. Extend the trigger finger along the trigger guard. Make sure the thumb is not exerting pressure on the top-lever.
2 Cant the gun clockwise (anti-clockwise for left handers). And, holding the grip firmly with rear hand, lean forward slightly.
3 Keeping the weight forward, bring the barrels up with the force of the front hand, pushing up on the forend while pushing down on the top of the grip with the rear. Throughout the process, the muzzles of the gun must be actively controlled downwards. The top lever should not be touched (it should be allowed to snap back into position under its own spring power).

Clients should be made to repeat the exercise several times until they feel comfortable with it (and reminded thereafter every time they fail to close the gun with control).

Repeaters
The normal procedure for a repeater would involve holding the gun so that the side of the stock touches the rib cage and the muzzle points diagonally downward as with a break action. The gun may then be rotated a quarter turn anti-clockwise (assuming a right-handed gun) so that the ejection port is facing

upwards. The action should be open and the safety applied. The right hand drops a cartridge through the ejection port and, in the case of semi-automatics, presses the action release catch or button allowing the working parts to move forward. If the gun is a pump, the left hand must operate the slide. (In the case of semi-automatics, you *must not* control the forward movement of the breech-block by holding the cocking handle when you press the release catch: it is possible that the mechanism will not lock up properly if you try to cushion the forward movement of the working parts. Similarly with a pump, do not be afraid of using normal force to close the action. Failure to do so may, again, result in a failure to lock up properly.)

With the action forward, the safety applied and a cartridge in the chamber, the right hand may load additional cartridges into the magazine through the loading gate (although it is difficult to conceive of any instructing situation that would require more than one cartridge in the magazine). Cartridges should always be pressed fully home with the pad of the thumb.

If it is inappropriate to direct the muzzles down when loading because of the nature of the firing point, repeaters may also be loaded with the muzzles pointing skywards at about 45 degrees.

Traditional method for closing break-action guns
Not recommended for basic training but useful for cross-barred cages
The traditional way to close a break-action gun is to 'bring wood to metal'. In other words, to hold the barrels at the forend with the weak hand while pushing the stock up at the heel. This method is fine in experienced hands (provided that it is not performed with too much gusto) but does not suit beginners who tend to lose control of the muzzles as the stock is pushed up, especially when the gun's action is stiff. The gun tends to rotate around the axis of their weak hand and may end up pointing at, or very near, a foot. By positively locating the gun stock between rib cage and forearm as the gun is closed, you may

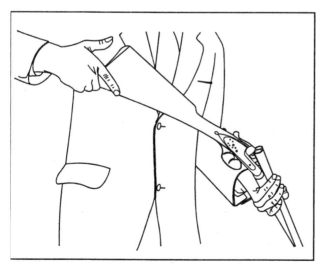

be sure of better leverage and much more positive muzzle control; this is a much more sensible method to teach the beginner.[2]

With any gun, what counts is firm control

The traditional method of gun closure – 'bringing wood to metal' – fine in experienced hands but does not always suit over and unders and can lead to problems with novices.

and muzzle awareness as the action is closed. Controlled opening and closing of the gun is one of the first things to teach new clients. I would usually start off by saying something like, 'You might have thought opening and closing a gun was simple, but in fact very few people do it well and safely. This is how to do it properly . . .' at which point I would talk through a physical demonstration. Someone taught to open and close guns carefully develops a cautious and respectful attitude that will extend to all their gun handling.

When to load and close guns

The gun should only be loaded and closed when one is about to shoot from a designated firing position (your choice as instructor), and when the muzzles are controlled in a safe direction. If the student is to shoot from a cage, the barrels should always be over the front bar.[3]

Use of the safety catch

Many believe a safety catch has no real function on a clay shooting gun. There is never a need to apply it. They say: you are either shooting or not and, if not, the action should be open. For this reason many clay shooting guns have non-automatic safeties which may be left in the off position permanently. Some clay shooters have their safeties modified so they cannot be put on 'safe' at all. This modification is not generally to be advocated (although one might make an exception for high level competitors). All shots should become familiar with the operation of the safety catch. When clay shooting, put the safety on and remove it before shooting as a matter of habit. This action, if habitual, also ensures the safety has not been left on mistakenly. One should also be in the habit of extending the trigger finger along the trigger guard whenever the safety is touched.

In the very early stages of instruction, the safety can be especially useful. The instructor may load the gun for the student and apply the safety while adjusting position or placing the gun butt at the shoulder. The safety may be disengaged by the instructor just before the shot is taken. This is an obvious means of increasing operational safety and control. Some instructors regard use of the safety as a hindrance. I do not agree: it is a useful option in some circumstances.

Safety catch and thumb position

Always be aware of the client's thumb position on conventional sliding safeties. Most beginners and many experienced shots are inclined to leave their thumb on the safety after disengaging it. This can result in a painful split thumb from the top lever as the gun recoils on firing.

When to unload

The gun should always be unloaded or checked unloaded immediately after shooting. If there is any delay during shooting (a trap malfunction, for example), unload. If you want to talk to the student, unload. If anyone is seen moving forward of the firing point, unload. If anything unusual happens which delays the act of shooting, unload. The basic rule is that the gun should be unloaded and open whenever possible.

Final actions

When shooting is over, the gun must be proven empty by the user (and, when instructing, by the instructor too: never trust the client to be safe) and left open before turning round to exit from the designated firing position. Some sloppy shots break the gun as they turn. This is very bad practice. These lazy types may walk off the firing point with an empty cartridge case – ejectors do not always function as they should – still in the gun. I have also seen people walk off the firing point with live cartridges in the gun for the same reason: they had a sloppy, undisciplined attitude. Very occasionally, disciplined shots will make the same mistake because they have been distracted. Happily, such lapses are usually picked up instantly by shooting companions.

Checking magazine tubes on repeaters

Another frequent breach of safety concerns the shooter with a repeating shotgun at a clay shoot who fails to check the magazine beneath the barrel after shooting a stand or station. The foolish assumption is that there are no cartridges left in the gun because two were loaded and two fired. Because it is easier to make a mistake with these action types than others, clients using semi-automatics and pumps must be taught safe unloading drills. These will differ slightly from gun to gun, but what counts is good control throughout and a final inspection of chamber and magazine tube as noted above. At the end of a shooting session, and after proving empty, the action of semi-automatics or pumps should be racked several times – as is common practice in the Services – with the gun pointing into the ground or skywards (the Army sometimes uses dedicated unloading bays). Dry fire into the ground or skywards and lock the action back, repeating your check of chamber and magazine. The gun may now be put away.

Loading when instructing

Unless the instructor is teaching loading, he should load for the client (it helps you to keep control). When dealing with beginners, only one cartridge should be loaded. Even with the experienced shot, you should only load one cartridge if a single target is being tackled unless you are specifically encouraging 'full use of gun' (the phrase used when two shots may be fired at one target).

Loading for the client is safer (because it keeps you in charge of the cartridges – nevertheless, always be aware that the client may have secreted some cartridges about his or her person). Loading for the client also gives an air of professionalism to proceedings, and it allows you to dictate the pace. Be careful of your fingers when loading for others, though: it is all too easy for an over–enthusiastic beginner to shut them in the gun!

Special care is needed with semi-automatics for instruction (which is not intended to put you off their use; they can be excellent tools for this purpose). When assisting clients to load a semi-automatic, you must be aware of the cocking handle protruding from the bolt. It can cause injury to you if the gun is accidentally discharged. If you place a cartridge in the chamber of an empty gun that the client is holding, you should apply the safety first and make sure:

1   That the client is gripping the gun firmly.
2   That the client's trigger finger is not on the trigger (tell him to extend the trigger finger along the trigger guard and to keep it there until told otherwise).
3   That the client's hands are well away from the cocking handle and its line of movement.

Beginners

A technique used by some instructors training novices with semi-automatics is to get the client to mount the gun with the action open. The instructor can position the gun at the shoulder (supporting the barrels as necessary). And, once everything looks good, can drop a cartridge in the open port and depress the release catch to bring the working parts forward. Finally, the safety catch may be disengaged. This can all be done very quickly and is my preferred way of operating at 'have-a-go' stands, offering both control and speed. If you try it, make sure you support the gun if required.

Misfires

Although misfires are much rarer than they once were, they are still a relatively common occurrence. They may be caused either by a faulty cartridge or by a problem in the gun's mechanism (such as a chipped firing pin or a weak mainspring). If you hear a click rather than a bang when the trigger is pulled, the proper procedure is to control the gun in a safe direction, wait 30 seconds and open the gun, taking care to keep the chamber mouths directed away from your face. Once the gun is open, remove the cartridge or cartridges and check for barrel obstructions. Examine the cartridge and its primer. Has it been struck properly? If the answer is yes, suspect a faulty cartridge.

If the strike appears very light, the problem is likely to be in the gun's mechanism – a weak spring, a worn or broken firing-pin, excessive head-space etc – although occasionally one encounters very hard or thick primers, or primers which are incorrectly positioned in the battery cup at the base of the cartridge. Do not automatically assume that a light strike indicates a gun fault, however: the pressures involved in firing the gun of themselves increase the indent on the primer. Indeed, most misfires appear rather lightly struck even when there is no problem with the mechanism. Whatever the cause of a misfire may be, the instructor should take careful charge of any suspect cartridges and dispose of them safely.[4]

Bloopers

If, on pulling the trigger, the gun goes off but the report sounds abnormal (a 'phut' instead of a bang), you must check the bore very carefully for obstructions. The weak report typically results from insufficient chamber pressure. It is possible that the cartridge had no powder in it or insufficient powder. The primer or powder may have failed to ignite because of contamination by oil or water. For whatever reason, if the gun is fired after an abnormal report, the likelihood of an obstruction is high. Chamber pressure may have been sufficient to push the wad through the forcing cone into the main bore but not powerful enough to push it out of the barrel. If you fire into the obstruction, a ruined barrel will be the least serious of the possible consequences. If a misfire or blooper occurs when you are instructing, you should take charge of the gun and deal with it. Explain to the client exactly what is going on and why you are taking special action.

Malfunctions in competition

If you have a malfunction in competition, you must not open the gun's action until it has been examined by an official. If you do, it may cost you a target. The FITASC sporting rule book – which on this subject is typical of most – states:

> In the case of misfire or any other malfunction, the shooter must remain in his place, the gun pointing safely down the range, not broken, and without touching the safety catch before the referee has examined the gun.[5]

Those with guns which are prone to misfire should note that the number of allowable misfires is usually limited to two before a lost target is recorded.

Ricochets

Shotgun pellets may be deflected off any hard surface: pattern plates, walls, trees and branches, pylons, hard or icy ground and also by water. I know of one case where an injury occurred because a pellet was deflected by a telegraph wire and another where an injury was caused when a pellet was deflected off the body of a low-flying grouse. Steel shot is much more prone to ricochet than lead shot. Shooting at metallic pattern plates with steel shot is especially hazardous (and to be avoided).

Carrying guns: clay shooting

Whenever a gun is carried out of a slip at a clay shoot, it should be unloaded and have the action broken (break-action types) or locked back (semi-automatics and pumps). This allows any third party to see that the gun is in a safe condition. With semi-automatic and pump-action types – which have chambers which are not easily visible – a handkerchief or purpose-made plastic breech plug with streamer should be placed in the chamber and ejection port. The principle, when carrying a gun at a clay shoot, might be summed up with the words, 'Safe and Seen to be Safe'.

Break-action guns should be carried broken, resting on the forearm (the best choice when uncovered) or, broken, resting on the shoulder with barrels pointing forwards and secured with one hand. Semi-automatics and pump-action guns should be carried, either resting on the forearm with the muzzles pointing at about 45 degrees towards the ground, or with the muzzles pointing straight up. They should never be carried 'at the trail'. As a general rule, the instructor

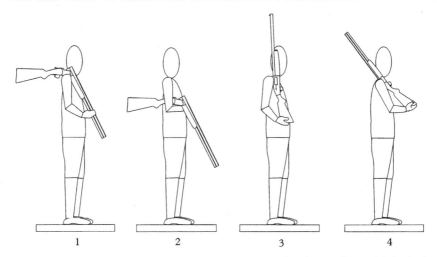

1   2   3   4

Methods 1, 2 and 3 are acceptable ways to carry guns on a clay shoot, 4 is not. Method 1 is not liked by some instructors, but is all right provided the barrels are *pointing forward* and are secured with one hand. In method 3, for repeaters only, the breech block must be locked back and, for those who want to show the care they are taking, a breech plug and flag may also be used. Between stands the ideal method of carry is in a slip (not shown).

should carry the client's gun out to the shooting field, unless the client needs the practice. Carrying the gun, like loading for the client, keeps you in control.

Slips
When shooting sporting targets, it is a good practice to carry guns from stand to stand in a slip (with muzzles pointing down: if the fastener fails, the gun will not fall out of the slip).

Beware of excitement
Many times, I have seen beginners turn or attempt to turn 180 degrees with gun in hands because of excitement at hitting a target. The instructor should always be in a position physically to intervene at all times. Because some beginners have this tendency to turn (especially women in my experience), the loading of one cartridge only is of critical importance in the early stages of instruction. Should other checks fail, there will be no live cartridge in the gun after the shot is taken. The layer system is in place.

Brain fade
Occasionally, one will see an experienced shot do something really stupid because of a momentary mental aberration. Some years ago I was at a well-known shooting ground near London. It was a practice day and I was waiting on the final stand – a simple driven pair – to complete the card. The shot in front of me went into the cage and began to call for his targets. He had his five pairs and kept going. Clearly something was wrong. He just kept shooting. Someone called 'That's your lot'. Then it began to get frightening. The head of the man in the cage began to move oddly, as if he were unsure of what to do

next. He had two cartridges loaded in an over-and-under and the safety was off. Suddenly, he turned. I had been standing immediately behind him. The muzzles of his gun pointed twelve inches from my chest. His finger was on the trigger; he was shaking, visibly sweating, and his eyes were glazed over. I remember thinking very clearly, 'This — idiot is going to kill me'. I could not move, for I sensed that the slightest movement might cause him to pull the trigger.

I stayed quite still and fixed his eyes with mine and began to speak in a quiet but firm voice, 'Very gently, very gently, I want you to break the gun, break the gun'. There was no reaction but I could see beads of sweat rolling down his forehead. I repeated my instruction, trying as best I could to control and soothe him with the tone of my voice. After what seemed an age, he did break the gun and began to shake his head in confusion, 'I'm very sorry, very sorry'.

If such an incident should ever happen to you, and I hope that it does not, do not grab the muzzles of the gun pointed at you. Stay calm. Do not react suddenly. I am sure I am alive today because I managed to communicate a great deal more calmness than I felt.

Gun Security
The security of firearms is a special nightmare for instructors who will often be responsible for a number of weapons. I suggest you get in the habit of having an equipment check at the end of the day. On location (or when dealing with groups on a shooting ground) a portable gun rack is very useful (it should be a firm rule that only the instructor is responsible for taking his guns from the rack or replacing them there). In some circumstances – country fairs spring to mind – it may be prudent to equip the rack with a lock and chain (even though it is positioned next to you), or to park your car next to the instructional stand so that you can lock your spare equipment in it (still making sure it is out of sight). Never be slack about gun storage, even though it may cause special problems when you are working 'off-site'. It may be useful to have your car alarmed and some sort of steel cabinet bolted to the floor of the boot. Whatever you do must be done on the basis of what is prudent under the circumstances. Should a gun go missing (God forbid) you must be able to defend your actions to the police and show that you took all reasonable precautions. You may also consider it worthwhile to photograph each of your guns, writing the details and serial number on the back of each print.

Group Instruction
Instructing groups is a special challenge, not least because one needs eyes in the back of one's head sometimes. Keeping control of the ammunition is critical (as always with beginners). Moreover, rigidly enforce a rule that *no-one* is to handle (pick-up, dry mount) guns unless they are under specific instruction.

THE TEN COMMANDMENTS

Here are ten commandments for clay shooting safety. You may copy them and give them to beginners or anyone else you think might benefit. A similar list for novice game shots appears at the end of the next chapter.

Safe And Seen To Be Safe
The Ten Commandments For Safe Clay Shooting

1 **Assume all guns are loaded:** if you do not wish to destroy it, do not point your gun at it.
2 **Check that a gun is unloaded**, when you pick it up, put it down, when it is passed to you or when you pass it to someone else.
3 The gun, if not in a slip, should be **carried action open**, unloaded, resting on the forearm or on the shoulder, barrels pointing forwards and secured with one hand.
4 You must enter the firing point with an **open, empty gun** and you must leave the firing point with an open, empty gun. The only time when a gun should be loaded and closed is on the firing point while waiting for a bird. (When trap shooting always make sure the gun is **open and unloaded** when moving from position 5 to position 1.)
5 Before loading, **check for obstructions** in the barrels such as mud, snow, a wad or a cartridge of a smaller bore.
6 **Close guns under control** with the muzzles pointing in a safe direction.
7 If your gun **misfires, control it**. A hang-fire might occur. Keep the muzzles pointing in a safe direction and wait 30 seconds before opening the action.
8 Make sure that a gun is in **serviceable condition** – well-maintained and in proof – before using it (if you have any concern at all, ask a gunsmith).
9 Only use **cartridges** in a gun **which are suitable** for it. Suitable in this context means cartridges which correspond to the proof marks on the gun both **with regard to pressure and to chamber length**. Most shotguns sold in the UK today have been proofed for use with 2¾ in. (70 mm) shells and an increasing number for 3 in. (76 mm) too. However many older guns have not, the old standard English proof was 2½ in. (65 mm). Modern 2¾ in. cartridges will fit into 2½ in. chambers, but if fired are potentially dangerous. The fact that an older 2½ in. gun may be marked for 1⅛ oz (32 grm) service shot load does not mean that a modern 32 grm cartridge may be safely fired in it; proof pressure and chamber length are determining factors.[6]
10 If you have **any doubts** about safety, **don't shoot**. You are responsible once you pull the trigger.

HEARING PROTECTION

Prolonged exposure to high, constant levels of sound (for example, the drone of machinery in a factory) or sudden exposure to high, peak levels of sound (as in shooting) is likely to damage hearing. In the first case, sound over 85 decibels is known to be hazardous; in the second, any exposure which exceeds 140 decibels will cause damage.[7]

The noise generated from firing a shotgun is derived primarily from two components: the muzzle blast of the gun (which is increased with short barrels) and the sonic boom created when the shot charge breaks the sound barrier. A shotgun blast typically registers a peak level over 150 decibels on a sound-meter; a full-bore rifle or pistol around 160 – 170. Thus, in both cases, the noise generated is well above the safe limit. If hearing protection is not worn, damage to the cochlea (the highly sensitive spiral tube in the inner ear which converts sound vibrations into nerve impulses) is most likely.

Hearing loss is an irreversible and progressive condition. Typically, the ability to hear the high frequency range of sounds (a range of hearing ability which also deteriorates with age) is likely to be lost first. This is the range which helps to clarify speech (which is normally heard in the range 500 – 4000 hertz.). If one loses the top end, it will be difficult to distinguish speech from competing sounds. Moreover, if high frequency hearing is damaged, it cannot be improved by a hearing aid. It is gone forever. As well as the danger of hearing loss or impairment, there is the risk of developing the debilitating condition known as tinnitus – a constant ringing in the ears.

Instructional duty

You must impress upon your students the importance of wearing effective ear protection. It goes without saying that you should wear it yourself – the more you shoot, the more certain it is that you will seriously damage your hearing if you do not wear protection.

You must also make sure that you can always provide ear, eye and head protection for all students, companions and staff. If you have an experienced shooter who insists on not wearing protection, explain that even occasional shooting without ear protection can cause permanent damage. If they say, 'I am not bothered, I am already a bit deaf', you must emphasise that protection can prevent further loss. You must *insist* that beginners wear ear protection. Hearing protection is now mandatory for Clay Pigeon Shooting Association registered competitions. Some instructors will refuse to teach *any* student who refuses to wear hearing protection.

What ear protection is best?

For sporting and game shooting I usually advise my clients to go for the disposable EAR type of plug. Surprisingly, these universal plugs offer one of the highest degrees of protection (because they expand to the size of the ear canal). They are also reasonably priced and easily replaceable. I do not advise the use of the small harder 'rubber' plugs or (Ear Defenders as they were called[8]), as once issued by the British Army and still on the back shelf in some gun shops. They are not very comfortable (even if one has the right size) and have been known to get stuck in the ear. Nor do I like the type of plug which has a soft rubber sleeve covering a small aluminium cylinder containing a mechanical valve. Although they may allow one to hear normal speech well, they are quite expensive, collect dirt easily (which can cause the valves to malfunction), and the rubber outer sections tend to tear if the plugs are used regularly.

Moulded plugs can be effective, but they tend to be expensive and the fitting must be done by an expert (or they will always have a tendency to fall out of the ear). The simplest and cheapest moulded plugs involve nothing more than a plastic substance being placed directly in the ear canal and allowed to set *in situ*. The resulting plug is large, relatively soft and tends to attract dirt. I do not think these give any great advantage over the cheap but effective EAR disposable type. More sophisticated, hard plastic, moulded plugs are made from impressions and may be fitted with some sort of mechanical sound attenuator or, in the case of the most sophisticated and expensive type, a combined electronic sound attenuator and amplifier, which restricts harmful sounds but amplifies others. Either hard plastic type can be an excellent choice for the instructor.

The advantage of plugs as far as shotgun shooting is concerned, is that they do not impede one's mounting or give a sense of psychological isolation as can muffs. One disadvantage, slight in practice, is that plugs can introduce foreign bodies into the ear canal or cause a build up of wax in some people. For trap shooting, I think muffs are to be preferred: the sense of isolation which they tend to create can be an aid to consistent concentration. It must also be said that for people who shoot a great deal, or who spend a lot of time in the vicinity of guns being fired, muffs will reduce the sound waves entering the bone around the ear. Research shows that this may be as damaging as sound waves entering the ear.

Many professional instructors favour electronic muffs. They are quite expensive (about £100 upwards at the time of writing), but effective, and also have the advantage—like the more expensive types of plug – of allowing the wearer to hear normal speech by means of an electronic amplifier. Electronic muffs or plugs, which control gun noise but do not suppress ambient sound, may also be preferred by some sporting shots who want to hear the traps being released. Those who are especially sensitive to noise may wear both plugs and muffs.

Before buying any pair of electronic muffs, you must try mounting a gun with them on—some types, on some shooters, hit the gun butt as it is brought to the face. The frames of spectacles can also be a problem with muffs: they can break the seal around the ear. Much depends on design of both spectacles and hearing protection, but the solution is simple: if a problem is identified, use plugs.

EYE PROTECTION

Too few shooters in Britain use eye protection (although it is 'strongly recommended' by the Clay Pigeon Shooting Association). It is much more common in the United States, where it is mandatory on most clay shooting grounds. Considering that our eyes are so vulnerable, our reluctance to protect them is strange. A shooting instructor should advise *all* his clients to wear eye protection (and clearly state that he will not be responsible for the risk of their not doing so). As with ear protectors, an instructor should always have a good supply to offer to clients, visitors and ground staff.

Protective glasses worn by the client also provide the instructor with an easy means of correcting some eye dominance problems (Ed Scherer always carried a chap stick in his pocket to place a smudge on his pupils' glasses when he suspected a problem; Chris Cradock used Vaseline; my own preference is a square of vinyl electrician's tape. If you want the ultimate – and can afford the luxury – there is the Magic Dot product made in the United States). In all cases, great care must be taken in placing the vision block in the correct location on the lens. The head must be properly positioned on the stock with good firm pressure on the comb, and the placement of the vision barrier must allow for head-lifting or turning.

Instructor requirements
For the shooting instructor himself, eye protection is a must at all times. An instructor is completely dependent on his eyes. The right pair of glasses will offer protection against ultraviolet light (which causes cataracts and should be of special concern to anyone who works outdoors), blow-back from propellant gases (quite common in semi-automatic guns – and felt all the more when you are standing to one side of them), stray pellet and – by far the most frequent cause of eye injury on shooting grounds – bits of broken clay.

I have acted on several occasions as a specialist consultant in cases where someone not wearing protective glasses has been blinded or seriously injured by a fragment of clay on a sporting layout. These tragic cases rarely, if ever, receive any publicity. If they did, more British shooters might be encouraged to wear glasses. I also know of many instructors who have had accidents or near misses with their eyes. The relative frequency of such incidents has changed my attitude to eye protection. I always wear it now, and I encourage others to do so routinely. Once one is in the habit, the absence of shooting glasses will cause psychological discomfort. To condition oneself in this manner makes the greatest sense.

Need for side protection
If my own experience of clay target related accidents is anything to go by, effective protective shooting glasses should offer protection to the side as well as the front (several of the cases I have reported upon recently involved an impact from the side). Modernistic, wrap-around glasses offer one (partial) answer (they do not offer complete protection and some may distort at the extremes of the visual field), as do industrial goggles, but side pieces may also be added to conventional glasses. Trap shooters use vinyl or card side pieces to cut out visual distraction from their neighbours; these are not intended for protection. Hard plastic, face-hugging, side-pieces are also available. Though they may not be described as protective (because of fears of potential litigation) they are much safer than bare frames. Considering the very active and innovative market in shooting glasses, and considering the real need, it is surprising that impact-resistant side pieces are not more readily available.

Specs for specs

Shooting glasses (prescription or plain) should have toughened glass or plastic (usually CR-39 or polycarbonate) lenses. Plastic-type spectacles are light, tough and less prone to fogging-up than glass. Of the plastics, CR-39 is more scratch-resistant while polycarbonate offers maximum impact protection. Whatever the material, lenses should be on the large side (but not so large as to impede mounting) and the bridge should be comfortable and low, so that the wearer is looking through the centre of the lenses when the head is positioned on the comb for shooting. An anti-UV coating is sensible for the reasons already noted, and an anti-reflective coating can be useful in poor light and for shooting under artificial light.

Tints

Bausch & Lomb introduced yellow-tinted shooting glasses in the USA in the 1930s.[9] Bud Decot (who pioneered rimless shooting glasses in the early fifties, plastic lenses in the mid sixties and interchangeable lenses in the seventies) has experimented with tints more than any other manufacturer in recent decades. Certain tints can offer competitors and live bird shooters specific advantages. Tints, however, should be no darker than required for given light conditions (otherwise they will cause the pupil to dilate excessively, which will result in a loss of depth of field, making focus more difficult). The requirements of different individuals may be quite different on the same day. Those with light blue eyes, for example, may need slightly darker tints than others because they have less pigment in their eyes and are therefore more prone to glare. One's natural eye colour, moreover, may affect one's reaction to different tints, so it is difficult to make generalisations. Here are some rough guidelines.

Yellow and orange lenses increase perceived contrast, and may be useful on overcast days. A rose tint is a good general purpose shooting lens and is especially good for increasing contrast on orange targets. Red and purple lenses also pull out orange targets (especially against a green background or when targets appear indistinct against the sky).[10] Polarising filters, which may be combined with many tints, reduce light transmission significantly and are useful in especially bright conditions. Brown and bronze are good colours for brighter conditions (and may be combined with a polarising filter). Gold lenses can help when light is poor and may be further enhanced by an anti-reflective coating. 'Blue-blocker' lenses are claimed by some to increase visual acuity. As is often the case in shooting, the best advice with tints is to experiment. Do not blindly accept someone else's advice and do not assume that the more or most expensive will necessarily be better. Most of all, do not buy shooting glasses without trying them first. One maker's red or yellow may be very different to another's. By way of a warning, I might note that I have a big box of shooting glasses which I do not now use, but for which I was once persuaded to pay hard cash.

Tints and correction for eye dominance

An interesting area, only recently being explored, is the idea that different tints may be used on different eyes as a means of combating master eye problems. I know of one international trap competitor who usually has right-eye dominance, but occasionally has a problem with the left eye taking over. He uses a clear lens over his normally dominant right eye, and an orange lens over the left. He swears that this has cured his problem, or so he claims. My own experiments have been less than conclusive, but it is an interesting area for further experiment.

Conclusions
All sorts of high-tech glasses have been produced with special tints or coatings. Whatever other properties they may have, glasses must work for the individual, feel comfortable, be free of distortion, and be impact-resistant. Small lenses offer less protection and the edges of their frames may disrupt one's field of vision; excessively large lenses and frames can interfere with one's gun mount.

Advice
My preference while instructing is for medium-tinted green or grey polarising lenses. I am also fond of non-mirrored bronze lenses; all these seem very easy on *my eyes* (which are grey-green). For those interested in sporting clays, I would recommend three pairs of specs: general purpose, impact resistant, 'sunglasses' in a tint that suits you, a really dark pair of polarised glasses for looking up in very bright conditions (for example, teal into the sun) and a pair of rose, red or purple glasses for 'pulling-out' yellow and orange targets. (When I am shooting, I use my red glasses more than any others). Game shooters who have not worn glasses before should be encouraged to do so. Clear, yellow, orange, amber and gold tints are well suited to this application.

What make? Decot, Zeiss, Oakley and Randolph all offer an excellent range of quality shooting glasses and there are many others too. In the UK, Napier offer a good range of cheaper glasses. At the other end of the price scale, John Bidwell swears by his 'Eagle lenses' (a polarised yellowish-green tint created by special organic dyes), offering more contrast and light transmission than many polarising lenses) provided by the American optometrist, Dr Charles Gilchrist. Generally, it is good advice to buy the best you can afford – many cheaper glasses are optically imperfect and the distortion they cause is more of a hindrance than a help.

Once bought, glasses must be kept carefully: a hard case is far better than a soft one. If not supplied, hard cases are obtainable at reasonable cost from any optician. A proper, optical-quality cleaning cloth will prevent scratching and makes cleaning much less of a chore, and much the same may be said of lense cleaning solution (Decot offer something called Plexus, $7.85 for 13 oz at the time of writing, which not only polishes your glasses but is good for putting a nice sheen on gun stocks as well!). Finally, I would note that getting the right prescription – if there is a need for correction – is even more important than getting the right tint (see box on page 82). And one more thing, eye protection is equally important for anyone standing near the firing point, not just the instructor or shooter.

OTHER SAFETY CONSIDERATIONS
Traps

Accidents involving traps and trappers are too frequent. Typically, a young trapper is hit in the head or hand by a trap arm because he was badly briefed or because his supply of clays has been positioned imprudently (the classic error is to place the store of clays too low, causing the trapper to bend down into a dangerous position every time he reaches for a new bird). Clay traps must always be treated with respect. Never walk immediately in front of, or to the side of a loaded trap. Danger areas, such as the ground in front of traps, should be marked off if there is any possibility of third parties walking near them. Screens should be used where necessary so that the shooting position, the spectator area and the routes to them cannot be reached by a clay, even if it comes off the trap arm at an eccentric angle.

Always release trap arms before walking forward of the trap, or if handing over to another trapper. If an automatic trap jams and you need to walk to it to sort things out, you must place the button somewhere safe or take it with you. Approach traps with caution and from the rear. When using voice-activated traps make sure the microphones have been switched off before going forward. Before trying to clear obstructions, make sure the arm is forward (most automatic traps have a release button) and the power is off. Do not load automatic traps while they are in operation. Never lift a trap, automatic or manual, which is cocked. Switch traps off and release them when they are not in use. All this is little more than applied common sense.

Instructors must become familiar with the operation of manual and automatic traps; indeed, most instructing includes an element of ground management. If you understand the Laporte automatic trap, you will understand most others since it is the most frequently copied pattern. As noted earlier, potential instructors should make an effort to gain experience as trappers. There is much to be learned that will be extremely useful. This knowledge extends far beyond the simple mechanics of traps and trapping. Among much else, you will learn to appreciate how clays are affected by weather conditions, you will become familiar with the trajectories and speed of various types of target and you will note the differences in timing and style of different shooters.

It is the instructor or ground manager's responsibility to make sure that trappers are properly briefed, equipped and insured. Two-way communications are useful but (in most circumstances) optional. However, every trapper must have suitable protective clothing, including gloves, goggles, hard hat (the type used on building sites) and hearing protection, and waterproof clothing as required. The type of industrial helmet which combines a visor with head protection is especially suited to trapping, and would have prevented most of the serious injuries that I have seen on shooting grounds.

Where needed, and in any situation where the trapper might have to come back towards the Guns, trappers should be given a red flag and have the clearest instructions about the procedures for its use. The basic instruction should be, 'If you have a problem, raise the flag and *wait* for assistance'. Similarly, you must make sure that the trapper is adequately shielded. Too often, a cosmetic approach is adopted. The test for any physical barrier between the trapper and the gun is whether or not the shielding will reliably withstand a direct blast from a shotgun at close range.

Finally, trappers must not only be properly protected, briefed and equipped to be safe, they must be adequately motivated and given regular breaks, food and hot or cold drinks as required. A few trappers are persistently blasé about safety. Do not let this pass. If you ever see a trapper raising his or her head to look at the Guns, or using equip-

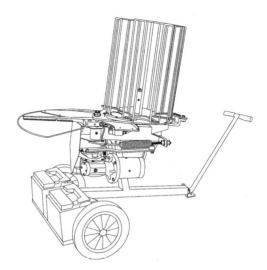

A mobile trap made by Andy Riva of A.A. Traps. I think this is an exceptionally fine design for the small ground or club or anywhere else where mobility of traps is important.

ment in a sloppy manner, be stern. If it happens regularly, you have no option but to find someone else to do the job. It is an inconvenience, but not nearly as much hassle or heartache as dealing with the consequences of injury or death.

Part of the downside of instructing is accepting the responsibility to make difficult decisions. An instructor can never afford to let danger or potential danger pass without taking action. The art is to be able to do this firmly but without causing offence. However, it is not always possible to be a good instructor and remain everyone's friend: the responsibility you have accepted always comes first.

Happily, most trappers will respond to good leadership and consideration. It is all too easy to forget about the welfare of trappers. Many times, I have seen trappers roasting unrelieved on a summer's day, or freezing or wet in winter. Think back to when you have trapped and what a thankless and uncomfortable task it was. Always thank your trappers at the end of a day's shooting. Sometimes it will be appropriate to offer the trapper the chance to have a few shots, either at the end of the day or on another occasion.

Setting up layouts – safety considerations

When you are setting up layouts for instructional purposes, be very careful that your clay flight trajectories are as safe as possible, not only as far as the shooting position itself is concerned, but also with regard to any area to which other people might conceivably have access. Always consider the fall-out area for the clays, and note how it might change if the wind shifts or if there is a trap malfunction. Always consider the arc of swing of the gun in the positions you create.

Ask yourself these questions: Is there a swing-through danger to other shooting positions or to anywhere else where there may be people? Have you built in an adequate safety margin? Do you have a full 300 yard safety zone? (Generally, normal birdshot falls at about 180 yards if fired at optimum trajectory. A three-hundred-yard safety zone is required because shot may travel for greater distances in some circumstances, for example, if the wind is behind it or if it balls.) Will the sun cause a problem on some shots? Have you considered how it will move during the day? Do cages or traps need extra screening? Are the traps properly secured?

As discussed, make sure you consider what may happen if a bird comes off the trap arm incorrectly. The release of a bird at an abnormal angle is not an uncommon occurrence when using automatic traps. Typically, it happens when the clay is gripped by the throwing arm. This might occur for a variety of reasons, most notably:

- a trap arm which is bent down, putting extra tension on the clay,
- a throwing plate incorrectly adjusted for height,
- inconsistent clay thickness/poor quality clays/re-use of recovered clays,
- a throwing plate obstructed by debris.

Trap Maintenance

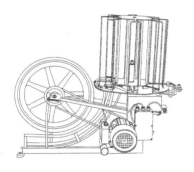

A rabbit trap made by Andy Riva of A.A. Traps.

Regular maintenance of traps is essential to prevent malfunction. The Clay Pigeon Shooting Association recommends that, 'traps should be maintained on a regular basis,' but does not go into more detail. In my opinion, traps should be serviced annually (or twice a year if the ground is very busy). Traps will need attention meantime, however. Regular greasing is important for the longevity of the mechanism. Throwing arm rubbers will need occasional replacement outside any service schedule (depending on wear); and adjustment of the throwing arm to throwing plate relationship must be routinely checked as must electrical connections. Occasional spraying of the throwing plate and the bottom of the carousel with WD40 can aid reliability. Moreover, traps should always be checked for smooth functioning before any shoot. Ideally, a service log should be kept; it is especially useful when large numbers of traps are in operation.

DUTIES OF CLAY SHOOT ORGANISERS

Target presentation: duties of shoot organisers

It is always the duty of the organisers to present targets which do not pose a threat to participants at a shoot. In setting up clay pigeon layouts, the organisers must ensure the safety of participants and employees at all times.

Judgement and experience must be used to present targets that are safe, and likely to remain safe in spite of changing conditions. Moreover, a shoot must be monitored throughout the day, and scorers, referees and trappers properly briefed. If weather conditions become really severe, there will be a point at which it will be the responsibility of the organisers to call off the shoot. Traps may sink into soft ground and require repositioning. A pro-active approach to safety must be taken at all times.

In recent years, many shoot organisers have restricted the targets they present in order to reduce danger. Birds driven towards and immediately overhead the shooter are, likewise, less often encountered than they once were. It is all too easy for fragments of such targets to strike the shooter or spectators, and even the habitual wearing of safety glasses will not eliminate all risk from low driven birds. (The problem can still exist when birds are driven to one side or the other. Low 1 and High 7 on a skeet layout require special care, as do some 'grouse' stands on sporting layouts. In the case of situations where a trapper is involved, it may be sensible to brief him or her to avoid presenting birds driven directly overhead the Gun.) Similarly, many grounds avoid having ground-level traps – even with screens – positioned behind the firing point.

Injuries from clays
It is surprising how much power there is in a clay, even one which appears to be 'spent'. Beware of clays and the potential danger from them. Keep guns in slips to avoid stocks being damaged. Wear a hat and encourage others to do so. Never attempt to catch a clay. On a properly designed layout, whole or broken clays should not be falling near the firing point.

Recommended Reading
CPSA Booklets
No.2 *How to Run Small Shoots*
No.4 *The CPSA Safety Guide*

How to Develop Places to Shoot
National Shooting Sports Foundation
(U.S.A.)
Flintlock Ridge Office Center
11 Mile Hill Road
Newtown
Connecticut 060470
U.S.A.
Tel: (00 1 203) 426 1320
www.nssf.org

Outdoor Section: NRA Range Manual Design and Layout Package (which includes information on 'Hunters Clays'
National Rifle Association (U.S.A.)
11250 Waples Mill Road
Fairfax, Virginia 22030
U.S.A.
Tel: (00 1 703)267 1000
www.nra.org

Sporting Clays Gun Club Manual
National Sporting Clays Association
(U.S.A.)
5931 Roft Road
San Antonio, Texas 78253
U.S.A.
Tel: (00 1 210) 688 3371
www.nssa-nsca.com

Storage of cartridges
Modern cartridges are extremely safe. Nevertheless, they should be stored securely in stable, dry conditions which are neither too cold or hot (about 60F).

Dampness will lead to corrosion of the metal rim (which in most cases is only plated steel and not the brass it appears to be). Paper cartridges are particularly susceptible to damage when they become damp and then dry: the crimp can be weakened and the propellant may be affected, causing loss of pressure and velocity.

Extremes of temperature may affect cartridge performance too. Very hot conditions, as sometimes occur when cartridges are left in a car in bright sunlight, will encourage propellent to burn more rapidly and hence will raise operating pressures and recoil. The reverse is the case in cold conditions. Some cartridges are more suited to very cold conditions than others (double base powders tend to work better in the cold because the addition of nitroglycerine improves combustibility). Cartridges should never be deliberately 'baked' in an oven or on a radiator. Some shooters still do this in the winter, but drying out the powder's moisture content in this way can have dangerous consequences as noted. An insulated cool box can be useful for storing cartridges in extreme conditions.

Propellent powders

As with cartridges, powders should be stored securely in cool, dry conditions and out of direct sunlight. They should not be stored with solvents or other combustible materials, nor should they be near heat sources (fires, furnaces, etc.), or electrical or mechanical equipment which is in operation. If you have large quantities of propellent powder to store, they are best kept in outbuildings. Never transfer powder from its original container, which is especially designed with safety in mind, to another.

Any locker or cabinet intended for the storage of propellent should be made with one weak wall, so that self-venting will occur should there be accidental ignition of the contents. A small, steel safe, by contrast, is a very poor place to store propellent: if there were

Black powder: storage and shooting

Shooting muzzle-loading weapons is great fun and growing in popularity. One sees an increasing number of have-a-go stands at country fairs and the like. However, there are a number of special safety considerations worth mentioning. First, black powder must be very carefully stored. Unlike modern propellents, black nitro is an efficient and potentially dangerous explosive. (Which is why the substitute Pyrodex was created. Introduced in 1976, it may be loaded bulk for bulk with black – not weight for weight – and is non-explosive and also cleaner-burning than the traditional sulphur, potassium nitrate and charcoal mix.)

Since black powder is an efficient explosive, its storage in domestic and commercial premises is strictly regulated by law. Black powder must also be handled prudently in the field. Quantities of the substance should always be isolated a good deal away from the firing point, so there is no chance of a stray spark or other heat source igniting them. An old wooden ammunition box is ideal for the transport and temporary storage of black powder containers. Do not store black powder and primers together, as both are explosive.

Because of the explosive properties of black powder, some users find alternatives for traditional powder horns and flasks which encourage relatively large quantities of powder to be kept near the body. Moreover, horns and flasks do not always throw a perfect charge. One good alternative to their use is to make up pre-measured charges of powder and place them in old plastic shotgun cartridge cases stoppered with corks. These can be placed in a conventional cartridge belt for extra convenience.

accidental combustion, the gases would be confined and an explosive effect would be most likely. In any room where propellent is kept, a 'No Smoking' sign should be prominently displayed.

Primers

Primers are highly explosive and must always be treated with special care. Storage conditions should be similar to those mentioned for propellent. Special care should be taken to keep primers away from oil or grease. Primers should be kept in their original packaging inside a wooden box. It is not prudent to store primers and propellent together. As with propellent powder, a 'No Smoking' sign should be displayed in the room where primers are stored. If reloading, no more than a hundred primers should be kept on the bench at one time.[11]

HANDLING MUZZLE LOADERS

When handling muzzle-loading weapons, the basic rule, as ever, applies: If you do not want to destroy it, do not point the gun at it. When you pick a muzzle loader up, check immediately that it is unprimed. You may also decide to use the ram rod or a cleaning rod to check that it is unloaded. There are many stories of muzzle-loading guns going to auction with ancient charges left in them! The essential safety problem is that one cannot immediately see whether muzzle loaders are loaded or not.

Loading

When loading muzzle loaders, priming *must* be left to last. The correct procedure with long guns is to place the butt on the ground or your foot and to conduct the whole loading process with the muzzles upright, but pointing away from your face (so if the gun should discharge, you would not be injured). Likewise, when holding the ramrod, grip it between the fingers; do not push it down with the palm of the hand. Keep it constantly in mind, while loading a muzzle-loader, that it could discharge at any instant because of a spark in the bore or from some other reason. If primed, muzzle loaders should be carried in the field at half cock. Hammers should only be brought to full cock with the muzzles pointing skywards and fingers around (and outside) the trigger guard. The hammer should only be lowered onto an empty nipple or fired cap. (Similarly with breech-loading hammer guns: they should

Loading position from a muzzle-loading. Note the barrels point away from the shooter (from *The Dead Shot*, 1866 be carried in the field with hammers in the rebounded position or at half cock, depending on design. Hammers should only be raised to full cock with muzzles skyward after the decision to shoot an identified target has been made.)

Eye protection

Eye protection is vitally important with all muzzle-loaders. There is a risk of primer fragmentation with percussion guns, pan flash with flintlocks, and burst barrels. Normal shooting glasses have insufficient side protection; light industrial goggles with all round protection are much to be preferred for this sort of work.

Hangfires

Hangfires and misfires are much more common with muzzle-loading guns than with breech loaders using modern cartridges. If one expects them, one will not be taken by surprise. One must also be aware of hazards such as pouring powder into a hot barrel which still has smouldering embers in it. Gun condition is another important safety consideration. Any muzzle-loader (other than properly proofed reproductions of modern manufacture) must be checked over by a competent gunsmith before use. He may well advise repair and reproof.

CONCLUSIONS: BASIC SAFETY

Shotgun safety is a huge subject which requires specific, methodical consideration. As far as instruction is concerned, it is tempting, but very foolish, to skimp on safety education. Some instructors see safety tuition as a sort of chore; they assume their pupils will be bored with it. Safety training need not be boring (although better bored than dead).

My own approach to safety is to teach it both as an end in itself, and also as a means to better gun (and mind) control. I use simple drills to teach gun closure and the removal of guns from slips. I encourage my students to take the greatest pride in safe gun handling, and I like to think of their going on to carry the message and set the example wherever they may later shoot and in whatever company.

An instructor, or indeed any shooter, should never be afraid to tell others if they are handling guns dangerously or carelessly. **Always be polite**. Being aggressive only causes offence and is unlikely to lead to a modification of the dangerous behaviour. If you see someone on a clay layout who is keeping his gun closed while moving from stand to stand because he is not familiar with clay shooting form, go up and say, 'I can see you may be a bit unfamiliar with this, but it's a firm rule when clay shooting that guns should always be broken when you move between stands. That way everyone knows the state of everyone else's gun.'

Many game shots are ignorant of what is considered safe on a clay layout, in much the same way that many clay shots are unfamiliar with the etiquette of formal driven bird shooting. In both cases polite assistance may be required. If you are sensitive to other people, you will usually get a positive response. On the rare occasions when you do not, be firm. If you still get no response, or only abuse (and that will be rare if you have handled the situation well), take action to expel the miscreant from the shooting field or, if you are unable to do this and can find no-one inclined to act, leave it yourself.

First Aid

Instructors should have some first aid skill for dealing with emergencies (I know of as many heart attacks that have occurred on the shooting field as impact injuries). In the United Kingdom, the Red Cross and the St. John's Ambulance Brigade offer excellent training from one-day introductions to comprehensive, certificated courses. Find out as much as you can about proper procedures in the event of gunshot, severe burns and head and eye injury. A good first aid kit – not the miniature variety available from chemists and motoring shops—should always be kept at hand, and it is prudent to have a nominated phone line or a mobile phone for emergencies. When working away from your home ground, make sure you know precisely where you are (a grid reference is ideal) so that you can give directions if need be (when in the field, a mobile phone should, of course, be switched off).

Insurance

The importance of adequate insurance cover cannot be overstressed. Risk can be minimised, but never eliminated. This is a subject to discuss with an experienced broker, but we can note here that you will need insurance which covers you, your clients, employees and third parties. You may be able to cover all or some of your equipment in the same policy. If you are a member of a shooting organisation or a professional body, it may well pay to discuss the subject with them in the first instance. It may also be useful to ask colleagues what sort of insurance they have, how much it costs and where they got it.[12]

NOTES

1 The phrase was changed in the 1970s because so many soldiers in Northern Ireland were falling victim to their own or their comrade's weapons. The Army considered the problem in depth and decided that the concept of an accidental discharge was erroneous.

2 It is sometimes suggested that the traditional method reduces strain on the gun's action. If we are comparing it to slamming a gun shut by throwing the barrels up, this is true. However, the traditional method itself can cause some people to close the gun with less than complete control in a rather abrupt manner. They are so concerned with being seen to perform in what they have been told is the right way that they forget the need for control and unnecessarily increase the stress on the gun's stock by performing the action with excess gusto. I suspect that this method of gun closure was introduced merely to ensure that the muzzles stayed down as the gun was closed.

3 Because they are a complicating factor, cages should be avoided in the *ab initio*, stages of instruction (especially narrow cages with crossbars). If circumstances force you to use a cage, make sure that you are always in a position to intervene instantly. This will mean being in the cage with the client, even if it is a little cramped.

4 There are various ways to dispose of misfired cartridges. They may be tried in another gun. If the cartridge still fails to go off, it may be made safe by cutting through the main body of the cartridge case with a sharp knife to remove the propellent powder. This still leaves you with two problems: what to do with the powder and what to do with the primer. The powder may be

scattered safely onto soil. The primer section is best buried (not burned: there is always a danger that it might fly from its pocket on detonation and cause injury). In the UK, it is (nonsensically) illegal to 'unmake' ammunition. N.B. faulty cartridges may not be returned to the supplier or manufacturer by post.

5 *Rules for International Sporting*, as revised in November 1991.

6 67 and 67.5 mm shells are another potential cause for confusion. Many are intended to be used in 2½ in. chamber guns, but some high pressure loads may be unsuitable. Be guided by the box label: if in doubt ask the manufacturer, the supplier or the Proof House.

7 These figures are taken from the legal requirements in Britain, where an employer is obliged to make hearing protection available on request when background noise reaches 85 dB(A)LepD. When background sound levels at the workplace reach 90 dB(A)LepD or peak sound levels 140dB, hearing protection becomes mandatory.

8 Although some obscure Victorian patents probably exist, it would appear that the need to protect hearing was first officially recognised in the First World War. The first commercial plugs of which I am aware are the Mallock-Armstrong 1915 Pattern Ear Defender which are advertised in some pre-WW II Parker Hale catalogues as being 'supplied to the British Admiralty'. In spite of their existence and occasional use, the enforced wearing of ear defenders when shooting in the British services only came into effect in the 1970s. Many older servicemen are hearing disabled as a result.

9 In the same era, J.H. Steward's of Bisley were offering 'Rectiform Sports Spectacles' with 'white or tinted lenses' and an option of 'unsplinterable glass' and 'Chromos' tinted lenses to reduce glare when shooting into the sun (see *Game and Gun* Vol 15 No. 159, 1938, page 710). Similarly Parker Hale offered Dr Fieuzal's 'meniscus' spectacles with 'yellow-greenish' tint in their 1936 catalogue (and, quite possibly before) noting that they overcame the disadvantage of ordinary sunglasses giving clear vision without unnatural colour or distortion. The meniscus lenses were billed as 'following the same shape as the eyeball'.

10 However, unless specially coated, red lenses do not offer protection from the harmful effects of solar radiation.

11 In England, private individuals are limited by law in the quantity of explosive (loose powder, made-up cartridges and primers) that they may possess. They may keep 15 kg of black powder (or 10 kg of black powder and 5 kg of nitro) *plus* 15 kg of powder of any sort providing it is in the form of loaded 'small arms ammunition and primers' (about 12,000 12-bore cartridges). No more than 5 kg of nitro-based propellent may be kept in loose form.

12 The most experienced broker in this field in the United Kingdom is Norman Cooper, who is also the Hon. Insurance Advisor to the Clay Pigeon Shooting Association. He may be contacted at: Rawalpindi, Foxley Drive, Bishop's Stortford, Hertfordshire, CM23 2EB, England, Tel: (01279) 652166.

CHAPTER 2

Game Shooting Safety

Game shooting is less predictable and less controllable than clay shooting and because of this, it is inherently more dangerous. For the instructor, teaching game shooting safety presents special challenges. Game shooting safety is a complex subject. Although there are very definite rules to enhance safety whilst game shooting (and they are presented here as comprehensively as possible), the matter cannot be reduced *simply* to a set of rules. It may be said, however, that game shooting safety *begins* by learning the rules, and this will take considerable time and effort. As far as the instructor is concerned, teaching must be imaginative (simulating field conditions when the opportunity arises), methodical (so there are no gaps) and progressive.

The education of the modern game shot should begin in the shooting school or in similar controlled surroundings. It should, ideally, progress to training in the field with an instructor. All instruction will need to be reinforced and refined by experience. The goal, as in clay shooting, is for safety to become part of a pattern of behaviour. Once the rules are assimilated and experience gained, the whole becomes greater than the sum of the specific parts and safety becomes habitual and (almost) instinctive. Because the process is more complex in game shooting, it will take longer for the average person to become a safe game shot than to become a safe clay shot.

Existing standards
Most game shots think they are safe; most are not safe enough. The idea that they might cause, or be the victim of an accident is all too distant. As in other forms of shooting, the enemy is poor education and human ego. Meanwhile, it is sometimes said (often by shots whose own behaviour leaves a deal to be desired) that standards in the field have deteriorated in recent years because more people are coming into shooting from an urban background. There is some truth in this, as evidenced by the horror stories concerning totally inexperienced and untrained 'Guns' being allowed to shoot game on certain commercial shoots (in Britain, a member of a shooting party is referred to as a Gun). But many, if not most 'non-traditional' entrants to shooting accept their ignorance and seek out further education, either at a shooting school or by attending courses such as those run by some shooting organisations. On the other hand, some of the least safe shots are experienced sportsmen *who do not realise that they are unsafe.*

Whether or not standards have fallen, and whoever may be the worst offenders, it may be noted that we have become far more aware of safety in recent years and demand higher standards. Gone are the days when a beater might be paid off with a sovereign for being 'peppered'; the blacksmith given a set of barrels to repair; or a boy sent off unattended into a field with shotgun or rifle.

Anyone who bothers to think about it, must note that this is progress. The 'good old days' were far more dangerous than we would like to imagine.

History's most dangerous Guns

The Duke of Wellington was by all accounts an exceptionally unsafe shot. He once peppered the unfortunate Lord Granville with nine pellets in the face whilst shooting at Wherstead. He is also on record as wounding a beater and an old lady doing her washing. By an interesting coincidence, Napoleon Bonaparte seems to have been as dangerous with a sporting gun. He shot his great Marshal, Massena, in the left eye and legend has it that he immediately turned to the long-suffering Marshal Berthier – another member of the imperial shooting party – and exclaimed, 'Why did you do that?'. In another famous incident during the Regency, Lord Clermont was shot by Prinny, eldest son of George III, *The Times* recording at the time: 'Lord Clermont, having too hearty a breakfast, sat in a resting posture behind a furze-bush. Two of the Prince's dogs scented the noble peer and came to a point. His Royal Highness let fly at the furze-bush, wounding Lord Clermont in the defence-less portion of his body. The Prince's gun hung fire, or the snipe would have received the full charge. Twenty-three and a half grains of Number 4 shot were extracted from his lordship's bum'.

THE BASIC RULES OF SAFE GAME SHOOTING

Muzzle awareness

As with all forms of shooting, if you do not want to kill it, do not point your gun at it. In the immortal words of Commander Mark Beaufoy to his son:

> *... Never, never let your gun,*
> *Pointed be at anyone;*
> *That it may unloaded be*
> *Matters not the least to me.*

> *... But at all times think of this –*
> *'All the pheasants ever bred,*
> *Won't repay for one man dead'.*
> (the full poem appears in the appendix)

One should not only be aware of one's own gunhandling but should take careful note of that of others.

Carrying guns

When shooting driven game, a gun should be carried to and from one's shooting position in a slip, muzzles pointing down. The use of a slip promotes safety (not least by removing the temptation to shoot when one is not in position) and prevents gun damage (a padded slip is better than a thin one for this reason).

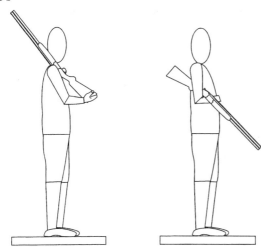

The traditional ways of carrying guns on a game shoot. The modern preference is for the gun to be carried open (and always unloaded) resting on the forearm. When moving between drives, the gun should be in a slip.

When it is appropriate to be walking with an uncovered gun, it should be unloaded with the action open whenever practical. It is bad practice to carry a closed shotgun (even unloaded with the safety applied), at any time when there is no need to. A few members of the old school, who habitually carry closed guns, will tell you that walking with an open side–by–side puts an extra strain on the action. There is a grain of truth in this, but the safety advantages of keeping a gun open outweigh it.[1]

When should the gun be loaded and closed?

The gun should only be out of the slip, loaded and closed, when you are in the process of walking up game, or in position in a line or hide ready to engage game. In such circumstances, the gun should, of course, always have the safety applied.

If shooting driven game, the gun should only be loaded and closed after the horn or whistle is blown at the beginning of the drive (unless other instructions are given: sometimes one is specifically told to load and be ready to shoot as soon as one reaches one's peg). The gun should be unloaded, physically proven empty, and immediately placed in a slip after the whistle or horn is sounded at the end of a drive (but not before, unless there is an emergency).

A loaded gun must never be put down when game shooting. A recent fatality occurred when this rule was breached: a dog stepped on the trigger of a gun which had been carelessly laid down with cartridges in the chambers.

Ready position

When standing or walking in line, one must be particularly careful not to point one's gun inadvertently at or near a neighbour. One must never hold or cradle the gun so that it rests horizontally across the arms. When loaded and closed, and with the safety applied and finger off trigger, the preferred position for the muzzles is pointing skywards at 45 degrees or above. It is also permissible to wait with the muzzles of the closed loaded gun, pointing into the ground at about 45 degrees in front of the shooter (again with finger off trigger). However, this waiting position has the disadvantage that one must move the muzzles of the gun through the horizon to engage a target. As beaters move

'The Gent from Town', (from the Badminton Library, *Shooting: Field and Covert* by Walsingham and Payne-Gallwey).

forward, it should always be avoided. As soon as the beaters come into sight, the barrels should be pointed upward. This should be achieved without the muzzles sweeping either the line of beaters or the line of Guns by moving the muzzles diagonally or by rotating the upper body rearwards and raising the gun from that position assuming that no one is behind.

Walking up game
When walking with a loaded gun one must be especially careful. If the ground is in any way suspect or any obstacle presents itself, open the action and unload. Two hands should be kept on the gun at all times (but one must guard against the tendency of the front hand to pull the muzzles back). The trigger finger should be extended along the trigger guard. If walking in a line or with a companion, you must constantly check to the right and left to make sure of the position of neighbouring Guns or Gun and to see if you are keeping up with the line. You must be especially careful of people creeping forward of the line on the flanks (and make sure you do not lag or creep yourself).

Target identification
Game shooting demands a cool head. Never shoot too fast. Never shoot where you cannot see. Never shoot at anything unless it is *clearly* identified. The student game shot must be familiar with the quarry he or she is likely to encounter (and it is part of the instructor's job to fill in any gaps in the students

knowledge). Moreover, one must always be aware of what might be behind, in front of or near a potential target. *Never shoot where you cannot see.* The driven game shot must constantly consider the position of beaters, pickers up and any other human or canine companions on the shooting field.

Ground game

Ground game has a special potential for danger: because it is at ground level; because it is easy to misidentify; and because it can tempt a Gun into swinging wildly or shooting into cover. I can remember a disaster concerning this sort of quarry which nearly befell me at the beginning of my shooting career. At the age of about 15, I was out shooting with a friend. I saw a large rabbit in a hedge and was in the act of bringing my gun up for a snap shot when the companion cried, 'Don't!' and grabbed my barrels. The rabbit, it transpired, was an old lady's head. She was lying on the other side of the hedge whilst picking blackberries, and had somehow contrived to twist her head sideways through a ground-level hole in the vegetation. I had expected a rabbit, so I saw one. I was very wrong. Only the timely intervention of my companion prevented a tragedy. Had I shot the woman, it would have been entirely my fault: for misidentifying the target, for being in too much of a hurry and, most importantly, for shooting where I could not see. I would prefer that my students learn such lessons less dramatically.

The problem of expectation

Noting my errors above, an interesting psychological point comes out of the incident: perception in human beings is affected by expectation and by the way the brain itself functions. Perception is an active process in which the brain processes input from the senses and considers it against memory. There is a tendency for the brain to complete a perceptual picture when the input is partial or ambiguous. It looks for patterns in the environment.

This has very important implications when shooting live quarry or when teaching people to shoot live quarry. Perception is not the absolute camera–like process most people think. Under certain circumstances, we can actually 'see'

'The Right Sort', from the Badminton, Library *Shooting: Field and Covert* by Walsingham and Payne-Gallwey. I would prefer to see the muzzles even higher.

something which is not there because the brain expects it to be there. To quote the psychologists Eysenck and Keane:

> ... the notion that perceptual analysis involves building up a representation of a visual scene from its individual elements may be misguided. Instead, initial global structuring is often fleshed out by progressively more and more fine grained analysis. There is obvious sense in having the perceptual system operate in this fashion, because it enables important objects in the visual scene to be identified and perceived with minimal delay ...

There is also an obvious danger in the context of shooting: one cannot immediately trust what one sees or hears. If you doubt this, look at the picture on the right. What do you see? An old lady or a beautiful girl? In other circumstances it might be a rabbit or a child.

Leepers' Ambiguous Lady

Foxes

It certainly ought to be an absolute rule not to shoot 'fur in front' (ground game or vermin in front of the line). Nevertheless, Guns are often put under considerable pressure to shoot foxes even when ground game is forbidden. Foxes usually present themselves in front or to the edges of the beating line. The temptation to shoot can be very great, but I have seen many shots taken at foxes which were not safe. Although there may be a certain glory in shooting a fox, I think they are best avoided because it is difficult to eliminate an element of risk: a shotgun firing bird shot is not a humane way to shoot these creatures anyway. The job is far better done with a centre fire .22 rifle (.22 Hornet, .222, .223 or 22-250 Remington).

Low birds

It is often said that one should never shoot at low birds. This is certainly true if one is shooting driven pheasant to one's front (where the old – and excellent – rule was always to see sky beneath the bird before considering a shot), and there are other situations in which it would be sound advice. When guns are placed in an arc rather than a straight line low birds may be especially dangerous. However, in some circumstances and with other safety considerations being satisfied, it will be acceptable to shoot lower birds: for example, when walking up partridges, when grouse shooting or when rough shooting in open fields. In such circumstances, one must be sure of the position of human and canine companions and of the ground behind the target. If one is walking up a

hedgerow, for example, low shots should only be taken away from the hedge
and with all other safety criteria being met.

When to shoot: rough shooting

First, the target must be a legal quarry species and it must be a safe shot.
Particular dangers while rough shooting are moving companions and cover.
Beginners, who tend to be impulsive, need to be taught to wait a moment
before firing when they flush a bird at close range. This avoids damaging the
meat and allows the bird to rise, thus giving one a little more time to assess the
safety of the shot. Beginners must also be taught always to pick a specific target. Shooting or 'browning' in the direction of a covey or flock is almost sure
to result in a miss and is extremely poor sportsmanship.

When to shoot: driven shooting

One must be in position on one's peg. One must have noted the positions of
neighbouring Guns and others who may be in the vicinity. The horn or whistle must have sounded (unless one has been given instructions to the contrary).
The target must not be prohibited and any shot at it must satisfy the basic
requirements of safety and conform to the rules of shooting etiquette. You
must teach your students carefully to assess the ground and surroundings as
soon as they arrive at a shooting position and to continue to do this as shooting progresses. If they have experience only on clays, you should have
explained to them just how different the driven shooting situation is and how
much more responsibility is placed upon them in it.

Safety zones for game shooting (after Churchill).

The 45 degree rule

As a general guide, a shot should never be taken (and the muzzles of a closed gun should never point) horizontally or vertically, within 45 degrees of any human being.

Arcs of fire

On driven shoots, one must also consider which birds one may properly shoot and which are best left for neighbouring Guns. A typical arc of fire when Guns are placed in a *straight line* might be about 90 degrees to one's front and rear (assuming there is no prohibition on taking birds behind the line). However, much will depend on the ground and the positioning of pegs. It may also be permissible to shoot birds outside this arc (the 45 degree rule above still being in force) if they have been missed or wounded by a neighbouring Gun.

It is impossible to lay down a general rule when the distance between Guns varies and the shooting line itself may not be straight. If one is positioned on the flanks of the line, a 180-degree arc may be safe. If one is in a staggered line (something to avoided when planning a driven shoot if at all possible), one might have a much reduced arc of fire on one side. Rather than get into complex geometry, I prefer to show my students a diagram of typical safe zones, and reinforce the really important and absolute rule: that no shot should be taken within 45 degrees of any person. Other rules of engagement relate to etiquette more than to safety.

Shooting 'down the line'

As far as driven shooting is concerned, novice game shots must fully understand the dangers of shooting or swinging 'down the line'. You will teach this as a matter of course. You must explain that there is a particular danger of swinging into a danger zone when taking a second shot at a bird which was missed on the quarter. The momentum of the gun combined with adrenaline-induced overeagerness – can carry the muzzles towards one's shooting companions, unless the movement is *deliberately checked*. Shooting at fast targets, like grouse, is especially dangerous because of this.

Crossing obstacles

When crossing obstacles such as gates, fences or ditches in the field:

1 Make sure the gun is unloaded and open.
2 If practical, before climbing over the obstacle, lay the unloaded, open gun down on the other side.

When shooting with a companion, one person should cross the obstacle first. The person left on the other side should then pass over both guns, stock first, having first proven them to be unloaded and unobstructed. When you come to pick up a gun that you have placed on the other side of an obstacle, or when you accept a gun from a companion, double check that it is unloaded and unobstructed stating the word 'clear' to show that you have checked its status.

Use of safety catch

The safety should only be disengaged once the target has been identified as safe (and licit), *momentarily before* the gun is raised to the face and shoulder. The index finger *must not* be resting on the trigger as the safety is removed. It is best placed extended along the trigger guard. If no shot is taken, the safety should be reapplied at once. It is a bad habit to remove the safety as the gun is mounted or to fiddle with it while waiting for birds.

The so-called 'safety catch' on most shotguns is often no more than a trigger block. A gun can still go off with the safety applied – a point which must be made very clearly to all students. Many cheaper guns do not have an intercepting safety sear – the device which usually prevents a hammer jarred out of position from falling on the striker – and even guns with intercepting sears are not infallible, as Robert Churchill was fond of demonstrating.

Though its action must not be relied upon, the safety does have an important function when game shooting. When properly used, it makes accidental discharge less likely. To fire a gun with the safety applied, two distinct actions are required: pushing off the safety and pressing the trigger. The possibility of nervous compression of the trigger is thus reduced. The safety should be applied at all times when the gun is closed, unless one is in the act of shooting.

Tradition and common sense dictate that drop or break-action game guns should be equipped with an automatic safety catch (consequently, when teaching game shooting, you should be using a gun with an automatic safety).[2] Its application cannot be forgotten under pressure. However, automatic safety catches are not foolproof. Although they may be applied automatically, they can be removed prudently or imprudently any time thereafter. Instructors and loaders should always be on the lookout for someone who has the tendency to remove the safety early when simulating, or actually shooting, game.

Use of safety catch: clayshooters shooting game

When you watch them game shooting, you will notice that many clay shots do not use the safety properly. This may occur either because they have not been taught how to use it correctly in a game shooting context, or because they are under pressure. It is a general principle of firearms training that individuals, when stressed, tend to revert to what is most familiar to them. Clay shots finding themselves shooting game may thus remove their safety catch too early – whether or not they know better – simply because they are used to removing the safety catch well before shooting in clay shooting. They may also forget to reapply the safety (especially if they are using a non-auto safe clay gun). The instructor, faced with a client moving from clay to game, must be aware of this tendency, and condition the client into a new, safer habit.

Hammer guns

Hammer guns should be carried uncocked or half-cocked (non-rebounding types) unless there is an immediate expectation of a shot. Barrels should point up when a hammer gun is cocked (it also makes cocking easier). Fingers must be around the trigger guard and the thumb positively located in the crutch of the hammer before cocking. Before uncocking, the gun should be broken and the chambers unloaded. The barrels should be controlled in a safe direction throughout.

Shooting 'Behind the Line'

Unless there is a specific prohibition, it will often be permissible to take a bird behind the line provided all other safety criteria are met. On many occasions in the field and, most notably when grouse shooting, this will be the best way to take a particular target. On all occasions, the shooter is responsible for confirming the safety of the shot before pulling the trigger. The specific danger when taking birds behind, is that one has not been watching that area as intently as one has been watching the area to one's front.

Teaching the turn

Turning is an awkward business for the novice. The time to introduce it is once you feel the individual is confident in his basic technique, and has developed a good, balanced stance and a smooth mount and swing (there is much sense in restricting novices to shots in front of the line in their first season's shooting). There are various methods for achieving the turn, but the crucial point is that, as the Gun turns, he must keep the muzzles well up, thus avoiding swinging or shooting down the line. The angle of the muzzles during the turn should be not less than 60 degrees. Good footwork is also important to stay balanced. The turn is considered in more detail on page 220.

Shooting from hides

The first thing to note is that there are important safely considerations in hide construction. A hide which is too small will be awkward and increase both the likelihood of accidents and the temptation to handle guns improperly. In particular, there must be sufficient room to the front to allow for safe loading and handling. Guns must never be loaded and propped up whilst waiting for a bird; if the gun is loaded, it must be controlled by the user.

The problems of shooting from hides are compounded when more than one person is shooting. Some experienced pigeon shots now consider it a bad practice for two guns to be simultaneously in use in a hide. They believe that during double occupancy, one person should shoot and the other should act as observer and spotter. Roles may change periodically. When they do, the observer/spotter's gun should be proven clear and placed in a slip. My own feeling is that two guns may be used simultaneously when one is shooting with a regular partner, but not initially at least in other circumstances.

Position in the hide is an important consideration in double occupancy. When two Guns sit side by side, there is always the danger, in the heat of the moment, of one person pointing a gun at the other. Loading is dangerous too. The best position for the non-shooting person is always to the rear. Moreover, the non-shooter should be positioned to one side (the right rear when behind a right-handed shot; and the left rear when behind a left-handed shot).

Lofting poles

A specific danger when decoying for pigeon is the use of aluminium lofting poles which, like carbon fibre fishing rods, can conduct electricity from high tension cables. The poles do not actually need to touch the cables either: the very powerful currents in pylon wires can jump to a nearby conductor.

The etiquette of formal shooting

In formal shooting, the line which separates safety and etiquette is not easily drawn. Much shooting etiquette is connected with safety. I am often asked by beginners for definite rules concerning shooting field etiquette and, as far as possible, attempt to comply with the request. I think by far the best advice one can give – apart from suggesting formal instruction in the field – is to tell students to find an experienced game shot who will stand behind them on their first few outings. Such a 'minder' will also explain the customs and terms of game shooting, things which are best learnt in the field. If I am acting as shoot captain, I insist that any shot new to formal game shooting be accompanied by a suitably experienced individual.

Nevertheless, there are some basic points of etiquette with which the novice must be familiar before he or she reaches the field. For example, one should not shoot at birds which are too close (although they may satisfy the requirements of safety), nor birds which are too distant and likely to be wounded. It is bad form to shoot a bird, even if it is within one's arc, if it is flying toward a neighbouring Gun, or would make a better shot for a neighbour than for you. If you are walking with the beaters do not shoot birds going towards the Guns, but only those birds which come back. If a neighbour on the line misses a bird, do not shoot until he has fired a second barrel or until it is apparent that he is not going to fire a second time. Never be greedy.

When positioned on a peg, keep still and keep quiet. If you miss a bird, forget about it (but if you wound one and it flies on, note carefully where it comes down). If you shoot a bird well, do not brag about it. Do not forget the peg number you draw and remember that it is normal to move up two positions between drives (but listen carefully for exceptions when briefed by the shoot captain). When you shoot a bird, note where it falls as precisely as you can (the eyes should be kept on the bird for a moment after the shot is taken), so that you may give instructions to pickers-up or retrieve it yourself at the end of the drive. (Following the bird visually after the shot is taken also ensures a good follow through).

Count your birds. Do not leave the field until your birds have been retrieved. Do not retrieve your neighbour's birds without asking. While shooting is in progress, do not be tempted to leave your shooting position to retrieve a bird, even if it is wounded (this is a point of safety as much as of etiquette). Do not shoot vermin on a driven shoot unless you have been told it is permissible. Similarly, do not assume that you can shoot pigeon (many shoot captains prefer Guns to avoid pigeon in the early stages of a drive). A useful general principle on any game shoot is: 'If in doubt, *don't*'. This obviously applies to safety, but it is also a good principle as far as etiquette is concerned.

If someone has been kind enough to invite you to a shoot, write a thank-you letter the evening after the shoot and post it as soon as possible. Never retract an acceptance of an invitation because a 'better' opportunity is subsequently offered. On the subject of tipping, the best advice to anyone who goes to a new shoot is to ask the other Guns what they usually give. Do not be stingy: tips are an important part of most gamekeepers' income, which at best is modest considering the skills and responsibilites of the job. Also remember to thank the beaters and pickers-up after a shoot: their hard work is too often forgotten.

Despatching game

All game shots have a duty to despatch their quarry as humanely as possible. Not all birds will be dead when they hit the ground (although the number of wounded birds will be reduced if: one restricts oneself to birds within sensible range; one's equipment is appropriate, and one has a responsible attitude toward improving and maintaining one's marksmanship skills). Some novices will attempt to pick up birds by their feet, rather than their necks. How to pick up a bird may seem obvious to someone who has done it all their life, but it is precisely the sort of point which needs explaining to a new or young Gun.

A good way to kill a wounded game bird is by a swift blow to the back of its head. This may done with a stout stick or a 'priest' – a metal or wooden truncheon made especially for the purpose. There are also pincer style humane despatchers. Birds should not be held by the head or neck and swung in an attempt to break their necks. This technique is used by some experienced countrymen, but there is a knack to it. It is easy to get it wrong and not kill the game cleanly. The novice is far better advised to buy or make a priest. Rabbits may be despatched with a karate-like chop to the back of the neck, or similarly with a priest, or by holding the neck with one hand and pulling the rear legs sharply with the other until the neck vertebrae are dislocated.

Finally, here are twelve commandments for game shooting safety. Note that the list is slightly different from the one that appeared at the end of the previous chapter on clay shooting safety.

SAFE AND SEEN TO BE SAFE
The Twelve Commandments for Safe Game Shooting
(again, feel free to copy this list and distribute it as you wish).

1 **Guns should always be handled as if they were loaded. If you do not want to kill it, do not point your gun at it.**

2 **Check that your gun is unloaded** when you pick it up, when you put it down, when it is passed to you, or when you pass it to someone else.

3 Before loading, **check for obstructions.** Mud or snow can block barrels and blow the gun up. So can a 20-bore cartridge, if your gun is a 12.

4 **Close your gun under control**, with muzzles pointing in a safe direction. Make sure the safety is applied and your **finger off the trigger** as you do so. Beware the beating line.

5 Only raise your gun to a **clearly identified target,** and if you are sure there is **nothing behind** the target.

6 Do not remove the safety catch prematurely. Keep your finger off the trigger until the safety is on 'fire'. If you do not fire, reapply the safety immediately.

7 **Always unload** a gun before crossing an obstacle such as a fence or stream. If you are crossing the obstacle with a companion, guns should be unloaded and open. One person should cross, and the other should then pass over the guns **stock-first** and with the actions still open.

8 When walking, keep the gun pointing **towards sky** or ground, muzzles forward. Note the position of companions at all times.

9 **Whenever practical, open the action** of your gun and remove the cartridges. Carry your gun action open resting on your forearm or, where practical, unloaded, muzzles down in a slip.

10 Never allow the muzzles of your closed gun to pass within **45 degrees** of a human being.

11 Make sure that a gun is in **serviceable condition** – well maintained and in proof – before using it. Only use **cartridges** in your gun **which are suitable:** i.e., which correspond to the proof marks on the gun with regard to pressure and chamber length Most shotguns sold in the UK today have been proofed for use with 2¾ in. (70 mm) shells. However, many older guns have not been. The old standard was 2½ in. (in which, subject to proof pressure, 65 mm and many 67 and 67.5 mm cartridges may be used). Modern 2¾ in. cartridges will fit into 2½ in. chambers, but if fired are potentially dangerous.[3] If you have any doubts, ask a gunsmith.

12 **Beware the invisible man.** If you have any doubts, **don't shoot.** You are responsible once you pull the trigger.

NOTES

1 The traditional methods of carrying uncovered guns on the game shooting field are either broken and resting on the forearm with the trigger guard behind the arm; or closed and unloaded, resting on the shoulder, trigger guard up, with barrels well up (45 degrees or more). I do not teach the latter method; when practised with discipline, it is safe and looks most elegant, but it is so easy for the muzzles to fall low inadvertently.

2 Many mass produced break-action guns are easily convertible – typically they have a safety bar which is pushed by the back of the bolt and itself then pushes back the safety slide. Conversion to non-auto function merely requires removal of the bar. Conversely, conversion of no-auto guns to auto function is also easily accomplished either by a proprietory part of by fabrication of a connecting rod.

3 65, 67 and 67.5 mm cartridges may, however, be safely fired in 2 ¾ in. (70 mm) or 3 in. (76 mm) chambers provided proof pressure criteria are met.

CHAPTER 3

Gun Condition and Proof

A shooting instructor must be able to assess the condition of a gun quickly, and he must have an understanding of proof and the ability to recognise and identify proofmarks. The two subjects overlap, but it is easier to consider them separately. Hence, in this section of the book, we shall look at general mechanical condition first, and consider proof in some detail thereafter.

To assess gun condition requires all the skills of a detective. Specifics are very important, as we shall discuss; but so is one's gut feeling, the reliability of which improves greatly with experience. Sometimes, for no apparent reason, a red light will flash when examining a gun. It should never be ignored.

When assessing the condition of a gun, the first thing to do – having proven the weapon empty – is to have a general look. Do you know the maker? How much has the gun been used? You can usually see immediately if metal or woodwork has been refinished (unless the work has been done by craftsmen of the first class), or if it has been abused. Having made a brief visual inspection, bring the gun to your shoulder. What is the balance like? Do the barrels appear short or long? Might they have been shortened? Are the stock dimensions normal? Open and close the action. Does it rattle? Could the gun be off the face? Is it very stiff? Has it been tightened? How do the safety catch and top lever function?

The 'Tap Test'
Prove the gun empty. With the locks cocked, tap the action with your hand and also tap the butt on a protective mat. If the sears are worn, the hammers may fall. Commonsense applies, as always. If this test is performed with excessive force, there is a risk of a broken stock, especially on guns which are thin in grip and/or heavily cast.

Strip the gun down
Noting these early impressions (which are especially important if negative, but not to be relied upon if positive), take the gun apart as if you were about to clean it. If the gun has a quick detachable locks, remove them as well. If the gun is a sidelock of conventional pattern, you may also decide to remove the locks. A gun is better examined with the locks off: stock cracks and poor repair work are made much easier to detect.

However, when removing locks you must use a turn screw or screwdriver of precisely the right size and you must make sure that you have adequate purchase on the screw head. If you do not have the proper turn screw, or if have any doubts about your ability to use one (and there is a definite skill to it), do not attempt the procedure: wait until you have been taught by a gunsmith. Nothing looks worse than a gun with spoilt screw heads.[1]

Start with the barrels

With the gun disassembled into its major components, pick up the barrels. Look at the surfaces very carefully. Are there signs of refinishing such as worn engraving on the rib? Does the blacking look too good for the age of the gun? Does it match the blacking on the trigger guard and other parts? Is the blacking dull or thin (as second or third class blacking often is), or does it have depth?[2]

Even when a gun has been refinished by an expert, if the rust pits have been deep, it is unlikely that they have all been removed. Look for minor external pit marks where they are most likely to occur: e.g., the trigger guard, tang and so forth. Also, note that many older guns were charcoal-blued, which virtually no-one in the trade nowadays can replicate. Bluing may appear perfect but not match the original.

Has the gun been sleeved?

Examine the piece meticulously. Although a gun which has been re-sleeved must be marked 'sleeved' by law in the UK, it is now possible (and indeed desirable) to use a TIG welder to disguise the telltale lines where the sawn-off chamber assembly is joined to new tubes. Welding may also be used to disguise the join, otherwise visible, under the extractors and at the rim recess. I have recently heard of a B25 Browning with one sleeved barrel disguised in this way. I anticipate that quite a few guns will arrive in the United States in years to come with dishonest sleeving (i.e., sleeved but not marked as such). There is no proof law to protect buyers of old guns in that country. (This is an objection to dishonesty rather than to sleeving, which can be an excellent way of giving an old gun a new lease on life.) In any cases of doubt, a gun may be x-rayed to confirm whether it has been sleeved or not.

Damascus steel

If the gun is old, look at the grain of the metal. Is it Damascus steel that has been blued? This used to be done occasionally to disguise twist steel. Now that Damascus barrels have become collectable, it is less commonly seen. We might note, moreover, that Damascus steel varies greatly in quality (and thus, safety). Unfortunately, it is very hard to detect the different qualities of Damascus steel by vision alone (which is why proof is vital). Cheaper Damascus barrels may have been made of skelp (a single strand process).

Visual examination of bores

Look down the barrels from both ends. Is there any pitting in front of the chamber or behind the chokes? What about the bores? Have the forcing cones been modified? Are the chambers pitted? Are the bores bright? Are they suspiciously perfect? Could they have been enlarged? A quick glance at the proof marks might be appropriate at this stage (measurement will come later, if you have the equipment).

Dents and bulges

The barrels must be checked for dents and bulges internally and externally. Gently squeeze the barrels between the pads of index finger and thumb and, maintaining a gentle pressure, run the fingers up and down the tubes. Touch is very sensitive and a good way of picking up flaws that might otherwise escape you. The barrel bores must be inspected visually too. It is easy to look through barrels, but to cast a shadow along their internal surface, as a barrel maker does, is a knack that must be acquired.

With the muzzles pointing towards you, pivot the barrels on the weak hand, with a bright but diffuse source of light behind (fluorescent light or, much better, clouded sky). Keeping the weak hand steady, use your other hand to move the muzzles through a small circle, so that you cast a shadow along the internal walls of the barrels. This shadow will show up the slightest flaw. Do the same thing with the chamber mouths pointing towards you and carefully inspect the chamber, forcing cone, etc.

Bulges, which can be serious, may have been formed because a dent was left unrepaired or because of a barrel obstruction in the past. (Ring bulges may occasionally be seen at the muzzles because of excessive choke constriction). Sometimes, what appears to be a dent or bulge is no more than a surface imperfection. Look carefully inside and out. Dents, usually, are not an especially serious problem. They are easily removed with a special lifting tool, but a little metal (perhaps a thousandth of an inch or two) is lost from the barrels walls when the job is completed by lapping out.

You will often come across a barrel which has been repaired in this way, but where the work is still visible on the surface (the telltale sign is tapping marks on the barrel surface). This occurs when the owner, or the gunsmith, did not wish to spend more money, or time, on complete refinishing.

The outside surface of the barrels must be examined for bulges or rivelling. Use the shadow casting method again for examining the outer surface. Cheaper guns, especially side-by-sides, will often have less than perfect external surfaces because they have not been 'struck up' adequately. As long as the bores and wall thicknesses are adequate, this is not a great problem.

Pimple bulges

To quote a special memorandum issued by the Proof Authorities:

> Since 1967 there have been increasing complaints of shotgun barrels developing small pimple bulges usually on the underside of the left barrel of double guns, or in similar positions in the second barrel of over-and-under guns. This unusual damage has mystified gunmakers and cartridge manufacturers and the expensive repairs have pained the unfortunate owners.

Apparently, the bulges are caused when pellets escape from poorly crimped cartridges (and especially poorly crimped paper reloads). They move forward along the bore and are struck by the rest of the charge on firing. The problem afflicts second barrels, because the escape of pellets is prompted by the recoil on firing the first.

PLATE 1

One must get in the habit of automatically extending the trigger finger along the trig-ger guard when handling guns.

Taking a gun from the rack. Note I am opening it with the muzzles still pointing up. Too many people are careless about muzzle sweep when taking guns from racks or removing them from cars.

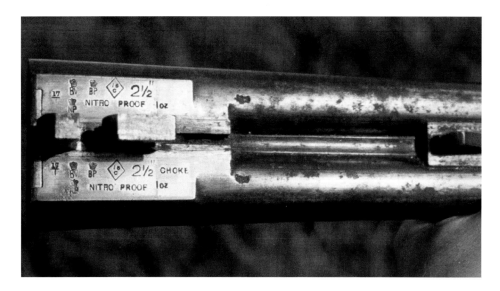

PLATE 2

(above) An instructor must become familiar with proof marks. This 16-bore has Nitro Proof for 2 ½ in. cartridges. Notice the barrels were originally made 17/1 ('seventeen over one'), indicating tight original bore dimensions. If over .662 at 9 in., it would be out of proof. BV stands for Birmingham View; BP for Birmingham Proof ; and NP for Nitro Proof. The 16 c in a diamond confirms standard chambers (16 'lc' would indicate 'long chambers'). The gun is proofed under 1925 Rules.

(below) Old guns may have very thick barrel walls or weak spots created by water penetrating beneath the rib. Always get a gunsmith to check out any suspect gun (and all old guns should be considered so) and always check for obstructions before loading lest this happens to you or a client.

Pimple bulges are rarely seen, and for this reason are only occasionally mentioned outside the gun trade, but they are worth knowing about both as far as assessing gun condition is concerned, and so that action may be taken to avoid them: i.e., beware of reloads with poor crimps, do not use cartridges in which there is any evidence of pellet escape, and make a habit of changing the second cartridge routinely if one is making a lot of first barrel kills.

Bent barrels

Your internal examination of the bores should not just concentrate on wear, damage or modifications. Looking down the line of the bore axis from the chamber-end of the barrels, one should be able to see a series of concentric shadow circles. If the circles are not concentric, the barrels are not straight. This is quite common on cheaper guns and is also an affliction of some mass-produced but relatively expensive weapons.[3]

The barrels of double guns are sometimes bent through heat distortion when ribs are re-laid. It is also advisable to check guns after (and before) such procedures, just to make sure this has not happened. All this said, many guns have barrels which are slightly out of true. As long as the condition is not gross and the gun is properly fitted and regulated, it may be ignored. Never tell a student that his barrels are bent - less than one barrel in a hundred is perfectly straight - unless you think something needs to be done about it! You will destroy his confidence in the gun.

Become a detective

One must become a detective when looking at guns. Little things are important. For example, the bead. Is it original? Study the muzzles. Are there any holes visible between barrel tubes and ribs? What about choke? Is there any? Have the barrels been shortened? If multichokes have been fitted, look at the rear of the choke tube in the barrel. Is it properly centred? Look at the front of the tube and at the barrel wall around it.

In some guns which have been fitted with multichokes after manufacture, the barrel wall at the muzzles may be very thin and the choke tube may appear slightly off-centre. Usually, this is just an aesthetic problem, but not always. If the muzzle walls are very thin, the gun may not be suitable for use with high pressure loads. Finally, remove the choke tubes; both to make sure they are not stuck and to check that there is no rusting behind the multichokes.

Internal dimensions

Shooters are becoming much more interested in the internal dimensions of their barrels than in the past, and not just for reasons of safety. The same instrument which can tell if pitting has been lapped out of the barrel by polishing (which could devalue an expensive gun significantly), can also tell you if a gun has a particularly tight or open bore, and tell you the precise choke restriction: all factors which will affect the way it shoots, and thus be of interest to both client and instructor. I think a bore micrometer is so useful (one measures chokes with it, too) that it really ought to be considered essential equipment. It is a much more flexible system than the older one of using bore plugs for ascertaining barrel dimension. Many gunsmiths and some professional instructors are also in possession of wall thickness gauges (see the end of the chapter for a list of commercial sources for the specialist equipment mentioned here).

However, measuring instruments are not infallible. With older guns, the combination of a re-laid rib (see below), and the removal of pitting from the bore, may materially reduce the wall thickness directly under the rib. Once everything has been put back together, wall thickness at this point will be impossible to measure. Renovated guns sent for proof sometimes split along this seam.

Joining and sighting ribs
Examine the joining and sighting ribs carefully. Ribs on older guns can detach themselves from the barrels because moisture has seeped between the rib and the tube. This is not necessarily a very serious problem, it depends on how deep the pitting beneath the rib is. When a loose rib is detected, it must be dealt with (gunmakers speak of 're-laying ribs') immediately. The structural integrity of the barrels may have been compromised, which must be checked. Also, if left unrepaired, a detached rib will allow moisture in between the barrels and rib, causing more problems.

The traditional way to test barrels for detached ribs is to suspend them vertically by the lump and then to tap them with a pencil. If they do not ring true (if there is a rattle rather than a ring, or a very dull ring), then there may be a problem with the rib.

Lumps
The barrel lumps should be examined carefully. Has a piece been dovetailed into the lump at the hook? Or has a centre punch been used to peen it and bring it up to the bearing surface of the hinge pin? (We shall consider the joint between barrel and action in detail shortly). If the lump is of the dovetail type, are there any signs of its joint to the barrel tubes failing?

Action
Having carefully examined the barrels, pick up the stock and action. Is there finish on the action? Is it original? Has the action been brush-burnished? Is the finish too good for the age of the gun? Are there signs of metal fatigue (look at the grain of the metal on the underside of the action)?

Look at the body of the action very carefully. If it is dirty, clean it. Are there any signs of cracking or weld repair on the action flats or face? On older guns, look especially at the area where the action face meets the action flats (remember, the action flexes on firing). Is there any pitting? Is it deep or superficial? Are there signs that the extractors are scrubbing the face? Is there a polished or scratched appearance to any part of the face?

Look at the knuckle of the action where it bears against the iron of the forend. Are there any score marks? If there are, look immediately at the forend too. Are there signs of galling on the bearing surfaces that mate with the action knuckle?

Try the top lever and safety catch again. Is their action crisp? Does the top lever spring need replacing? Using a block against the action face, try the triggers. What do they feel like? Is there creep? Are they very light or heavy? What about the impact of the strikers? Is it strong or weak?

Triggers

A gun in serviceable condition will have trigger pulls which are firm and crisp. Trigger pulls would normally be about 3½ lb (front or first) and 4 lb (rear or second pull), athough there are some significant exceptions – some trap shots prefer very light pulls. (It is worth making up your own pull gauge from a set of fishing scales and some wire.) It is inadvisable to try to instruct someone with a gun which has poor trigger pulls. Light pulls are dangerous because they may go off unexpectedly, heavy pulls require too much muscular effort and put a beginner off. Trigger pulls affect timing profoundly. I believe good pulls – crisp and not too light or heavy – are as important to good shooting as good gunfit.

If the gun has a single trigger of the inertia type, one may move the barrel selector or administer a sharp blow to the butt sole to trip the mechanism. In double guns especially, look at the trigger blades carefully. Have they been twisted at their base? In other words, was the gun made for a left-hander originally? Careful examination of the stock may also reveal a conversion: there may be signs of bending at the wrist, or the comb cast may not look quite right.

With the strikers visible, examine their tips with a magnifying glass. Are they well shaped, or are there signs of chipping or other wear? Have the strikers been fouling the extractors? Look at the holes through which the strikers protrude. Are they disc set strikers? Is there evidence that they have been removed (such as re-blacking)? Does the gun have gas venting channels around the striker holes (common on Victorian guns and some Continental copies of English guns)? If the gun has hammers, do they match?

Examine the lockwork. Are there signs of inept repair? Does the quality of the normally hidden lockwork match the apparent quality of the gun? Some cheaper sidelocks look pretty on the outside, but the lockwork gives away their true value. On the other hand, occasionally, one will see a very plain, border-engraved gun, which has locks of the first class.[4]

Jointing

Assemble the gun, but leave the forend off. Holding the gun with one hand at the grip, try and rattle the barrels. Is there any sign of movement? Hold the gun up to the light. Can you see a gap between the barrels and action face? (A very slight gap between the flats of the barrels and the flats of the action is essential. The action flexes when the gun is fired. If there were no clearnace built into it, it might crack.) Another method for checking the jointing involves holding the gun vertically and placing the stock between your thighs. The muzzles should be secured skywards with one hand, while the other holds the action at the joint and gently applies pressure from side to side. Any looseness will be immediately apparent.

Even slight movement indicates that the gun is 'off the face' and requires re-jointing to bring it back into serviceable condition. If you fire a gun which is off the face, it will recoil excessively and put unnecessary stress on the action and lumps. It is a problem which only gets worse. Nevertheless, you will find that many older guns are loose; and, among modern guns, some Brownings and nearly all Winchesters have a tendency to rattle a bit after some years of use. The Webley 700 series also has a tendency to do this (not because of its solid hinge pin design as sometimes thought, but because of the design of its hook which is prone to bending open under stress). Many shots use loose guns in this state for years, oblivious to the fact that recoil is gradually increasing. You should always advise immediate repair. This is not necessarily an expensive operation, although beware of gunsmiths who shortcut the proper procedure by squeezing actions in the vice, peening the lump and the like. To bring the gun back onto the face may require a new hinge pin and work on the lump. In the old days, a piece of new metal was dovetailed into the bearing surface of the lump. Today, a neater job can be accomplished by TIG welding and remachining.

Ejectors

To check the timing and power of the ejectors, one requires an assembled gun and a pair of identical snap caps. Prove the gun empty, load the snap caps, and dry fire both barrels of the gun in a safe direction. Open the gun slowly and fix your eyes on the snap caps. As the ejectors are tripped, they will fly out. Watch their flight. Are both together in the air? Or did one eject first? With well-timed ejectors, both snap caps should be next to each other in flight. If this is not the case, the ejectors may need retiming.

Woodwork

Carefully examine the stock and forend. Use a magnifying glass if necessary. If possible, remove the stock from the action. In the case of sidelocks, examina-tion will always be easier with the locks off. At the risk of repeating myself: look very, very carefully. Faults in stocks, such as hairline cracks, are hard to spot and drastically affect value.

Pay particular attention to any area where wood meets metal. The head of the stock, the grip and the area immediately behind top and bottom straps are all common sites for cracks. Look at the main body of the stock. Are there any flaws in the wood? Is there any sign of wood lifting? Do forend and butt wood match? If they do not, or if the chequering is different, it may be a sign of restocking. Has the gun an extreme of cast? If so, pay special attention to the grip. Less reputable parties have often filled cracks in the wrist with a mixture of shellac and wax, hiding the start of a crack.

Forend

With the forend, the procedure is very similar. Again, pay special attention to the area where metal and wood meet. Some guns are very prone to cracks in the forend: the Winchester 101 for example. It is often possible to repair cracked forends almost invisibly by squeezing 'SuperGlue', or something similar, into the crack and clamping. A little wire wool and some linseed oil will finish the job. The same method often works with stock cracks too.

Repeaters

In Britain, we are not that familiar with repeaters. However, much of what has been written above applies to them as well. There are some special points. On pumps, cycle the action. Does the action lock tightly when the bolt moves forward? With the action locked, try to cycle the action without pulling the trigger. It should hold firm. Does the forend appear very loose? Carefully examine the surface of the magazine tube along which the forend trombones for wear.

Look at the extractor. Broken extractors are a common problem with older repeaters. What about the surface of the bolt face? Is it pitted? Disassemble the gun. If it is a gas-operated semi-automatic, note whether it has been properly cleaned around the gas port. Are there signs of heavy carbon deposits? If so, it may not be a serious matter, but rather an indication that the owner was not keen on cleaning and a possible cause of malfunction. Look at the magazine tube. Has it been converted to restricted capacity by crimping? Does it bear the appropriate proof house stamps? Returning to the action, note the slot for the cocking handle at the rear of the chamber port. Occasionally, cracks form here in guns which have been very heavily used. This is an occasional problem with the otherwise excellent Remington 1100.

Conclusion

An instructor should make it his or her business to learn as much as possible about the things which commonly go wrong with guns, and the procedures for putting them right. However, leave the gunsmithing to the professionals. Although there are some small jobs which you might be tempted to do, pass them on to an expert. Many times a gun which goes in for repair of something simple turns out to have something else wrong with it which only a trained gunsmith would have spotted.

Sources of Measuring Instruments

Jim Wills of Bath makes an excellent wall-thickness gauge which is exceptionally good value. He also operates an efficient mail order service and may be contacted at 4 Gloucester Street, Julian Road, Bath BA1 2SE. Tel: (01225) 4450621

In the United States, bore micrometers, wall-thickness gauges and just about anything else you might imagine – from a recoil pad to a lathe, to a can of spray on grit (for improving grip on synthetics stocks) – are available from Brownells Inc. at Route 2, Box 1, Montezuma, Iowa 50171, USA. Tel: (00 1 515) 623 5401; Fax: (00 1 515) 623 3896, www.brownells.com.

If nothing else, get in touch with this first-class firm and acquire a copy of their magnificent catalogue: it is a valuable reference work in itself.

US barrel maker, Stan Baker, is well known for his bore and choke gauges, as well as for his innovative work on back-bored barrels. He may be contacted at 10,000 Lake City Way, Seattle, Washington 98125, U.S.A. Tel: (00 1 206) 522 4575.

PROOF

Proof relates to serviceability, and is a vitally important aspect of gun safety that every instructor must understand. It would be too much to ask instructors to be truly expert in this complex subject, with all its international ramifications; but they must develop a working knowledge of British and the more common foreign proof marks; and must moreover be able to recognise the limitations of their knowledge. If in any doubt on a question of proof: consult a gunsmith, an experienced member of the gun trade or, best of all, one of the proof houses. You will find both Masters extremely helpful.

Notes on the Proof of Shotguns and Other Small Arms, a booklet produced by the British Proof Authorities, should be a compulsory purchase for any instructor operating in this country. Moreover, instructors will be well advised to acquire the more detailed *Rules of Proof, 1989,* as well. Both publications are available from the Proof House, 48 Commercial Road, London, E1 1LP, (Tel: (020) 7481 2695); or the Gun Barrel Proof House, Banbury Street, Birmingham, B5 5RH, (Tel: (0121) 643 3960). The proof houses also provide other publications at nominal cost including memoranda on sleeving, pimple bulges on shotgun barrels, and the proof of guns for magnum cartridges.

History

Proof, which involves test firing guns with an especially powerful proof load, was introduced both as means of ensuring public safety, and as a form of gun trade protectionism. In the early days of the gun trade, many people (who were not gunmakers) attempted to make guns. The Gunmakers' Company of London was first granted a Royal Charter in 1637, and from its earliest days was involved in proof testing; the Birmingham Proof House was established in 1813, although private proof houses had existed in Birmingham before that date.[5]

The idea of the proof test is to show up any material weakness in the steel. There is an argument that the firing of high-pressure proof loads might itself weaken a gun, but centuries of experience have proven the efficacy of the present system. Guns do fail proof quite regularly. Indeed, I have seen a number which have failed it most dramatically; several of these were of modern manufacture. Proof is no academic consideration.

The law on proof is extensive. There are Gun Barrel Proof Acts of 1868, 1950 and 1970, and there are also Rules of Proof which supplement the Acts. The most important Rules of Proof are those of 1925, 1954, 1986 and 1989. The 1986 Rules introduced the metric system to British proof.

The Proof Authorities state:

> The provision of the [proof] Acts apply to all small arms, whether of present use or future invention, within certain fixed limits of bore size and projectile weight (with

the exception of some military arms made for the use of H.M. Forces). Air guns, not being firearms, are specifically excluded.

The Proof Acts lay down no small arm may be sold, exchanged or exported, exposed or kept for sale unless and until it has been fully proved and duly marked. The maximum penalty is £1,000 for each offence, but with provision for higher penalties ...

Arms previously proved and bearing apparently valid proof marks are deemed unproved if the barrels have been enlarged in the bore beyond certain defined limits or if the barrel or action has been materially weakened in other respect.

All new guns sold in Britain have either been proofed in the country by one of the two proof houses, or by a recognised International Proof Commission (CIP) proof house in another country. In Britain we recognise the proof marks of: Austria, Belgium, Chile, the Czech. Republic, Finland, France, Germany, Hungary, Italy, the Russian Federation, the Slovak Republic and Spain.

United States and Japan

There is no equivalent of national proof for sporting guns in the United States or Japan, where manufacturers test their own products Thus guns coming into the UK from these countries, and others which are not members of CIP, must routinely be proved in London or Birmingham before retail sale. Hence you will note English proof marks on most Japanese-made Brownings sold in the UK (a few may have Belgian marks instead).

Types of proof

There are basically, five types of proof: definitive proof, which covers any arm; magnum proof, which covers arms intended for use with magnum loads; high performance steel proof, which covers arms intended for use with high performance steel cartridges; provisional proof, which applies only to shotgun barrels at early stage in their manufacture; and blackpowder proof, which applies to guns which are intended solely for use with black powder. We may also note the existence of reproof, which might be applied in any of the above categories (save provisional proof), and which applies to any gun which falls out of proof (see below).

Definitive proof, which we might call standard proof, is seen on most guns. The information given by definitive and other proof marks will vary depending under which set of rules the gun was proofed. For example, under the latest 1989 rules, definitive proof marks will note: the minimum proof pressure (e.g. 850 BAR), the nominal chamber length in millimetres (e.g. 70 mm in the case of 2¾ in. chambers), the nominal gauge (displayed in a triangle in the case of London proof), and the bore size of the gun as measured in millimetres 9 in. from the breech (in the case of a 12-bore, anything from 18.9 mm down to 18.2 mm). There will also be symbols on barrel and action to indicate that the gun is nitro proved.

Under the 1954 rules of proof, the pressure would be given in tons per square inch (e.g.: 3, 3¼ or 3½), but this pressure would not be the minimum proof pressure as marked today, but the highest mean service pressure. Nominal chamber length would be marked in inches (for example 2½ in.). The bore size as measured 9 in. from the breech, would be marked in thousands of an inch (for example .729 in. in a twelve-bore). The nominal gauge would appear in a triangle, as it still does.

Under the old 1925 rules of proof, the gun would not be marked for pressure, but with a maximum shot load in ounces (for example: 1⅛, 1¼ or 1½). Nominal chamber length would be given in inches. The bore size as measured 9 in. from the breech would be given as 12/1 (.740 in.), 12 (.729 in.), 13/1 (.719 in.) and 13 (.710 in.). The nominal gauge would be given in a triangle, for example ◺12.

Bore size

For proof purposes, bore sizes are measured by plugs. Under the 1925 rules, if a plug gauge of .729 in. diameter – but not one of 740 in. diameter – would enter the bore to a depth of 9 in. from the breech, that barrel would be marked 12. Under the 1955 rules, the same method was used, but the marking would have been .729 in. Under the 1989 rules, the same system is used but the tolerance has changed from 10 thousandths of an inch to .2 mm (8 thousandths) on a 12-bore. Thus, under the old rules of proof, if the bore of a 12 were enlarged by .010 in. more than the marked size, it was out of proof. Under the new rules, it may be enlarged by only .2 mm (008 in.) before going out of proof. Note, however, that the Rules of Proof in foce at the time the gun was proved determine whether it is 'in' or 'out' today. Thus guns proved under 1955 rules still have a 10 thou tolerance (guns proved under 1875 rules have a full bore size tolerance.)[6]

Magnum Proof

Magnum proof is designed:

> ... to cover loads developing pressures in excess of normal service loads, either as voluntary proof to satisfy a particular requirement or as a compulsory proof where the arm is designed for use with unusually heavy loads.[7]

It was introduced in the late 1960s because Eley had introduced a range of high performance, magnum cartridges. Under the older rules of proof, a magnum proofed gun would be marked 4 tons per square inch. This referred to the highest mean service pressure. Under modern rules it is marked 1200KG or 1200BAR. This refers to the minimum proof pressure.

To quote the British Proof Authorities memorandum on the subject:

> Since the rules of 1989 were introduced and marking was brought in line with CIP Rules and Regulations, the position of Magnum Cartridges has been clarified. All guns which have been proofed to accept magnum cartridges will be marked with the minimum proof pressure of 1200BAR or 1200Kg. This covers all calibres from 4 bore down to .410 and with the exception of the 73 mm chamber for .410, all chambers will be 76 mm or longer. Only guns marked as above, under current Rules are suitable for magnum cartridges . . . For older guns it is recommended that only those with chambers of 3 in. or more, and marked 4.0 TONS or more should fire magnum cartridges. This does assume that these guns are in proof and in good

condition. [Anyone with any doubts whatsoever about magnum proof should consult one of the proof houses.]

Steel shot

The introduction of steel shot has considerably complicated the business of proof. The British Proof Authorities are not completely in agreement with CIP over the matter. Let us start here by considering common ground. As we noted earlier, two types of steel cartridge are now recognised: standard steel shot and high performance steel shot. These are defined according to certain velocity, pressure, momentum and shot size maxima. Steel shot proof requires the proof cartridge to deliver a shot of a defined hardness and size to a certain minimum velocity. This is the first time velocity has been considered in the proof test of sporting arms.

A standard steel shot cartridge is one which has a maximum velocity of 400 metres per second (as measured 2.5 metres from the muzzles), a maximum bar pressure of 740, a maximum momentum of 12 Newton seconds and maximum shot diameter of 3.25 mm. A high performance steel cartridge is one in which the maxima are 430 m/s, 1,050 BAR, 15 N/s (raised from 13.5 in 1988), and 4 mm respectively. A 12-bore high performance steel cartridge will be marked, 'For a weapon steel shot proved to 1370 BAR' on each cartridge.

Proof levels for steel shot

The proof level for standard steel shot is set at the same level as definitive nitro proof. However, a new category of steel shot proof has been created for guns which will use high performance steel shot cartridges. Even this does not include all the steel shot cartridges available, the most notable exception being the – as yet CIP-unapproved – US 12-gauge 89 mm (3½ in.) load. Nevertheless, many guns are now routinely proved for high performance steel shot.

CIP advises that high performance steel shot cartridges should only be used in suitably proofed guns with .5 mm (half) choke or less. The British Proof Authorities believe the half-choke restriction should also apply to guns proofed for standard steel shot and high performance steel shot. Moreover, several independent experts believe that CIP may have set the velocity minima too low to ensure effective performance on live quarry at range.

Provisional Proof

Provisional proof is voluntary, and is utilised by the makers of good quality guns early in the manufacturing process to avoid expending effort on unsound barrels. Black powder proof is compulsory for black powder guns. Guns bearing black powder marks, must not be used with nitro powders unless subjected to nitro reproof.[8]

Reproof

Reproof may be voluntary or compulsory. It is compulsory when caused by wear in the gun or work on the gun which causes a gun to exceed its proof limits. Reproof is commonly carried out whenever a gun's bore is enlarged beyond its proof limits (as may happen when lapping out after repair of a dent or, more certainly, when a gun is back-bored), or when any welding is carried out. It may also be carried out: when a gun is converted to fire a cartridge of greater length than the one for which it has been proved (the conversion of 2½ in. game guns to 2¾ in. is very common); when it is converted from non-ejector to ejector; when it is converted from black powder to nitro; when a gun is rebarelled; when it is converted from fixed to interchangeable chokes; and, as noted, under any other circumstances where there is an indication of material weakness or weakening.

Enlargement of bore

Before the introduction of the new proof rules which are oriented towards a metric system, British 12-bore guns of the modern era were usually made with a bore diameter of about .729 in. and went out of proof when they reached .740 in. (these measurements being taken at a point 9 in. from the breech face). The 1989 Rules of Proof subsequently changed this (although bore dimensions are still taken at the same point). The table presented here shows how nominal bore sizes are marked under 1925, 1954 and 1989 Rules:

Examples of proof marks impressed on the flats of 12 bore shotgun barrels.

Rules of Proof	London			Birmingham		
1925	12	NP ♔ ♔	⟨12/C⟩ Nitro Proof 1⅛oz	12/1 BV BP NP	⟨12/C⟩ 2½"	Nitro Proof 1⅛
1954	.729"	NP	⟨12⟩ 2½" 3 Tons	.729"	BNP	⟨12⟩ 2½"- 3 Ton per □"
1989	18.3	NP	⟨12⟩ 65mm 850 Bar	18.3	BNP	12-65 850 Bar

Under current rules, bore size is indicated in finer gradations than was heretofore the case: in the case of a 12-bore, anything from 18.9 to 18.2 mm. This is useful in that one may now get a more precise impression of the size of the bore by looking at the proof marks.

Semi-automatic and pump-action guns

Since the amendment of Section 1 (3) of the Firearms Act, 1968 – by the Firearms (Amendment) Act of 1988 – pump and semi-automatic shotguns are considered in Britain as firearms (that is, subject to the same controls as rifles and pistols), unless:

1   They have been converted to hold no more than two cartridges in the magazine tube, and,

2 That conversion has been carried out by approved methods (usually by crimping of the magazine tube), and subjected to proof authority inspection (as evidenced by the stamping of the magazine tube with a proof mark and the issuing of a certificate by either the London or Birmingham Proof Authorities).

Sleeved barrels

After the last war, a clever method of restoring side-by-side shotgun barrels was invented called sleeving. It involves cutting off the old barrels just in front of the chambers and, after machining, inserting new barrel tubes into the remaining breech assembly. It is similar to the 'monobloc' process used to build most mass-produced over-and-unders today.[9] The great advantage of sleeving is that the original ejector mechanisms, rib and barrel lumps may be employed. It is a much simpler, and cheaper process than making completely new barrels and, consequently, many thousands of old English guns have been restored to shooting condition by this method.

A gun which has been sleeved, must be subjected to reproof and is stamped 'sleeved' by the proof authorities. Because it affects originality and (insignificantly) the strength of the barrels, sleeving has a profound effect on the value of a gun. Moreover, there have been a few occasions when the unscrupulous have (illegally) obliterated the special proof markings in order to pass the gun off as being in unusually good condition for its age. When buying (or advising on buying) any older English gun, it is always wise to check the external (and internal) finish of the barrels very carefully. Refinishing may disguise barrels that have been badly pitted, it may disguise twisted Damascus steel, and it may be an indication of sleeving. The usual telltale sign of sleeved barrels, apart from the proof stamp, is a very feint line where the new tubes have been mated to the old sawn-off breech assembly – find a legitimately marked gun and you will discover exactly what to look for (although some recently sleeved guns, as noted earlier, may be TIG welded to disguise this join).

Proof: conclusions

Just because a gun has valid proof marks does not guarantee it serviceable – it might have been damaged since proof. As part of their training, all instructors should arrange a visit to one of the proof houses, by writing to the Proof Master in London or Birmingham at the addresses given earlier.

From our point of view, an instructor has, primarily, two things to consider regarding proof:

1 Is the gun the student is using in proof?
2 Is the cartridge the student is using (and which the instructor may have supplied) safe to use in the gun? Many older (pre-1950) English guns are proofed for 2½ in. cartridges (in which, subject to proof pressure, 65 mm and most 67 and 67.5 mm shells may be used) and must never – if so marked – be used with the more modern 2¾ in. (70 mm) loads *even though these may fit in the chamber.* Since there is insufficient length of chamber ahead of the cartridge, the crimp will open into the bore itself creating a

constriction and excessive pressures. Some old guns are proved only for black powder; they should never be used with modern cartridges unless reproofed.

Recommended reading (proof)

Anon., *A Short Account of the Worshipful Company of Gunmakers, 1637-1979.*
Clive Harris, T*he History of the Birmingham Gun Barrel Proof House.*
The various Rules of Proof and Proof Acts.

NOTES

1   As a matter of interest, spoiled screw heads can be repaired relatively easily. They may be welded up and the slots re-cut or re-made and re-engraved. Nonetheless, there is no excuse for damaging them in the first place.

2   Blacking, also called blueing, like the older decorative browning, is a process which involves the controlled oxidation of the barrels in certain, usually very poisonous, chemicals. The quality of blacking is affected by three factors: the polishing before treatment, the chemical formula itself and the expertise in its application. It is easy to get any of these wrong. The traditonal blacking process is 'rust blacking' in which the outside surface of the barrels is painted with a special solution, the barrels are then hung up in a cupboard in which the realtive humidity is controlled. On removal the surface is brushed off and the process repeated. Traditional browning uses the same procedure. The modern method of blacking makes use of a hot bath of chemical solution in which the tubes are left for a number of minutes (typically about twenty) before being removed and washed off. It is quicker than the old system and can give extremely good results. There are also cold processes. Touch-up cold application solutions and pastes are available and may be used to camouflage wear or damage. Their existence is especially worth noting in the context of this chapter, since they may be used to conceal signs of wear.

3   Single barrel guns which are accidentally bent may be straightened relatively easily by an expert barrel maker. They may, less advisedly, be straightened by others too. I know of one case, not apocryphal, in which a very famous American shot came to shoot Sporting Clays in the UK and was having particular difficulty on one stand. He excused himself from his companions and walked over to a convenient tree with a forked trunk. He placed the barrel of his repeater in the fork and applied considerable pressure. Having bent his barrel thus, he returned to the stand and straighted it!

4   I have a best W & C Scott sidelock pigeon gun which cost 60 guineas in 1896 - a very considerable sum at the time - which has very plainly decorated locks. I like the severe elegance of this style.

5   Prior to 1637, gunsmiths had belonged to the Armourers' or Blacksmiths' company.

6   If the flats of a shotgun are marked 'NOT FOR BALL' it is proofed under 1875 rules (introduced for the new choke bore guns). In 1887 the rules were changed and NOT FOR BALL was replaced by 'CHOKE'. Thus NOT FOR BALL on the barrel flats may be used to date a gun between 1875 and 1887.

7   *Notes on Proof of Shotguns and Other Small Arms*, p. 4.

8   As a matter of historical interest, Nitro proof marks were introduced in the 1887 Rules, but Nitro proving was not made compulsory until 1925.

9   This, to the best of my knowledge, was introduced by Beretta early in the twentieth century.

CHAPTER 4

<u>Shooting Vision</u>

To shoot effectively, we must locate, centre and sustain focus upon a moving object. The visual act begins when the rod cells in the peripheral region of the retina first pick up movement of the target (a primal response to danger). This induces a reflexive flick of the eyes towards the movement (properly called a saccade). The 'extraocular' (external) muscles then lock vision onto the moving object (called pursuit), as the 'ciliary' (internal) muscle adjusts focus and, by altering the size of the pupil, light levels.

Binocular vision
Human beings, like other primates, have a highly evolved binocular vision system. This increases our field of vision and allows for a better judgement of distance, speed and angle; it also facilitates hand-to-eye co-ordination. To maintain the perception of a single image requires higher cognitive processing and the most accurate co-ordination of eyeball movement. Mechanically, this movement may be inward (convergence) or outward (divergence). Divergent movement of the eyes is more common in shotgun shooting than in other areas of life because the target is usually retreating from the eye. Divergence requires a relaxation of the eye muscles and is more difficult to control than convergence.

Breakdown of binocular vision
Squints, defects in the nervous system and severe refractive errors may cause normal binocular vision to break down with double vision (diplopia) resulting. However, double images in our peripheral, unfocused vision are perfectly normal. This may be simply demonstrated. If you point at a distant object with an extended arm and index finger (or a gun), and focus upon it, you will still see two images of the finger in peripheral vision. If focus converges back on to the finger, the two images will merge into one as two images of the distant object form in peripheral vision. We have an innate or learnt ability to suppress one image from consciousness.

Should we use one eye or two to shoot?
The simple answer is 'two', if possible. When both eyes are kept open, the perception of distance and angle is enhanced, tension is minimised, and natural hand-to-eye co-ordination is enhanced. Two-eyed shooting allows for precise location of the target in 3-dimensional space (shotgun shooting presents a special visual challenge in this respect simply because the target is moving in space without reference points to give visual cues). The prescription for two-eyed shooting is not absolute, however. It depends on the individual's eye dominance.

Anatomy of the Eye

Each ball is about 25 mm in vertical diameter (there is little variation in size in adults) and located in a protective bony socket, or orbit. The distance between the eyes is subject to significant individual difference and this, like the width of the head, is an important consideration in gunfitting. In adults, it is in the range of 56-72 mm (pupil centre to pupil centre), with the average for men being about 66 mm and for women, 63 mm.

Twin lens system *Each eye has two lenses: the cornea; and behind it, a lens which can change shape in order to focus at different distances. When the lens of the eye is referred to, it is this inner lens which is meant. It is flattened to see objects at distance, and made more spherical to see objects close-up (this is called accommodation). Between the two lenses is a fluid called the aqueous humour.*

Muscular control *Six small 'extraocular' muscles control the movement of each eyeball externally. There is also an internal, ciliary, muscular system which controls both focusing and pupil size. It is a ring-like structure, connecting the base of the iris to the front of the retina. The iris itself functions much like an automatic camera aperture control. More light leads to contraction of the pupil, reducing the light entering the eye and increasing depth of field.*

The retina and visual perception *Light passing through the lenses of the eye is projected onto the retina, stimulating photoreceptor cells which send impulses to the visual cortex of the brain via the optic nerve. Each retina has a small central depression (the fovea) containing a high concentration of cone cells. These are used for detail and colour perception. The surrounding peripheral region contains a much larger number of rod cells, which are sensitive to movement and also provide us with a night vision capability.*

An upside-down world *The image projected on the retina is actually upside down; the brain interprets this and inverts it. This is an important point: visual perception involves a large element of learning and interpretation. Our eyes work with our brain and create images in the light of experience. Our visual system is far more than a mere camera.*

Most adult males have one eye which dominates pointing. That is, if they point at a distant object with a finger, there will be a straight-line relationship, from one or other eye, to the finger and on to the object. Two fingers would be seen in peripheral vision, but one image would be dominant and the other suppressed from consciousness. 60-70% of men have an eye dominance which matches their handedness. They can shoot from the writing-hand shoulder with the same eye controlling pointing. In the remaining 30-40% of the male population, however, the opposite eye is dominant (cross-dominance): neither eye is dominant (central vision)[1], or there is some other condition other than absolute dominance in one eye. Usually, these individuals cannot shoot from their writing-hand shoulder *keeping both eyes open*, unless the gun is substantially modified. If they attempt to, they may align the barrels with the wrong eye, causing a massive aiming error, or suffer from visual confusion (typically, seeing two sets of barrels and not knowing which to use for alignment)[2].

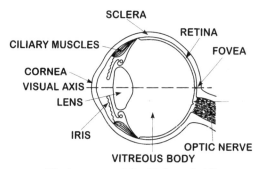

SCLERA

RETINA

CILIARY MUSCLES

FOVEA

CORNEA

VISUAL AXIS

LENS

IRIS

OPTIC NERVE

VITREOUS BODY

The human eye (after Dr Laso Antal).

Sex and age differences

It is rare for women or children to have eye dominance matching their handedness. Indeed, absolute eye dominance of any sort is the exception in women and children. These groups, like a minority of men, may require that the vision to one eye be obstructed by some means at the moment of shooting. These phenomena are considered in more detail in the eye dominance section of the gunfitting chapter. Meantime, we may note that some people who ought to keep both eyes open will shut one eye unnecessarily through habit (thus losing the benefits of binocular vision); others, who need to block the vision to one eye (or alter their stock), will keep both eyes open and end up shooting to one side of many targets (the classic symptom of an undiagnosed eye dominance problem).

As well as testing for dominance, shooting instructors must make note of any tendency by the client to close or squint an eye while shooting. If the tendency is observed, the instructor must ascertain if the client does this throughout the shooting process, or only when the shot is being taken (one may also note a tendency to squint an eye on particular shots). It is possible for the cross-dominant or semi-dominant sporting or game shooter (using a conventionally stocked gun) to pick up the target with two eyes open and shut, or squint, one eye as the mount progresses. This technique allows some of the benefits of binocular vision to be gained in the earlier part of the mount and swing. Notably, it makes target location easier. This technique is not advised for trap shooting, however, where it may cause visual confusion on targets of unpredictable line. In these circumstances, better to close one eye or squint before the call.

Eye focus

Focus should be maintained on the target once visual contact is established; the sighting bead and barrels should be seen only in peripheral vision. This was (most famously) the advice of Robert Churchill, who noted that if one watched the bird and forgot about everything else, the subconscious mind and the momentum of the gun would

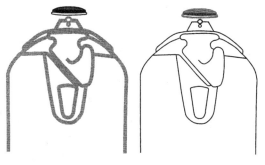

Clients must be trained to sustain focus on the bird. The gun should be seen only in peripheral vision.

automatically apply the needed forward allowance.[3] Whether one accepts the subconscious forward allowance theory entirely or not, it is a fact that many misses occur because the firer takes his focus off the target and brings it back to the gun (which typically causes the gun to stop and may also cause the wrong eye to take over in some circumstances).

Shooting optometrist, Dr Wayne Martin, goes further than advocating mere focus on the target. He refers to the need for shooters to centre on the 'primary zone' of the target (which might be the centre or the edge, depending on direction of travel), defining it as, 'that area of the target in which your vergence must be centred to strike it squarely'. He defines the secondary zone as, '… the target as a whole or any of the surrounding area non-specific in direction for accurate performance'. Martin notes with the conviction born of years of observation, 'Insecurity of performance, lack of concentration, and glancing back within the secondary zone to see what the moving target is doing, causes confusion, indecision and misses.'[4]

Corrected vision

Good vision is obviously essential to the shooter. To achieve this, the lens system of the eye needs to match the length of the eyeball. If not, correction is required. Those who are short-sighted (myopic), have a an eyeball which is too long and thus require concave lenses to focus on distant objects. Those who are long-sighted (hypermetropic) may be able to see objects at distance, but only with undue muscular tension. They have short eyeballs and require convex lenses to see at distance without undue effort. Those with astigmatism have an eyeball which may be more like a rugby ball than a sphere. This causes visual distortion and may require correction with special lenses too.

From the mid-20s there is some decrease in visual acuity. From the mid-30s, the eye becomes significantly less flexible, focusing becomes more difficult (presbyopia) and glasses may be required. There is also a deterioration in low light vision with age. Lightly tinted lenses may be used to improve perceived contrast in low light, but they reduce the overall amount of light entering the eye. This disadvantage may be outweighed by the enhancement of contrast, provided the tint is not too dark (see page 38).

Behavioural optometry

This is quite a controversial area, but worthy of mention. Behavioural optometrists believe that the primary reason for poor vision is not refractive error in the eyes. Rather, they believe that stress, chronic anger or anxiety and old emotional pain may cause vision to deteriorate. Poor vision is a symptom of closing ourselves off from life. Their approach to improving vision involves the release of 'emotional blockages' and the reduction of physical stress on the eyes themselves. Dr Jacob Liberman, a modern behavioural optometrist who follows in the footsteps of the early twentieth-century pioneer, William Bates, notes, 'The most important aspect of clearing your vision is simply the willingness to consider new ideas, to be willing to experiment and discover what works best for you.'

I was very sceptical of these ideas until I tried them on a friend, a keen shot, who suffers from rather poor vision. By simply encouraging David to relax neck and shoulder muscles and diaphragm effectively, his vision without glasses improved by a remarkable 3-4 lines on a standard eye-test chart. Initially, when looking at the chart, he would complain of visual fuzziness followed by occasional flashes of clarity. With improved relaxation and self-trust, the periods of clarity were significantly extended. Encouraged by these results, I have tried the method on others with equally good (and equally surprising) results. It really does appear that relaxation can improve visual acuity (and that anxiety, stress and physical tension may disturb vision). The secret to Bates' approach,

PLATE 3

(above) Shooting instructors must continually emphasise the importance of sustaining visual contact with the target. I will often ask the client 'to look for the ridges on the bird' or 'see the reflected sunlight'. Shooting vision is a skill which must be developed.

(below) This young lady's corrected vision has been no barrier to shooting success. Note how focused she is and the position of her hands. In other cases the front hand would be too far back – but it looks perfect for her.

PLATE 4

You can just make out the shot string on the way to the target in this picture. Position is good, there is excellent facial contact with the stock and a good follow through. The shooter has locked focus on to his bird. The clay will break.

A nice style – alert but relaxed with good visual concentration.

it appears, is in not forcing vision but letting clear sight happen naturally once a state of relaxation has been achieved.

Anyone with sight problems is well advised to experiment (and persist) with these methods. There are, moreover, implications for all those who shoot. Good visual contact is undoubtedly critical to good shooting, but it may be a mistake to try too hard to achieve it. The eyes should not be squinted, nor the surrounding muscles tensed unduly to achieve focus. My own approach is to concentrate all energies on the bird while physically relaxing. I seek not only to focus on the bird, but to make it brighter in my mind's eye by an awareness of it. I am feeling the target as well as seeing it. At beginner, novice and even intermediate levels, this may be too much to ask. At these levels, simple emphasis on focus will bear much fruit. At higher levels of development and performance, a more sophisticated – more Zen-like – awareness of the target should be encouraged. Learning to focus physically on the target is just the beginning. At the ultimate level, the goal is no conscious separation of ones self from the target.

Alternating focus between muzzle and target
Some shots alternate focus between gun and target as they calculate a lead. This is nearly always inadvisable (though it may be forced on one-eyed shots in some circumstances). Sustaining focus on the bead of the gun, as if rifle or pistol shooting, can usually be considered an absolute fault in shotgunning. It is easier to identify than you might think: people who do this seem to labour in the aim, and the gun's barrels will appear to judder as they search for the clay. Poor light, tiredness, distraction, an excessively deliberate approach to shooting, eyesight problems, past training with rifles and pistols, an over-dominant bead and, not least, a simple misunderstanding of what ought to be done, may all cause focus on the bead or muzzles.

How the target is seen relative to the muzzles
Some shots will be used to seeing a larger vertical gap between target and gun bead than others. This is a significant individual difference. Deliberate shots – those who focus more on the bead than perhaps they should, and who have a tendency to 'measure' birds – may see little or no gap as they align the muzzles with the target. Their requirement will be for a flatter shooting gun. Because there is a potential for confusion and individual difference, one should always explain to beginners (and accompany the explanation with simple demonstrations) precisely how you want them to relate the muzzles to the target.

Vision is a skill
Although we have extraordinary abilities, shooting vision is best considered a learned skill. Whether beginner or international competitor, the client must understand exactly what it is he ought to be doing with his eyes; and he must develop a visual strategy to make sure he does it. If you ask the average shot whether or not he looks at the bird when shooting, the typical answer will be: 'Of course I do!'. But most do not really understand the need to *sustain* sharp

EYE EXERCISES

Here are some of the exercises with which I have been experimenting recently:

Rotations   Stand or sit erect. Look ahead, keeping the head still. Shut the eyes. Look right, look left. Look up, look down. Rotate the eyes clockwise half a dozen times, repeat anti-clockwise. This may initially cause some odd sensations. Continue until you can perform the rotations smoothly. Finish by 'palming' (see below).

Basic convergence exercise   Bring an object (a pencil or finger) close to the eyes to a point just before double vision occurs. Look at a distant object and hold the focus for a count of three. Bring the focus back to the close object. Repeat.

The Yardstick   This was one of Ed Scherer's favourites. One takes a yard rule and holds it horizontally about one foot in front of the face with the left hand. The right hand, meanwhile, holds the chin to prevent head movement. Keeping the head directed forwards, one looks to the extreme left. Next, one shifts the eyes to the extreme right (the 36 in. mark). Scherer advises continuing this exercise for 5 minutes each day, turning the rule to a vertical position halfway through (*Scherer on Skeet II,* p.58).

Watching a swinging ball   A ball of about 3 in. diameter (a tennis ball is ideal) is attached to a string suspended from the ceiling. Dots are marked along the ball's equator. As it is set in motion, one dot – the target dot – is fixated. The head is kept still; only the eyes move as the ball swings back and forth. The length of the string may be varied, as may the position from which the ball is viewed. Wayne Martin recommends trying this while trampolining!

The binocular string   This is described in detail by Martin and also by Tom Migdalski, the Yale shooting coach. It requires about 10 feet of string and three small balls of different colours with a central hole drilled through the body. The balls are positioned about two feet apart. The string is attached at one end to a door handle or something similar, at the other it is held to the nose. One focuses on the first ball, at which point the string will appear to divide into two. Focus is maintained for a count of three and focus is moved to the centre ball. One holds again for a count of three and then focuses on the far bead. Martin notes that the exercise is strenuous and that one should rest if tired.

The clock   Copy the chart shown here, and place it a sufficient distance from the eyes for the figures to be slightly blurred. Centre on the clay. Keeping the head still, move the eyes to 12 and back to centre, to 1 and back to centre until you have returned to 12.

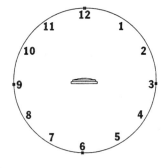

Palming   This is not so much an exercise as a relaxation and visualisation technique. Sit down at a table upon which you have placed a pillow to rest your elbows. Shut your eyes and cover them with your slightly cupped hands. Relax. The bottom of the palms should locate on the cheek bone and the finger tips of one hand should overlap the other on the forehead. Do not touch your eyes. Become aware of your breathing and visualise a clay going away from you in slow motion. See as much detail as possible, including very slight rocking movements of the birds and the glint of the sun on its rings.

Swinging Another relaxation technique which, like palming, was advocated by the late William Bates, the pioneer of behavioural optometry. It merely involves relaxing while gently swinging the body from side to side with the arms hanging loosely. The eyes should be allowed to wander. Bates believed that this exercise, like palming, might result in 'clear flashes' (episodes of well-focused vision) in those who had refractive errors of vision.

focus on the target, or a part of the target, *throughout* the shooting process. Prolonged focus on a moving object requires considerable effort. It is instinctive to flick one's eyes towards a moving object momentarily in order to recognise it, but to continue to lock focus on the target after recognition – and in so doing to gain full benefit from our remarkable powers of hand-to-eye co-ordination – requires discipline, training, and good natural or corrected vision.

Trained eye muscles and good visual preparation will prevent straining and help one towards the end of relaxed concentration, aware of nothing but the clear image of the moving target and the sense of being locked into it.

Where the eyes should look before calling for the target

When one looks at a clay being thrown from a trap, there is a place along the line of flight where one begins to see the clay as an undefined blur. This will extend into a streak of apparent movement and lead to a point where one first sees the target as a solid, defined object. My own approach to gun-down skeet and to sporting is to take the eyes back to the place where the target begins to be seen as a streak (but not right back to the trap), while holding the muzzles just under that point at which the target is first seen as a distinct object. This is generally good advice for these disciplines.

Directing the eyes into this area, minimises violent saccadic (flicking) movements and ensures the smoothest possible transition into the pursuit phase of the visual act (i.e., where it is first seen in sharp focus). Gun swing usually begins as target direction is confirmed. It must be neither rushed, nor hesitant. Timing is controlled by the eyes. Generally speaking, the gun should not start moving until fine focus on the target is achieved (although this may be done very quickly if the eyes are looking in the right place). There are some occasions in sporting and skeet, however, where it will be natural to move the gun before fine focus is achieved, i.e., reaching to the blur of target movement, with focus being achieved as the swing progresses.

The danger of moving early is that one may commit oneself to the wrong line.

Therefore, moving before full focus is achieved may be considered an absolute mistake in trap shooting where precise target direction is unpredictable. Moreover, the technique for applying forward allowance may be a significant factor – those who swing through (and therefore hold the gun nearer the trap) may react more often on the blur than those who maintain a lead or pull-away.

A few might make the same point concerning all targets. However, after much experiment, I have confirmed the advice in the preceding paragraph. Some targets are simply too fast to wait for fine focus before moving (if one did, there would not be time to build a lead picture and shoot with control). The tempo of other – typically longer and slower – shots allows for a different approach. Waiting for fine focus does improve accuracy, but the downside is the time penalty. Having become aware of these factors, each individual must experiment to find out what works best in which circumstance. The important thing is to become 'focus aware', taking special care with visual pickup and gun hold points.

Taking the eyes right back to the trap can often be considered an absolute mistake. It is also an error to take the eyes too far forward (for the sake of argument, let us say significantly forward of where the target is first seen as a solid object), or away from the immediate area of the flight line. Another absolute mistake is to hold the muzzles so that they obscure the pick-up of the target (one-eyed trap shots are not advise to adopt high holds for this reason).

Need for visual strategy

The Sporting Clay or Skeet shooter who lacks visual discipline and a definite visual strategy (knowing approximately where he is going to look for the target and how he is going to react to first sight of it), is making the act of shooting less consistent than it might otherwise be. Two common symptoms of poor visual discipline are excessive muzzle movement and target chasing. If the muzzles are held too high (above the line of sight to the flight line), a downwards correction will be made as the target appears. This will nearly always overcompensate for the original mistake, and a second – upwards – movement will be needed to achieve correction to flight line level. If the barrels are held too close to the trap at the outset, they may rush through the target, brake, come back, and then chase the target again. Pick-up point and gun hold must be chosen to allow for the smoothest possible start.

Zone shooting: game

The game shot (assuming a driven bird situation) needs to scan the area to his front. He can establish a broad zone in which targets are likely to appear. The most significant visual pitfall, and one which will prevent sustained focus on the target, is to be distracted by another bird. Once a safe and legitimate target is identified, the eyes must stay with it. The easiest way to ensure this is to sustain focus on the head or beak rather than generally on the body mass.

Zone shooting: trap

The trap shot can direct his gaze towards a narrower zone or 'window', in front of the trap where the bird will appear. The focus must not be directed at the trap house: one must look beyond it into this area (typically 6 to 8 ft wide) where the bird will be seen as a blur. Many instructors talk of a 'soft focus' in this area. In other words, one prepares in such a way that the eyes will have to do as little work as possible when the bird actually appears in the zone. As we have already noted, it is a particular mistake for one-eyed trap shots to hold the muzzles too high as this will impede efficient pick-up at the emerging target.

Conclusions

To summarise all of the above, the instructor must consider:

• The client's visual acuity.
• Whether binocular vision is appropriate or not.
• The direction of the eye or eyes in anticipation of the target.
• When the client should begin moving the gun – before or as fine focus is achieve.
• The point of focus during the act of shooting.

Few shots use their eyes as well as they might. After decades of shooting, they may still be unaware of how important **consistent, sustained, focus** really is.

Recommended Reading

The Athletic Eye by Dr A. Seiderman and S. Schneider
The Bates Method: Better Eyesight Without Glasses by William Bates
Better Sight Without Glasses by Harry Benjamin
The Complete Book of Shotgunning Sports by Tom Migdalski
An Insight to Sports, Featuring Trapshooting and Golf by Wayne Martin
Natural Vision Improvement by Janet Goodrich
Take Off Your Glasses and See by Jacob Liberman
20/20 Is Not Enough by Arthur Seiderman.
Vision Training by Natural Eyes
The Visual Handbook: The Complete Guide to Seeing More Clearly by John Selby.
You Can Improve Your Vision by Robert Kraskin

NOTES

1   True central vision is comparatively rare.
2   Many clients have an eye problem relating to eye dominance (and/or visual acuity – the keenness of vision) but are not aware of it. Some, for example, believe themselves to be absolutely dominant in one eye, when in fact the dominance is only partial (requiring a modification of technique or equipment to achieve consistent performance). Eye dominance may change after puberty and in middle age and may also be affected by ill-health, tiredness, light conditions, severe refractive errors and gunfit. The diagnosis of eye dominance (see the Eye Dominance section for testing procedures) and the manner in which the client should use and train his eyes are matters which must not be rushed or glossed over. It is a matter of the greatest importance. If you get gunfit and eye dominance diagnosis right, you are more than half way to getting the client to shoot well.
3   Churchill's advice (taken up by Macdonald Hastings, Major Ruffer and many others) has caused much argument. Clearly, Churchill never meant that you should shoot at the target when shotgunning, as has sometimes been stated. He merely suggested that if you watch the

target carefully – focusing hard upon it – and forget the gun, it appears as if you are shooting at the target provided you do not check the swing. In the words of Macdonald Hastings (who was the editor of Churchill's famous work *Gameshooting*): 'The secret of shotgun work . . .is to forget all about "forward allowance" and rely on your eyes, combined with a smooth swing and balanced body movement, to make a necessary allowance for you. The eye is never wrong.' (*How to Shoot Straight* by Macdonald Hastings, p. 37.)

4   Martin's book, *An Insight to Sports: Featuring Trapshooting and Golf,* is essential reading for any sports instructor. Dr. Martin is a great advocate of visual discipline. He believes, moreover, that with training almost anyone can shoot with both eyes open. My own opinion is not quite as strong. I believe that some must shut an eye even though the benefits of binocular vision will be lost to them. In these cases, as revealed by testing and observation, the benefits do not out-weigh the potential confusion caused by cross-dominant or partially dominant two-eyed vision. It may still be the case, though, that with persistence and absolute discipline concerning focus on the target, some shots with less than absolute dominance in one eye may be trained to shoot with both eyes open. I have noted recently, for example, a client with central vision and a con-ventionally stocked gun, who was able to shoot well at driven targets after focus training, with both eyes open. However, he was still completely flummoxed by crossers unless he dimmed one eye before firing. There is one other piece of research worth mentioning, conducted by Professor Michael Land of the University of Sussex. It focused on cricketers but may well have application to shooting. Land's experiments showed that on some occasions professional crick-eters looked *ahead* of the ball once they had picked it up. Andy Perkins of Holland and Holland noted a similar phenomenon in the shooting context many years ago. My teaching still empha-sises the critical importance of visual contact but the fact that some experienced shot may focus *in front* of the target in some circumstances is certainly worthy of note. For those interested in pursuing Professor Land's research, the reference is, 'From Eye Movement to Action: How Batsmen hit the Ball', Michael Land and Peter McLeod, *Nature Neuro Science*, Vol. III, p 1340 - 1345.

CHAPTER 5

Shooting Technique

Introduction

Every individual evolves a different style of shooting to good or bad effect. The instructor must be able to stand back, and analyse technique dispassionately. He needs to know what to teach, to whom, and for what purpose. He needs to be able to identify absolute faults, acceptable individual differences and areas where change may improve performance. To do these things, the instructor must have a sound understanding of the classic styles and he must also be able to break down any specified or observed technique into its component parts. Careful observation and a methodical approach are required because of the interaction of the variables and because of the complexity of an act which integrates both mental and physical processes. Where do we begin? I would suggest the following basic ways in which individual technique varies. Each is worthy of deeper consideration:

1 The way the eyes are used (considered in the previous chapter and in the Eye Dominance and Gunfitting chapter).
2 The stance adopted.
3 The manner in which the gun is held.
4 The style of gun mount employed.
5 The trigger pulling technique.
6 The way in which forward allowance is achieved.
7 The acceleration of the barrels during the swing (which is related to forward allowance, but not synonymous with it).
8 The psychological approach of the individual (which will be considered in the Psychology chapter).

STANCE

All sorts of conflicting, or apparently conflicting opinions have been uttered concerning where the feet and centre of gravity should be positioned when shooting. To cut through some of the contradiction and opinion, let us first note that each person must find a balanced way of standing which suits his physique, his technique and the type of target he is about to engage. Feet should not be set in concrete like the impressions at Mann's Chinese Theatre in Hollywood. Foot position and centre of gravity may change from one shooting situation to another. Generally speaking, a close stance promotes good rotation; a wider one, stability – *provided the arc of swing is not too long, and the feet are not placed too far apart.*

The most common recommendation is to stand obliquely to the target with the bulk of the weight on the front foot for all shots. This was – most famously – the advice of Charles Lancaster and Percy Stanbury. Stanbury suggested

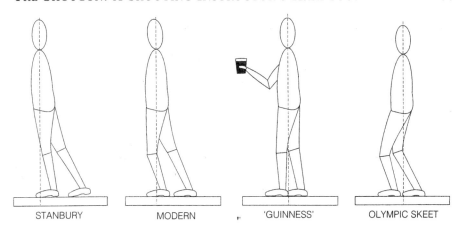

| STANBURY | MODERN | 'GUINNESS' | OLYMPIC SKEET |

Various stances. Note: the straight front leg and raised heel of Stanbury; the bent knee with flat rear foot of the modern stance; the more relaxed and upright Guinness stance; and the double bent knees and even weight distribution of this Olympic skeet stance.

that the feet should be positioned at 1 o'clock and 3 o'clock (when the shooter faces 12 on the clock face), with heels fairly close together (about 8 in. apart), the rear heel slightly raised, and the front leg kept straight.[1] In this stance, it is notable that the weight is over the front foot (but not significantly forward of it). The back is straight or nearly so. A subtle variation of the Stanbury style – and one well suited to clay shooting – brings the heels a little closer with no pronounced forward lean (or a less pronounced forward lean). The front knee is not kept rigidly straight (nor any part of the body held stiff). We might call this a *Relaxed Stanbury* stance. George Smith, Stanbury's predecessor as Head Instructor at the West London Shooting Grounds, advised that the feet should be kept a little closer when shooting pheasant than when shooting grouse. (I have tried this and it seems to work. The closer foot position is certainly better for the higher, slower bird. A wider foot position can aid balance and power of swing with low fast targets, although an excessively wide stance will make body rotation more difficult and may check the swing.

Churchill stance
Robert Churchill (as Norman Clarke and Rex Gage later) advised a quite different stance. He stated that one should stand nearly square to the target, 'with the weight evenly supported on both legs'. Heels are narrowly spaced 'three or four inches apart' (although they often appear wider in the photographs which illustrate his books). Quite unlike Stanbury, Churchill advocated a transfer of weight according to the shot – on to the right foot for a shot to the right, on to the left for a shot to the left. This involved a distinct raising of the heel of the foot opposite the direction of swing as it was used to push and pivot the body weight around the other foot. One sometimes sees the Churchill stance referred to as the 'British method' in American shooting literature; although in my experience, the Stanbury system – or variations of it – have been far more popular in Britain.

The Churchill technique
will bring the weight onto
the right foot for birds to
the right and for many
overhead shots.

The Churchill stance can be useful for people who are short and well built – like its inventor, or for those who have difficulty moving their back or hips. It can be adopted instinctively when gameshooting (especially when one is a little flustered by a bird on an unexpected line); and when clayshooting, if a pair is thrown in opposing directions and there is no time to change the orientation of the stance between shots. I do not believe that conscious weight transfer should be taught as a primary technique to most people (it makes following the precise line of the bird more difficult and inhibits body rotation). Nor do I believe that most shots are generally well advised to stand square or nearly square to the direction of fire. Nevertheless, weight transference and a squarer stance have their uses.

The Modern stance

A commonly encountered stance – I shall call it the 'Modern Stance'[2] – falls somewhere between Stanbury and Churchill. The leading knee is *relaxed* (which has the effect of bringing the rear foot into firmer contact with the ground) but the rear leg is straight. The feet are positioned at (or just past) 12 and 2 on the clock face (a little squarer than Stanbury, but not as square as Churchill); the heels 8 in. or so

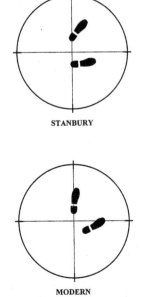

STANBURY

CHURCHILL

MODERN

PARALLEL

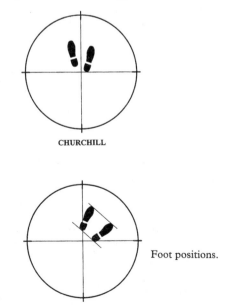

Foot positions.

A celebrated Victorian pigeon shooter, Capt. Brewer using a very erect stance and forward hold (from *The Gun and Its Development* by W.W.Greener).

Another famous pigeon shot, J.A.R. Elliot (from *The Gun and Its Development* by W.W.Greener). An early exponent of what might be termed the Modern Stance, with bent front leg but straight rear, the position is to be contrasted to the more upright stances.

apart; and the centre of gravity is slightly forward (but not as far forward as in the classic form of Stanbury). In this stable and determined position, the muzzles, front hand and front knee all point together as the mount and swing progress (as in Stanbury). The front 'cracked' knee acts as pivot, while the straight rear leg helps to power the shooter through the swing (it acts as the driving leg). The heels remain on the ground (although the rear heel may be unweighted on occasion). One advantage to a slightly squarer stance is that a left-hand bird may be taken more effectively.

Bending both knees

Most Olympic Skeet shots (and a few Sporting shots who may adopt the stance routinely, or only for lower birds) bend both knees to a greater or lesser extent, while keeping lines drawn across the toes and heels more or less parallel. Such a foot position is referred to as 'the Parallel Stance'. The weight is evenly (50:50), or almost evenly (60:40) distributed; in the latter case, the front foot is slightly favoured. Bent knees and an even, or nearly even, weight distribution can be an aid to smooth gunmounting from the awkward low-start position of Olympic Skeet. Bent knees (or indeed, a bent front knee) can also help with fast, low, crossing targets. If overdone, however, knee bending can look rather odd. Barry Simpson, once a keen Olympic Skeet shot, and always an elegant Sporting performer, uses a slightly bent stance deliberately for some sporting targets: 'I find it helps me keep on the line of low birds for anything eye level and below. I adopt a more conventional stance for higher birds.'[3]

Straight leg stances

Many successful shots keep both legs straight (but relaxed) with the feet fairly close together (shoulder width or closer). Peter Croft is a well known exponent of this style and it is popular with other international competitors. It has been called 'the Guinness' style by Peter and Ken Davies – standing as one might in a pub with a glass in hand. Again, lines drawn across the toes and heels may be parallel (and consequently, this may also be referred to as a 'Parallel Stance'). Again, weight is evenly (50:50), or near evenly (60:40) distributed. Nothing is locked or hunched; it is a relaxed position which keeps the shoulders above the heels. This is an elegant, erect style well suited to Trapshooting and, *for some people*, Skeet and Sporting Clays as well.

In certain circumstances, however, it can encourage head lifting because the centre of gravity is so central. A close-footed, straight-legged stance also lacks the element of controlled aggression which some competitors need in order to perform well. Proponents of the stance might retort that it obviates the need for an exaggerated body twist as you swing back to the hold point in anticipation of target release (in the straight-leg stance, the upper body rotates back much like a tank turret), and also that it makes it easy to keep the shoulders level. This is true, but it is also notable that beginners who use this stance (in reacting to – or in anticipation of – recoil), frequently allow their weight to come back onto the rear foot, almost guaranteeing recoil discomfort and a loss of balance rearwards when the gun is fired.

My frequent advice to beginners is to crack the front knee while keeping the rear leg straight, as described in the Modern Stance (although much will depend on what looks comfortable for the individual and the bird being presented). In other situations, I tailor the stance to the individual's physique and the shooting situation (most of my own sporting and game shooting makes use of the Relaxed Stanbury Stance which my body itself has evolved from the more rigid technique taught to it in adolescence). An erect, straight-legged, fairly narrow stance is often more natural on higher birds. A bent front knee works well on lower birds but will not suit everyone. Many experienced shots will find themselves alternating between the two unconsciously.

'Rifle shooters'

Those who are influenced by rifle shooting – particularly former or serving soldiers – may stand very erect and edge-on to the target, with the feet widely spaced and the back arched rearward. In America, a nation much influenced by the rifle, this stance is commonly encountered. A wide, edge-on stance is also encouraged when walking up game. Such a stance – sometimes called the 'long-bowman stance' in Britain – is not be generally recommended. It makes swinging the gun more difficult (especially to the left for right-handers), and can encourage head lifting and back bending because of the central or rearwards weight distribution. Beginners will often adopt a wide stance like this with one hip pushing forward if they are not corrected.

Differences in British and American shotgunning styles

Why do British shotgunners tend to stand with their feet more closely positioned than their American counterparts? British styles have been greatly influenced by driven game shooting in which there was little walking and the arc of presentation of targets was fairly predictable. Interestingly, if one looks at British shooting prints from the eighteenth century – an era before the introduction of driven shooting as we know it – one sees a much wider, edge-on, style. Some of the wide stances illustrated in Charles Lancaster's *Art of Shooting*, show an interesting transitional phase, wider and more upright than most modern stances, but not as extreme as the wide-footed 'prancing' position sometimes adopted by the shooters in eighteenth century prints.

Unusual stances

In considering more eccentric positions, we might note that a few suggest that one should take up a position square to the target with the feet fairly wide spaced (in imitation of the style once adopted by George Digweed). Such a stance, although it looks a

Orientation of stance: zone shooting and point shooting

This is a most important subject. The Stanbury and Churchill styles were created to deal with unpredictable live birds. The lithe Mr Stanbury pivots on the front foot and rotates from the hips to allow for variation in angle to right and to left, while the more portly Mr Churchill transfers the weight to right or left foot to achieve the same end. Both techniques allow for a wide arc of engagement with no change in direction of the feet. They are what I call 'zone shooting methods'. Trap shooting requires a similar approach: there is no time to move the feet, so one must address a zone rather than a known 'killing point' or 'sweet spot'. Stance and body movements must suit these imposed conditions.

In Skeet and most Sporting shooting though, one knows exactly where the target is coming from and, most usefully, where it is going. This intelligence should always be used when setting the foot position to make shooting as consistent and effortless as possible. Orienting one's stance towards the killing point encourages an uncoiling action of the body into the target. Those shots who set themselves up towards the trap or creep towards the trap as their shooting progresses (hence impeding their swing towards the target) will lose birds unnecessarily. The tension in the swing causes misses behind and off-line (it is a common cause of 'rainbowing').

In the Modern stance described in the main text, the leading foot should point towards the anticipated killing point or just past it. Another way of considering this – and one which may be adapted to other stances – is simply to pick up the gun, and, pointing down-range, take up an 'address' position with butt down and barrels held up at about 45 degrees. To where does the gun naturally point? Now, step round until this natural point coincides with the estimated killing point for the target. You have guaranteed a free swing 'into' the target.

When shooting skeet and sporting, I typically end up with the rear foot at 90 degrees to the killing point. Sometimes, I will want to be a little squarer, in which case I point my leading foot to the killing point, or to the centre of zone where I expect to engage targets. When Down-the-

Line shooting, for example, I usually point the leading foot towards the marker stake (positioned some 50 yards to the front of the trap on each firing point). In this case (as in driven game shooting), one is setting oneself up towards a zone in which targets are anticipated, rather than towards a specific point. In Trap shooting, however, the act of centring oneself to that zone needs to be really precise. Setting the stance at each shooting position must become a ritual in all forms of clay shooting.

Moving the feet

Many game and clay shots fail to move the feet although they have the opportunity to do so. When shooting a high driven bird to right or left with a Stanbury or similar method, rather than rely on body rotation alone (and suffer unnecessary body tension which may impede the swing), it is advisable – when the opportunity arises – to 'step into the line' of the bird, leading with the front foot, the front arm and the muzzles moving together with it. The rear foot naturally ends up at about 90 degrees to the anticipated killing point. Good footwork is the mark of a good game shot. It is another means of orienting the body to the anticipated killing point to achieve a smooth controlled shot.

bit odd, can be effective for Sporting Clay shooting (and is used by a number of successful, self-taught Sporting shots). I would not normally teach it, however. Much the same comments apply to the extraordinary 'lavatory crouch' position sometimes seen in Olympic Skeet shooting.

Overhead birds

Shots overhead are a particular consideration when considering stance. Some will keep their weight on the front foot even when taking a bird which is straight above them, as Stanbury advocated; some will follow Churchill's advice, changing from one foot to the other depending on the line of the bird; some will move onto the back foot for most or all overhead shots, while some will keep their

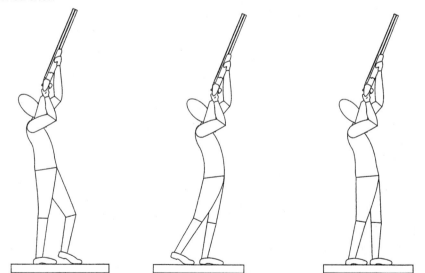

The right technique for overhead shots is the one which suits the client. Method 1 - keeping the weight on the rear foot, Method 2 - keeping in on the front foot (Stanbury) and Method 3 - a more even weight distribution between the feet. 2 looks the most elegant, but some people will not be comfortable with it. Comfort and balance are of paramount important as anything which causes tension or checks the swing will lead to misses behind.

centre of gravity between the feet. As with Basic Stance, it should all depend on what suits the individual as discovered by experiment. For my own shooting, I usually try to keep the weight on the front foot, having been taught the Stanbury method at an impressionable age (in which case the rear heel raises as the swing progresses). However, when suffering from a stiff or painful back, I sometimes bring the weight on to the rear foot by necessity (in which case the front heel rises) or, on occasion, adopt a narrow stance keeping both feet firmly planted on the ground. I have no problem with others doing any of these things, provided it is intentional and not the result of a loss of balance rearwards as the swing progresses. Ideally, I take my bird before the vertical at about 60-70 degrees as this reduces body tension and allows for a follow through into or just beyond the true vertical position.

Conclusions

The instructor must learn to read the body of the client, noting his build most carefully. Consider first the centre of gravity, the relative position of the feet, the distance between them, heel/ground contact, the straightness or bend in either leg, and the orientation of the feet to the killing point. When developing a stance, the position and suppleness of the back must be considered too; the shoulder width relative to height, the capacity for body rotation and the strength and length of the legs. Centre of gravity must be observed, not just in a static position but as mount and swing progress. A common error, and one often indicative of a poor stance, is for the centre of gravity to come back during the swing causing the gun to stop and the head and barrels to raise. Most of the stances discussed can work well. My general advice in *ab initio* situations would be to teach the Stanbury style to would-be game shots and the slightly squarer, cracked front knee, straight rear leg Modern Stance – which provides a very stable platform when two birds at different angles must be engaged – or the Guiness stance to would-be clay busters. Each must be adjusted as necessary to the individual and to the shooting discipline. There are no absolutes: you must find a stance which maximises stability (throughout the mount and swing, but most especially at the moment of firing), but which does not restrict gun movement. Once this optimum stance is identified, you must ensure that it is orientated (wherever possible) to the appropriate killing point or zone. You should always be willing to change stance if it offers an advantage in certain situations.

HOLDING THE GUN

This business of the hands is subtle and requires some thought to avoid confusion and apparent contradiction. We shall start by considering the least controversial first: hand position.

Rear hand position

The rear hand should be positioned well back; the base of the thumb should be comfortably located on the flute beneath the nose of the stock comb. The front of the thumb should be wrapped around the grip (not left resting on the safety catch or top strap). A good gripping technique (and a well-shaped grip) should allow for the trigger finger to be extended to allow for a straight pressure on the trigger. Bringing the web of the rear hand too far forward or too high on the grip – and in so doing, preventing a straight pull and a consistent grip – is a common fault in inexperienced shots and will also have a detrimental effect on mounting. It may be aggravated by incorrect placement of the trigger finger (placing the trigger in the crack of the first joint, which I do not usually advise, can cause the problem) or by a poorly positioned safety which requires the thumb of the rear hand to move too far forward.

Front hand position

There are fewer absolutes as far as the position of the front hand is concerned. About mid-way on the forend of over-and-unders, or near the tip of the fore-end on a side-by-side is usually the best advice. Some shooters prefer to bring the front hand closer to the action for some or all shots (George Digweed, for example, who brings the hand back when he wants speed of swing). This can be an acceptable technique to increase the speed and ease of swing; an aid to rapid cycling on pump actions; or a fault in need of correction. A short hold can work well for those with strong arms and shoulders, but it can lead to a loss of control for those with less developed muscles. The instructor must weigh up the pros and cons. As always, extremes are rarely to be advised. Positioning the front hand far beyond the fore-end, which was once fashionable among driven game shots (in imitation of the style of George V), creates tension in the swing which can lead to misses behind (it may also cause the barrels to be pulled down off-line on the crossing shots, leading to misses below). However, a forward hand position can properly be used as a temporary remedy for too short a stock. A short front hand position, on the other hand, may help with a heavy gun (or, if adopted instinctively, may be an indication that the gun is too heavy).

Many instructors suggest that the index finger of the front hand should point toward the target (either following the bottom rib of a side-by-side, or positioned along the bottom edge or side of the fore-end of an over-and-under or repeater). It helps to make full use of natural pointing ability. I usually advocate this too, but note that a few people find it uncomfortable, in which case it should not be forced on them. We might also note that it is not necessarily comfortable for the fore-end to be supported with pressure directed straight up through its bottom centre. The more natural hand position – allowing the front

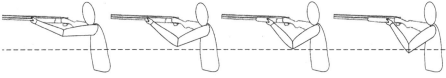

Front hand position can be used to compensate for a stock which does not fit for length. It may also be used to modify the handling characteristics of the gun (some bring the hand back when they want a faster swing). An excessively long hold – as some game shots favour – can impede swing. When the stock length is correct a mid-way hold is usually about right on an over-and-under.

forearm to adopt an angle of about 45 degrees without any cocking of the wrist – may favour one side.

Grip tension

The great D. Lee Braun stated that the fore-end should lie across the palm, 'as though you were holding a handful of eggs'. Peter Croft also emphasises the importance of a light front grip. Percy Stanbury suggested that the rear hand should grip tighter than the front. Similarly, Fred Etchen notes: 'The trigger hand brings the gun to the waiting shoulder and cheek while the left hand serves only to balance the piece.' (*Common Sense Shotgun Shooting*, p. 109). Chris Cradock follows Churchill in advising a grip which incorporates what we should now call isometric tension: the front hand pushing forward as the rear hand pulls slightly back. This tension is maintained during mount and swing and may reduce felt recoil. In *Gameshooting*, Churchill notes,

> ...the left arm pushes forward while the right finally neutralizes the push and adds the bit extra that brings the gun back. Thus the left arm absorbs a large proportion of the recoil which would otherwise be received by the shoulder. The pressure of the stock against the shoulder by the right hand involves the necessity of gripping with the right hand and so avoids the occasional trouble of too slack a grip. You should actually be pulling the gun between your two hands as you fire (*Gameshooting*, p. 46).

I have found this a useful concept, but difficult to teach. I will on occasion say, 'Imagine the action is made of rubber and you are trying to stretch it as you fire'. Generally, though, I find that clients get rather confused by talk about the opposing action of the hands. So while I agree that there should be an opposing action – to a greater or lesser extent – I do not usually choose to emphasise it. My own preference is for equal grip tension, or for the front hand to be slightly more dominant – depending on individual and discipline. Too often, in my experience, the rear hand dominates; and some training of the naturally weaker front arm is required to achieve a well balanced gun-holding style. Does this contradict the light front grip school? Not necessarily. Greater use of the front arm and improved pointing with the front hand does not imply that there need be an excessively tight grip. Excessive pressure in either hand or arm will impede or distort movement; insufficient muscular tension will reduce muzzle control and increase felt recoil.

Precise requirements will change, moreover, with individuals and with the discipline being shot. Olympic Skeet, with its difficult low starting position, requires a style in which both hands work together (and where, by necessity, the lifting role of the leading arm and hand is increased). The needs of Trap shooting (where some of the best shots favour a light front grip to encourage free movement), and Sporting (where the role of the front arm and hand is critical in picking out certain targets) are significantly different. On some sporting targets (for example, crossers at range on a difficult line) I am aware of front arm and hand tension increasing as the mount and swing progress to achieve the required muzzle control. One of the most useful Sporting and game shooting tips ever given to me was by an old Norfolk gunsmith Paddy Woods, who,

PLATE 5

I like the whole demeanour of this skeet shot. He is clearly in a state of 'relaxed concentration'. His grip is not hard, but he is in complete control of the gun.

I recommend left-handed pistol shooting as cross training for clay shooting. It strenghthens the left arm and improves concentration and visual discipline (although the point of focus is different to shotgun shooting). By using a low-powered air pistol it can be conducted indoors provided one is safety conscious.

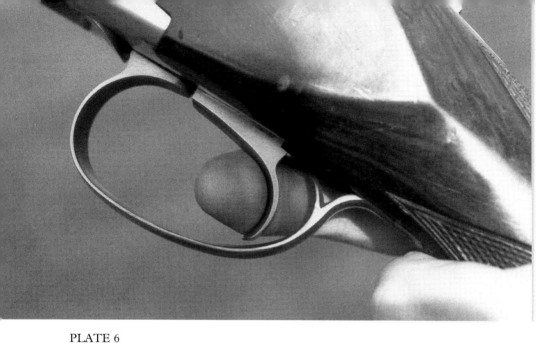

PLATE 6

I favour using the pad of the finger on the trigger rather than the first joint as is some-times recommended.

This is my completed mount. Note the elbow positions (both at about 45 degrees), the use of the front hand, and the position of the head and eyes (which are just about level as they should be). Nothing looks strained.

having watched me dry mount a gun a few times in a gunfitting session, observed, 'You shoot pretty well, boy, don't you? But you need to learn to shoot with the tip of the gun'. He had observed that I pointed the gun accurately, but was not using my front hand as well as I might to control the muzzles during the mount.

For beginners, with whom subtleties have little place and for whom recoil control is paramount, a slightly firmer grip with both hands is often advisable. One must also emphasise the need for shoulder contact with the butt sole and facial contact with the comb. One can grab the barrels of the mounted and proven unloaded gun from the side, and simulate recoil by a sharp – but controlled – rearwards push. It is soon apparent if the gun is not being gripped tightly enough, or alternatively with a teeth-gnashing-holding-on-for-grim-death determination.

For advanced shots this business of hands is more subtle, and the prescription for any individual will depend upon careful analysis and trial. Instructors must become aware of the pressure exerted by the hands as well as their position. Watch the fore-end in recoil, and note if the hand is slipping due to insufficient pressure, or if the knuckles are white and the swing impeded through the application of excessive pressure. Observe the grip pressure before and at the moment of firing, and note the degree of muzzle control.

Position of the trigger finger
It is often suggested that a shotgun trigger should be positioned on the crease of the first joint of the trigger finger. After years of rifle and pistol shooting, my preference is the middle of the front pad of the trigger finger. This is the area of maximum sensitivity. By comparison, there is little feeling or 'give' in the crease. Moreover, those who use the crease may bring the web of their hand too far up the grip and, if one considers it, one may not use the crease to pull both front and rear triggers on a double-trigger gun. A poor hand or finger position, a poor grip design, a misshapen trigger, or an adjustable trigger in the wrong position may all lead to a poor trigger pull. A good grip combined with good gripping technique will allow for a well-controlled, straight-rearward pressure as already noted.

Elbow position
Some would suggest that you bring the rear elbow up high, others that both elbows should be held in a natural position with both forearms at about 45 degrees to the ground. I tend to the latter camp, although I acknowledge the need of some Trap shooters to raise the right elbow position because it locks the cheek into the gun and creates a better shoulder pocket. I feel, however, that a high elbow on the rear arm cramps one's movements as far as other forms of shooting are concerned, although many have advocated it. Beginners and those with experience in rifle shooting may adopt an almost vertical position of support with the front arm and elbow (to compensate for the weight of the gun), typically with a bent back. This is an absolute fault in shotgunning and should be corrected.

H.A.Thorn (aka Charles Lancaster) demonstrates the mount – note how similar this is to the Stanbury style. (From Lancaster's *Art of Shooting*).

Save for a slightly lower starting position of the muzzles because I am addressing a lower bird, my stance and mount look very like that of Charles Lancaster.

THE GUN MOUNT

A good gun mount – and we have already covered some points in considering gun hold – is one of the fundamentals of good shooting. Great shots usually have great gun mounts. The tip of the gun is controlled perfectly. The head remains still, eye focus is directed forwards, the gun comes to face and shoulder with a minimum of movement. Anyone who wishes to improve consistency of technique is well advised to practise the gun mount in the same way that Karate enthusiasts practice their 'kata'. Most really good competitive shots perform dry practice drills (which may be no more than a few dry-mounts) on a daily basis.

Gun-up or gun-down?

Apart from *ab initio* instruction, where most will take their first shots gun-up, the great majority of British shooting instructors advocate a 'gun-down' position for general shooting. A gun-down position makes it easier to shoot with good timing and it allows for better visual contact with the target. Gun-down shooting is certainly the method of choice for Sporting Clays (with certain target exceptions, e.g., long quartering targets and Trap-like teal birds which may be better shot gun-up or nearly gun-up); and it is essential for good game shooting. It is required in Olympic Skeet and FITASC, although the former demands an abnormally low – and rather unnatural – starting position with the toe of the stock on a line level with the crest of the hipbone. Few would adopt this by choice.

Specialist disciplines like English and NSSA Skeet are often shot gun-up. Many of the best English and NSSA Skeet shots shoot this way. Typically, the pre-mounted style is justified by the cognoscenti as a means of eliminating the possibility of a mismount. It may well be so, but I note that superb scores may be made gun-down too, and the latter has the advantage of being a less specific style of shooting. Someone who masters gun-down shooting may apply that technique to game, Sporting or Skeet.[4] Trap shooting is another matter, although it can be shot gun-down, a pre-mounted gun is the only way to succeed.

In gun-down shooting, there is much variation in starting positions: one extreme being the Olympic Skeet start mentioned previously. Rules apart, some advocate a fairly low starting position for the stock: say, with comb parallel to forearm (Stanbury's advice). Others suggest that the heel of the stock should be about level with the armpit or, in some cases, just out of the shoulder. The latter position has specific applications in English Sporting and English Skeet. Instructors influenced by Churchill may even suggest that the butt should nestle under the armpit. In this position it must be pushed forward of the shoulder before being pulled back, an action which prevents the butt sole's dragging against the shoulder area and which promotes a clean mount. It can be a useful way to make novices mount their guns properly but I do not advocate it generally as it may cause the momentum of the mount to be checked. I certainly find that a gun-down start is advisable in Sporting, but it should be modified according to the target presentation. On some shots, the best position will be just out of the shoulder; on others, a lower start may encourage good gun movement.

Muzzle position

Some would suggest that the muzzles should be kept well up, with the tip just below the line of sight to the target (Stanbury). Others, Robert Churchill and John Bidwell included, prefer a lower starting position. Churchill stated that the barrels must be raised 'parallel to the line of vision', and contrasted it with the technique whereby the gun is raised at an angle to the line of vision (as in Stanbury). 'In this practice ...' he noted, '... not only is the line of vision temporarily intercepted by the barrels, but the gun is spinning windmill fashion,

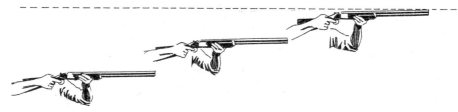

A Churchill mount with the muzzles being raised parallel to the line of sight. In such a mount
the gunstock would usually being underneath the armpit, forcing the firer to push
the gun out and pull it back.

A classic mount as advocated by Stanbury with the muzzles beginning just
under the line of sight.

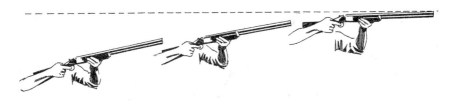

This is the mount that I would usually advocate now (starting a little lower than the illustrations
on p. 98). The muzzles begin as if one was pointing at the target. This ensures a smooth progressive mount with the maximum economy of movement, falling somewhere between
Stanbury and Churchill.

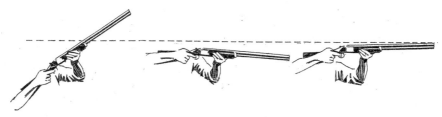

Starting with the muzzles above the line of sight is a classic error made by game shots when first
attempting clays. It ensures that one must make a zigzag correction before getting on to
the line of the bird.

and it has to be got out of its spin before firing takes place.' (*Gameshooting*,
p. 49).

Although I used to adopt the high Stanbury position in all situations, today I
usually advise (in the case of crossing and quartering targets) that the barrels
of the unmounted gun should point at the flight line of the bird (lower than
Stanbury and higher than Churchill). This promotes maximum economy of
movement and allows one instantly to relate the muzzles to the bird when it
appears. The high Stanbury start makes sense when using a swing-through system of forward allowance however.

I know of only one old-school instructor who would suggest that the muzzles should start above the line of a crossing or quartering target. In such a position – common to game shooters first exposed to clays – the barrels are forced to come down through the line of the bird and rise to it again. This zigzag action is not conducive to good shooting.

Mechanics of the mount

Robert Churchill advocated that the gun, starting with butt just beneath armpit, and barrels 'parallel to the line of sight', should be pushed out towards the target before being pulled back to the shoulder. In his early work, *How to Shoot,* he noted that the right hand should bring the gun back 'smartly' to the shoulder. In *Gameshooting*, he notes that the right arm merely 'neutralises the push' of the left arm. The three key points of the Churchill mount are: the starting position of the butt; the relatively low position of the muzzles at the beginning of the mount; and the use, indeed, dominance of the leading arm which lifts and guides the barrels.

The Stanbury mount is different, but not in all respects. The starting position has the gun butt slightly lower, with the stock comb in line with the forearm. The gun is still pushed toward the target (as it is in most modern sporting styles); but rather than being pulled back to the shoulder, the shoulder moves in to meet the butt sole as the comb of the stock comes to the face. The muzzles are controlled so that the bead remains just under the line of sight to the target throughout this process. It is a very elegant action (and generally my preference). The key points of it are: the starting position of the butt in line with forearm, the relatively high position of the barrels and the forward movement of the firing shoulder.

Mounting for pre-mounted disciplines

As already noted, many English and most NSSA Skeet shots – and just about all Trap shots – shoot pre-mounted. It is worth noting, however, that a pre-mounted gun does not obviate the need for a good initial mount. If pre-mounting for Trap, I advocate starting the mount with the barrels pointing at about 30-45 degrees skywards. This start seems to lead to a cleaner, more consistent, mount than any other and it allows one to come down on to the trap house. Others prefer a horizontal pre-mount or a pre-mount 'into' the trap house. Whatever pre-mounting system is adopted, the stock should be brought to the face during the motion. It may be considered an absolute mistake to bring the face down onto the gun once the butt sole is in the shoulder. Similarly, a good mount requires that the head be kept still and eye movement minimised (to see why, try mounting or pointing a finger whilst moving the head).

Where should the gun come to at the shoulder?

It is often said that the sole of the butt must come to the shoulder pocket, that is, the natural pocket between the shoulder joint and collar bone. For many people, this is good advice, but some very good shots mount their guns on, or partially on, the shoulder joint because they have a very narrow shoulder pocket. Frequently, this works perfectly well. Mounting the gun on the arm, as will happen if the stock is too long, may be considered an absolute mistake. The instructor may ask beginners to fold their arms across their chest, so that he can place the butt in the correct position for them. As for height, much will depend on the line of the stock. Generally speaking, the heel of the stock in a *well-fitted* gun should be no higher than the top of the shoulder. When teaching beginners, I sometimes get them to practise raising the shoulder and rolling it forwards. Some – notably those with longer necks – seem more naturally inclined to raise/roll the shoulder than others.

Pushing and pulling

The distinction between those who push their guns toward the target and bring their shoulder in behind the butt sole; and those who pull the gun back to the shoulder, is worth further consideration. For Sporting and game shooting, most prefer the former style, but the latter is used by many trap shooters (although some Trap instructors caution against it). The manner in which the gun is mounted has clear implications for grip design. Someone who pushes his gun toward the target will want a less acute grip than someone who pulls the gun back and locks it into the shoulder (who might, for example, benefit from an acutely angled Etchen-style grip).

Action of the hands

Most instructors would agree with Churchill that if any hand dominates the action of the mount, it should be the front – the pointing hand which begins the action of the mount. The front hand and arm play a key part in applying lead and following through. Most shots do not understand this, and may not have sufficient muscular development of the 'weak' hand and arm for really good shotgun marksmanship (see Exercise section).

Churchill writes in *Gameshooting*:

> The left hand must not be considered simply as a lifting lever. You will shoot just wherever you put it. Therefore, *the left hand must point the barrels at the target during the whole movement of gun-mounting and trigger pulling* [my italics]. If you misuse your left hand simply to lift the gun and then, in a separate movement, try to poke it at the target, you will miss. If the left hand is moving continuously on to the mark as the gun is mounting, the barrels will be on mark too.

I do not agree with everything Churchill wrote, but in this I think he is absolutely correct. Moreover, I would note that in gun-down shooting: if the rear hand dominates, the gun tends to move at the fulcrum of the front hand. Typically, it chops under the line of the bird as the gun is mounted and a correction must be made. A smooth pushing mount involving both hands acting in concert, or with the front hand slightly more dominant is far more economical of movement and follows the line of the bird better. Another important feature of a good mount is that it must start slowly. Far too many shots rush the first stage of the mount.

TRIGGER CONTROL

This is a subject which is given insufficient attention in shooting literature (and what little that has been written is not always sensible). My own experience of regular gun testing for the shooting press has led me to conclude that trigger pulling technique, and the quality of trigger pulls, are of paramount importance. I can shoot with a gun which does not fit, but find it much harder to adapt to a gun with poor trigger pulls. The adaption can be made with a conscious effort, but only if one has mastered the art of trigger control.

It is sometimes suggested – often by those who also advise that the blade should run in the crease of the trigger finger – that the trigger of a shotgun should be pulled more forcefully than that of a rifle or handgun. I think any suggestion of 'slapping' a shotgun trigger is mistaken. While it is true that the time one has for pulling the trigger in shotgunning is limited – once the target is launched one is committed to shooting it without delay or hesitation – trigger control is still vitally important. Eastern European and Russian competitors, most of whom were introduced to serious shotgunning via precision target shooting, often proved this point with their extraordinary scores. Their shotgun training regimen emphasised the importance of trigger control far more than was the case in other countries. Petrov, the great Russian Skeet shot and coach, noted, 'I fired 5,000 shots just learning how to pull the trigger'.

Most good clay shots are very fussy about the quality of the trigger pulls on their guns (which is further circumstantial evidence for the importance of fine trigger control). Those who know no better than to slap or yank their triggers can never expect to achieve their full potential. A shotgun trigger, like a rifle or pistol trigger, requires a delicate touch if shooting is to be accurate and consistent. A good trigger technique, and the timing that comes from it, is essential to good shooting.

FORWARD ALLOWANCE

The key skill in shotgunning, safe gunhandling apart, is to get in front of a moving target. In other words, *you must shoot where the target is going, not where it was*. Simple though this may sound, there has been endless debate on how one should achieve the requisite forward allowance. Usually it is suggested that there are four basic systems: one may *swing through* from behind the bird (the 'smoke trail' method); one may *maintain a lead* in front (keeping the barrels ahead of the bird all the time); one may start on the bird and *pull away*; and one may *intercept* the bird either by shooting at a spot in front of it instinctively, or by waiting and ambushing the target with a stationary or nearly stationary gun. To limit our consideration of lead to only four systems, however, would be an over-simplification. To really understand forward allowance, there is a need to go deeper.

Variations of swing-through and maintained lead
For example, in swing-through, one may distinguish between those who start

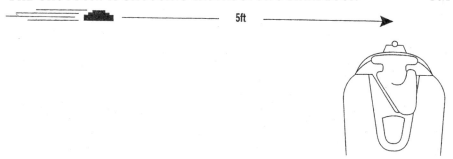

At 30 yards the actual lead required to kill a crossing or driven bird is about 5 feet.

just behind the bird and those who begin from a considerable distance behind it (a practice which may lead to slashing but can be useful on very fast, distant targets). With maintained lead, one observes some people who stay in front of the bird during the whole process of shooting but apply lead instinctively (John Bidwell); and those who stay in front and *deliberately* measure a specific lead and *sustain* it (the late Ed Scherer). The latter technique can be devastatingly effective at Skeet, where targets are launched at known speed on fixed trajectories, but it is usually unsuited to situations where target speed and angle are less certain.

Variations of pull away

In the pull-away technique (as developed by Clarrie Wilson and now taught by the CPSA), the gun is mounted onto the bird, the bird is then tracked momentarily before the barrels move ahead and the gun is fired. There are three distinct movements. It is an excellent method for teaching novices, and it can be useful on any bird where the speed and angle are difficult to assess and where there is sufficient time to apply the technique. The act of locking on the target greatly aids the assessment of speed and angle. Pull-away cannot be used for fast Trap shooting disciplines (and I would not advise it for others), nor would I usually advise it for the second bird of a pair when birds are thrown in different directions. The technique works best when there is plenty of time to shoot the target, it can break down if rushed.

Having considered the well-known version of pull-away, I would also identify here another more fluid and faster technique with which it is sometimes confused. In this, the tip of the gun starts with – or very slightly ahead of – the bird, and smoothly moves further ahead to fire as the swing progresses. There is no prolonged tracking, and the gun is unmounted until the muzzles move in front of the bird. This is the method adopted in my Positive Shooting system. It may be used for *ab initio* instruction, or it may be taught as a natural progression from the CPSA or traditional swing-through methods.

Controlled pullaway

This is a method mentioned by Dan Carlisle and Dolf Adams in their book, *Taking More Birds*. They suggest inserting[5] the gun, 'in front of the bird at increasing distances for increased lead'. (*Taking More Birds*, p. 72). Depending on range, one may begin on the front edge of the bird for a 30-yard target, a foot in front for a 45-yard bird, and two feet in front for a target at 55 yards (their variations actually go into inches). Dan is one of the world's most successful shotgun marksmen, but I have not been able to make this method work for me. That is no reason for you to reject it. Try it along with the others mentioned.

Interception

Finally, the interception methods: there are those who instinctively snap shoot at a point in front of the target, and those who deliberately ambush a target appearing on a known trajectory. The first method is performed with the gun out of the shoulder and with a comparatively normal mount (but little, if any, swing or follow-through); it is used by many live quarry shooters and sometimes by clay shots. Done well, it has its uses – one does not have to 'poke' when shooting in this manner. The second technique is likely to be performed with the gun in – or just out of – the shoulder. It may be a flaw in style requiring correction if applied universally, or it may be a sensible tactic for dealing with certain awkward clay targets. For example, the rabbits sometimes seen on a Sporting Clays layout that must be shot between two posts, or the crossing target that briefly appears between two trees. Ambushing in such circumstances can buy time. Sometimes, it can be the only way to shoot a target.

One could develop endless permutations and combinations based on all the above, but I would suggest limiting the consideration of forward allowance to eight distinct methods:

1   Close swing-through (barrels start just behind the bird).
2   Extended swing-through (barrels start a considerable distance behind the target).
3   Maintained lead (where forward allowance is applied instinctively).
4   Sustained lead (where an exact, measured lead is deliberately held).
5   Pull-away (tracking the target with a mounted gun before moving the barrels forward).
6   Positive Shooting (pull-away without tracking, and with an unmounted gun for most of the swing).
7   Snap shooting (where there is a mount and abbreviated swing, but where the gun is stationary or nearly stationary when fired).
8   Ambushing (pre-mounted or nearly pre-mounted, with a stationary or near stationary gun).

A competent instructor should be able to demonstrate all of these. For teaching absolute beginners, I would recommend methods 1, 3, 4, 5 and 6 (with 4 and 5 being especially useful for one-eyed shots or those who have problems with co-ordination). By preference, I would start with 1, 3 or 6. But you must discover what works best for you, and (more importantly) for your client. That will require experiment. For experienced Sporting shots I would advise 1, 3, 5 or 6 as primary methods (but knowledge of methods 7 and 8 will be essential too in order to tackle specific situations). For my own Sporting shooting these days, I use the Positive Shooting method as the core technique for most birds inside 30-35 yards. Occasionally, I use pull-away on targets that present themselves at what I believe may be a deceptive angle (especially if I note a lot of people having trouble with the bird). Instinctive maintained lead, snap shooting or ambushing are required on some targets where time and space are limited. Close swing-through – which allows one to establish line better than any other technique – can be extremely useful on longer birds where special care with line is required. It can also be a useful technique for slower short-range crossers, where there is a danger of shooting in front with maintained lead. Extended swing-through is a means by which momentum may be gained on some very fast, long-range birds, but is not to be generally recommended for clays because it lacks control. For game shooting 1, 2, 3, 6 and 7 all work, though the last technique is best restricted to closer birds. On the Skeet field 3, 4 or 6 would be my methods of choice.

Ballistic lead

As well as considering specific techniques for applying forward allowance, I also think it useful to consider mathematical or, as it might be termed, 'ballistic lead'. This is the exact distance that one must aim in front of the bird to achieve a kill; taking the velocity of the target, the velocity of the shot charge, and the distance from gun to target into account. According to that ever useful little publication, the *Eley Shooter's Diary,* the precise forward allowance required for a target crossing at 40 miles per hour would be (using no. 6 shot in a standard load): 5 ft 6 in. at 30 yards, 6 ft 8 in. at 35 yards, 8 ft at 40 yards, 9 ft 6in. at 45 yards and a whopping 11 ft 1 in. at 50 yards. Note that the difference between the required leads at 30 and 50 yards is greater than one might predict. This is because the pellets are slowing down considerably at longer range and forward allowance must be increased to allow for this (the use of a higher velocity cartridge does not make much difference to required forward allowances – the essential problem is one of air resistance). It is worth making the point, moreover, that the average shooter has no idea that he needs to be 8 feet or more in front of a crossing target at 40 yards.

Most clients will, on occasion, need to be given precise instructions for the amount of lead to be applied (although it should not be the norm in teaching). A specific instruction may be required when a more experienced shot is facing a very high or distant bird, and has no comprehension of just how far in front of it he needs to be. The verbal instruction should be backed up with some clear visual indication of the lead required – either using the hands as if indicating the size of the 'one that got away', or by referring to the lead required in gun lengths, or by comparing it to some nearby object such as a gate or car. The client must relate to any figures or instructions given. One man's 3 feet may be another's 3 inches (because one is seeing the lead at the muzzles and the other at the target). One must also explain to the client to look for all this *at the target,* keeping the sighting bead and muzzle in peripheral vision.

Simple and complex lead [6]

Simple lead refers to those situations where lead is only required in one direction. A complex lead is one which requires consideration of both vertical and horizontal axes. The consideration of complex lead implies a deliberate approach to the shot. Its main application in Sporting shooting where one might sometimes 'box' a target, giving it, for example, a yard in front combined with a yard under (see page 208).

Positioning the gun
The way the gun is held in the vertical and horizontal planes in anticipation of the target is critical. Whenever there is the opportunity, one should select gun hold and visual pick-up points. These will differ with individuals; most notably, they are affected by the technique selected for applying forward allowance. For example, if one is to maintain a lead instinctively in the Bidwell manner, the gun will need be held further out and lower than if one is to swing through.

Pick-up point
In disciplines where the direction of flight is known, the eyes should look at the area where the target begins to be seen as a blur. When faced with a situation where birds may appear at random angles, gun hold (and stance) ought to be a compromise to best engage birds within a defined arc and the eyes should be directed with a soft focus into the zone where birds will first appear. If I were waiting for birds in a flurry, for example, I would position the muzzles of the gun to my front just beneath the middle of the zone that my eyes were scanning for the arrival of targets.

THE ACCELERATION OF THE BARRELS

This is another neglected subject. Different methods of applying forward allowance imply a different type of accelerative action. For example, swing-through and the CPSA style of pull-away require a very different movement. One requires a stroking action; the other a more deliberate technique with a period of constant velocity while the target is tracked, followed by an acceleration phase as the barrels move ahead. Within the context of a particular lead technique, individuals will move their gun barrels very differently. Some start relatively slow and finish fast; others (including many beginners) rush to slow down. Some just rush. Instructors must be able to spot these differences whatever forward allowance system is being used. They are not always obvious. Although there are exceptions like Mickey Rouse, an exceptionally fast shot, most champions appear to move quite slowly. Generally, one might say that if the client is rushing, something is probably wrong. Often one notes slow target pickup because of poor pre-shot preparation, followed by wild movements of the gun in an attempt to make up for it. Barrel length and weight may also profoundly affect acceleration and the perception of leads.

Acceleration and the perception of lead
The acceleration of the barrels (and consequently barrel length and balance) may affect the perception of lead. One who moves his gun too fast – a slasher – usually sees less lead than one who moves it with more finessel. Rapid swings,

The Swing

A good swing is one of the great foundations of consistent shotgun marksmanship. There should be economy of movement, flow and power. Horizontal movement of the gun should be generated primarily by movement of the body not the arms (although vertical movement of the gun and fine muzzle-control are provided by arms and hands). The shoulders and the gun itself provide momentum. It is often said that the upper body should move like a tank turret. This is usually true, and unless deliberately intended, the shoulders should remain level during the swing (dropping the shoulder is a common problem but there are odd occasions in sporting shooting where there is a requirement to do it. However, good upper body rotation is not the whole story. The feet play an important role too, providing balance and driving the gun. In a Stanbury stance or one of its derivatives the front knee and gun move together in the swing. If the knee is not moving with the gun – pointing where the gun points as the swing progresses – something is usually wrong.

The swing should usually begin with body rotation, well before the gun is fully mounted (it is a common error to mount the gun too early). The swing and mount should be a flowing, unchecked motion. The action must not be sluggish or wild (another common fault). There must be power in the swing and, as noted, it comes from the upper and lower body rather than the arms. It is also important that the gun barrels relate well to the line of flight and do not roll off line (as they may do if one drops a shoulder because of poor footwork which required one to extend the swing too far beyond the 'sweet spot' for shooting the target – i.e., when one fails to set the stance towards one's tended killing point or when one fails to step into the line of the target). Moreover, it is essential that in the final phase of swing and mount that the upper body, gun and head are locked together as a single unit – though this may only occur momentarily and must be achieved without checking the swing. One problem of long birds – where the greatest leads will be required – is that they tend to encourage a slower swing than on close targets. A particular effort therefore needs to be made to keep the upper body and gun moving. Sometimes it will be appropriate to ask the client to exaggerate the follow through to achieve this. One may also need to encourage sustained facial contact with the stock after the trigger is pulled. Setting the feet slightly beyond the killing point can also help by encouraging 'unwinding into the target'.

In the Churchill technique, the swing is abbreviated. It is more a point – some might unkindly say a poke – than a swing. There is minimal body rotation as weight is transferred from one foot to the other. Nevertheless, one aspect of the Churchill system (see box on page 112) is applicable to nearly all swings – good use of the front arm as an aid to pointing. Although the power for the swing must not be created by the arms, the front arm in particular has a very important role in completing the swing – most sporting shots do not use the front arm well enough in my experience. Nor do most people realise the strength behind the swing of most top shots.

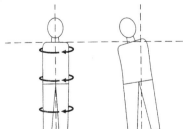

A good swing requires good body rotation and it starts from the ground up. In most situations the shoulders should remain level throughout the swing. When you see uncontrolled weight transference, poor body rotation and wild arm movements which bring the gun off the line of the bird, correct it.[7]

which increase gun momentum, may be adopted instinctively because a client has found it hard to apply the required lead in a more controlled manner. The original problem may be no more than a failure really to understand the full requirement for forward allowance. Rapid, violent, uncontrolled swings may also be the result of poor gun placement. Having been taken by surprise by the appearance of the target, the shooter is forced to rush in compensation.

Rhythm and tempo

This is another way of looking at acceleration and speed of swing. Most gun-down shooting is (or ought to be) performed to three beats, hence old phrases like bum: belly: beak (specific to swing through) ; and you: are: dead; or indeed John Bidwell's move: mount: shoot. However, inexperienced or poorly trained shots will often be seen to shoot with two beats. They mount the gun jerkily back to the shoulder on the first beat and slash at the target on the second.

It is a useful exercise to get beginners, or anyone else who has not got a sense of shooting rhythm, to call out the three-beat time aloud as they mount the gun: one: two: three (almost as if they were waltzing). *One* as first visual contact is made, *two* as the gun begins to move, *three* or, more descriptively, *threeeee* as the gun moves ahead of the target and the trigger is pulled). After doing this a few times, they can practise the same thing non-verbally. This three-beat system can be adapted to most methods of forward allowance.[8]

The Stanbury Method

The most obvious thing about the Stanbury method is the elegant, oblique stance. The weight is kept on the front foot (the left in the case of a right-hander) for all shots. Whether one is shooting to the right, left or vertically above, the weight is kept on the ball of the front foot, with a straight - but not locked - front leg and the heel of the rear foot slightly raised.

Stanbury suggests that the muzzles should be 'held on the line of flight all the time while the gun is mounted'. He also advocated a front hand position forwards of the fore-end.

Beginners nearly always hold a gun with the left hand too far back. If they also adopt a tight grip and have fingers or thumb on top of the barrels, they tend to look over the top. Sighting thus becomes wildly erratic. There is no specific position along the barrels where the left hand must be positioned, but a straight or very nearly straight arm is recommended. (Shotgun and Shooter, p. 26).

Contrary to some interpretations, Stanbury's is a short-swing-through system. He advocated starting with the tip of the muzzles on the tail of the bird. As the body pivots and as the mount, progresses, the muzzles are pushed in front. The gun is fired as the shoulder meets the butt. Stanbury was very critical of those who laboured in the aim with muzzles following a bird: 'It is very bad style; and even if its followers sometimes score a hit, they rarely scarcely deserve to.' (p. 29, *ibid.*). As far as lead is concerned, Stanbury preferred the conscious approach. He talks about 'seeing' lead: 'It is not a distance measured in feet but a "picture".' (p. 33, *ibid.*]. I was taught the Stanbury method by his apprentice, Michael Rose. It is a very stylish way to shoot game. Some people of wide frame may find it hard to conform to Stanbury's advice on stance; moreover, the style of stance – with the stiff front knee and raised rear heel – is not so well suited to competitive shooting.

The Churchill method

Robert Churchill, who was a much squatter man than Stanbury, taught a squarer, narrower-footed stance. He also advocated a start position for the gun with the butt under the armpit and with the barrels parallel to the line of sight. Churchill suggested that for a shot to the right, the weight should go on to the right foot; and for one to the left, on to the left foot. Thus, with Churchill's method, the weight may sometimes be on the back foot when taking a bird overhead.

Churchill's is an instinctive style (and he created his fast handling, short-barrelled gun to go with it). He did not talk about forward allowance in the same way as Stanbury; rather, he told his protégées to focus on the bird and forget everything else: the momentum of the gun and subconscious hand-to-eye co-ordination would do the rest. Churchill did not teach (as has often been stated) that one should shoot *at* the bird. His advice was that if you learned to mount the gun well (and he especially emphasises the importance of the forward hand in the mount), and kept your eyes on the bird, then it would *appear* as if one were shooting at the bird. 'The whole secret,' he wrote,

... is to regularise your movements and mount the gun properly to the shoulder so that the hand and eye co-ordinate. Your barrel must always be aligned precisely where your eye is looking. The eye learns its job quickly enough. Apparently you are shooting straight at the bird, but unconsciously you will be making the necessary forward allowance. (How to Shoot, p. 46).

Churchill was a larger-than-life character and, because of his success, has been much criticised. He started a storm of controversy over his guns and shooting method. Both work to a degree. I have found that shorter, heavily-built people tend to stand in Churchill's position naturally and they also tend to transfer their weight as Churchill did. His technique is also useful for people with back problems.

Churchill's starting position, with the butt under the armpit, can be a useful way to teach beginners how to bring the butt sole to the shoulder properly. As far as his ideas on lead are concerned, many experienced shots (unwittingly) use the Churchill method of unconscious allowance. However, the unconscious approach to forward allowance will not work all the time. There are times when a more conscious approach must be taken, even by the most experienced shotgun marksman. Moreover, as far as teaching novices is concerned, the great majority will need to be told to shoot in front of their first birds.

Tempo is also important. A long crosser will usually require a slow tempo mount and swing, and a close quartering bird a fast one. If facing a simultaneous pair, one may need to shoot the first bird with a faster tempo than one would like in order to buy time for the second. It is rare that two targets require the same tempo. David Peckham, a great Sporting Clays course designer, told me in discussing a draft of this book that he often tries to fool guns by changing the tempo required of two shots within a report pair in competition. Experienced shots will, consciously or unconsciously, note this and take appropriate action; inexperienced shots will fail to notice the difference, fail to adapt their timing, and come off the stand scratching their heads wondering why they missed such a seemingly straightforward pair of birds.

Conclusions

Many shots have no idea of rhythm or tempo. Instruction should therefore help to develop a better sense of both. A conscious sense of rhythm and tempo is a

Positive Shooting

My own Positive Shooting system, the primary application of which is Sporting Clays and Skeet, was developed after watching some of the best competitive clay shots in action. The Positive Shooting system especially stresses the importance of preparation – what in golf is called 'approach work'. It notes the need for careful assessment of the target before shooting (so that gun hold and visual pick-up points may be established precisely); habitual alignment of the feet to the estimated 'killing point'; good visual contact with the target; and mental generation of a positive result before calling for the bird.

Rules permitting, the Positive Shooting system advocates that one should mount the gun onto the anticipated killing point of the target and wind back (gun still in shoulder) to the chosen gun hold point as part of one's pre-shot ritual. The gun butt may then be lowered, and the muzzles positioned so that they point at (not above) the line of flight. This allows for the smoothest possible mount and swing with the greatest economy of movement.

The Positive Shooting method clearly distinguishes between the preparation and performance stages of shooting. The former is occupied with a specific sequence of thoughts and actions, to set oneself up to shoot the target as efficiently as possible. The latter is concerned only with good visual contact with the target and smooth body motion. The bridge between the two stages is positive visualisation as mentioned – seeing in the mind's eye a decisively broken target.

A key concept of Positive Shooting – inspired by Churchill – is that deliberate forward allowance is not required on *most* targets *after* initial training. The right lead will be applied sub or semi-consciously as long as there has been *proper preparation* and as long as *visual contact is sustained while shooting*. However, the importance of preparation as a prerequisite to the unconscious approach is much more strongly emphasised than in Churchill's writing. Moreover, the Positive Method is not dogmatic, acknowledging that some targets will require a more deliberate approach to forward allowance.

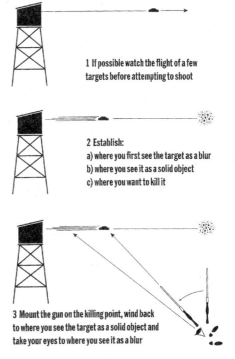

1 If possible watch the flight of a few targets before attempting to shoot

2 Establish:
a) where you first see the target as a blur
b) where you see it as a solid object
c) where you want to kill it

3 Mount the gun on the killing point, wind back to where you see the target as a solid object and take your eyes to where you see it as a blur

The Positive Shooting method might be summed up:

- Always select the point where you first see the target, so that you will know where to look and where to position the gun.
- Always select a killing point and set up your stance to address it.
- Always visualise what you want to achieve – a break – before calling for the target.
- Always maintain visual contact throughout the shooting process.

great aid to smooth, consistent shooting. Timing in all its aspects is just as important a factor in understanding how someone shoots as the precise system of forward allowance used. Poor visual pick-up often leads to poor timing.

SHOOTING TECHNIQUE: FINAL CONCLUSIONS

Which combination of all the physical factors mentioned above is best? The question has no simple answer. Most of the components of physical technique described have an application, although some are more generally applicable than others. As an instructor, you will see individuals doing all sorts of strange things with their bodies and guns, sometimes by accident and sometimes by design. Through experience, you will be able to differentiate between individual difference and absolute error. Sometimes it will be obvious, as with the beginner who lets the weight go too far back or lifts the head (two related conditions resulting in recoil discomfort and misses behind and above). Sometimes it will be so difficult to diagnose that no definite answer will be found. Do not be afraid to be unconventional. Regard the factors we have analysed as building blocks. You could, for example, combine Stanbury's stance with Churchill's watch-the-bird-and-forget-everything-else system of forward allowance. But do not be unconventional for the sake of it. The classic styles became famous because they worked. A shooting routine applied to every target, or pair of targets, will improve performance with any technique.

Recommended reading
Advanced Competition Shotgunning by Ray Forehand
The Art of Shooting by Charles Lancaster
The Better Shot by Ken Davies
Clay Shooting by Peter Croft
Clay Target Games by Ed Migdalski
Claypigeon Marksmanship by Stanbury and Carlisle
Common Sense Shotgun Shooting by Fred Etchen
Competitive Clay Target Shooting by Paul Bentley
Complete Book of Shotgunning Sports by Tom Migdalski (Ed Migdalski's son)
The Complete Clay Shot by Mike Barnes et al.
Experts on Guns and Shooting by Teasdale Buckell
Finding the Extra Target by Linn and Blumenthal
Gameshooting by Robert Churchill
The Gun Digest book of Trap and Skeet Shooting
Hartman on Skeet by Barney Hartman
Illustrated Skeet Fundamentals by E.F. Sloan (NSSA)
An Insight to Sports featuring Trapshooting & Golf by Dr. Wayne Martin
A Manual of Clayshooting by Chris Cradock
Positive Shooting by Michael Yardley
Scherer on Skeet by Ed Scherer
Score Better at Skeet by Fred Missledine
Shooting Made Easy by Mike Reynolds and Mike Barnes
Shotgun and Shooter by G.L.Carlisle and Percy Stanbury
Shotgun Marksmanship by Stanbury and Carlisle
Shotgun shooting: Techniques and Technology by John Brindle
Skeet and How to Shoot It by Bob Nichols

PLATE 7

Take pride in all your own shooting. Here, I am demonstrating the Stanbury address which might be used for game or clay shooting. Note the weight is well forward with rear heel slightly raised.

Here, I am taking a high bird off the rear foot in the Churchill style. I would not normally do this, but for people with back problems or backs which are less than flexible, it can be a good method.

PLATE 8

(above) Group instruction is always a challenge. Alan Rose demonstrates stance and front hand position.

(below) Ian Cawthorne instructing a game shot. Ian is concentrating as hard as the client. Alan Rose looks on. We cannot see the client's feet but his weight is nicely forward and his hand and head position are excellent.

Skeetshooting with D. Lee Braun
Sporting Clays by A.J. Smith
Successful Clay Target Shooting edited by Tony Hoare
Trapshooting with D. Lee Braun
You and the Target by Kaye Ohye

As well as acquainting yourself with some of the above, take a look at Richard Faulds' excellent new website, www.richardfaulds.com. You should also apply to the Clay Pigeon Shooting Association (CPSA), or similar bodies abroad, for the rule books of specific disciplines. Shooting instructors should make an effort to learn the rules (especially of the domestic disciplines) carefully; you will often be asked about them. One simple way to improve your knowledge is to qualify as a referee in the various disciplines (and a very good way to build up expertise about shooting technique is to work as a referee). Similarly, I suggest that every potential shooting instructor should qualify as a CPSA Club Safety Officer (it is now a prerequisite for attending the CPSA's own instructor courses).

NOTES

1   Stanbury himself said that the stance, 'should be comfortable and, although it may vary a little according to the build of the shooter...The general attitude is that of a half-turn to the right front. Common faults are feet too far apart and the right foot nearly alongside the left, so that the shooter's chest is almost facing his target instead of being at an angle of about 45 degrees to the line of fire. Nearly all the weight is on the left foot; the right heel is just clear of the ground, and a slight forward lean induces a feeling of mild resistance in the left hip; it is not a tension, for the whole body from the hip must be able to rotate right or left for slightly more than a right angle without the feet being moved. The left knee is not bent, and it is the only joint that is kept stiff during the rotating movements.' (G. L. Carlisle and Percy Stanbury, *Shotgun and Shooter*, pp. 923-924).

2   Although its use goes back at least to the Victorian era – see, for example, the illustration of J.A.R. Elliott's 'Position at the Trap' on p. 462 of the ninth edition of Greener's *The Gun and Its Development* and reproduced here on p. 90.

3   Conversation with the author, November, 1999.

4   Might this be the way to rescue Skeet from its current decline? I certainly believe gun-down skeet – skeet as it was devised originally – to be a more challenging and useful game than the artificial discipline which has since developed. The long runs of gun-up skeet champions are remarkable – a triumph of mind over matter – but skeet could have a much broader appeal if the gun-down rule were reintroduced. (I do not advocate an extreme rule as in UIT, merely 'below the armpit'). The concept of the game, with its twin traps and semi-circular range, which allows for so many angles to be practised, is brilliant.

5   The term 'point of insertion' is sometimes used in modern shotgun literature to refer to the point at which the gun first comes to the flight line of the target when trying to establish a lead.

6   As far as I am aware, Don Carlisle and Dolf Adams were the first to use this term.

7   With some high, rising, driven pheasants shot at quartering angles (notably the shot to the left for the righthander), dropping the gun shoulder may allow one to stay on the bird's line more effectively.

8   The old idea of 'brushing' the birds out of the sky (as opposed to poking at them) achieves something similar. It is most applicable to swing-through systems of forward allowance and can be a useful concept when over emphasis on beat may cause excessively deliberate shooting. It is a particularly useful concept for gameshots and also for clay birds off the high tower.

CHAPTER 6

Instructional Technique

General Principles

Every shooting instructor must develop his or her own personal style. It would be a dull world without individual difference. Some abilities, however, are common to all good teachers. The effective instructor must be able to:

1 Communicate effectively
2 Assess character
3 Quickly gain confidence
4 Assess ability
5 Motivate
6 Maintain control
7 Criticise and correct without offence
8 Recognise when his teaching method is not working and adapt accordingly
9 Maintain interest

Each of these is worth more study

Communication

We are often told that we live in a 'communications age', yet despite all the talk of media and message one of the key problems of our time seems to be a lack of effective inter-personal communication. We are all wary and suspicious. Poor quality or misleading information bombards us on all fronts, creating confusion and anxiety. Filtration – the sorting of wheat from chaff – has become a key survival skill. The good communicator has the ability to cut through the interference, in the shooting context: to identify the key skills and information and transmit them. Verbal, written, non-verbal (e.g., the use of body language), visual and tactile techniques of communication may be required in different situations.

Clear thinking and sensitivity are always important. Speech must be concise and diction good. All instruction should be unambiguous, gently persuasive and, in so far as is possible, incapable of misinterpretation. Effective communication requires that you direct your efforts not just to the client's intellectual self – the rational, thinking self – but to his feeling self as well. You must develop muscle memory as well as intellectual understanding. The conscious and unconscious aspects of personality must be engaged. Most of all, you must believe and have confidence in what you teach. It must be 'right'. If it is, and you have put the hours, days and years into discovering what works, the client will recognise the truth of it. The more effort you put into the content of your teaching, the easier communication will become.

Assessing character

You must become something of a psychologist. You should note whether the client is confident or anxious by nature. Is he in control of his body? Is he self-disciplined? Is he likely to do something unpredictable? What is his attention span? Some people will need to be pushed, others will need reining in. Some are sensitive, others are more resilient. You must ask yourself: 'How does this person see himself?'. What clue does his body language give? Is he relaxed or 'uptight'? Will a relaxed or a more formal teaching style be most appropriate? (Doctors sometimes distinguish between Type A personalities – those who are driven, hard working, impatient and demanding – and Type B personalities who are relaxed and easy going).

Teachers soon discover that people respond to instruction very differently. Some can transform instruction into action easily; others find it very hard to modify their behaviour even though they appear to understand what they ought to be doing (for example, the person who shoots behind the target every time, no matter what the instructor does or says). There seems to be some barrier between thought and action. Patience, gentle handling and good humour are required in these circumstances. Those who appear to grasp something intellectually but continue with the wrong physical action repeatedly may respond better to demonstration, or manually assisted instruction than to verbal instruction. The fundamental problem is one of effective communication. You may have reached the thinking self, but not the feeling self.

I categorise some clients as 'feelers' and others as 'thinkers'. The feelers are not inclined to intellectualise. The thinkers, on the other hand, will want to understand the smallest detail before acting. Feelers may need to be taught to think – to become more consciously aware of what they do; thinkers may need to learn to let go or to direct their thought process to useful activity rather than potential distraction. You will also meet clients who might be labelled as a bit neurotic. Their thought process seems to suffer from continual 'interference'. They have an inability to focus on the key point without being distracted. In such cases, be friendly but firm. Offer them clarity to cut through the confusion. If you do not plot a clear course you may become the victim of their confusion.

In all cases, one should be in the habit of treading carefully. The individual and his needs must be respected. The challenge is to develop real communication and trust. Most people prefer first names but some do not; some will want you to be hard on them, some will not; most clients will not mind if you touch them, a few more prickly customers will feel very uncomfortable indeed (they may even be concerned if you stand too close). Be sensitive, patient and trust your instincts. Learn to understand people. Regard difficult personalities as a professional challenge. Win them over.

Gaining confidence

The easiest way to gain the confidence and respect of your pupils is by demonstrating your own competence. In the context of shooting instruction, this does not mean that you should start off by proving to the client what a good shot you are; you must demonstrate what a good instructor you are. The client needs to feel you are a completely reliable and trustworthy source of information and advice; he must feel that you are listening to what he is saying, and that you are sensitive to his needs. All your own gun handling must shine with competence. You must have confidence in yourself and, not least, you must be able to get results quickly in terms of perceived improvement on the part of the pupil.

Assessing ability

Most experienced shooting instructors have developed a pretty shrewd idea of the client's ability level long before the first shot is fired. Make a point of asking a new client about his shooting experience. Watch him handling the gun in the club house, note the level of safety awareness. When you are dealing with a more practised shot, make sure you that you test his technique thoroughly. Many of us have a flaw or a 'hole' which may not be immediately visible. It may be something fundamental, such as a tendency to lift the head or stop the gun; or it might be a difficulty with a specific target or situation, such as long-crossers, tower birds, rabbits, teal, floaters, the pair on station 4 at Skeet, the straight-aways or extreme angles at Trap, the last bird when we are on for a straight, shoot-offs and so forth. It is your business to discover such problems and overcome them.

Motivating the client

The greatest motivator is success, so put the client in a position where he can achieve it regularly. He will also benefit from frequent positive reinforcement from the instructor. This might take the form of an immediate, 'Well done!' or 'Well shot!' after a bird is broken in good style. Your style of instruction and interaction with the client should be positive. Keep the lesson varied and interesting. Practice on easy birds in the early stages of learning, but do not keep the client rooted in the same spot forever. Move around, offer frequent (attainable) challenges. You must keep up interest to avoid boredom and to maintain attention and effort. Set goals and offer small rewards: a few extra shots 'on the house', a coffee in the club house, or what ever else to motivate the client to do something specific. You must set up the instructing situation to give meaningful and memorable rewards to your clients. For example, you might present 10 easy birds to help them towards their first 10 straight.

Instruction should not be too easy, nor too hard. If the situation is too easy, little will be learned and the positive reinforcement of successful performance will lose the power to motivate. If the instructional situation is too testing, despondency or even despair will set in, which is disastrous. Clients will always need targets adapted to their needs. One of the great problems with Sporting shooting today, as far as the novice or the less able is concerned, is that standards generally are so much higher than they were. The gap between the novice and the average shot has widened. A course which may not appear difficult to experienced shots may be a quite unsuitable place for basic instruction. In the final analysis, maintain a positive approach and be aware of what motivates people, then use your common sense and allow your instincts to direct you. Ultimately, the shot who wants to succeed must motivate him or herself.

Maintaining control

As an instructor, it is your responsibility to maintain control throughout the lesson (one simple aid to this is to keep the cartridges and to load for the client, which – all the safety benefits apart – ensures that you control the pace of the lesson). Be friendly but professional and politely firm when required (which should not be often). With beginners, you must be in a position physically to stop them doing something dangerous. Never let little points of safety or technique slip by. Intervene to correct them as soon as possible. With the right approach, most clients will become self-disciplining very quickly.

If you have someone in a group who is really causing a problem by poor behaviour (and the situation arises very rarely) try a humorous approach first. Some teachers will put troublemakers in a situation where they know they will fail. I think that should be a last resort. Humiliating any pupil – even the most irritating – is a very bad idea. Try winning them over instead. If need be, take the offender aside and say, 'You know, you really are making life a bit difficult for me'. The last time I needed to do this – and it was some years ago – the culprit replied to me brightly, 'Yes, I know, I am being a real arse****, but I think you're dealing with me very well'. And he meant it! He was easier to deal with thereafter, but not much.

Very occasionally, you may think negative reinforcement necessary. This might take the form of a sterner tone of voice when someone repeatedly fails to do something you have asked them to do. However, be very careful that the reason for the client's failure is not your own failure to communicate effectively. Negative reinforcement must always be used very, very carefully – it is all too easy to create resentment and to destroy the mutual trust the client-

---

CASE STUDY Jerry D

Jerry, 53 was and is a keen club shooter. He had been shooting for quite a while, and with work, his averages were creeping up. A competent, well motivated, shot, he was very hard on himself and, as a consequence, subject to the odd collapse in performance (one miss, could lead to a spate of lost targets). A few years before I had helped to sort his gun out, now his main problem was psychological. Jerry was a 'thinker', he liked to calculate everything and here was the root of his problem. He kept on calculating once he had called for the bird – the phase when he should be 'feeling' the bird rather than trying to use internal trigger-nometry to work out where he should be shooting. When Jerry missed, it was all too clear that he was disconnected from the bird. Taking a holistic perspective, it was clear that the bits were not coming together towards the same end. His body, the gun, the target, they all seemed to have their own agendas. All Jerry needed was a little more confidence in himself and his natural abilities. We devised a personal 'contract', a stated self-command, to stop thinking so consciously (which invariably caused his focus to shift to the gun and his swing to slow) and start looking more intently at the target – once he called 'Pull!'. With that and a little more refinement of technique (for example, taking more care with orientation of stance and hold) Jerry is now fulfilling his potential. He is shooting AA scores in club shoots and is quite capable of a AA CPSA average. He has learnt to befriend himself.

instructor relationship requires – but it is all the more powerful if your norm is positive. Some people will need encouragement one day and gentle scolding the next. Your experience will tell you what is required.

Criticism and correction without offence

If you maintain a kind friendly manner, and the client knows that you have his welfare at heart, you should run into few problems when criticising. Women are usually easier than men in this respect. Some men see their shooting as a projection of their egos: they can be highly sensitive to the slightest suggestion that they have done anything wrong (often to the extent that you wonder why they have come for a shooting lesson). They need firm but very careful handling. Note their worst error; correct it; prove that you can improve their performance. Never lose your temper or use foul language with anyone: the limit of my own admonishment is, 'Well, you made a bloody mess of that, have another go'. With delicate blooms or the self-important, even that could be going too far.

Recognising when your teaching is not working

This is not always as clear as you might think. Usually, the problem boils down to communication or asking the client to do too much. Always be ready to stop and to try to explain something from a different angle. When building up shooting skills, one must do so bit by bit. If a client runs into a problem as instruction progresses, it may be sensible to backtrack. For example, when a client can hit a target from 30 yards,

Effective Instruction.

Here are 20 specific points arranged in four blocks to prevent information overload.

Block 1
* *Consider the client.*
* *Be clear and concise.*
* *Explain to the client what he should do, rather than what he should not do – a positive approach is preferable. (There will, of course, be times when you have to tell clients not to do things, but the emphasis of your instruction should be positive.)*
* *When a client makes a mistake, consider WHY he has made that mistake; not just where the shot has gone.*
* *Correct one fault at a time.*

Block 2
* *Direct instruction to the feeling as well as the thinking self. Seek confirmation that the key message has been 'received and understood'.*
* *Be truthful. If you didn't see what the student did, admit it. Similarly, admit your diagnostic errors – you will make them. Don't bullshit; the client will see through it.*
* *demonstrating technique, make sure the client can see clearly. (For a right-hander you would normally be on the right side, and for a left-hander on the left. When you demonstrate to a right-hander, you will often be working left-handed; for a left-hander, right-handed. This is sometimes referred to as the mirror image principle. All shooting instructors must learn to become ambidextrous to a greater or lesser extent.)*
* *Use body language and tone of voice to help communicate the idea. For example, 'I want you to shoot this one smoo-oothly/slooooowly'.*
* *Having identified what it is that motivates the client, encourage the setting of personal goals (short, mid and long-term). Organise instruction to provide both intrinsic and extrinsic reward (see: Psychology chapter).*

Block 3
* *Enjoy yourself (it's infectious).*
* *Make instruction enjoyable and challenging, and match it to ability level*

so that confidence is routinely bolstered.

- *Supply the client with simple learning aids such as handouts explaining and illustrating safety and basic shooting positions (i.e., stance and how to hold the gun).*
- *Do not cram too much into one lesson or into any one part of the lesson.*
- *Do not shoot too much. Once an initial success has been achieved, consolidate it. The driven student's inclination to steam on may need to be resisted.*

Block 4

- *Be polite and patient at all times.*
- *Do not be afraid of repetition when appropriate (but avoid boredom by changing the scene, if required). Make sure that at all stages of instruction, you return to, revise the basics.*
- *When you are confused by a client's inability to perform a certain action or hit a certain target, go back a stage (your teaching should be progressive) and consider the problem again.*
- *Routinely boost confidence (do not ask too much of the client).*
- *Finish on success.*

but not 40, go back to the 30 yard mark and move to 40 in increments of a couple of yards. This usually works. Sometimes, however, you will simply reach a ceiling to the client's ability and you must stop or move on to something else. (Try to avoid ending in failure. Go back to the target the client can hit, achieve a couple of breaks and then move on or complete the lesson.)

There may appear a great deal to take on board, but most of the above is common sense. You will find that with experience, most of it will become second nature. The mistakes that inexperienced instructors tend to make usually follow a fairly clear pattern. Failing to match instruction to the needs of the pupil is very common, as is failing to consider why a shooter is doing something wrong—seeing the symptom but not the disease. For example, it is absolutely no good telling someone that he is shooting behind a bird and not telling him that the reason for this is that his feet are pointing in the wrong direction. Similarly, if a client is lifting his head and missing over the top because his weight is too far back, the important advice is to tell him to get his weight forward, not just to keep his head on the stock.

Other common mistakes include talking too much – confusing the client with useless information rather than sticking to the key point – and speaking when the client has the gun in the shoulder (when only single words or clipped phrases, if anything, should be used). Good communication is all-important. What you say must be intelligible to the client. You must create a bridge of understanding. You must be flexible – the same approach will not work for everyone – and be able to empathise. You will discover that voice is a wonderful and most flexible tool. Tone, emphasis and cadence of speech are all important, as are specific words and phrases and good diction. By borrowing and inventing, every instructor develops a 'library' of his own key words and phrases. Some examples from mine follow and they apply to many different shooting methods and situations. Note the italicised words, which are stressed when spoken. This helps focus attention on the point you are trying to get across.

For beginners

'Let's have a *look* at a clay.' [for familiarisation]

'I'll *show* you a bird.' [signalling this is a time for attention]

'The bird is coming from *that* trap.' [to avoid confusion]

'The bird is coming *now.*' [this was one of Chris Cradock's favourites – it tells the client exactly when the target will be released and promotes psychological focus]

'The bird will come when *you* call 'Pull!'.' [to hand over control to the client]

'Call for the bird when *you* are ready.' [to give the client a sense of control]

'*Touch* [the bird] and *Push* [ahead]

'I want you to point a finger at the bird and *keep it* pointing *at the bird* like this. [if you can get a finger pointing at the target, you can get a gun pointing at it]

Now, I want you to keep pointing at an imaginary spot ONE FOOT ahead of the target. [Some clients will not need a special instruction but some do]

'If that was one foot, give me *two.*' [if the one foot instruction would have led to a miss behind]

'Just let the bird *sit* on the bead like this.' [demonstrating muzzle-target relationship with barrels and clay; beginners may have no idea of what is required]

'Just let the bird *sit* on the barrels and gently pull the trigger.' [for beginners, but also to encourage more experienced shots to take a calmer approach on certain targets where no lead is required]

'Imagine the barrels are twenty yards long, and you must keep them *touching* the bird.' [another means to establish a relationship between gun and moving target]

'We'll shoot this one *together.*' [the shot is then taken with the instructor's hand supporting forend]

'Shoot where the bird is *going*, not where it *was!*' [adapted from Ed Scherer]

For focus and awareness

'Keep your eyes glued to the *target.*' [to promote visual contact]

'*Fine focus* on the bird.' [as above]

'*Lock* your focus/eyes onto the *front edge* of the target and keep them on the *target.*' [the same]

'Make a real effort to sustain *sharp focus.*' [the same]

'Vision is a *skill.* You need to train your eye muscles to sustain focus on a moving a object.' [the same]

'Imagine you are fighter pilot *locking* his guns onto an enemy aircraft.' [the same]

'*Grab* the bird with your eyes.' [the same]

'*Watch* the target, nothing but the target.' [the same]

'*Focus fast!*' [the same]

'Look for the precise *shape* of the target this time.' [the same]

'Can you see the *ridges/rings?*' [the same]

'Can you see the reflected *sunlight* on the surface of the clay?' [the same]

'Where do you first see the target as a *blur* or *streak? Where do you first see it *distinctly as a solid object?'* [to establish visual pick up and hold points]

'*Be* the target, imagine you are the target, notice every slight movement, every subtle change of light and movement.' [the same]

'*Slow* the target down, see it rocking in the air, watch its rings.' [as above]

For the call

'Go on! Sound as if you *mean it* when you call for the bird.' [to build determination in the meek]

'Match your call to the *target*. If you are going to shoot fast, call *fast*. If you are going to shoot *slowly*, call more *slowly*. What do you think you should do here?' [the way one calls for the target has a significant effect on how one shoots it]

'Don't call so *sharply*. Relaaaxxx.' [to slow down the tense or aggressive]

For head position

'Keep your head on the stock until you see the target break.' [to promote follow through]

'Keep your head on the *stock* and *follow through*. Exaggerate it.' [the same]

'I'll tell you when you can *lift* your head.' [to modify the behaviour of chronic head raisers]

'Keep your head *glued* to the stock.' [to prevent head lifting]

'Keep your head *steady* as you mount the gun.' [to improve visual contact and hand–eye co-ordination]

'Don't bring the face to the gun, bring the *gun* to the face. Like this...' [demonstrating]

For smooth movement, control and timing

'*Brush* the bird out of the air, as if you were using a *broom.'* [to encourage flair and timing]

'Don't rush. I want you to shoot this one with *smooth* control.'

'Stroke the bird out of the sky.' [as above]

'Don't *slash.'* [negative, but sometimes required]

'Don't be *wild.'* [as above]

'S-L-O-W—D-O-W-N.' [tone of voice and speed of delivery are critical here; one should exhale as one speaks]

Try this one in *slow motion*. Mount the gun as *slowly* as you can.' [to prevent rushing and improve the timing of the mount and swing]

'Get the barrels swinging *before* you mount the gun.' [to prevent premature mounting]

'Keep *swinging* until you see the target break.' [to promote good follow through]

'You *stopped* the gun. Why?' [to focus attention on this cardinal sin]

'This time, I want you to be aware of how your gun moves *after* you've fired the shot.' [as above]

'Why *rush* to stop?' [the same]

'Keep the barrels moving *smoothly.*' [the tone of voice will have a great effect on whether this achieves the desired result]

'Keep *swinging* until you see the target break.' [again, to promote a better follow through]

'Don't *hang on* to the bird. If you try to *make sure* of it, you will probably miss it.' [deliberate shooting is one of the most common causes of missing behind]

'Don't poke, *push.*' [negative, followed by positive instruction]

'*Push* the barrels *smoothly* through the bird – use the left arm more.'

'Don't *check.*' [Lord Walsingham's famous advice]

'Start the gun *just behind* the bird [to encourage more control in swing-through]

'Remember: *bum: belly: beak!*' [to improve control and timing when applying close swing-through]

'*you: are: dead!*' [might be used to improve timing for any 3-beat system of shooting]

'I'll call out the timing for you—*one: two: threeeee...*' [to slow down the swing and improve follow-through]

'Shoot with an *accelerating* gun.' [a check to deliberate shooting, well-suited to swing-through and pull-away]

'Take the tip of the gun to the bird, *track* it for a moment, then *push/pull* ahead.' [to explain the pull-away technique]

'*Look: lock: lead.*' [used by Roger Bryan]

'*Pick it up: pull ahead: shoot.*' [fo the CPSA method]

'Start the gun ON the bird, then *pull away.*' [another way of explaining pull-away]

'*Track* the bird, then *pull away/accelerate in front.*' [as above]

'*Move: mount: shoot.*' [John Bidwell's famous phrase, associated with his maintained lead technique]

'Hold it: hold it: hold it.' [Ed Scherer's words for his sustained lead technique.]

'*Don't track the bird. Start building your lead picture as soon as you see the target clearly.*' [Positive Shooting system]

To improve rotation

'Move your upper body and gun like a *tank* turret.' [to promote controlled and fluid rotation]

'Use the rotation of your upper *body* and *shoulders* to keep the barrels moving. Let me show you....' [as above]

'Generate the *power* for the swing from the body, not the arms.' [the same]

'Move from the *hips*. Like this.' [the same]

'Let the movement come from the feet up.' [the same]

'Don't *arch* your back, rotate the upper body.' [the same]

'As you swing to the left, keep the back straight and bring the right hip forward.'

For shoulder awareness

'Tense your shoulders...*tight*. Now...*let go!*' [to make the client aware of shoulder tension]

'Can you feel the tension in your shoulder?' [as above]

'Let *go* of the tension between your shoulder blades. Here.' [gently tapping between the shoulders]

'Keep the shoulders *level* as you swing. Use the *front* arm [demonstrating] to keep the gun up.' [rotation and good support of the gun from the front arm will prevent the back arching]

'Don't drop your *shoulder;* don't *rainbow.'* [as above]

For the hands and arms

'Use your *front arm* more.' [to improve swing and muzzle control]

'I want you to use the front arm more this time.' [as above]

'Feel the *muscles* in your front arm working this time.' [as above]

'I want you to feel these muscles working.' [gently squeezing]

'Use both hands *together.'* [to encourage a co-ordinated movement of the hands and the rest of the body]

'Don't let your rear hand control the mount. *Point* the gun with your *front* hand. Let it do the work.' [demonstrating a controlled motion with the front hand and arm as if holding the forend]

'Push the muzzles in front of the target...use your front arm more...*push!'* [again, to encourage use of the front arm, the second *'Push!'* is given during the swing]

'Control the *tip* of the gun. Think about shooting with the last two *inches* of the barrel.' [to promote muzzle control and good style]

For specific targets

'Miss this one *in front.* I mean it.' [to achieve break-through on forward allowance]

'See a larger *gap* between the gun and the target this time. More daylight.' [as above]

'Give me *three* feet more.' [as above]

'Miss this one *two* yards in front. Go on, *risk it!'* [the same]

'Shoot in front of the bird by the length of that *gate/shed/car/bus/barn.'* [the same]

'If that was three feet, give me *six* this time.' [the same]

'Fifty per-cent *more.'* [the same]

'Now double it!' [the same]

'Shoot the *front edge.'* [useful for some quartering birds]

'Shoot *at it* this time.' [if client is overleading].

'Knock the *hat* off this one.' [to prevent undershooting while still executing a controlled movement]

'Shoot the *top* edge .'[as above]

'Shoot the *legs/undercarriage/wheels/bottom edge* off this one.' [to prevent over-shooting]

'Remember – *grouse wear spats.'* [as above – the traditional remedy for shooting over the top of low driven targets]

'Give me a foot *over* the first and a foot *under* the second.' [for easy, vertically up, presentations of double teal]

'Take the *rear* bird first. Don't move against your *natural* swing.' [as is all too common]

'Give me a *gun length/x feet* under.' [for droppers]

'Pull *under* as you fire.' [as above]

'Take the *eyes* up, but not the gun.' [for overhead shots from behind]

'Don't take the gun so far *back.*' [as above and also for quartering shots]

'Confucius say: ' "Battues need 50% *more lead*".' [to prevent underleading typical mid-to-long range battue presentation]

'Take the *rear* bird first, then swing on to the front.' [to prevent movement against the natural direction of swing]

'Shoot the bird which *dominates* your vision first.' [an occasional qualification to the above]

'Shoot the *faster* bird first.' [the same]

'Shoot the bird which is going to become a *problem* first.' [the same]

'Don't rush. Just take your *hands* and *gun* to the bird decisively.' [for use at station 8 at skeet, a bird which may easily be over or underled]

'Imagine a box a *yard/foot* square . . .The target is top right, you need to shoot bottom left.' [this 'boxing' technique has many applications, including incomers and chandelle targets]

'I want you to imagine you are *bayonetting* the target as you mount the gun.' [used on going-away birds, this has the effect of getting the client to push the gun towards the target during the mount]

'Clear your mind...I want you to forget everything *except...*' [to promote attention on one aspect of the shot, for example, visual contact or proper use of the front arm]

For imagery and feel

'*See* the bird breaking in your mind's eye before you call for it.' [to promote positive visualisation]

'Close your eyes, imagine a clay, see the *ridges* on it, the *exact* shape, now that is what I want you to look for.' [to promote visualisation and actual focus]

'*Feel* it this time, don't think it.' [to encourage a more instinctive, right-brain approach]

'*Trust* yourself.' [as above]

'Don't calculate, keep your eyes on the target and let it *flow.*' [the same]

For stance

'Stand square, take half a pace forward with the *left* foot, bring your weight on to it and relax the knee.' [a simple way to get a beginner or anyone else into a relaxed basic stance]

'Imagine there is a post going through your *front* shoulder, *front* hip and down into the ball of your front foot.' [to encourage a forward centre of gravity]

'Keep the weight *forward* . . . on the *ball* of the front foot.' [as above]

'Weight on the front foot, head on the stock.' [especially useful for novices]

'Keep your centre of gravity more *central*. Imagine a rod going down through your spine and into the ground between your heels.' [for those who tend to lean to far forward or back]

'Just stand naturally, as if you were holding a pint of *beer* in your hand.' [Peter Croft's Guinness stance]

'Relax, unlock the *front* knee.' [which may have the affect of putting the rear heel in contact with the ground in the case of a Stanbury shooter]

'Keep the rear leg *straight*.' [to encourage a 'driving' action of the rear leg]

'Don't lean so far *forward/back*.'

'Try standing a little *squarer*.' [for those who are adopting a very edge on stance]

'Keep the heels *closer together/a little further apart*.'.

'Position the feet about *shoulder width apart*.'

'Don't stick it out! Keep your *bum/bottom/posterior* underneath your shoulders.' [use to promote an elegant style with straight or nearly-straight back, although it may not always be good advice for women who often need to feel they *are* sticking their bottom out to counter their natural tendency to thrust their hips forward.]

For reaction

'Don't call for the bird until you are *ready*.' [to encourage control and better visual contact]

'Wait until you can see the bird *clearly* before you move.' [to prevent premature movement]

'Don't move *until* you can see the bird *in focus*.' [as above]

'Push off *smoothly* when you first see the target *clearly*.' [self evident]

'This target is very fast. Start the swing as soon as you see the first *blur* of movement/as soon as the *direction* of flight is clear.' [to modify the client's reaction – the first is a faster start than the second but has dangers because one may misread the line]

'*Move* as soon as you see it.' [similar]

For preparation

'I want you to *wind back*. Muzzles where you first see the target *in focus*. Eyes directed to the zone where you see the target as a *blur*.' [to promote good preparation]

'Where do you *first* see the target? Where do you *want* to shoot it.' [as above. but shortened]

'Have you worked out a *plan* for this one?' [the same]

'Time spent in *reconnaissance* is never wasted.' [the same]

'You won't need to chase the target if you get the barrels and eyes in the *right place* before you call.' [the same]

'Hold the muzzles *just under* the spot where you first see the bird in focus.' [the same]

'Imagine a line from your eye to target, hold the bead *just under* it.' [the same]

'Don't start with the barrels pointing *above* the flight line.' [the same]

'Imagine you are *hip* shooting, the barrels should point to the *line* of the bird.' [as above - it creates a lower starting position]

'Rear foot at 90 degrees to where you want to *break* the target, please. *Every time.*' [to ensure minimum tension at the moment of firing]

'Is your front foot at 12 o'clock/1 o'clock to where you are going to *kill* the target? Are you sure?' [the same]

'Point your *navel/belt buckle* at the Low House.' [similar for skeet]

'Set your stance up for the *second* bird...that way you will naturally swing on to it.' [the same]

'If you feel you have time, *move* your feet.' [the same]

For encouragement

'*Thank you!*' [a favourite of Alan Rose's when the client breaks a target having followed advice]

'*Well done!*'

'*Well shot!*'

'*Great!*'

'That's *really* good!'

'*You've got it!*'

'*First class!*'

'*Excellent*'

These words and phrases may sound simple, but they contain a great deal of information. You will note the vast majority are positive. With a few exceptions, the negative comments are followed with a positive instruction. Why the need for so many ways of saying the same thing in

Demeanour and dress of a shooting instructor

You can only make a first impression once. A professional shooting instructor should dress smartly. I usually favour a cotton or woollen shirt combined with a woollen or manmade fibre tie (silk ties are easily ruined by rain). To wear a tie is a sign of respect for the client and for one's profession. Similarly, the best shooting vest and jacket that can be afforded should be acquired. There are many excellent shooting jackets available today, some lined with breathable materials like Gore-Tex: they are perfect for instruction in cold and wet weather. Cords or moleskins are the trousers of choice. Sleeveless vests are a way to keep you warm in winter without excessive bulk. As far as footwear is concerned, medium-weight, brown brogues or Oxfords are ideal for summer. I prefer stout rubber soles to leather ones. Good quality Wellingtons (such as those made by Hunter, Barbour, Aigle and Le Chameau) are a necessity on most sporting grounds in winter, and useful at any time when conditions are wet and muddy. Leather-lined Wellingtons are much more expensive but well worth the cost. A hat or cap will help keep you warm (a great deal of body heat is lost through the head) and dry and offer some protection from falling clays.

Amateur instructors should also look well turned out: it is a sign of respect for the client and inspires confidence. If you have earned an instructional qualification from one of the shooting organisations, do not be afraid to wear the badge on a shooting vest; but I suggest that if you want to avoid ribbing from your friends, you only wear that vest when you are instructing! No instructor should wear camouflage-type jackets or trousers. They may be comfortable (and are useful for pigeon shooting and wildfowling) but they give entirely the wrong impression while instructing.

Personal hygiene *This is a delicate subject, but there is nothing worse than to be taught by someone who smells unclean or has bad breath. Unfortunately, we do not always know if we do suffer from such afflictions. Indeed many people with BO and bad breath are unaware of it. Every shooting instructor should ask a spouse, or close acquaintance for an honest answer; both problems are easily put right. I might also add that even a normally sweet-smelling instructor can put his* *clients off if he has eaten a lot of garlic the evening before teaching!*

Smoking *I am no rabid anti-smoker, but it is poor form to smoke cigarettes while engaged in instruction. It not only looks messy, but is potentially dangerous because it occupies a hand (however briefly) and distracts the attention.*

Drink *An instructor must not drink during the day. Like a pilot or a surgeon, he has a legal and moral responsibility to be absolutely sober. Excessive drinking in the evening may also result in an inability to perform properly the following day.*

some cases? Because people are different, and because one must vary what one says to maintain attention (especially when it is an instruction that needs to be repeated many times, as those relating to visual contact do). There may appear to be some contradictions, but people and techniques are different: what is right for one won't work for another. Once you have accepted that what the client is trying to do is right, your task is to help the individual apply that aspect of technique consistently. If someone is learning the Stanbury stance, putting too much weight on the right foot is an error; if they are learning Churchill, the weight will have to be transferred to the right foot when engaging birds to that side. Right and wrong must be considered within the context of the style being taught.

You will also note that the words and phrases above are often combined with demonstrations (verbal and visual modes combined – see next chapter). Some also involve physical contact ('Relax the tension here', 'Feel these muscles working'). Sometimes one can say as much without speaking. I will occasionally place the palm of my hand behind the client's shooting shoulder to prevent the weight coming back. This is helpful both for beginners and for more experienced shots who are in the habit of coming back as they swing. Very occasionally (and only with prior consent), I will gently insert my hands under the client's armpits from behind to keep the shoulders level during the swing.

The aim is always to create an effective bridge of communication, verbal or non-verbal, to get through to the client and then to shape or re-shape behaviour as effectively as possible. The way the words are used is important. If one wants to encourage, one must sound encouraging. If one wants to stop something, a firmer sharper tone may be required. If one wants to impose clarity on confusion, one's words must be clear and concise. They need to have a rhythm. Repetition of a key word is often called for. By way of example, 'Watch *the target*, nothing but *the target.*' It is almost a form of hypnosis. The voice is used to promote the client's focus and to create mental grooves. One is creating order out of chaos. One is passing on a part of oneself.

Diagnosis

When in the field instructing, one often knows that the client is going to kill the bird well before the trigger is pulled. How? No magic, it is simply that all looks right: the client is 'locked in' to the process of shooting, and one can see that everything is coming together toward the desired end. One is observing control, co-ordination and relaxed concentration. It reminiscent of the concept in Japanese archery that arrow, archer and target are part of the same whole rather

than separate entities. When you notice this wholeness – and it is easy to identify with experience – the end result is predictable.

Conversely, there are occasions when one recognises something is out of
place, when the separation of shooter, gun and target are evident. The problem
may be immediately apparent – an obvious flaw in technique or failure to read
the target – or, it may be hidden, with only intuition telling you that something
is wrong. To help in such circumstances, I refer to my 'triangle of Universals'
– a simple device designed to remind one of the requirements for the perfect
shot. First set out in a series of articles and then in my book, *Positive Shooting*,
it is not a complete answer to diagnosis but I have found it useful. Initial concentration on the Universals reduces the number of things one is looking for in
the first instance and identifies an area or areas worthy of further consideration.

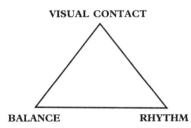

When considered together, the Universals give one a holistic impression of
any individual's performance. If there is a problem with any corner of the triangle, the individual concerned will not be shooting as well as he or she might.
The great advantage of the holistic approach to diagnosis is that it limits what
must be carried in one's conscious mind, and it gives a clear way to proceed
even when a specific flaw in technique momentarily escapes you. Noting a
problem in one or more corners of the triangle will almost always lead you to
a clear plan of action.

Visual contact

Visual contact is one of the great secrets to good shooting. Someone who has
the discipline to maintain good visual contact with the target is going to shoot
better than someone who has not. Good visual contact—making the effort to
focus on the bird—promotes concentration and purpose; it is associated with a
certain determination. On the other hand, poor visual contact can have some
strange consequences, erratic gun movement, head lifting and weight shift rearwards among them. Even the best shots can fail to maintain visual contact
sometimes. Sustained focus on a moving object is not a natural ability: you
must train your eyes and mind to achieve it.

There are many ways an instructor can improve visual discipline, not least by
simply saying, 'Watch the target' to the client before shooting or by emphasis-
ing the need to see the exact shape of the target rather than a vague black mass.
You may also tell the student to look at a particular part of the target. For
example: the front or bottom edge of a clay, or the beak or head of a live bird.
You can also give the student specific exercises to improve shooting vision.

PLATE 9

(above) Although this skeet shooter's stance is very wide, he looks in balance, well focused and as if he had found his rhythm. The shot was taken during a successful attempt at a world speed shooting record.

Double gunning requires balance and rhythm, not to mention an empathy with one's loader. Note how the loader here (Trevor Scott) directs the muzzles of the second gun down as he closes it.

PLATE 10

(above) Note my position here. We are both concentrating. I like the client's position – the front arm and hand are working well. The head is well down and his eyes are on the bird. Could the stock be a bit short, though?

(right) A good professional in action - the client has her weight on the front foot, I would lay money on the fact that her head is on the comb too. Note the smart but practical clothing of the instructor and the cartridge bag he carries so that he can load for the client.

(See Eye section of Shooting Technique chapter.)

As well as the failure to understand the need for sustained sharp focus on the target, poor gunfit (notably too low a comb), poor gun-mounting, looking for the target in the wrong place, poor psychology, lack of background contrast or a visual impediment may all cause poor visual contact.

Balance

The good shot always appears to be in balance. His stance must promote stability throughout the mount and swing. Every shot must find a way of standing suited to his physique and style. The stance may need to change to suit different circumstances (for example, on poor ground or for an overhead driven bird). Poor balance will be recognised instantly. In novices who are afraid of the gun, you will see the tendency to hold the gun at arm's length with the head held back. This is disastrous for balance. In more experienced shots, outrageous body positions may evolve in a mistaken attempt to improve balance. However, good balance is rarely achieved with exaggerated or ungainly body positions. Balance may also be impeded by lack of strength or fitness. To achieve good balance, a degree of muscle tone is required. Strong arm and shoulder muscles are obviously important, but a strong neck, back and legs are needed too.

Poor balance is often the result of addressing the target badly. Novice instructors sometimes change the stance of a client without real need, when all they need to change is the client's orientation to the target. For example, many clay shots face the trap rather than the intended killing zone. They run out of swing and end up being unbalanced at the moment of firing. Similarly, many game shots do not move their feet as much as they might. Consequently, they may run out of swing and end up shooting behind a bird. Like focus, balance may be considered at a level beyond the simply physical. The perfect shot is striving for mental and physical balance as well as a solid stance. The mind and body need to be in synch.

Rhythm

Good rhythm concerns the business of shooting smoothly, as if to a beat. It is unhurried and promotes elegance and economy of movement. Developing good rhythm – or timing, if you prefer – is vital but difficult. One sees many Guns who have shot for years and never learned it.

The instructor can use his voice to encourage good rhythm (calling out the time for the student), or he may ask the student to verbalise the rhythm as he shoots by saying ONE: TWO: THREE or something similar during the gun mount. Another good way to improve rhythm is for the student to shoot with really good shots as often as possible. Unconsciously, he or she will begin to adopt their timing (the reverse is also true, which is why anyone seriously interested in improvement should avoid the company of poor performers – which is one reason why an instructor's own shooting may not be improved by his work). Visual discipline, balanced body position, good gunfit and a moderate recoiling gun will also be aids to acquiring good timing.

Check list for instructors

I do not advise that you use the Universals exclusively for diagnosis, they are only an aid. I am fond of the system because it gets me thinking holistically before considering specifics. More traditional methods remain important. When looking at a client's shooting, you must obviously consider:

1   Safety.
2   Vision in all its aspects.
3   Physique.
4   Gunfit and suitability of equipment.
5   Stance and centre of gravity.
6   How the gun is held.
7   Address to the target and pre-shot preparation.
8   The reaction to the initial appearance of the target.
9   Relationship of muzzle to flight line.
10   When the gun comes to the shoulder.
11   Body rotation and the relative height of the shoulders during the swing.
12   The system of forward allowance employed.
13   The speed of swing.
14   Any trend in missing.
15   How the gun is controlled in recoil.
16   Adequacy of follow through.
17   Disguised, but fundamental errors (such as eye or head-lifting, checking the swing and flinching).
18   Body tension.
19   Consistency of technique.
20   Obvious problems (e.g., a poor mount or difficulty with specific targets).
21   Individual psychology.

This will lead you to ask questions like:
• Does the client have any physical or visual impediment that I have, as yet, failed to identify?
• Is the gun and gun fit adequate? Are poor trigger pulls, or excessively short or
    heavy barrels preventing progress?
• Is the trigger finger properly positioned? Does the grip shape impede trigger finger placement, or cause the wrist to cock excessively?
• Can the client see the target? Is a low stock causing head lifting? Does the client have problems with rising targets?
• Is there any indication of the left eye taking over on occasion? Is the head twisted on the comb?
• Is the client's basic mounting technique sound? Might it be improved by dry-mounting exercises? Does the stock need an alteration? How much of the butt
    sole is in contact with flesh? Is anything snagging?
• Is the butt coming to the shoulder too early in the swing?
• Is the head moving more than it should?
• Is the rear hand too dominant, or the muzzle held too high causing the barrels to see-saw during the mount?

- Is the front hand being used effectively?
- Is there any unnecessary movement of the gun muzzles?
- How is the client's weight distributed in the chosen stance?
- Does the weight distribution change as the mount and swing progress? Is it moving back? (A very common fault which will lead to head raising and misses behind and above.)
- Is the client prone to rushing or stopping?
- Is the client 'rifleshooting', i.e. being too deliberate?
- Is visual contact sustained for every shot?
- Is there any sign of gun judder during the mount and swing? Do the eyes seem disconnected from the gun?
- Is the client persistently behind or in front of the target? Is it an eye dominance problem.
- Is the client persistently above or below the target? Is it a gunfit or technique problem?
- Is lead achieved by a flick or a smooth push?
- Does the client really understand forward allowance?
- Is he reading the target well?
- Does he chase the target? Is this because the gun is starting in the wrong place?
- Is the client keeping the shoulders level during the swing? Is the back arching to compensate for poor rotation and arm use? Is part of the reason poor address to the killing point for the target?
- Are the barrels canted when they should not be?[1]
- Is the barrel dropping on long crossers? Is the problem poor front hand position or lack of arm strength? Is the gun too heavy?
- Does the client set his feet to favour the second target?
- Are the feet moved when the opportunity arises?
- On report pairs, is the client trying to ambush the second target with a stationary gun? (i.e., not returning to pick up the second target).
- Is the client confident?
- Is there any sign of body tension?
- Is he shooting too quickly?
- Is he consistent?
- Is his style elegant?
- Is it effective?
- Does anything else look wrong?

Common problems and their causes

The shooter is placing his shot pattern behind the bird

Common causes: Insufficient understanding of the need for lead, i.e., the client is never catching up with the bird. The client is stopping as he pulls the trigger or failing to follow through. The target has been misread. The orientation of the stance is incorrect with regard to the anticipated killing point (causing the swing to be checked). The stance is unsuitable (for example, the feet are too far apart). Focusing on bead rather than bird. The client is shooting deliberately (as if using a rifle). Poor visual pick-up and gun hold preparation. The gun is too heavy for the client. Excessively heavy trigger pulls. Undiagnosed eye dominance problem. Poor gunfit (too long a stock, or wrongly cast). The front hand is extended too far forward.

The shooter is placing his shot pattern in front of bird
Common causes: Misreading target. Moving too quickly. Undiagnosed eye dominance problem. Poor visual pick-up and gun hold preparation. Use of maintained lead technique. Too much instructing (would-be instructors please note!). Use of short-barrelled gun. Lightweight gun. Light-barrelled gun. Front hand is positioned too close to the action. Poor gunfit.

The shooter is consistently over the top of target
Common causes: Head raising. Gun mounted too low (causing head raising). Leaning back (causing head raising). Poor gunfit (stock may be too low (causing head lifting and overshooting, or too high, also causing overshooting). Gun badly regulated (notably a high shooting top barrel on over-and-unders) or too long. Shooter is misreading target. Shooter is moving too quickly. Gun or barrels are too light. Shooter is firing as the target passes the apex of its trajectory. Psychological reluctance to get under low targets. Shooter is off line of target.

The shooter is consistently underneath the target
Common causes: Bad mounting.

Flinching

Flinching can be a most awkward problem. It takes several forms. The worst sort of flinch (we shall call it type 1) is a complete inability to pull the trigger. This may not occur on every shot, indeed, typically, it might occur in only a few shots out of a hundred. When it does happen it is, of course, most disconcerting The more common flinch (type 2) involves a violent involuntary spasm upon pulling the trigger, usually accompanied by closure of the eyes and a downwards jerk of the gun barrels (occasionally, this 'left arm flinch' is seen in isolation – type 3). It afflicts many shots including beginners who fear the gun and experienced shots who have over-trained or who are suffering from fatigue. Frank Little notes:

> I have been watching other shooters for all my shooting years, and I have come to the conclusion flinching is caused by one of two events: a shooter whose timing does not match his bird/bead relationship or a shooter who is a trigger squeezer. (The Little Trapshooting Book, p. 96).

I am not sure that I agree with the last point – I advocate a controlled trigger release – but I do believe that both very light and heavy triggers may aggravate or cause a flinch.

With beginners, who frequently suffer from a type 2 flinch, the right gun, lightly loaded cartridges, and good instruction in the basics of hold, mount and stance should deal with most cases. When a flinch is identified in an experienced shot it must be taken very seriously. The shooter will be aware himself if he suffers from a type 1 flinch. The the presence of a type 2 or 3 flinch may be confirmed by surreptitiously loading a snap cap into the second barrel and observing the client's reaction on pulling the trigger. Unless there is an obvious reason for the flinch – such as a gun which recoils excessively – the best prescription is a lay-off for at least a month, during which time the client should be encouraged to get fit and rested. After a rest, his mind and body may be retrained. This can take various forms.

My own approach uses the psychological technique of behavioural modification. I advocate repeated dry firing with snap caps whilst simultaneously concentrating on relaxation, muzzle control and visual contact with a designated target (which need only be a spot on the wall). The client may also make use of an air rifle, shooting in a warm and comfortable indoor environment or even a de-activated double action revolver (which may be repeatedly snapped whilst simultaneously making an effort to relax the muscles of neck and shoulders). One has to break the conditioned response that has developed in association with the subconscious fear of pulling the trigger. This is made much easier by being able to practise the essential skill with no fear of recoil or muzzle blast. Training should take place for five or ten minutes twice a day. Repetition is the key to success. Training must continue for a couple of weeks after the flinch appears to be cured.

Once this regimen has been completed - and it requires considerable motivation to persist with it – shotgun shooting may continue, but not before equipment has been thoroughly considered. Trigger pulls should be checked because excessively heavy or light pulls can be a factor in flinching. Gunfit (stock length, comb width and angle, excesses of cast, purchase on grip and forend) and weight are also important factors. Choose a soft-recoiling cartridge, consider the fitting of a recoil pad and limit the client's shooting over a period of three to six months. This may sound like an awful palaver, but a flinch is a very serious problem for the committed shot. It must not be ignored or it will get worse, the type 2 flinch evolving into a type 1.

I might add as a postscript that Chris Cradock sometimes recommended a double trigger gun as a cure for flinching. 'The thing about the double trigger,' he told me once, 'is that the action required from the user is different. With the single trigger, one must pull-release-pull; with the double there are two pulls.' Many American Trap shots who have developed a flinching problem – and flinching may be more common among American Trap shots because they shoot so much – opt for a release trigger. This is a trigger which is armed by compression and released by letting go.

Dropping shoulder and rolling off line of target due to poor body rotation.[2] Shooter misunderstands the 'picture' for which he should be looking. Flinching. Poor gun fit with regard to drop and pitch. Muzzle-heavy barrels.

The shooter is being hurt by recoil

Common cause: Gun is being held improperly. Shooter fears gun. Lack of strength or body mass. Poor gun-fit (too short a stock, too much bend in the stock, too angled a comb). Gun is too light. Cartridge is too powerful or payload is excessive. Gun is too tightly bored or (more arguably) has short, sharp, forcing cones. Ill-health or tiredness.

The shooter is slow to react to the bird

Common causes: Poor visual contact. Pick up point or gun hold are wrong. The bird is too fast for shooter's ability level. Poor eyesight.

Erratic shooting

Common causes: Poor basic technique. Lack of preparation prior to the shot. Insufficient motivation or poor psychology. Focusing on the bead. Bad eyesight. Undiagnosed eye dominance problem. Failure to maintain visual contact with the target throughout the process of shooting. Rifle shooting style applied to clays.

Hesitation

Common causes: Poor confidence. Fundamental misunderstanding. Watching bead instead of bird. Lack of basic technique

Seeing the shot

An effective shooting instructor

must be able to 'see the shot'. Though they might tell you otherwise, the truth is that most instructors cannot see the shot all the time. A really good instructor might see the shot 80-90% of the time (though some may claim even more). How is it done? It is a knack. (This talent, it appears, was first publicly claimed by H.A.A. Thorn, better known under his trading name of Charles Lancaster.) First you must know what to look for. No-one sees individual pellets in flight. What you see is a swarm of pellets (and the air disturbance around them) travelling towards the target. The shot will be observed as a relatively small, very fast moving darkish mass; or as Robert Churchill called it, 'a ghost of a shadow'. Usually, shot is easier to see on a slightly overcast day. It is very hard to see against a green background (although nickel plated shot is easier to see than other types in this situation). If you want to see the shot, you will need to stand beside and behind 'your gun'. If you are too close to the gun, muzzle blast will prevent you from seeing the shot. Your eyes should be looking a few inches above the muzzles of the gun, not focused on the gun but directed several yards ahead.

The more you look for shot, the easier it will become to see it. And, as Robert Churchill notes:

> The trained coach sees a great deal more than merely the flight of the swarm of projectiles. He sees the flight of the charge with the centre of his eye but he is aware of the gun-muzzles on the outer edge of his field of view...he sees how the gun comes up, whether steadily or jerkily, whether it checks or wavers, how true the alignment on the target is...he is also able to detect, from muzzle movement, errors of gun-mounting. (*Game Shooting* by Robert Churchill, fifth edition, p. 220.)

NOTES

1 In a simple mount, one without swing, it is an absolute mistake to cant the gun. However, some start the mount for a crossing bird with a slight natural cant when they wind back to pick up the target. This is not necessarily a fault. Similarly, when taking driven birds quartering high to either side, those schooled at West London may maintain (assuming an over-and-under) a perpendicular relationship to the flight line.
2 Flexing the back and dropping a shoulder rather than rotating the body and keeping both shoulders level is a common error when tackling crossing birds. The remedy is to encourage a better mount and swing in three phases. First, set the stance to the killing point; next, demonstrate the importance of rotation from the hips; finally, show how the front arm is used to keep up on the line of the bird as the upper body rotates to the killing point. The action should be akin to that of a tank turret. When game shooting stepping 'into the line' of the bird, anticipating the killing point, will help to keep the shoulders level.

CHAPTER 7

Psychology

What is psychology? It is merely the science of the mind. How can psychology help shooters and shooting instructors? It provides us with another way of looking at the complex skills involved in our sport. It is a way towards a deeper understanding of our technique and of ourselves. All good instructors are already psychologists. We note how state of mind affects performance. We note how the individual reacts to stress, how he is motivated and how far he may be pushed. We may note whether he has a rational or an instinctive approach to the sport. These are all psychological observations. A more formal consideration of psychology does not make this any the less important. It just enables us to do it in a more sophisticated and methodical way. Ideas are examined in this chapter from formal sports psychology and sports science and also from works of popular psychology and self-improvement. The purpose is to get over the importance of the psychological dimension and to give you a number of ideas with which to experiment. We will start with a consideration of skill.

Skill

Barbara Knappe in *Skill in Sport*, writes that a skill is the 'learned ability to bring about pre-determined results with maximum certainty, often with the minimum outlay of time, energy or both.' Sport scientist, Wilf Paish, notes in reference to Knappe's definition that, 'skill implies quality and efficiency of movement. It will involve mental and physical abilities. It is not instinctive. It is dependent upon learning and practice.'[1] Matt Jarvis, a sports psychologist, highlights a distinction between skill itself and those innate physical attributes that will determine our potential to develop skill (a similar distinction is made by many other commentators). A skill, is, in essence, about control and consistency. It has mental and physical components. It must be learnt and developed by practice. It should be distinguished from 'natural ability'.

In the shooting context, unlike field athletics, developed skill is arguably more important than innate physical ability (though instructors should always be sensitive to variation in motor abilities such as strength and gross body co-ordination; and psychomotor abilities such as reaction time, dexterity and aiming ability). The possible proof of this, is that no one becomes a shotgun champion without a long, hard, apprenticeship. A famous American trap shot once quipped when asked to what he put down his great success: 'Natural ability and a million registered targets.' Slow starters (people who seem to have little natural ability), by the application of sheer determination, can become great shots. At the elite level, innate physical abilities (such as better-than-average eyesight and excellent hand-to-eye co-ordination) are clearly significant, but determination and the will and need to win are, in my opinion, the key factors in taking you to the top in competitive shotgunning. You could, of course, argue that such psychological qualities are themselves innate attributes of the individual.

Describing skills

Psychologists categorise skills in different ways. *Fine* skills, involve fine movements (as in sewing or precision shooting disciplines). *Gross* skills, involve large muscle movements (as in throwing a javelin or weightlifting). Shotgunning falls somewhere between the two. The swing and mount require both gross movement and fine motor control (we might conclude therefore that fine and gross are best considered as poles of a continuum rather than as absolutes).

Psychologists also talk about *closed* and *open* skills. Closed skills are those which are performed in predictable environments and have a definite beginning and end. Open skills are those which are performed in more fluid situations.

Some closed skills can support open ones. In Karate, for example, the performance of Kata - the repetition of a fixed routine of blocks and punches - is a closed skill which will help when one is in an open fight. In shooting, developing a good gun mount with dry practice (a closed skill) will be a great help in all subsequent live firing situations, not least when facing unpredictable driven birds in the field. Skills, moreover, may be *internally* or *externally* paced. Releasing an arrow or firing a bullet at a static target is internally paced as is hitting a golf ball: one decides when one does it. Catching a ball is externally paced (the pace is dictated by the arrival and speed of the ball). The act of shooting a clay begins when we call, 'Pull!', but is affected by the speed and trajectory of the target. Internal and external factors are both relevant.[2] What about game shooting? Here the bird dictates pace and this is one reason why it is usually more difficult to shoot game than clays. However, the really good game shot is able to impose a degree of internal pacing by carefully selecting his birds and refusing to rush.

Learning skills

Researchers Fitts and Posner (1967), noted three stages in the acquisition of a skill. The first is *cognitive*, when we try to understand what is required of us: we talk, watch, imagine and try; a so-called 'motor programme' is created. This may involve holding a lot of information in memory and results are likely to be messy. The instructor's job at this stage is to offer the feedback to the client, to point out what feels right and what does not. The second stage is *associative*: in this we have an idea of the skill and can now move on to develop a feel for it, a 'muscle memory'. The client is able to offer himself some feedback in this stage, but the role of the instructor is still critical (and there will be greater detail in his feedback to the client). The final *autonomous* stage is when we are able to practise the skill without conscious thought and without a constant need for feedback from the instructor or coach. At this stage, our mind becomes free to consider other things relating to the application of the skill. For example, once we have learnt to mount the gun, we are free to consider the importance of focus on the target.

Types of instruction

When skills are being taught, various techniques can be employed to transmit the instructor's knowledge to the pupil. In the shooting sports context, as in many others, three are notable:

- *Verbal:* hearing the expert describe the skill;
- *Visual:* watching an expert perform the skill ('vicarious experience');
- *Manual:* direct assistance from the expert involving touch.

Verbal and visual instruction may, of course, be combined: 'Bring the gun to your face like this ...'; as may verbal and manual instruction: 'We'll shoot this one together (with instructor supporting forend). We'll take the tip of the gun to the bird and pull away ...'. Verbal and visual guidance are used most commonly in shooting instruction; manual guidance is the hardest technique to master but most useful on some occasions. It might involve placing a gentle - unseen - hand behind the client's shoulder to prevent the weight's coming back during the swing or helping a beginner to achieve the right forward allowance by supporting the forend of their gun. More rarely, one might place one's hands underneath the client's armpits from behind to prevent him rolling his shoulders during the swing and mount and to encourage proper upper body rotation. (I only use this particular physical intervention as a last resort when verbal instruction and demonstration have failed.)

Practice
Practice is required to perfect any skill, but the nature of the practice may differ significantly. Skills may be practised in *part* or in *whole*. Part practice allows some skills to be broken down into their component parts. It is especially useful when teaching beginners complex skills, or when refining or modifying the technique of the more experienced. Part practice training is also useful when one is dealing with situations requiring multiple skills: for example, the collection of techniques required to deal with a fur-and-feather stand (a rabbit followed by a bird in the air) on a sporting layout. Learning to shoot the rabbit and the bird as single targets first and then put the two actions together is a beneficial training exercise. The linking movement, one might add, is itself a skill. (Which is why the pick-up for the second bird should be planned to maximise performance.)

There is also a distinction to be made between *mass* and *distributed* practice. If an action is repeated many times without a rest – say ten consecutive shots at the same single target or ten consecutive gun mounts – it is termed mass practice. *Distributed* practice involves short practice sessions with other things happening in between: for example, alternating practice between several different targets on the same stand. While mass practice carries a risk of boredom and fatigue, distributed practice may fail to inculcate the skill adequately. In the sporting shotgun context, there is often insufficient mass practice in the teaching of basic technique (the situation in the military and the martial arts is quite different with repetitive drills being the primary method of basic instruction). In sporting shooting we shy away from mass practice and because of this, many shotgunners fail to master basic skills such as gun-mounting and sustained visual contact. Those with less motivation and attention span will usually prefer distributed practice, elite level performers (and beginners if properly encouraged) can make good use of mass practice to perfect a specific skill or movement. Do not take this as a licence to bore beginners to death with 20 shots at the same bird! The real application of mass practice is in things like teaching a good, rhythmic gun mount. I know of one champion skeet shot who will shoot *hundreds* of cartridges at a single station if he misses a bird at that position in competition. He has shot more 100 straights than any one else I know.

Having noted that mass practice has its uses, we might observe that the practice required in basic training or to overcome a specific technical fault is rather different to the type of practice which we undertake to improve our general game. Practice in the latter case should not be too easy or stupidly difficult (it must stay within what we might call the 'zone of benefit'). It should be planned and goal-oriented. It must stretch ability to isolate faults in technique or in areas were work is required; and it must be fun; or intrinsically motivating in another way (for example, in presenting a challenge). Unless practice makes these demands, fundamental flaws or weaknesses in technique may remain undiscovered and full potential may not be achieved. How many club shooters have had a rude awakening when shooting away from their home ground? The man who can manage 40 ex 50 (80%) regularly on the home layout may struggle to break 65 on a championship course. The moral is to create practice which develops experience of different targets and situations and which is constantly pushing you or the client forward.

The value of this has been brought home to me over a series of visits to a well-known shooting ground in southern England. The ground is famous for

---

Preparation and performance routines

I have done much work in recent years on creating routines of thoughts and actions (thus combining the mental and physical aspects of the game) to increase individual awareness and consistency in the shooting process. I want to offer my clients a precise set of instructions which they can take away with them when the lesson is over and which, when consistently applied, will offer them a long-term improvement in performance. Such routines are also useful to the competitive shot. They occupy the mind at a vital time: focusing energy, preventing distraction and anxiety, and boosting confidence and consistency. In all cases they ensure that practice or competitive performance is as efficient as possible (indeed they blur the distinction between practice and 'real' performance). Awareness and self-knowledge, encouraged by a routine and basic skills which are well refined, are the keys to successful shooting. The right way becomes the familiar way, and deviation from the mental and muscle memory is easily picked up.

The expert shot usually has a much higher level of awareness of his own actions because he applies such a routine consciously or unconsciously. *He knows what feels, looks and thinks right.* The expert knows what to look for and what precise technique to use in a particular circumstance. So-called concentration is easier for him, *because he knows exactly what to concentrate upon.* In the first phase of preparation he gathers intelligence; in the second, he applies it to his set-up procedure. In the performance stage of shooting, which begins as the decision is made to call for the target, he concentrates on sustaining focus on the bird. The expert's energy is disciplined and directed. His concentration is the product of experience not a mystical power.

its well-presented, thought provoking, targets. The shooting of the regulars I know there has been absolutely transformed over the last three or four years. The ground offers a constant challenge, many great shots shoot there. The course designer, a keen shot and skilled instructor, has a deliberate policy of stretching the ability of his patrons but without ever going over the top. The benefits of such an approach are self-evident and to be contrasted to another club which I sometimes visit and where that challenge is always lacking. Most of the birds at that venue are boring, but one can usually rely on the fact that at least one bird will be presented at ludicrous range or from a firing point facing in the wrong direction. The regulars there, and they are dwindling in number, never seem to improve.

Arousal and performance

This is another area of psychological research which has a clear application to shooting. An individual's level of arousal (and arousal is closely related to stress and anxiety) has a great impact on his performance. There are different components to arousal, the most important being cortical arousal, during which electrical activity in the cortex increases, and autonomic arousal, during which activity in the autonomic nervous system increases.

The autonomic system is so important to sporting performance that is worth considering in some detail before going further. It is the mechanism which regulates normally unconscious body functions such as heart beat, respiration and blood pressure. The autonomic nervous system is split into sympathetic and parasympathetic sub-divisions. Essentially, the sympathetic system speeds things up (making us ready for 'fight or flight') while the parasympathetic system slows us down. For example, if a stimulus requiring immediate physical action is perceived, the sympathetic nervous system will usually increase heart beat, blood pressure and breathing (to increase the oxygen supply to the brain), increase muscle tension and raise production of epinephrine (adrenaline). Perspiration will be initiated (to reduce body temperature), salivation decreased and sugar and fat released into the blood stream. This is the physiological nature of arousal. When the need for activity is past, the sympathetic system brings down heart rate, constricts the bronchial tubes and stimulates digestion (which is suppressed during arousal)[3].

Bringing some autonomic functions under more conscious control is a valid goal for all serious sportsmen, not least because it may allow us to master our emotions. The experience of emotion relates not only to an emotion inducing context, but to our perception of things like heartbeat and respiration. Arousal may be emotionally ambiguous until we have scanned our environment for clues to fathom out just why we feel so aroused. Increased arousal might be interpreted as either excitement or anxiety depending on situation and individual attitude. Someone really skilled in the mental game may even be able to reinterpret the emotional label they attach to feelings of increased arousal - 'I'm not scared, I'm excited'.

The relationship of arousal and performance

So much for what arousal is and how it may be interpreted, but how does it effect sporting performance? The psychologist, C.L. Hull, developed something called Drive Theory in the 1940s and 50s. It suggested that for a simple task and a well learnt skill, higher arousal was likely to lead to higher performance. The relationship was a simple linear one. If the task was complex, or the skill (the response to the task challenge) was not well learnt, high arousal would lead to poorer performance. The theory suggests that expert performers with well learnt skills will achieve their best results in competition (where arousal is high). It also suggests that those just starting in a sport (or anyone who has poor basic skills) should train under conditions of low arousal in order to maximise performance. All of which appears to make good sense but it was not enough to satisfy the psychological researchers.

The 'inverted U' model was popularised in the 1970s (but based on much earlier work). It suggests that in any situation requiring the application of skill, there is an optimum level of arousal: exceed this and performance will deteriorate; fail to reach it and the individual will not be performing at his full potential. This relationship can be shown graphically as an inverted U. The ideal level of arousal will change depending upon the complexity of the skill; fine motor skills require lower levels of arousal than gross ones. Wherever shooting may fall on fine-gross continuum, most of us have experienced occasions when under-arousal (as in being lackadaisical) or over-arousal (as in being nervous) has damaged our performance.

Catastrophe theory

The inverted U hypothesis itself has been challenged in recent years. In the late 1980s, psychological researchers, Fazey and Hardy, discovered that at low levels of anxiety the inverted U model worked; but at high levels of anxiety, the model was not accurate in predicting performance. At these high levels, a small increase in arousal could lead to a sudden dramatic fall in performance (whereas the inverted U hypothesis would predict only a gradual one). To further complicate matters a Russian psychologist, Hanin, has noted that individual response to anxiety (which is related to arousal - see below) may be very different. He proposed that each sportsman has a zone of optimal functioning (ZOF). This certainly seems to ring true to my own experience of people and might lead anyone serious about their own, or a client's performance to consider the ZOF and how one might contrive to reach and stay within it.

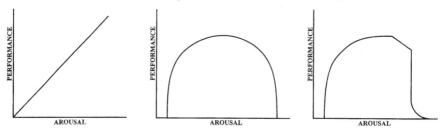

Theories of performance and arousal. Notice the sudden fall-off predicted by catastrophe theory when arousal passes a certain critical point.

Arousal and state of mind

Barbara Woods notes (as common sense might also suggest) that top class sportsmen may be able to cope with higher levels of arousal *if they are self-confident*.[4] Apter has shown that our reaction to arousal may be dramatically different, depending on our state of mind. If we are in a *telic state*, which is serious and goal directed, we will find excessive arousal unpleasant because we are seeking to reduce anxiety to achieve the goal. If we are in a *paratelic state* - in which excitement is sought deliberately – we are more happy-go-lucky, more interested in the here-and-now than something over the horizon. In this state, we may find very high levels of arousal enjoyable. We can alternate between the two states very rapidly, which may explain why over-arousal causes problems (such as anxiety) in some situations and not in others.

Arousal and personality

Personality may also effect how we react to arousal. The British psychologist, Eysenck created a model of personality (not to mention a questionnaire-based method of testing it – the EPI Eysenck Personality Inventory – which included, most famously, an introversion-extroversion dimension). He noted that the introvert is more easily over-aroused than the extrovert (and hence avoids excessive arousal). Over-arousal in the introvert leads to anxiety and poor performance. Whereas, the extrovert, may seek arousal. According to Eysenck, these differences are primarily determined by individual brain physiology.

Arousal for dummies

So much for the psychological and physiological theory. How do we achieve an optimal level of arousal in the real world? By understanding our own reaction to arousal by maintaining adequate levels of motivation, by using stress and anxiety (see below) as allies, and by using specific routines and techniques for winding up and down. Most top-level athletes develop complex rituals to get themselves 'psyched up' before battle commences. These rituals are extremely personal: they may be short, mid or long-term and they must be constructed to suit the individual. They may involve thought alone (as in mental imagery) or, they may be physical (a warm up) or, they may integrate thoughts and physical actions (as in my Positive Shooting System - applying the routine of which is designed to keep one in what amounts to a ZOF). Many professional sportsmen make use of inspirational music to get them in the mood. There are infinite possibilities. The All Blacks dance and shout. It is a case of whatever works for you.

In the competitive shooting context, the process of psyching-up might commence early in the morning (though it could start weeks or months beforehand) with attention being directed to a personal goal. For example: 'Today, I will make the extra effort to maintain visual contact with every target.' The process continues as equipment is checked and other preparations are made. On any day of competition one usually needs to 'wake-up', consider the objective, engage with it and relax. Positive imagery and mental rehearsal might be used on the way to the shooting ground provided such activities do not become obsessive and provided they do not interfere with relaxation and clarity (I prefer to listen to music or simply chat to a friend). Warming-up (see next chapter for more detail) on arrival is useful because it not only limbers one up but gets the blood flowing and the brain functioning. 'Walking the course' which combines gentle exercise with useful reconnaissance always makes sense.

Some find shooting before the main event helpful – for example, participating in a pool or practice shooting on another ground or layout. Although it can be useful, one should not become dependent upon it – it may not always be possible to shoot before competition (an alternative is mental rehearsal). Meals need to be planned so that performance is not hindered. The wrong meal at the wrong time may have a soporific effect on mind and body, when just the opposite is required. Some may find that they perform better at a certain time of day and plan accordingly. The danger with this sort of approach is that, on occasion, the plan will inevitably be broken and negative thinking may result: 'I never shoot well in the morning'.

Switching on and Switching off

During competition, different levels of arousal will be required at different times: one needs to learn to 'switch on' and 'switch off', if one is going to direct maximum energy at the critical moment (usually just 2 or 3 seconds). It is certainly not a smooth upward curve. There should be peaks and troughs of arousal before shooting commences. For example, when I first go to a sporting stand I will have a look at the birds, note where they are coming from, what targets are being used and the effects of wind and light. Doing this methodically will, of itself, raise arousal levels significantly, but the method and mental occupation will also act as a check to excessively high arousal. If the targets are being missed, I will look for the reason, 'the where and the why'. I will always establish a strategy, a plan, for the stand, including the technique or techniques to be used on the individual targets (for example, does the first bird need maintained lead or ambushing to buy time?). I will decide more or less where I want to kill the target; where I will first direct my eyes; and where they will need to go for the second target. Having completed this basic assessment, I will relax and chat (if I am in the mood) and wait my turn. (If the stand is a very hard one, it may make sense to devote more energies to analysis and forgo the socialising – it is a question of personal priority. Champions care about every target. Their success is directly proportional to the mental effort put into each bird. They may accept, indeed prefer a degree of isolation to achieve their goal. But this is not always the case. George Digweed was noticeably gregarious between stands during his phenomenal performance at the 2000 British Open at High Lodge.)

I usually start to 'change heads' (i.e. my arousal levels begin to rise) when I note the competitor two cards in front me going to the stand. Keeping silent, I will stand behind and to one side, watching his birds and confirming my strategy. When possible, I will stand directly behind the next man. If I need to psych-up more than usual at this stage (which I may need to do if my motivation is low), I will rehearse the strategy with mental imagery (and may make the decision to call for the birds with a bit of aggression or decide to shoot with more choke than is ballistically necessary). If I need to psych-down because I am over-aroused or anxious, I may use a simple breathing and/or relaxation technique (and make a mental note to call for the birds in a more relaxed way and/or determine to shoot with perfect visual contact and gun movement). The goal is to step into the cage in a relaxed but engaged state with a specific plan. The feet are set to the killing-point according to the gathered intelligence but are not set in stone if the first pair indicates a change to the plan. Hold and pick-up points are confirmed but subject to adjustment if required. A mental programme is now running. All input irrelevant to the job in hand is automatically blocked by one's complete involvement in the execution of the specific stages of the task in hand. (Should concentration be broken by a disturbing external stimulus, mind and muscles should be relaxed and one should break the gun and return to the beginning of the routine.)

Loading can be used both as a signal that one is about to 'shift up a gear', and as a sort of mini-meditation (some may choose to align case heads as part of their ritual). It is a cue for muscular relaxation and mental focus. One becomes single-minded. The end is in sight. As the gun closes, mental energy increases. In the address position it rises further and slight muscular tension in the front arm is noticeable and proceeds immediately to a rapid mental rehearsal (the imagery of two smashed targets) before the call. Arousal approaches its peak at this stage. The call is made with absolute attention on the bird (even though as yet one cannot see it). The target or targets appears: swing, mount and triggering follow. Arousal peaks[5]. To ensure follow through as arousal drops, a special effort needs to be made to maintain focus on the bits of the broken target (momentarily for a the first bird, somewhat longer for the second). Relaxation ensues, but within the now established cycle. One must pace oneself and never rush. One must not allow one's timing to be dictated externally (other than by the bird). After shooting, forget the misses – you cannot change history – and return to relaxation and friendly banter if appropriate.

Trap

At trap, a good signal to start focusing one's energies is when the Gun two positions down has finished shooting. When the next door Gun has fired and opened his action, I will immediately close mine and go into the rest of my performance routine. After the shot I relax, consciously un-tensing my shoulders, waiting to begin the cycle again. At skeet, I operate to much the same principle, but specifics depend upon where one is placed in the shooting order. The general principle is never step onto a stand and shoot 'cold', one should be using a routine of thoughts and actions and pacing oneself to create a rhythm. One must have attuned oneself to what is going on first, attended to the situation fully and created a plan. If you have a specific winding up and winding down strategy, it is much less likely that you will be caught unawares.

Stress

This is a word which is much used in modern life but not often defined. We all regard some situations as especially stressful: A-levels, the driving test, not having enough time to get a piece of work finished, the hundreth bird after a run of 99. Technically speaking, these are *stressors* which may lead to physiological and psychological responses and the psychological and physiological experience of stress. Hans Seyle, the pioneer of stress research, noted three stages of stress: first was an *alarm reaction* during which the physiological changes associated with 'fight or flight' occurred[6]; next comes a *resistance* stage, in which our heightened physiological[7] and psychological responses lead to greater activity and finally comes the *exhaustion* stage – we cannot stay at red-alert forever.

Stress is very closely related to arousal. It is not necessarily bad: it is the body's means of preparing us for battle. A degree of stress (like a degree of arousal) is essential for peak performance, it keeps us alert and energised. Without some stress, life would be very dull. However, stress can become a problem if it is intense or prolonged. Excessive stress over long periods, moreover, can lead to physical and mental illness. In a sporting context, too much stress (or a poor reaction to it) can lead to impaired performance

Anxiety

A predisposition to anxiety – apprehension about future misfortune – may be related to personality, which would be termed *trait anxiety* by psychologists (at its extreme, a disorder of personality); or it may be a response to stress brought about by specific situations, which is known as *state* anxiety. Martens et al. (1990) suggested three components to anxiety in competitive situations: cognitive anxiety (negative thinking, fear of failure etc.), somatic anxiety (stomach cramps, perspiration, elevated heart beat), and a self-confidence factor involving the anticipation of success or failure. This seems a useful model. Martens and his team created a questionnaire which could be used by coaches to monitor anxiety. Such an approach backs up the coach or instructor's intuition concerning those competing at the highest levels. A simpler approach would be simply to rate one's mental and physical anxiety on a scale of 1 to 10 and use these figures as a base line for action.

We cannot run away from stress or anxiety – competitive shooting is a stressful activity and should be recognised as such – but we can learn to respond to stress positively and to control or accept our anxiety. Both trait and state anxiety may be dealt with in a similar manner as far as routine shooting instruction is concerned. If the client has a fear of failure, you should arrange situations which initially induce anxiety but which provide opportunity for repeated success. If the client's anxiety is specifically associated with competition, the answer is to encourage him to shoot more competitions. The best practice for competition is competition itself. In this case, one may either encourage the client to jump in at the deep end by entering major events straightaway; or to take a gentler approach, by shooting smaller competitions on a regular basis and building up to progressively larger ones.

Clinical psychologists would call the first process *flooding* and the second *progressive desensitisation*. For example, someone with a fear of spiders might be introduced to the thought of very small ones first. Then they might be shown

PLATE 11

Trap shooting requires that one learns a cycle of concentration and relaxation. One can see that the shooter's body and mind are locked in to what he is doing. The gun to his left relaxes but remains engaged. Note also the close stance both have adopted: this reduces tension in the swing when there is a wide arc of fire and no opportunity to move the feet.

Clay shooting can be a great sport for the disabled. Wheel chair position requires just as much thought as foot position if good breaks are to be achieved consistently. This Gun is alert without being over stressed. All of us can use our sport as a means of self discovery. Focus on achieving your best not beating someone else. Winning is an occasional bonus.

PLATE 12

(above) A student instructor watched by Alan Rose - note that the Guinea Pig (Andy Hudson - a fine shot) has no left hand.

Good shooting technique should combine disciplined preparation, economy of movement and relaxation. I do not see psychology as a separate subject – it is part of the shooting process which is a sequence of thoughts and actions. Body and mind are part of the same whole.

a photograph of a small spider. At a later stage, they may be invited to handle a plastic pot containing a tiny arachnid, eventually they may be able to pick up a huge, hairy Tarantula with far diminished fear. A similar technique may also be used for problem targets. If there is an unresolved complex about a certain bird – teal, rabbits or whatever else may create the clay pigeon shooting equivalent of arachnophobia – arrange for an easy presentation. Then check technique, modify it as required, achieve success, and make the target progressively more difficult until the largest and most hairy specimen holds no fear (indeed, until the client enjoys it).

Another useful strategy for dealing with the fear of failure is to concentrate on the perfection of technique and to place less emphasis on result. On some occasions, one might even suggest to the client that he should accept failure: 'Forget about breaking the bird; assume you won't.' This is not to be recommended generally because it introduces an element of negative thinking, but it can be used as a tactic to shift mental focus from failure and on to some aspect of technique. More commonly, one might say, 'Shoot the target with good style; if it breaks, it's a bonus.' Everyone wants to break birds, but to achieve this consistently, technique must be perfected first. There is a most memorable section in *Zen in the Art of Archery* where the master gets angry with the student for getting the right result the wrong way. I know how he felt! One meets rather too many poor or 'not-good' shots who think because they can hit a bird occasionally that they know how to shoot it[8]. In Zen, perfection technique is the prerequisite to enlightenment. A similar approach may be applied to shooting style by those of mature mind who appreciate beauty of form. The perfection of technique as an end in itself may not appeal to everyone, but those who are only interested in results must still acquire technique before, they can 'forget' it. Many people have not the patience or determination to work at the basics and because of it, they never achieve their potential.

Stress Busting
Fitness and feeling good make one more resistant to stress and thus make an anxiety response less likely; we become better able to cope with the slings and arrows of outrageous fortune. Competence (improved ability) is another great stress buster. Professional sports psychologists might advise checking arousal levels prior to competition to make sure that one begins in the right arousal zone. They might further suggest that one should always start from the same baseline. Moreover, they might advise using a mental technique such as imagery to deal with psychological anxiety; and a physical one, such as a relaxation exercise, to deal with anxiety which is producing physical symptoms. There are a whole range of techniques and therapies, mental and physical, conventional and unconventional, which might be tried by those who suffer from stress and anxiety or who just want to improve self-mastery or explore human potential. Here is a brief overview of some of them for those who wish to experiment (although my best advice is start by getting fit, the body will lead the mind). More information may be found at your local library, health food shop or on the net.

Massage is an ancient technique for stress reduction. It has been practised for millennia. There is no need to pay someone for the service (although a first class professional masseur or masseuse is well worth the cost). Buy a book or two, a packet of joss sticks and some suitable oil and contract with your partner for a weekly or bi-weekly mutual massage session. Who knows where it may lead! You can also buy massaging back cushions and foot stools, not to mention various hand held devices. Some are surprisingly effective and may be used while watching the box or as part of a more focused relaxation routine.

Meditation does not require paying vast sums to a beaded guru in a saffron robe: it need be no more than sitting down for fifteen or twenty minutes each day in a comfortable chair and making oneself still and quiet. Some forms of meditation involve the repetition of a holy word or mantra. This is practised by Buddhists, Hindus and some Catholics. However, meditation need not have religious overtones: one might repeat the word 'one' or 'peace' rather than something overtly sacred. As you learn to meditate, all sorts of distracting thoughts may come into mind initially. Do not resist them, but do not pursue them either, just let them pass by. If you meditate regularly, you will discover that there really is another you (or something) which exists beyond the turbulence and trivia of your conscious mind.

Yoga means yoking or union in Sanskrit (the yoking or union of the individual with the divine consciousness). It is about bringing the instinctual and reasoning selves together and releasing creative energy. Classically there are eight stages: yama (restraint or abstinence), niyama (observance and devotion), asana (the physical postures), pranayama (breath control), pratyahara (sense withdrawal), dharana (concentration – focusing the mind's energies on a single point), dhyana (meditation) and samadhi (the bliss of self-realisation). Patanjali who wrote the first account of Yoga nearly two thousand years ago (and the practice is much older) called Yoga: 'the settling of the mind into silence'. All of this may sound a bit esoteric, but Yoga may be used simply as a technique of relaxation and a form of exercise. There are many forms: some are less physically demanding than others. Hatha Yoga, the predominant school of Yoga in the West, uses breathing and relaxation exercises to achieve the classic positions without straining. Power Yoga, a modern variant, is more vigorous. Raja Yoga is the highest form and is concerned with mind and spirit rather than body. By this 'Royal Path' intense concentration is fostered and (according to its exponents) psychic powers.

Tai Chi, widely practised in China, is increasingly popular in the West. Its elegant, slow-motion, dance-like exercises are rooted in Taoism and (like Yoga) based on the observation of animal movements. They are intended to restore the natural balance of yin and yang by improving the flow of energy through the body and bringing internal and external energy into balance. Tai Chi improves breathing, posture and flexibility. It is excellent for spotting tension in the body and can also improve strength. Tai Chi is another great stress buster. Advanced practitioners may use it as a martial art. I think that the rhythm of Tai Chi makes it especially well suited to shooting sportsmen, most of whom need to slow down. I do not know if Shan Zhang, the 24 year-old

Chinese girl who shot 200 straight at Skeet at the 1992 Barcelona Olympics (and then 23 ex 25 in the final), was a practitioner of Tai Chi or not, but some special discipline allowed her to enter 'The Temple of the Undistracted Mind' and achieve a perfection of form which led to the overall Gold medal and not inconsiderable resentment from some of the male competitors she beat. Her extraordinary performance led to a change of rules separating the sexes in future competitions.

Hypnosis, from the Greek Hypnos (the god of sleep) is widely practised, as any copy of the *Yellow Pages* will reveal. Essentially, it is about inducing a state of relaxation and then making positive suggestions. Does it work? Academic research suggests no qualitative difference between an 'hypnotic state' and deep relaxation; although this hardly explains the extraordinary antics of individuals who fall victim to stage hypnotists or why Sigmund Freud used hypnosis to access the subconscious before he rejected it in favour of his free association technique. (The main advance with free association is that it works with more people than hypnosis). A friend who is a 'co-operative' hypnotherapist (and an airline pilot with a scientific education) recently told me: 'Hypnosis is not magic; it is one of many methods used to induce trance. The method by which trance is achieved is un-important but what is useful to know, therapeutically speaking, is how susceptible a person may be to suggestions whilst in this relaxed dream-like state. The hypnotherapist uses his voice and non-verbal communication– such as matching the clients rate of breathing – to make subtle, indirect suggestions towards the client's goal. The authoritarian or stage hypnotist commands "sit in this chair and go into trance"; whilst the co-operative hypnotherapist might say, whilst indicating two chairs, either of which the client might choose: "in which chair will you find it easier to go into trance". The client then sits down, accepting the pre-supposition that not only will he go into trance but that he will do so easily. I am convinced hypnotism works and that many people use its techniques without even realising it. As for the question of cost, the price of a visit to a professional may seem exorbitant, but the client may learn self-hypnosis at an early stage and become self-sufficient. I like to give clients a tape of a session. They can pull out images and may repeat "anchors" for the trance such as a squeeze of arm or knee. Such a personal tool is going to be much more effective than a tape made for a more general audience.' If you are interested in hypnotherapy – which has potential dangers as well as benefits – make sure that you deal only with a professionally qualified person willing to give references.

Imagery, which we shall look at in more detail later, is commonly used to induce relaxation. One might visualise oneself escaping to a quiet river bank on a summer's day, a wood in spring or lying on a sun-soaked beach listening to the waves (we shall note shortly, how similar techniques may be used for mental rehearsal of shooting technique). Imagery may be used within meditation or hypnosis and might be combined with breathing techniques or positive self-talk (see below)

Neuro-linguistic Programming (NLP) is a term which originates from the work of Richard Bandler and John Grinder. NLP is, in essence, a recipe book of imaging and other techniques used by hypnotists and other therapists. An example of an NLP technique might be as follows. An individual comes to a hypnotherapist expressing the desire to relax and increase confidence. He is led into trance and the therapist notes: 'Imagine a room, a control room, in your mind. In this room there are many switches and dials and indicator lights. Switches are dials for all sorts of things. Over there on one side you can see a sliding-dial for your breathing. See how it is set, almost near the bottom, the light is dim. The pulse slide is also at "low". The switch for walking is off and the light above it out. The switch for your eyelids is in the down position. There many other control switches. Now take your time, explore, make some adjustments. See the slider for confidence. It can be set at Very High, High, Medium, Low and Very Low. Where is it now? Reset it.'

Autogenic training (AT) is a form of stress control involving self-hypnosis and requires professional instruction. It involves a series of mental exercises designed to suppress the 'fight or flight' reaction and to develop deep relaxation. These take three forms: passive concentration on the body; key words or phrases to induce feelings such as warmth and heaviness; and placing the body in positions to 'block out' the exterior world.

Aromatherapy uses 'essential oils' to address all sorts of conditions, but, most commonly it is sold as an antidote to the stresses of modern life. The oils are massaged into the body, inhaled or sometimes taken orally. Aromatherapists claim to be able to treat a wide variety of conditions including stress and anxiety. If nothing else, aromatherapy is a very pleasant and relaxing experience.

Reflexologists believe that pressure points in the hands and feet are associated with different organs in the body. These points may be 'blocked' and by applying intense, localised pressure, better functioning of the organ may be promoted. Reflexology can be quite painful but, like aromatherapy, it can be very relaxing.

Shiatsu is similar to acupuncture but uses pressure instead of needles to stimulate key points along the meridians (paths of energy) in the body. Shiatsu may be used both to psych up and to psych down depending on which points are stimulated.

Of the many **breathing techniques** which might be practised, perhaps the simplest are most to be favoured. Relax the neck, shoulders, back and abdomen. Focus consciousness on your breathing. Breath in and out slowly so that the abdomen moves in and out. Continue until you feel relaxed and focused (with practice, one full cycle in and out can have a significant effect). Another simple breathing exercise involves no more than being aware of the cold air entering your nostrils and the warm air leaving them.

Positive self-talk might be saying to oneself, 'I feel great,' 'I am relaxed,' or 'I am going to kill this pair; I've killed the last six.' **Negative self-talk** is an interesting mind game whereby you tell yourself the opposite of what you want to do: 'I'm not going to kill this pair.' Positive self-talk should always be honest and concise. I would not say, 'I feel great', when, in fact, I felt lousy. Better to focus the mind on something specific. Positive self-talk may be used almost as a mantra: 'Focus', 'Don't slow', 'Lock-on', 'Steady', 'Follow Through'. **Key words** which elicit a specific response.

Progressive Muscular Relaxation (PMR) is a routine whereby one becomes aware of and learns to tense and relax one's muscles progressively. It was developed in the 1920s and has achieved widespread popularity. There are various ways in which the technique may be applied. Typically the body may be split into various sections (usually four), but I prefer to consider individual muscle groups - temples, eyes, jaw, neck, shoulders, arms, hands, chest, upper back, lower back, stomach etc. Starting from top or bottom, tense for five seconds and relax for ten or twenty. One may associate specific actions such as relaxing the area between the shoulder blades with a more general relaxation (one of the benefits of PMR is that conscious relaxation of voluntary muscles will lead to relaxation of involuntary muscles as well). I use this technique - relaxing the area between the shoulder blades – whenever I perceive myself being tense in competition. It is one of my **planned responses** – a predetermined response to a specific situation or event.

Biofeedback involves the use of equipment (ranging from the highly sophisticated EEG machines to monitor brain waves, to miniature watch-style, heart-rate monitors to track the pulse, and the simple but ingenious 'Biodot' patch which changes colour as body temperature rises (an index of relaxation). The core idea is that if we have accurate feedback of these autonomic functions, then we will be able to bring them under more conscious control. Biofeedback techniques have been used with success by sportsmen (including some shooting sportsmen). For example, if we are affected by anxiety or negative thinking, this can also affect heart-rate (pushing it up or down in different circumstances). A heart-rate monitor could then be used – once one has studied one's reactions to emotive situations with an expert – to provide feedback on when one was straying outside the optimum performance zone. Biofeedback may appeal to those who prefer the scientific approach to training (though be warned, there is quite a lot of pseudo-scientific clap-trap in the advertisements of some devices).

In the 1970s, a consideration of **Bio** or **Circadian Rhythms** became fashionable. Human beings, like most other animals, display a rhythm in many of their physiological functions which is linked to the light and dark of a 24 hour day. Our heart rate, metabolic and breathing rates, and body temperature peak in the late afternoon and are at their lowest levels during sleep and in the very early morning. This may sound logical enough, but the periodicity of these functions remains even if our normal pattern is suddenly disrupted (one reason why jet-lag is a problem). Any sportsmen may find it useful to ascertain what his personal pattern is and try and compete within it when possible (subject to warnings already given). When travelling abroad, moreover, the psychological research[9] would seem to indicate that at least a week is required to adjust fully to the disruption of one's Circadian pattern and for the patterns themselves to adapt to the new cycle of light and dark.

Thus far we have mainly considered sophisticated and exotic techniques, but there are many more mundane ways to beat stress, gardening for example and listening to classical or otherwise inspiring music (the latter, may of course, be used as a method of psyching-up too). There is no need for complexity or novelty unless it provides better results for you. But every serious competitor should consider these issues and consider the mental aspects of their game and how they might be improved.

Use your nervous energy

Anxiety will never be entirely eliminated. Indeed, it is most important to explain to clients that it is OK to be a little anxious in situations like competition, where stress is intended and arousal is a prerequisite of performance. One must accept one's natural response. If you try to ignore anxiety, or push it out of your mind, it is only likely to get worse.

Planned response to anxiety and negative thought

Anyone who feels anxiety coming on, is well advised to develop a plan to deal with it. I have already noted how I may relax the area between my shoulder blades if I notice myself getting tense (which might otherwise lead to a miss behind). I may also make myself aware of my breathing, followed by honest self-talk: 'OK, I feel a bit nervous, but that is just my body responding to the situation. Now I am going to use that energy; I am going to throw it down the barrels; I am going on the attack.' The particular dangers of anxiety for shooting performance are the disruption of gun movement and visual focus. Another technique is to use imagery to stop or contain a negative thought. If you note yourself thinking negatively ('Oh, I know I am going to drop a bird here'), imagine a stop light or a frontier barrier closing. Literally stop the thought. If one uses such imagery, it is much easier to do this. The 'treasure box' technique involves creating an imaginary box with your greatest achievements or most precious thoughts contained within it. If anxiety or negativity is caught creeping into one's head (or if one needs a boost), one may open the mental box. Another tactic is to have an imaginary friend, a great master of the sport, 'find' him when you are challenged or in need of assistance and do as he would do in the circumstance. May the force be with you!

Specific *refocusing plans* should always be used to deal with distraction. After a 'no-bird', I always lower and break the gun and return to the beginning of my shooting routine. Otherwise I might shoot in a state of muscle fatigue and with diminished concentration. One other tactic might be mentioned whilst we are discussing relaxation and anxiety. We made reference earlier to Apter's Reversal Theory. It suggests that a sportsman in a telic (serious and goal-directed) state has two options if anxiety becomes debilitating: reduce arousal or, and this is most intriguing, shift into the happy-go-lucky paratelic where the anxiety creating situation may be re-interpreted as fun.

One target at a time

In all forms of shooting, it is vitally important to focus all one's energy on the job in hand and forget the targets that have gone before or will come after. One must stay, in so far as it is possible and practical, in the present moment. The act of shooting should become a meditation in itself. When a bird is missed, it is vital not to linger on the thought of it. Some people find this very hard, but the necessity and wisdom of putting it behind you are clear enough: major championships have been won many times after a lost bird or a poor start. The positive-minded shooter may even use an early miss as a bonus: 'Good, I was not concentrating hard enough. Now I can really begin to make the effort.' I do this routinely in sporting competition and have found it really useful (so much so, that I almost look forward to missing an easy bird early on in proceedings, I know it will make me try harder).

Warming up

A gentle pre-shooting physical warm up loosens the body, promotes mental and physical focus, and may also help with muscular tension. If the brain notes such tension, it may produce an anxious response. 'My muscles are tense, therefore I must be worried'. Conversely, muscle relaxation – even if consciously performed – brings with it a sense of peace and well-being.

The Iceberg profile

Twenty years ago W.P. Morgan, a sports psychologist, compared the mood states of successful elite athletes with unsuccessful ones with regard to six factors: tension, depression, anger, vigour, fatigue and confusion. When the scores for these factors were plotted in a graph, the profile of the two groups was quite different. The results are shown below.

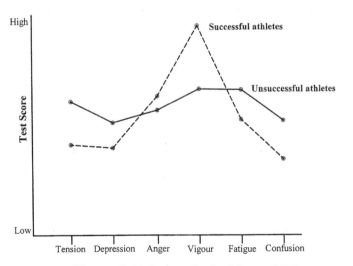

The so-called iceberg profile after Morgan (1979).

Subsequent research has shown that this holds true over a wide variety of physical sports, including shooting.

Motivation: intrinsic and extrinsic

Motivation is another key to peak performance. Psychologists talk of *intrinsic* and *extrinsic* motivation. Intrinsic motivation comes from within: for example, the sheer satisfaction when one first learns to hit the really high birds off a tower. Extrinsic motivation is the result or prospect of an external reward. It might be a word of praise from the instructor or it might be a trophy waiting to be won. The instructor should understand both types of motivation and which is most applicable to the client and when (see for example, the section on learning skills above).

Achievement motivation

Some people appear more motivated to achieve success, and others seem more motivated to avoid failure. The first group tend to look for challenges, are not afraid of failure, welcome constructive critical comment and enjoy having their performance tested (for example, in competition). They attribute both success and failure to internal factors. If they succeed, it will be because of hard work; if they fail, it might – quite rationally – be put down to a lapse of concentration or a failure of technique. Those who are motivated to avoid failure are dominated by the recurring thought of failure. They avoid challenges and testing. They attribute failure to external factors: unfair conditions, poor equipment, bad luck, etc. As a shooting instructor, you will meet both types (and all shades of grey in between) but the second group will usually be the greater challenge. Recent research indicates that the fear of success may be a significant motivational factor too. I have to confess that this has afflicted me on occasion. I can on several occasions recall being in a position where I could win a championship – where my abilities were clearly up to the challenge and where, for example, I may have posted the highest qualifying score – only to crack at the thought of being so close to success. Physician heal thyself.

Confidence

Confidence – based on real skill and firm, focused, determination – is unquestionably the X-factor which separates brides (champions) from bridesmaids (runners-up). Winning becomes a habit. Going to the opposite end of the scale, negative thinking (or mental distraction) will bring the mental and literal focus back to the gun. The typical result in shooting is frustration and 'inexplicable' misses above and behind (because the gun stops and the eyes or head are raised).

Psychologist, Richard Cox writes:

> The notion of self efficacy is synonymous with an individual's belief that he or she is competent and can succeed at a particular task. An individual who enjoys a high level of self-efficacy enters into a competitive situation with enthusiasm and self-confidence. The degree of self-efficacy possessed by an individual will determine whether that person will approach or avoid an achievement situation....Bandura's theory (1977, 1982) proposes that self-efficacy is fundamental to competent performance. In competitive situations, the higher the level of self-efficacy, the higher the performance accomplishments and the lower the emotional arousal...' [10]

In considering confidence, you must explore the motivation for any individual's shooting and note whether or not he is 'self-reinforcing' and personally secure or not. Insecure people may be thrown out of kilter by a single poor performance, or by the knowledge that they are being observed by others. Once such problems or traits are identified, training can be constructed to overcome them. For example, simulation training may introduce the stress of competition or audience observation into what would otherwise be a simple practice session. Training must also provide the opportunity for repeated success (an especially important factor with the young). Nothing will damage confidence as badly as repeated failure combined with a feeling of powerless to overcome it. How do you gain confidence? Focus on success. Repeat it whenever you can. Train methodically. Use performance routines. Make an effort. Control as many of the controllables as you can. Teach the client to expect success.

Positive thinking

Most us could do with thinking a bit more positively about ourselves and our potential. In his excellent book, *Gold Minds,* professional coach Brian Miller describes the 'Success Cycle'. The concept apparently originated in East Germany, and was designed to highlight the relationship between how an athlete feels about himself and how he is likely to perform. Miller notes that if one's self-image is positive, one's general attitude is likely to be positive. This, in its turn, leads to higher expectations and improved behaviour. One is likely to take better care of oneself. Performance is boosted. Self-image is improved and so the cycle continues upward. A negative image can have the opposite effect and may create a downward spiral.

Many sports psychologists note the need to make frequent 'positive affirmations'. Psychologist Stephen Bull and his colleagues encourage sporting clients to write down a list of personal positive affirmations. 'We get athletes to write their personal affirmations on a card and then read this card several times a day

The Success Cycle [after Miller]

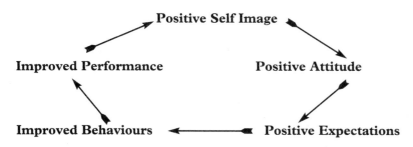

on a daily basis. Eventually, the affirmations seem easier to repeat with conviction and the athlete becomes more comfortable with the whole process of positive thinking'[11] The sort of statements he suggests include:

I am confident in my ability
I feel mentally strong
I can stay positive throughout competition

Perhaps the greatest exponent of positive thinking in the shooting context is American rifle marksman, Lanny Bassham, an Olympic and twice World Champion. He wrote a book called *With Winning in Mind* and it laid out the principles which brought him Olympic gold. They might be summarised as:

- Decide to be a winner.
- Set specific written goals with time limits for their achievement.
- Use visual rehearsal as often as possible.
- Never consider what you have done wrong, only what you *should* be doing.

Bassham advises that you should write down what your goal is every day. Similarly with visual rehearsal. It takes some presence of mind to this, let alone to find the time and determination actually to sit down quietly every day and practise your sport mentally (in our case, watching yourself shoot 25 or 100 straights at skeet and trap; or in sporting, seeing yourself shoot every type of stand with success). Bassham would suggest that you should also regularly see yourself winning in your mind's eye to the extent of accepting the trophy or walking to the podium to get the medal. Bassham is not the only person to advocate this. Among my clayshooting friends, I know that Kevin Gill is a great believer in positive visual rehearsal.

Focus and flow

Focus relates to absolute attention on the skill being executed. The aim is to enter a state of Zen-like meditation. This leads to 'flow', or being 'in the zone'. One is completely focused, so utterly engrossed in execution, that one is unlikely to be distracted: one is not self-conscious; one is not consciously involved in decision-making. 'It' is happening. In the words of the old Zen masters: archer, arrow and target are one. There is no separation. It may sound like hocus-pocus, but once experienced, it is very real and remarkably simple. Everything comes together without boundaries. Your engagement with the activity is complete. There is no you and it.

To achieve focus and flow is the key to high levels of performance. We have noted how shooting routines – good approach work in the preparation phase and disciplined visual contact in the performance stage – can aid concentration. They teach us precisely what to focus upon at any particular time. There is a special need for this sort of discipline, not just to apply technique effectively, but to eliminate distraction. Achieving flow, however, requires an extra magic ingredient, which will come of its own accord if one practises the discipline of focus sufficiently.

Our body is designed to react to danger instinctively – loud noises, movement and signals from the other senses. Psychologist James Manktelow[13] points out that in a sporting context, these reactions may need suppression. The same flick of the eyes to a person moving in the fringe of our field of vision – a primal response to potential danger – may disturb concentration and distract us from shooting the next target. 'Part of learning flow,' he observes, 'is learning to isolate the important stimuli for the sport from the irrelevant ones that cause distraction. This will involve learning to selectively override your

Mental rehearsal and white magic

Mental rehearsal (also called visual rehearsal or imagery) is a very widely used technique in modern sport[12]. An example would be to shoot 100-straight at skeet in one's head—including 100 decisive kills – the evening or morning before a major competition (or nightly) as a means of improving concentration and focus. Alternatively, one might choose mentally to rehearse just one perfectly smooth swing and follow-through. Ed Scherer used to say, 'You know, I shoot 25 birds in my head every morning, and you know what? I shoot 25 straight each time and each bird is centred!'. Jack Nicklaus has noted that he uses imagery before every shot. First 'seeing' the ball where he wants it to finish, 'nice and white and sitting up high on the bright green grass', seeing its trajectory, 'and even its behaviour on landing' and then watching himself making the perfect swing 'that will turn the previous image into reality'.

My Positive Shooting System, which integrates mental and physical processes, advocates positive visualisation of a smoked target between the preparation and performance stages of shooting. The act of visualisation creates a bridge from preparation to performance. Mental rehearsal promotes focus and concentration on the correct execution of the skill. It is a reminder of what one needs to concentrate upon, and it allows for the comparison of physical movement with the perfect image. Mental rehearsal has a physical element as well: it may activate the neural pathways that will be used in actual performance. One can use imagery from an internal perspective, or one can 'observe' oneself from outside – the external perspective.

Apart from affecting final outcome positively, mental rehearsal can create a situation which has not yet been experienced; it can allow for the development of responses to unusual situations (such as planning what to do when distracted); and it is a means by which a complex skill can be broken down into parts – slow motion in the mind's eye. Some serious competitors use video of themselves or of masters of their sport as a starting point for visualisation. A portion of the tape is played repeatedly until the memory is assimilated. I found making several films about shooting, some of which required the reshooting of certain sequences many times, and the subsequent editing process has much improved my visualisation skills. Everyone who shoots should experiment with video in my opinion. It gives you a much better sense of your own and other people's performance. Subtleties emerge which may have been missed before. The use of video as a training aid will improve the quality of subsequent attempts at visualisation.

brain's natural reaction to stimuli.' Manktelow also notes that flow is easiest when:

- One realises one's skills are up to the challenge
- One is paying complete attention to performance without any thought of analysis.
- One is relaxed but alert and thinking positively.
- Attention is trained.

Whether one considers it from a Zen or psychologist's perspective, flow must be allowed to happen, it must not be forced. Susan Jackson and Mihaly Csikszentmihaly (who developed the concept of flow a generation ago) write: 'Flow is found by listening to your inner voice, which can tell you what your true interests are; by developing skills necessary to become immersed in a chal-

---

Goal setting

This is a very fashionable area in sports psychology and one increasingly adopted by the corporate world. Goal setting is a means of accelerating progress by improving motivation: it defines one's commitment level, creates as action plan, identifies key skills and boosts motivation and confidence. When goals are achieved, new goals may be set. An example of a sensible goal would be: I will shoot 3 registered competitions a month for the next three months.

Whatever goals are set, it is important that they be:

Agreed (with the instructor/coach)
Written down
Worthwhile
Well defined
Open to modification if required
Relatively difficult
Time limited
Regularly reviewed and assessed

Goals can be outcome or performance based. An outcome goal might be winning a specific medal or being selected for a county or national team. Performance (sometimes called process) goals are generally to be favoured, because they are definitely achievable: for example, 'I will shoot three registered competitions a month for the next three months.' Provided the effort is made, the goal will be met. It is completely under the control of the individual who set it. This does not mean that outcome goals should never be set (if you want to be the best, you must dare to think it) merely that performance goals should be used more often. Whenever goals are considered, priorities should be set and goals should be written down in order of importance. Provided plenty of thought, effort and feeling is put into the creation of the goals, goal setting really works. It is just a question of making the effort. Try it.

---

lenging activity; by learning to focus on concrete goals and on subtle feedback. However, flow is not guaranteed. It is not a state of mind which can be manufactured...'[14] The most one can do is to behave in a manner in which the experience of flow is most likely to occur.

Performance profiling

This is a useful and very practical technique for the shooting sports. The performer is asked to consider what the important qualities for success are. These might include physical attributes (such as fitness), technical skills (such as a good gun mount), and psychological factors (like confidence). Having isolated 20 key attributes, the performer then ranks himself on a scale of 1-10. The information is displayed as in the diagram below or in simpler bar chart form. It shows what the individual considers important and will encourage targeted training to meet those specific needs. It may also be used as a means of monitoring performance and is useful for 'post-mortems' after a competition.

What would your 20 factors be? Here are my 20 points for Sporting (although my factors for skeet and trap would not be greatly different save for items 13-17):

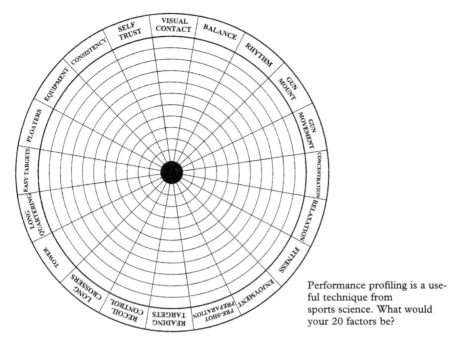

Performance profiling is a useful technique from sports science. What would your 20 factors be?

1 visual contact
2 balance
3 rhythm
4 gun mount
5 gun movement
6 concentration
7 relaxation
8 fitness
9 enjoyment
10 pre-shot preparation
11 reading targets
12 recoil control
13 long crossers
14 tower birds
15 long quartering
16 consistency on easy targets
17 floaters
18 equipment satisfaction
19 general consistency
20 self trust

These factors are those that I consider to be training and performance priorities for my shooting (several personal weaknesses are included). They chart the dimensions of performance that I regard as important and record an interest in performance is some highly specific situations.

The Inner Game approach

This is something rather more esoteric, but extremely interesting. In the early 1970s, a young tennis pro called Timothy Gallwey wrote a best-selling book called *The Inner Game of Tennis*. It was such a success than *The Inner Game of Golf* soon followed (not to mention *The Inner Game of Music*). Gallwey had been involved with Eastern philosophy and also with the human potential movement. Basically, he suggested – having noted 'conversations with himself' whilst playing tennis – that we all appeared to have two selves. One is rational and conscious, 'the teller'; the other, instinctive, an 'unconscious, automatic doer'. This concept accords quite well with the scientific distinction between the left and right brain. The left brain is concerned with logic and language; the right brain is concerned with creativity, co-ordination and synthesis. When one tells oneself to keep one's eye on the ball or to bend the knees on a tennis court, it is Self 1 talking to Self 2.

The essential problem in sporting performance, according to Gallwey, is that the rational Self 1 tends to be over-dominant. We do not trust Self 2 sufficiently, though it is capable of extraordinary results if properly programmed – better results than we could ever calculate our way to with Self 1 in charge. Nevertheless, most instruction is still directed toward Self 1. I discovered Gallwey only recently, but I had come to very similar conclusions while experimenting with technique for my book *Positive Shooting*. In clay shooting, conscious activity should, in the main, be limited to the preparation phase of the shot. Once the target has been called for, focus should be locked onto it and directed instinct should take over.

Where Gallwey is especially useful is in giving us specific principles that will allow Self 2 to function more effectively. He suggests that we should establish a gentle, polite, relationship between the two selves. We should observe our behaviour non-judgementally. Having noted what we want to change, we should *ask* Self 2 to help, not command it to. We can tell Self 2 what is required – reprogramme it – by means of awareness, feeling and image. Then we should just let it happen and observe the results. Gallwey advocates minimum intervention in teaching: few words, a light touch and key images.

Gallwey cautions against an overemphasis on mechanics (he does however emphasise the importance of visual contact, advocating, for example, that tennis players should look at the seams of the ball just as we enjoin the client to look at the target). His goal is literally the inner game, the game that we play for mastery of ourselves. He argues, most powerfully, that we should free ourself from the desire to win in order to achieve freedom and (paradoxically) peak performance. The game: tennis, golf or shooting, is merely the vehicle by which we can develop. He suggests a complete change of attitude, the acceptance that we are using the game for this purpose. Interestingly, he also opposes the 'positive thinking' approach, arguing that it is a form of 'self-hypnosis', inextricably linked with the negative (and therefore part of the same mind-set as the negative). It is directed at the 'ego mind' of Self 1 – the mind which can interfere with our performance.

I am a convert to the Inner Game, but I do not believe that it does away with

Psychological warfare

Psychological warfare can be considered from two perspectives – victim and attacker. In the former case, one should always remember that if someone is bothered enough to put you off deliberately – and this takes many forms: 'sledging' (unpleasant personal comments), making a disturbing noise, being boorish, excessive 'barracking', 'hexing', invading your personal space, giving false information ('You've got to shoot straight at those'), playing mind games ('I wish I could shoot them as fast as you'), ejecting cartridge cases towards you, shooting with a rhythm designed to put you off – it is invariably because they fear you or because they have a personal problem.

Once you see them in their true light, they should become far less of a threat. Your awareness disempowers them. If you feel affected nevertheless, you may elect to open your 'treasure box' (to take out a positive thought to counter a negative one), you could enlist the help of the imaginary friend, a virtual reality George Digweed), or you might imagine their attack as pebbles bouncing off the armour plate of a tank. An alternative strategy is to take all they can give, then smile, and break your bird or birds in fine style knowing it will irk them all the more (in club situations or minor competitions such a statement of confidence can prevent a recurrence). You might choose just to make them irrelevant, by focusing completely on the execution of technique. Let them fade into the distance.

As far as psychological warfare as attacker is concerned, I would note that my advice is limited. I enjoy using tight chokes because they allow me to see how I am killing a bird, but also because they smoke targets. I get a buzz from that; the opposition may not (on the other hand, they may think I am idiot for using so much choke when less will kill the bird). In serious competition, I make an effort to remain happy and relaxed. I may sometimes choose to be a bit distant. If someone is trying to attack you at a psychological level, this is a good countermeasure because they perceive that they cannot make destructive contact. Some good shots deliberately change their timing in a shoot-off to put off inexperienced opponents. Frankly, it seems a waste of time, it is more likely to put you off your own shooting.

In a shoot-off situation - and never pass up a chance to take part in one, the more familiar you are with the situation, the less daunting they will become - it is usually sensible to shoot first if the opportunity arises. This puts the other shot (or shots) under pressure. I may also think to myself, 'Well, someone has to win this. It might as well be me,' or, 'Win or lose, I am going to watch every bird and shoot with style.' Such action crosses no great moral Rubicon. Beyond these things, I will not go[15]. I hate to see poor sportsmanship on the shooting field and would prefer to lose or see my clients lose than win by adopting underhand methods.

the need for learning good basic skills in the traditional way. Moreover, I think the inner game concept requires a qualification. Self 2 should be trusted more. Once one is in the habit of trusting Self 2 to do most of the work, one must recognise those situations where Self 1 can help. For example, on very long crossers (let us say those targets requiring 4 or 5 yards of lead), I find I need to extend my leads consciously if I want to shoot them consistently. On the other hand, at Trap I am 100% Inner Game – all my shooting is based on visual contact and 'instinct' (sublimated skill). If I see the ridges on the bird, I know it will break. Perhaps if I had more faith the IG approach would work in all situations. I am working on it!

Winning

Winning is a habit. The more you win, the more you are expected and expect yourself to win. The reverse is also true. In some people, winning is a real need (and one which can dominate their lives if they are not careful). For this reason, I believe some people are by temperament more likely to become champions than others. As we discussed at the beginning of this chapter, natural ability is probably less important than this hunger for success.

Frank Little was one was one of the world's great trap shots (holding a 99% average for 21 consecutive years). His opinion on winning has obvious weight:

> Winners expect to win and losers expect to lose...A winner's performance is usually the result of past successes. A winner usually expects excellence and has a plan to make it all work. This kind of confidence is the result of knowing you have the right equipment and a plan and technique that works. A successful plan usually includes a few personal touches during the 'get ready' process. Winners have a plan that works for them and practice zero deviation from that plan. If you have ever felt the bottom dropping out of your game, it was probably because you failed to develop a disciplined plan before you called for the target. Usually, this is the result of a lackadaisical attitude and decreased desire to succeed.[16]

I would agree with all of that, but my own prescription for winning is a little different. Develop your basic technique until it is as perfect as it can be. Compete so much that competition becomes your practice. Set realistic goals. Integrate the mental and physical aspects of your game. Get fit (physical fitness improves both your physical and mental stamina). Be determined in your approach (but not obsessive). Push yourself to achieve. Once you have created and are committed to a plan for success, be disciplined within it. But be kind to yourself too. No one wins all the time whether they visualise being given the trophy or not. Winning a prize is a bonus. You win every time you do your best.

Conclusions on psychology

Do not discount the psychological aspects of shooting. Once basic technique is perfected shooting is 80% mental. Make the client more aware of the psychological aspect of shooting, note individual strengths and weaknesses, integrate the mental with the physical game. Just as one might consider stance and forward allowance when considering physical technique, rate the individual on personal confidence, motivation, anxiety and general psychological awareness. Take the mystery out of the mental game by offering specific prescriptions (individually tailored arousal, imagery and relaxation techniques, performance profiling advice, preparation and performance routines, systematic goal setting and assessment). Remember that male ego can be a great barrier to improvement, but it is also a very powerful motivating force if properly directed. Do not over complicate the issue. As with physical technique, keep it as simple as possible. Good psychology boils down to nothing more than having the mental discipline and control to apply a technique which one has proven on every shot, eliminating all interference to its implementation. Shooting psychology has as much to do with learning how not to think as learning what to think.

Having said all this, I might note that I now tend to the Inner Game

PLATE 13

(above) This is Arnie Palmer after winning the White Gold Cup some years back. He is not unhappy – just tired after giving it everything he had. After one has shot really well, it is common to feel drained. It shows one made the effort.

Here a student instructor demonstrates foot position. His client is obviously paying attention. She is learning the importance of getting the details right. Too many experienced shots are distracted by trivia (such as their choice of cartridge or choke) and forget to direct their energies into the fundamentals. Just doing that is the basis of good psychology.

PLATE 14

A study in concentration. More than anything else, good psychology is about getting rid of the interference. Focusing all one's energy on a few simple points will pay enormous dividends if one develops the discipline to do it every time.

Never foget that the purpose of recreational sport – shooting or any other – is to have fun. A good instructor must always be a good entertainer.

approach, using my sport as a vehicle for broader development. But there are still concepts from sports psychology and science that I have found most helpful. For example, Fitts and Posner's ideas on acquiring skills, and Catastrophe Theory are very useful models which help one to understand and predict client's performance at different levels. I also relate well to Bassham's concept that one should focus on what is right and never on what is wrong (I often use it as the basis for 'treatment' of some of my more neurotic students – those who suffer from a mental confusion which leads them to consider everything except what is really important – they worry about the gun, the cartridge, the choke, but forget to keep their eyes on the bird).

Let us end by noting that the first and last piece of psychological advice to give your clients or yourself is to go out and have fun. Peak performance, the inner game, flow, or call it what you will, the goal is the same – to be in kilter with oneself. Mental skills can and should be taught, but they should not be considered too obsessively. Control the controllables. Do not focus on 'am I doing well?' but rather ask yourself 'am I doing everything right?'. Be disciplined and determined by all means – a great score is built one target at a time – use the power of your imagination, but do not become a control freak. Take time to 'smell the flowers'. Modern psychological techniques are a fascinating voyage of self discovery. If applied sensibly, they can lead towards the goal of self-mastery, but never forget that if one does not enjoy oneself and grow wiser along the way the whole process is pointless.

Recommended Reading
Applied Sport Psychology: Personal Growth to Peak Performance by J.M. Williams.
Applying Psychology to Sport by Barbara Woods
Coaching Sessions - A Guide to Planning and Goal Setting [National Coaching Foundation]
The Complete Manual of Sports Science by Wilf Paish
Exploring Sport and Exercise Psychology edited by J.L Van Raalte and B.W. Brewer (A publication of the American Psychological Association)
Guide to Natural Healing by Geddes and Grosset
Gold Minds: the Psychology of Winning in Sport by Brian Miller
Handbook of Research on Sports Psychology edited by R.N. Singer and M. Murhy and L.K. Tenant
In Pursuit of Excellence by T. Orlick
The Inner Game of Golf by W. Timothy Gallwey
The Inner Game of Tennis by W.Timothy Gallwey
The Inner Game of Music by W.Timothy Gallwey
Mental Skills - An Introduction for Sports Coaches (National Coaching Foundation)
Sports Psychology by Martin Jarvis
Sports Psychology: Concepts and Applications by Richard Cox
Sports Psychology in Action by Richard Butler
Sports Psychology in Performance by Richard Butler
With Winning in Mind by Lanny Bassham

NOTES

1   *The Complete Manual of Sports Science*, p. 84
2   There is one interesting potential exception: John Bidwell claims to apply the same speed of

gun movement to all shots. He calls his Move: Mount: Shoot method a 'speed of motion technique.' It is, he notes, 'the only method which does this. It removes the variables; one is not necessarily moving at the speed of the target; rhythm and tempo remain constant: Move: Mount: Shoot for every bird.'

3   However, the relationship between the components of arousal is not quite as simple as this. There are some circumstances where we may be highly aroused, but where our heart rate is low. In considering the research of Lacey (1967), Barbara Woods writes 'in behaviour involving reaction time (such as saving a penalty in soccer) heart rate is lowered but skin conductance is usually raised. When stressful cognitive activity is involved, such as deciding how to play a difficult shot at golf, both of these are usually lowered.' (*Applying Psychology to Sport*, Hodder & Stoughton, London, 1998). These intriguing observations are useful not only because they help us understand the interaction of the components of arousal but because they show just how subtle the reactions of our body and mind can be to specific sporting situations. 'Common sense' would not necessarily give us the same answers.

4   See *Applying Psychology to Sport* by Barbara Woods, p.106.

5   If one is dealing with a report pair, there may be a significant trough between the peak arousal levels for the two birds. Sometimes, it may be appropriate to make a deliberate effort to relax, for example, when one changes foot position between shots.

6   The sympathetic nervous system is brought into play, which in its turn prompts the adrenal medulla to release adrenaline and noradrenaline into the blood stream. These are associated with increased blood pressure, blood sugar and dilated pupils. Blood flow to the muscles is increased.

7   In the resistance stage the body chemistry changes significantly. Adrenaline and noradrenaline production decreases, but production of the hormones which control the release of glucose in the blood - such as cortisol and corticosterone - increases.

8   I know one rather foolish individual who demands 'good targets' at every sporting ground to which he goes. His definition of a good bird would seem to be one he cannot hit consistently. If he manages to break two or three of eight he behaves as is if he has mastered the situation and demands a fresh challenge. He will never learn to shoot properly because he is unable to apply himself to the mastery of basic technique. It is interesting to note, moreover, that this person is always the first to complain and constantly changes guns and cartridges. His very presence, unnerves other shooters. He talks constantly, and carries mental chaos in his wake. In truth, he is rather sad. Seek out shooting companions who make you feel better about yourself and your shooting performance.

9   See, for example, *The Mind Machine* by Colin Blakemore, BBC Publications, London, 1988.

10   *Sports Psychology – Concepts and Applications*, p.219.

11   *The Mental Game Plan*, p. 44.

12   The technique is, however, an ancient one. To take one of many examples, the Jesuits advocated the use of mental imagery so that recruits could imagine themselves in the presence of Christ. The extraordinary achievements, iron faith, and courage in the face of death displayed by many Jesuits may, in part, be linked to these techniques. They amount to a sort of brainwashing. Should one brainwash oneself for sport? That is a question each individual must decide.

13   I developed a much more sophisticated understanding of flow thanks to an essay, Sports Psychology, written by Manktelow, and posted on the Internet (www.demon.co.uk/mindtool/page11.html).

14   *Flow in Sports*, p.161.

15   Well, not quite true, I once tried to use the imagery of the archery match in Errol Flynn's Robin Hood to my advantage. After Robin's opponent the Captain of Archers hits the bull, a voice is heard to say 'but no man alive could beat that shot' after which Robin splits the arrow. I remembered the line, visualised the scene, 'drew my bow' and missed the target!

16   *The Little Book of Trapshooting.*

CHAPTER 8

Nutrition, Sleep and Exercise

Good nutrition is obviously important for any serious sportsman. Indeed, a considered diet is necessity for anyone with common sense and the desire to live a long and healthy life. Unless you have been living on another planet, you will be aware of the need to stop smoking and to reduce saturated fat intake. The consumption of refined foods should be limited too, and one should reduce the consumption of sugar and salt (it is not just a question of eliminating them as supplements; one should be aware of their use as flavour enhancers in many products). This may be disguised in the case of salt, where lists of ingredients may note 'sodium' rather than salt content. Refined sugars are not only high in calories, they increase mouth acidity, causing tooth decay. In prepared products (including biscuits and many sweets) sugars are typically combined with saturated fats. Excessive salt consumption raises blood pressure and may be a factor in heart disease and strokes.

Pasta, chicken, pulses, beans, brown rice, wholemeal bread, low-fat bioactive yoghurt, game and fish all get the thumbs up, preferably accompanied by plenty of fresh, lightly cooked vegetables (protein should only be a small part of the meal – meat and three or four vegetables is to be preferred to meat and two vegetables. Crisp salads are also to be encouraged. Amazing though it may sound, some vegetables can significantly reduce the threat of cancer. Broccoli, cabbage, Brussels sprouts, spinach and wheat bran all have strong anti-cancer properties. Oat bran and garlic lower cholesterol. The Omega 3 fatty acids in oily fish like salmon, mackerel and sardines are good for the heart, unlike the saturated fat in butter and red meat. Just eating oily fish twice a week can reduce your risk of heart attack by 30%.

Olive oil should be used (but not in excess) for cooking and plenty of garlic (unless one is instructing, in which case an odourless garlic supplement may be advised). Avoid chips (but baked potatoes are fine). Meat should be lean and eaten in moderation (in which case, there is no harm in the odd red meat treat, but consumption of red meat should be limited to no more than four small portions per week. Mince should be made from lean cuts. Sausages should be grilled and preferably 'low fat'.). Grilling, baking and poaching are better than frying (unless one is frying in olive oil and garlic). Skimmed milk and cottage cheese should replace the full-fat variety. Fruit is an excellent snack, and water, the perfect drink. Caffeine (as found in both coffee and tea) is a stimulant and is to be avoided, if possible, unless required through poor pre-match planning (e.g., when you had to leave at 4 am to get to the competition!).

Obesity
Many shooters suffer from obesity. A fat-free, or reduced fat diet and plenty of enjoyable exercise (see below) is the only effective way to lose weight in my

experience. If exercise is not enjoyable, you will not persist with it. Similarly with diet: healthy alternatives must suit your palette, if you are to alter your eating habits permanently. It may take a bit of time and effort, but with motivation – and it all boils down, as it were, to your decision to stay fit – alternatives which really taste good can be found. Once you are in the habit of eating well, the wrong food will actually taste bad. Do not attempt crash diets. Rather, aim to lose a pound a week for three months. Achieve that goal (which is just less than a stone) and set another. The key to success is a long-term change in your eating and exercise habits. 'Quick fix' approaches will not resulting in lasting changes.

Eating before and during competition
The timing of main meals should allow for about two hours before performance. Some foods tend to make us sleepy (such as heavy, greasy meals) so it may be prudent to avoid them before competition. Any pre-competition meal should not be excessive and should be carbohydrate rich. A plate of pasta would ideal, as would cereal with milk or yoghurt, rice or noodles or a baked potato. Late meals should also be avoided because digestion is less efficient at night. (Anyone interested in losing weight should also be careful of eating very late in the day.)

Snacking
It is worth putting to rest the idea that a sugary snack such as bar of chocolate can give one's blood sugar a boost at a critical moment. It is a bogus concept invented by confectioners. A bar of chocolate is more likely to lead to an insulin reaction. An apple or a banana or a pot of natural yoghurt would be much better (and should be carried in the kit bag along with a small bottle of water, unsweetened fruit juice or well diluted squash). Rather than buy greasy burgers or sausage sandwiches for lunch, take a Tupperware box with your own healthy alternatives. Ultimately, eating well, like healthy exercise, is a decision – a commitment to make the effort.

Vitamins
A multi-vitamin a day can do no harm and may be a real benefit to those who persist in eating refined foods and for those who smoke. Select one without iron unless you know you have an iron deficiency; men, in particular, should be careful of iron supplements as their bodies cannot dump the excess. As for individual vitamin supplements, five are worth consideration (subject to medical approval): Vitamin C (500 mg per day) to fight 'free-radicals' and boost the immune system, Vitamin E (400IU per day) to help repair the damage to the body that many sportsmen suffer (in moderate doses it also seems to reduce the risk of heart attack which may relate to its vasodilating and anticoagulant qualities but note that pregnant women should not take Vitamin E.), Selenium, which works synergistically with Vitamen E and appears to be anti-carcinogenic (and may even prevent dandruff!), a 'B Complex' to combat stress and keep us mellow, and Folic Acid (400 mcg) which helps to produce red blood

cells and aids in protein metabolism and which counters Folic Acid depletion caused by increased Vitamin C intake.

Following my grandmother's never forgotten advice, I also believe in cod liver oil. A daily teaspoon of this wonderful but initially foul-tasting stuff is good for the heart and joints. Cod liver oil is a natural source of Vitamin A and D as well artery-protecting Omega 3 fatty acids. You may also decide to invest in an 'anti-oxidant' supplement containing beta-carotene (another source of Vitamin A). Beta-carotene is found naturally in carrots, spinach, broccoli and apricots and may help to reduce age and UV-induced free radical damage to the eyes and other tissues. It is good for vision and skin and may be especially useful to those who work outdoors. Large doses should be avoided. All these supplements have the added advantage of being relatively cheap; the benefits of more exotic and expensive supplements are much more debatable (with the possible exceptions of Coenzyme Q10, a powerful anti-oxidant which helps to release energy from the body's cells, and Glucosamine sulphate, which is good for joints and cartilage). If you combine specific supplements with a multivitamin, make sure that you do not exceed recommended daily dosages where it may cause a problem (as it can with Vitamin A). Also, be warned that some recent research indicates that vitamin supplements may not be as beneficial as previously thought. If you have doubts ask your doctor or pharmacist (dieticians in my experience seem to be rather anti-vitamin).

Sleep

If you are having problems with sleeping, few cures are more effective than regular exercise (although avoid working out late in the evening). Those who are fit tend to sleep better than those who are not. One should avoid heavy, greasy or especially spicy meals the night before competition. It is also bad idea to go to bed on a full stomach (dinner should finish at 8, if lights are out at 11). There is nothing wrong with a glass of wine or a pint of beer, but alcohol consumption should be very moderate and accompanied by a glass of water before bed to prevent any ill effects the next morning. One of the reasons the French are able to drink so much wine is that they are constantly drinking water with it.[1] Diluting wine with water is common on the Continent and it is an excellent way to drink when in company without looking fanatically teetotal. Caffeine in tea, coffee, hot chocolate and cola may prevent sleep, as may anything which causes you to become excited or tense (argument, loud music, late-night work). A hot bath with salts or something like 'Radox' added is relaxing and may be used to promote sleep, as may soft music, moderate reading or sex which does not try to simulate the Kama Sutra.

It is obviously inadvisable to get up before dawn to drive to a competition; much better (both for sleep and for the control of stress) to travel the day before or – better – a day or two before a competition (which will not only allow you the chance to settle into a new environment, but will also provide you with an opportunity to make a reconnaissance). If you have no option but to drive early the same day to an important event, try to get someone else to do the driving. If not, get everything packed bar your gun the night before. If you are inadequately rested or stressed by a long drive (in which may have to use your eyes in poor light for an extended period), your performance will suffer. Good planning can prevent this. If you are travelling to compete abroad across a time zone and the event is important to you, try and combine shooting with a holiday. Ideally, you should allow *at least* a week to allow for sleep and other body rhythms to adjust. I shoot abroad a great deal and always find it usually takes several days before I feel like picking up a gun.

How to react to a sleepless night before competition
If you find yourself unable to sleep because of nervousness, clinical and sports psychologist Richard J. Butler recommends three techniques:

- Concentrating on feeling heavy, 'So heavy that the muscles feel like dropping through the bed.'
- Developing a shallow breathing pattern.
- Imagining a small blue dot against a green background. 'Picture the small dot very slowly and gradually expanding in size until it consumes the total visual field. (Usually sleep occurs before the background is fully covered.)'[2]

The shooter's equivalent of counting sheep might be shooting a 100 straight on a simple bird. My own technique when suffering from insomnia is to stop trying to sleep. Instead, let the mind and body 'do their own thing'. Relinquish any attempt at control, become an observer. Say to yourself, 'Well, I may not be able to sleep, but I do have the chance to rest.' Let your mind wander where it wants. Sleep usually ensues. Even if you do not get to sleep, do not give up. Peter Croft, recently told me about his experience at the European Olympic Trap Championship of 1980:

> I was awake half the night and half an hour before I was due to shoot, I was sitting on my own in the team tent shaking like a leaf. When I walked on to the line, however, I went cold as ice, the nervousness evaporated. I won on 197 including 50 straight that day. The first British win since 1961.

Exercise
The sheer physical effort of shooting, especially competitive shooting, is considerable. The energy expended in the course of a day's competition is far more than in many sports which may appear more athletic. Without a good level of general fitness and the ability to pace oneself, performance will suffer. Building stamina is reason enough to get fit, but specific fitness (such as building up the muscles of the left arm or neck) and flexibility training is also important to the serious competitor. It aids technique and may prevent injury. As if all this were not enough, exercise promotes good health and well-being. The right exercise can help to maintain the natural balance and flow of energy through the body. A recent study at the Appalachian State University in North Carolina confirmed that moderate exercise boosts the immune system and reduces the risk of upper respiratory tract infection (competition and excessive exercise can increase the risks, however). The benefits are evident, but exercise must be planned and progressive to be effective. Moderation is important to avoid

undue stress. Overtraining can cause you real damage (allow 48 hours between aerobic training sessions to allow for recovery).

Take your resting pulse now (assuming you have not just run up the stairs). If you are fit, it might be in the 60's (or less in the case of athletes). If it is much above 80 after resting, you are probably unfit or ill. Everyone is well advised to consult their doctor before beginning an exercise regimen and it is absolutely essential if you have high blood pressure, heart disease or back trouble *or if you are planning to exercise intensely*. A sensible exercise routine for shooting sportsmen and women will consider four things:

1   Aerobic fitness to counter fatigue and promote well being.
2   Specific muscle fitness to help in the execution of technique.
3   Stretching to increase flexibility and protect from general injury.
4   Action to counter the effects of recoil.[3]

For serious competitors, the ideal cross-training exercises for shooting are tennis, rowing, cycling, cross-country skiing and swimming. These have the advantage that they improve aerobic fitness (and with it stamina) and also strengthen the muscles of legs, back, shoulders and arms. Tennis has the additional bonus of requiring visual contact with the ball. It was especially popular with Eastern European shotgun teams in years past. Squash and handball are also good for general fitness (but the pace is fast and will not suit everyone). Circuit training – typically the performance of a series of about ten exercises each stressing a particular muscle group for about 30 seconds before a 30 second recovery phase – is another good choice for dedicated competitors (or anyone serious about fitness) provided the circuits have been well conceived. Initial supervision is much to be recommended.

Aerobic classes are an interesting and surprisingly tough alternative which would benefit any male or female shooter. Those who are unfit are best advised to start with 'low-impact' aerobics. 'Aqua-fit' programmes, where limbs are worked out in resistance to water, are also to be recommended (and are especially good for those returning to exercise). There is absolutely nothing wrong with traditional jogging and running but they can be a bit solitary initially (getting started is the difficult thing; once one is in the habit of an evening or morning run, motivation is less of a problem). Weight bearing exercises – which include jogging, power walking and most forms of aerobics – increase bone density and resistance to osteoporosis in old age (the latter is a particular problem for smokers whose habit saps calcium from the bones).

For serious training for high level athletes in good physical condition, Fartlek (speed-play) running is especially good, but very demanding. It was devised in Scandinavia and is now much used by athletes and by the military. It combines steady pace running with sprinting and striding over varying terrain. It is a very efficient but tough way to boost an athlete's aerobic fitness and recovery time. If you are really serious about training, you might acquire a heart rate monitor. These watch-like gizmos provide instant feedback on your pulse and, in conjunction with professional advice, allow you to optimize your training regimen. For those who are not quite so committed, ordinary running or jogging may be

---

Major shoulder and arm muscles

The deltoid lifts the arm. It is one of the main muscles of the shoulder.
The trapezius is a large muscle which lifts and stabilises the shoulder and side bends the neck.
The biceps flexes the elbow/forearm, rotates the palm up and stabilises the shoulderblade.
The triceps extends the forearm and brings the arm back.
The supraspinatus is used in moving the arm outwards and in raising the arm. It also stabilises the shoulder joint.
The pectoralis major (and minor underneath) brings the shoulder forward.
Other muscles used in shooting include the **Latissimus dorsi** of the upper back which rotates the arms inwards and braces the back and shoulder; the **flexor** (bottom side) and **extensor** (top side) muscles of the forearm; the **abdominal muscles** and the **obliques** to either side.

---

combined with walking. If even this seems too energetic, simply get into the habit of climbing stairs and walking. One highly successful RAF pistol shot of my acquaintance used to cycle during the evening news on an exercise bike parked in front of the television! Any exercise is better than none. Simply walking at a brisker pace than normal for 15-20 minutes or more will achieve significant aerobic conditioning if undertaken two or three times a week.

The neck

The neck is especially important in marksmanship training. It controls the head which is the chassis for the eyes. Smooth eye movements require good neck control. The following routine (adapted from an exercise suggested by Olympic pistol shot Dr Laslo Antal) might be used on its own for strengthening the neck or as a mini warm-up or as the completing stage of a comprehensive warm-up.

Shrug the shoulders (bringing them as high as you can). Drop them. Repeat. Yawn. Turn the head to the right and then to the left. Repeat. Next, bend the head to the right and then to the left, bringing the ear towards the shoulder while looking forward. Repeat. Bring the chin to the chest looking down and bring the head up (avoid bending the neck right back which may cause excessive compression of the vertebrae). Repeat. Move the chin in a circle clockwise, then anti-clockwise. Repeat. Breathe in deeply through the nose.

My physiotherapist has come up with an additional neck exercise specifically to counter the effects of recoil for the right-hander. I perform it as part of my warm-up and at the end of a shooting session. Rotate the head to the right keeping the eyes level. Bring the left ear toward the chest (without straining). Repeat 4 times. Her other exercise for right-handed recoil is:

1   Stand square.
2   Drop the left hand and shoulder, causing a lateral flexion of the trunk and the raising of the opposite hand and shoulder.
3   Rotate the torso gently anti-clockwise (opposing the spinal compression which may occur in recoil for the right-hander).

All rotations should be gentle.

The scientific description of limb and muscle movement

Flexion occurs when a limb is bent.

Extension occurs when a limb is straightened.

Abduction is when movement is away from the mid-line of the body: for example, when you raise an arm to the side.

Adduction is when movement is towards the mid-line of the body: for example, when you lower the arm.

Rotation is the movement of a bone around its longitudinal axis: for example, when you turn the neck to one side. If it is outward, it is lateral rotation; if it is inward, it is medial rotation

Lateral flexion is moving the head or trunk sideways without rotation.

Elevation is moving the shoulders up.

Suprination is the act of rotating the palm up as most shooters do to hold the forend.

Left (or front) arm

As a right-hander, I have found left-handed air pistol shooting a useful and enjoyable means of toning the muscles of the left arm and hand. I have made it a habit. I prefer to use a 'double action' CO_2 pistol (one in which pulling the trigger cocks the hammer as well as releasing it) to increase the effort required.[4] The weaker hand may also be used for brushing the teeth. An effective approach to exercise incorporates it into the routine of daily life.

Another specific way of increasing left arm and shoulder strength, and one often used by pistol shooters, is to use a large elastic band attached to floor, ceiling or foot at one end and to the left wrist at the other. There is something called a Theraband (which you may be able to purchase at your hospital or through a physiotherapist). It is a brilliantly simple exercise tool consisting of nothing more than a long strip of rubber sheet. It looks as if it had been cut from a tyre's inner-tube, but it is durable and of just the right elasticity. What do you do with it? There are all sorts of possibilities:

- Put one end under the foot and hold the other with the hand, raising the arm as if simulating pistol shooting. A similar exercise may be performed to the side. You may also choose to extend the index finger of the lifting hand while focusing on a 'target', making this a pointing and visual exercise as well as a simple muscular one.
- Attach the band to a solid object to one's side and hold the other end with the left hand. Create tension. Bring the extended (or three-quarter extended) left arm horizontally across the body. Turn 180 degrees and repeat the exercise so that you are overcoming a force from the opposite side. You may devise something similar by securing the Theraband under the heel and bringing it from behind your body across the back of the leg to your front.

The band can also be used in front of the chest like a chest expander, above the head or behind the neck. Thinking about the muscles used for shooting will lead to the creation of a number of other sport-specific exercises. The Theraband has the advantage over weights that strain is unlikely (but not impossible, if you exceed your limits) and it can be used to target muscles which conventional gym work may leave out. Best of all, this brilliantly simple training aid may be slipped in the pocket and taken anywhere.

Drymounting

Dry mounting one's gun at home is an excellent way to develop sport specific upper body strength. It is possible to obtain weights to place in the barrels to increase the effort required. I have experimented with these, but whilst advocating regular dry-mounting practice, prefer to use the gun in its normal and familiar state. If need be, the number of repetitions may be increased.

More traditional exercises

Pectorals and triceps are given a good work-out by press-ups. Start with five or ten (if you feel comfortable), and build the number up by one a day until you can manage twenty or more. Keep your chest off the floor! Women, or anyone who finds a conventional press-up difficult should attempt the exercise using the knee rather than toes as the pivot point; one may also perform push-ups leaning against a wall. Pull-ups are a tough exercise but good for pectorals, trapezius and back. If you try them, control head movement but avoid tensing the neck excessively. Anyone with blood pressure problems or who suffers from obesity would be well advised to avoid heavy anaerobic (when the muscle is operating starved of oxygen) exercise such as press-ups and pull-ups (and heavy weight lifting) and, subject to medical advice, concentrate on circulation improving, low-impact aerobic activity.

The tummy zone

Abdominal muscles also need specific toning, not least because doing so will reduce the strain on one's back and because it is the area of the body most easily forgotten by shooting men. Traditional sit-ups can cause back problems. Better to perform a 'crunch' (which is especially good for the upper abdominals). Lie down with the feet comfortably apart and hips pulled forward (which will keep the back flat). Take your fingertips to the side of your head near your ears. Raise the shoulders about 6 in. so that you can see your knees. Hold it for a moment and lower yourself into the starting position slowly. Repeat as many times as you can without discomfort. One can apply a similar technique in leg raising (which works the lower abs). Keep the knees bent and, with back flat, lift the heels 6 in. or so and hold and lower. Repeat ten times. If you attempt either exercise with straight legs you can strain your lower back.

Back

Gentle exercises for the back include: pelvis lifting (Lie down with the neck supported. Raise the knees keeping the feet flat. Push the pelvis up, keeping the

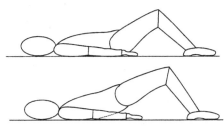

shoulders and upper back on the floor); and the hamstring stretch (Lie down with the neck supported, knees raised and feet flat on the floor. Raise one bent knee, lifting the foot off the ground. Hold under the knee with both hands. Pull it back towards the chest gently and straighten the leg).

Another good exercise for building leg and back strength (provided one's knees are in good condition) is to sit against the wall with the palms of the hands flat against the wall. Try it for 30 seconds initially and build it up until you can manage several minutes. Squats – as if one was sitting on a horse – are also good for back and legs (with the same qualification concerning knees). Keep the back straight, the feet more than shoulder-width apart (about two feet), bring the bottom down slowly (and do not go lower than 90 degrees). Feel the effort in the thighs and the bottom of the back. Do not lean forward. As with wall sitting, try to hold the position for 30 seconds initially.

Flexibility training

This is of special importance to the shooter. Shots are frequented missed because of restricted movement. Many of the activities already mentioned (such as swimming and aerobics) are good for flexibility. Less conventional alternatives might include dancing, yoga, tai-chi, judo, akido and karate. (The only disadvantage to the martial arts is the great dedication they require and the significant risk of injury which could disrupt shooting training.) If you are not inclined to pursue any of these on a regular basis, you can work out as I do with an old broom in the garden. I hold it behind the shoulders and bend right and left, forward and

back (if you have a back condition, ask your professional advisor). I also work out in the hot tub of the local pool, holding the grab rail that circles the tub with tummy up and both arms stretched back behind the head. Keep the body straight and the feet together. Rotate the legs and torso right and left. This is also good for the arms and shoulders. Another good exercise is simply be to sit on a stool with hands on head. Rotate the torso gently right and left. Complete ten rotations to each side. Now repeat the procedure with hands on the chest (right hand just above the left breast, left hand just above the right). Sitting down isolates the back and makes the exercise especially efficient. All flexibility training must be preceded by a warm up (and nothing in this case could be better than swimming).

Warm-up

One should always warm-up before exercise. It will help to prepare the body for what is to come. It increases heart rate and breathing and ensures that enough blood is available for the muscles to function effectively and to prevent injury. A warm-up before shooting has the added benefit of improving movement. If you are stiff when you start shooting, there is every chance that it will cost targets. Warming up is also important for proper functioning of the eyes, to combat tension and to achieve optimum arousal levels. It gets you in the groove, physically and mentally, to break the first target decisively.

All the exercises within a warm-up routine should be gentle; nothing should wrench or cause pain or discomfort. Many of the movements will be wide and sweeping. The idea is to raise the blood temperature. Ten or fifteen minutes walking is a good, discreet warm-up or you can create a routine similar to those used by athletes. It makes sense to develop it with a professional advisor. This is one I sometimes use:

- Begin marching on the spot, simultaneously opening the hands wide and closing them to form a fist (continue for 30 seconds and stop).
- Put the hands on the hips. Look right, focus on a distant object. Look left and focus. Look forward and sway the hips in a circle as if you were using a hula-hoop. Complete ten rotations in each direction.
- Extend the arms vertically and bring the hands back down to ear level. Repeat ten times. Extend the arms to the side and start to make large circles in the air. Repeat ten times clockwise and ten times anti-clockwise.
- Interlock the fingers behind the head. Moving from the waist turn to the left and alternately to the right, bringing the elbow forward as the torso rotates. Ten times in total. Bend forward gently without twisting. Repeat five times.
- Bring the right elbow down and to the left, and the left elbow down and to the right. Ten times in total.
- Squat, keeping the back straight; rise still keeping back and neck straight. Repeat five times.
- Spread the legs and, with hands to the side, bend (without straining) to the right and to the left, moving the tips of the fingers down the 'trouser seams'. Five times on each side.
- Touch *towards* your toes without straining. Repeat five times.
- Go back to marching on the spot. Raise the knees higher. Try and bring the thighs to the chest (continue for 30 seconds). Finish by hugging each knee to the chest.
- Touch the right hand to the right shoulder and the left to the left shoulder. Raise the elbows to the horizontal and out to the side. Move them in a circle clockwise five times and anti-clockwise five times.
- Take each hand over its shoulder and reach down as if trying to touch the middle of the spine. Ten times in total.
- Take the right arm behind the back with the knuckles touching the spine. Reach up to the shoulder blades. Repeat with the left arm. Ten times in total.
- Looking forward, shut the eyes. Moving the eyeballs only and keeping the eyelids shut, 'Look' left. Look right. Look up. Look down. Rotate the eyeballs clockwise and anti-clockwise. Open the eyes. Extend the arm. Focus

on the fingertips. Take the focus to a distant object. Hold it. Bring it back to the fingertips.

The neck exercises mentioned earlier might be inserted into this routine. Mental rehearsal might follow physical exercise (my warm-up routine finishes on the image and feel of the perfect shot, followed by visualisation of a very bright, very clearly defined target). Whatever routine you create, a warm-up should always begin very gently. It should last for about five to ten minutes.

Professional advice
As was noted earlier, it is important to get a health check-up from your doctor before beginning serious exercise. Men over 35 are well advised to ask for a cholesterol test at this time (you may not be offered one unless you ask). If it comes back high, or if the check-up reveals high blood pressure or obesity, there will be an even greater motivation to take up a healthier life-style. Always exercise with prudence. Do not overdo it. If you feel pain or dizziness, stop. If you are really serious about getting fit, visit a good gym and enlist the help of a professional trainer for a couple of sessions (or more if you can afford it). The cost is relatively modest and will ensure you develop an effective physical training programme.

Recommended Reading
Advanced Physical Education & Sport by Honeybourne, Hill and Moors.
The Complete Manual of Sports Science by Wilf Paish
Foundations of Sport and Exercise by R. Weinberg and D.Gould
The Heart Rate Monitor Book by Sally Edwards
Peak Performance by John Hawley and Louise Burke
Reader's Digest Good Health Fact Book

NOTES
1   Note, however, that carbonated water may increase the speed with which alcohol enters the bloodstream.
2   *Sports Psychology in Action*, p.29
3   The consequences of a continual, one-sided pounding of the body are not to be under-estimated. When one watches a shotgun being fired in slow motion, the effects are quite shocking. It looks as if the firer, however experienced, is being punched by Mike Tyson. The head comes off the stock, the jowls shake, the shoulder is driven rearwards. Such profound physical stress can cause injury – which is the reason for the introduction of 24 gramme loads in so many disciplines - and it may result in contracted or contorted positions becoming habitual.
4   But any airpistol may be used with benefit.

CHAPTER 9

Eye Dominance and Gunfit

For most people, shotgunning is easier and more effective with both eyes open. Binocular vision facilitates the estimation of distance speed and angle, and helps one to get the full benefits of hand-to-eye co-ordination (if you doubt it, try catching a ball with one eye shut). There are other benefits to binocular vision such as reduced tension and fatigue. However, do not believe those who tell you simplistically that everyone should shoot with both eyes open. It is just not that simple (which condemns more than a few shooting tomes to the pyre): the critical consideration is eye dominance.

It is a curiosity of the binocular system of human vision (at least in most adult males) that one eye tends to control pointing. If a finger were pointed at a distant object, there would be a straight line relationship from object to finger to eye. The pointing eye, whichever it may be, is called the dominant or master eye. The majority of adult men have eye dominance which matches their handedness (and, once this is confirmed, are well advised to shoot with both eyes open). There are other possibilities. Some may be cross-dominant (e.g., right-handed with a left master); a few have central vision (neither eye dominating); and others may be predominantly but not fully dominant in one eye. For those shooting a standard gun who fall into one of these categories, the best advice is usually to shut or squint an eye. In women and children, absolute dominance in the eye overlooking the breech is the exception, and one-eyed shooting is often the simplest remedy too.

Eye dominance is an intriguing phenomenon in which biological, environmental and experiential factors appear to play a role. Eye dominance in boys typically becomes more absolute with advancing years.[1] In middle-aged men, however, it may become less absolute. It may be affected by training (disciplining oneself to sustain focus on the bird and ignore any 'ghost' image), but results are unpredictable. It is (largely) unrelated to visual acuity (one can have poorer vision in one eye yet it can still be more dominant as far as the control of pointing is concerned). It can vary in the same individual. It can be disturbed by fatigue, ill-health, staring at computer screens, long-distance driving and low light levels. It is not just a physical phenomenon, but a mental one as well. Having considered some of the scientific literature while researching this book, it appears that gunfitters may have a more profound understanding of eye dominance than anyone else (especially with regard to sex and age differences).

The diagnosis of eye dominance certainly involves far more than a simple – and potentially inaccurate – observation that an individual is right or left eye dominant (any testing method that only gives 'either/or' results is worthless). It is common, for example, to find a male client who has what might be called 'pseudo-dominance', i.e., when tested, one eye appears to be almost – but not quite fully – dominant. Such a condition is easily overlooked by an inexperienced or sloppy instructor (typically being misdiagnosed as full dominance). However, the effects on shooting can be profound. Typically, there will be many inexplicable misses on quartering and crossing targets where the lead does not favour the dominance.

It is not uncommon, moreover, for shooters to be wrongly advised to switch shoulders having been told they were cross-dominant, when in fact their dominance in the opposite eye was not absolute (much better and simpler advice would have been to stick to the 'strong' shoulder and squint an eye). All of which leads me to conclude that the precise diagnosis of a client's eye dominance is one of the most vital considerations in shooting instruction. One need make no apologies for dealing with it in the most scrupulous manner.

Testing procedure

Before carrying out any test for dominance, you should ask the client if he suffers from any known eyesight problems and determine whether a visit to an optician has been made within the last couple of years. If not, advise one. (Shooting, not to mention the general enjoyment of life, can be drastically improved by the right pair of glasses or contact lenses. Similarly, some basic visual defect must always be considered a possibility when one has eliminated all other reasons for poor performance during instruction.) The next step in the procedure is to ask the client to confirm his handedness: left or right. I also ask: 'Have you ever been ambidextrous or been tempted to play games like cricket, tennis or golf as a left-hander?' If the client says yes or notes that sometimes he sees two guns, the probability is high that his handedness and eye dominance do not match.

Preferred test for eye dominance

There are a variety of ways of testing for eye dominance: I usually start with a simple finger pointing routine. I ask the client to stand about 10 feet away, facing me squarely in a relaxed stance. I ask him to let both arms fall by his side and then demonstrate the action of pointing with an outstretched arm and index finger. I position my index finger so that the nail is just under my right eye and say, 'Keep both eyes open; focus on my finger tip... now, with an extended right arm, point your index finger at my eye just as I did at you'. I observe the result and ask the client to drop the arm. I then ask for the left hand to be pointed, 'Now point with the left'. (I have found this use of both hands to be more effective at detecting anomalies than merely pointing with one hand.)

If eye dominance is absolute, a direct unhesitant action immediately putting the client's finger in line with one of his eyes will be noted. If the client's finger wavers slightly before settling in alignment with one eye, the opposite eye may well be causing a disturbance. If the finger is aligned between his eyes precisely in line with the nose, central vision is a possibility. If the client complains as his finger waggles in space that he sees two fingers and is not quite sure what to do next, it is another highly significant discovery.

Finger pointing and the 'circle method as described'.

Now – unless there is no question in your mind – it is time to move on to what I call a circle test. This is accomplished either by asking the client to make a circle, 'by bringing the tip of the index finger and thumb together', or by offering the client a curtain ring, or something similar, to hold between the fingers. Those who enjoy gadgets can attach a ring (about 2½ - 3 in. in diameter) to a pistol-like handle as Chris Cradock advocated. This has the advantage over a bare ring in that it can only be held in the correct manner. The finger-circle (or ring method) has the advantage that the circle in either case can be brought back to the eye from the fully extended position.

After a brief demonstration for clarity, testing is repeated holding the circle at arm's length. Absolute eye dominance will place the eye in the middle of the circle from your point of view, anomalies of eye dominance will put it to one side (or occasionally high or low). The final test should be with a proven-empty gun. This tells the fitter/instructor more than any other method (and, if I were to choose one test from all those mentioned, this would be it). The subtleties of vision described are more easily identified and one also gets some idea of gunfit and the client's mounting and pointing skills.

I always prefer to use the gun with which the client normally shoots (modified with a comb raiser if the stock is clearly too low). Explain that this is a special circumstance – one of the very few times when it is permissible to point a shotgun at a human being. Make sure the client has no cartridges in his possession and prove the gun empty with him, inserting your fingers in the chambers if possible. Dry fire the gun if you know it will do it no harm to the action, and apply the safety catch yourself (*under no circumstances use snap caps*). Ask the client to mount the gun and to aim at the your master eye (which you should indicate with the tip of your index finger or thumb).

Any of the variations in eye dominance mentioned above may be noted again. If, while keeping both eyes open, the client's head seems well above the breech and strangely angled, it is often the sign of an eye dominance problem. If, on asking the client to close an eye, the character of the mount changes dramatically – and the open eye suddenly takes up a normal position looking down the

PLATE 15

The circle test has revealed that this shooter is not absolutely right eye dominant, note the 'pull' from the left eye. A finger pointing test might not have shown this so clearly.

Frontal view of the completed mount. Note my right eye dominance and also note the position of my head (with eyes nearly level), the natural position of elbows and the foot position.

PLATE 16

(above) My son, Jamie, then aged 11, under instruction from David Etherington at West London. Note David's hand on Jamie's shoulder to keep the weight forward and also note the small white patch on the shooting glasses. Like many young men, Jamie has inconsistent eye dominance. The patch was required because he found squinting one eye difficult.

(below) I believe that air-rifle shooting under proper supervision is the ideal way to introduce a young person to shooting. Although the aiming technique is different it teaches the basics of safe gun-handling and there is no recoil problem and less weight if the gun is well chosen. This is my son Harry aged 7, another keen shot.

rib, another most important discovery has been made.

Action after diagnosis

A right-hander with a left master eye (or a left-hander with a right master eye) has a number of options. One of the easiest, in the former case, is to shoot from the right shoulder but closing or dimming the left eye prior to firing. Rather than keeping the eye shut throughout the pickup, swing and mount, it will be better for most sporting and game shots to dim the eye as the gun comes up to the shoulder. This way one gets some of the benefits of binocular vision and has an increased field of view during the critical pickup phase. It is a definite mistake to dim the eye only at the last moment as this may be visually confusing.

Eye patches

The offending eye may be covered with a patch (although instructors who inflict this on novices should try it themselves), or if the student wears spectacles, a block to vision may be placed over the appropriate lens. This need not be a full-sized patch but may be a much smaller block, refined so that it is no more than ½ in. across. One may use electrician's tape, a smudge of Vaseline, chapstick, typing correction fluid or a Magic Dot[2] on the lens to achieve this (once the position and size are confirmed, glasses may be permanently and neatly modified by sandblasting in an optical workshop).

In all cases, the block to vision is best positioned with the instructor in front of and facing the client; with the client resting the muzzles of his proven-empty gun on the instructor's shoulder; and with the client's head positioned on the stock comb as if firing (if you try and do this with the client merely looking at you without a gun, the spot will, inevitably, be wrongly positioned). Account must be made of the fact that in the field, the client may raise or rotate his head when firing (not to be encouraged, of course, but the block must be positioned to take this into account).

Obturators

Another option for side-by-side users is to equip the gun barrels themselves with a mechanical barrier to vision such as a hand-guard obturator. Thomas Gilbert patented a device in 1884 which was attached to the top of the barrels near the breechface. It consisted of a post with a hinged flap to one side to block the vision of the left eye. Ian Crudgington and David Baker have unearthed an 1885 patent of W.W. Watts, chief instructor of the London Sporting Park,[3] which consisted of a ring with obturator disk attached, designed to be worn on the left thumb. Kay Ohye, the famous trap shot, developed a 'blinder' to be attached to the rib near the muzzles of over-and-unders. It has subsequently been manufactured by several firms. Another clever device consists of a U-shaped channel with a flourescent rod sight at one end. This may be attached to the barrel and when in place, the brightly-coloured insert can only be seen by the eye looking along the rib. A similar effect may be achieved by using the thumb on the forend to block the vision of the eye not

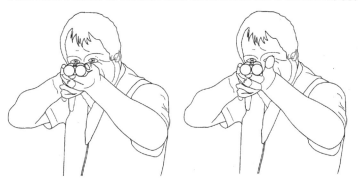

Using the thumb to block the image of the target to the left eye.

looking down the rib (as practised by both Robert Churchill and Barry Simpson).

Supplementary sighting devices

Supplementary devices allow for mounting on the usual or strong-side shoulder, but sighting with the opposite eye. The most famous of these is the Monopeian sight consisting of two gun-metal arms protruding for 2 in. or so from the side of breech and muzzles.[4] There are other similar systems involving projections permanently or temporarily attached to the gun barrels. Some years ago, I fitted a Beretta 687 with a replacement foresight consisting of a small brass rod screwed horizontally into the rib at the muzzles and bent to create a new foresight approximately one inch to the side of the old one. The client did not want cast and insisted on keeping both eyes open, though his right eye was not dominant. This simple, even crude, arrangement boosted his score at clays by more than 25%. One modern device developed by Andy Perkins, an instructor at Holland & Holland, offers a complete carbon fibre rib running parallel to the original.

Cross-over stocks

The most expensive option, and the one that still delights some London makers, is to make a cross-over stock gun: a gun which has a bent action and a stock with a very obvious dog leg in it (these guns allow the shooter to mount the gun on one shoulder while using the eye of the opposite side). I am no great fan of cross-over stocks: they feel odd, recoil badly and are subject to cracking; but they can make driven birds easier as both eyes can be kept open.

Shooting from the opposite shoulder

A traditional remedy for those whose master eye and handedness do not correspond, is to learn to shoot from the left (or weak) shoulder with or without a suitably adapted (cast-off changed to cast-on triggers reshaped) gun. I do not usually favour this course (though it is sometimes appropriate). The advantage of binocular vision may be outweighed by the awkwardness of the manoeuvre. It is my experience that few of those who are forced to take this route develop into really first class shots (although many one-eyed shots, beating the odds, do).[5]

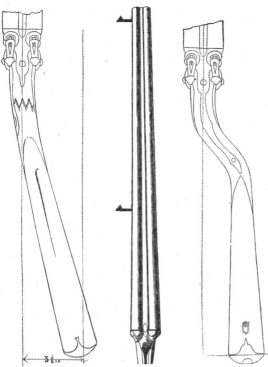

<- 3⅝ IN ->

Three ways of overcoming the same problem: two
types of cross-over stock and the 'Monopeian'
sighting system.

Central vision and other variations on the norm

A few people will have so-called 'central vision' whereby neither eye is truly dominant; others will have one eye only slightly more dominant than the other. These differences in vision (like full cross-dominance) will have the effect of pulling the muzzles to one side of the target or the other, if the shooter habitually keeps both eyes open. In the old days, English gunmakers used to adjust cast rather liberally to accommodate such problems, up to and including the semi-crossover stock. I believe, however, that the best route for people who have significant eyesight anomalies – which, bear in mind, can change – is simply to get into the habit of clos-ing or dimming the eye. This is not universal advice, though. Some women and some youngsters have particular difficulty with winking. They may be best served with a small, but carefully located, barrier to vision attached to one lens of their protective shooting glasses. You must experiment and find something that works and which is comfortable for the individual.

Finally, beware: not everyone shoots as their eye dominance – as tested – might suggest. Some may be able to shoot well with both eyes open, even though initial testing without a gun indicates a dominance problem. Some will have inconsistent eye dominance (my own normally right-eyed dominance fades and can even switch when I get tired). Some will have a master eye sig-nificantly weaker than the other as far as visual acuity is concerned. Inability to focus can undermine eye dominance. (Sometimes those with contact lenses who have a slight eye dominance problem, may be advised to shoot with the left lens removed.) Some people's eye dominance is affected by the choice of gun. Short guns and side-by-sides tend to cause more problems than the more pointable long-barrelled over-and-unders. Changing to longer barrels can help someone with a mild eye-dominance problem. The only really reliable test of shooting eyesight is to observe a person shooting on several different occasions with all of these things in mind. No one can concoct rules that will work in every case. However, it may be said that: *Shooting instructors should take the greatest care to diagnose eye dominance thoroughly. Its importance to good shooting cannot be overstressed. Test for it. If you have doubts, do not be afraid to test and test again. Get the eyes right and everything else will fall into place.*

Case Study Joe J

Joe, 62, had had a distinguished career as a trap shot (winning two national championships) and came to me when he noted that his sporting scores were falling. He was convinced that his age was the root cause of his problems and that his shooting was 'falling to bits' as a result of it. His basic technique was, in fact, very sound. He had a good relaxed stance and prepared for his targets well. When he shot there was good gun-movement, nice timing and a good follow with sustained facial contact. Nevertheless, he was continually shooting to the left side of birds presented from the right. It was soon apparent that his problem was an undetected change in eye dominance. His biggest difficulty was on fast quartering birds from the right (which may easily be missed in front by someone with 'normal' right-eye master dominance, let alone by someone suffering with partial left eye dominance). On examining his gun, I noted that it was very straight with respect to cast and the comb was quite thick. The net effect was to give the gun cast-on (though Jimmy was right-handed and might be expected to require cast-off). Jimmy was also wider than average in the face. The prescription was simple enough, a thinned comb and some extra cast-off (the eye dominance problem was not so severe as to require him to close an eye or change shoulders). Until the gun was altered, we developed a tactic whereby Jimmy might shoot straight at most birds from the right, rather than attempt to lead them significantly. Once Jimmy understood that there was a simple explanation for the dip in his performance, he was well pleased. Realising that there was life in the old dog yet, his old shooting confidence returned.

GUNFITTING IN BRIEF

Having written a book about gunfitting, I am the first to admit that it is possible to overcomplicate the subject. So let us note at the beginning of this section that the basic purpose of gunfitting is simply to make a gun shoot where the client is looking (usually by getting the master eye just over and in line with the sighting rib). A gun which shoots where one is looking makes good shooting as instinctive as possible. A well-fitted gun must also control recoil effectively, and it must be comfortable and consistent to mount. People can sometimes shoot with badly fitted guns, but they will shoot better with well-fitted ones, especially when they are tired or conditions are poor.

Advanced gunfitting – which is a time-consuming business – requires that the client be able to shoot proficiently in the first place. In all cases, serious gunfitting requires that a gun mount and shooting style have been developed. The situation with beginners and novices is less demanding. They need a gun which is a reasonable fit in respect of stock length and comb height and which is of appropriate weight and has reasonable trigger pulls (you will note I define gunfit broadly: fitness for the person in every sense).

A basic requirement for gunfitting is a safely positioned range with a pattern plate. If the ideal, a 6 ft-square steel plate, is not available, one may construct a temporary or permanent frame of wood or steel to which large sheets of paper or card may be pinned or clipped. A try-gun is not essential (indeed, because the balance of try-guns is odd, I always prefer to work with a client's own gun or one of very similar type), but the gun-fitter will require some means of measuring the gun. A six-inch rule or tape measure is indispensable. A length-of-pull gauge is useful (especially when measuring the length to bump and toe), as is a bend stick (see diagram).

Most shooting schools have special cradles or jigs for measuring drop and cast. Traditionally, they are bulky affairs, but an excellent modern version is made by Helston Gunsmiths (see appendix). Apart from giving confidence to clients (and a lot of gunfitting, like instruction, is about giving confidence), cradles greatly facilitate the process of accurate measurement, particularly of cast. An alternative method of measuring cast is to place the gun in a vice with protected jaws, and then to attach a piece of string with a small loop over the bead. Bring the string straight back, following the centre line of the rib, and extend it beyond the heel. With practice, one may measure cast at heel quite accurately in this way, cast at toe may be measured using a plumb line attached to the same piece of string.

The gunfitter will also require a notebook, butt extensions in various lengths (avoid the bulky leather type, and, not least, comb raisers. 'Blu-tack' or some other putty-like substance may also be useful for building up combs (the comb is built up to requirements then taped-over), as will moleskin (otherwise designed for foot problems). Vinyl electrician's tape (which, if used carefully, does not remove stock finish as other types may) should form part of the gun fitter's standard kit (you cannot buy too much!), as should: a pen knife or razor, a set of small turnscrews, snap-caps for common bore sizes and printed forms for gunfitting measurements.

Getting on with the job
Once eye dominance is established, consider the individual's physique, especially noting the length of the neck, the length of the arms, the width of the shoulders and chest, the width and height of the head, the shape (triangular or square), abnormalities of cheekbone, and the distance between the eyes. The sex and age of the client will usually tell us a lot. Women and children tend to have small heads and will require a higher comb to get the eye in the right place, just above the rib. Women, and anyone with a well developed chest, may also require a reduced toe measurement. The existing measurements of the client's gun (including grip and forend type) should be recorded at an early stage and you should observe the client mounting the gun at a specified mark to assess mounting style and level of expertise. After these things are done, work can begin in earnest.

Length
The gun should be as long as is consistent with comfortable mounting. A gun that is too short does not control recoil as well, but too long a gun is hard to mount. One way of deciding whether or not the length of a sporting clays or

game gun is right is by setting up a high overhead bird. A gun is too long when it cannot comfortably be swung and mounted at a vertical target. Generally, beginners will want slightly shorter guns than experienced shots, who have refined their mounting technique. Moreover, the high bird technique for assessing length is not suitable for beginners because they tend to have difficulty with this target. The best method for checking the length of stock for beginners is to place the stock in the shoulder for them and, making sure their head is firmly down on the stock, measuring the gap between the tip of the nose and the base of the thumb of the rear hand. Ideally it wants to be about 1½ in. (which is about two finger widths) for a sporting gun, perhaps 1 in. for a game gun (which may be used in heavy clothing).

Length is traditionally measured from the middle of the trigger to the middle of the butt sole. It is also measured to the bump of the butt sole (the slight protuberance visible on many guns just below the heel – see diagram) and to the toe. The last two measurements will affect the pitch of the gun (see below).

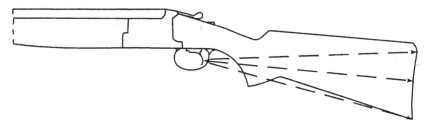

Length to bump, middle and toe.

Drop

The drop (or bend) of the gun, arguably the most important gunfit variable, is usually measured at comb (the front of the comb) and at the heel of the stock. It may also be measured 'at face'. Drop dictates the relative position of the eye over the barrels. A secondary, but nonetheless important, function of drop is to locate the butt sole at the shoulder. Ideally, the butt sole should be supported in a good position on the pectoral muscle between the shoulder joint and collar bone. However, in some people, the shoulder pocket is very small. Mounting on or near the shoulder joint may be acceptable in these cases (what is absolutely wrong is to mount the gun on the arm). Some shots prefer a low style (mounting on the chest is popular among some Italian trap shots). Generally, I like to see the heel of the stock about ¼ - ½ in. below the top line of the shoulder.

A typical drop measurement on a classic English gun would be 1½ in. at comb and 2 in. at heel. A typical measurement on a new Continental over-and-under would be 1 3/8 in. at comb and 2 1/8 in. at heel. The drop at face would be much the same in either case, but the over-and-under would have less felt recoil if the English measurements were applied (because they reduce the slope of the comb). Some older American guns (circa 1900) and ancient (pre-1800)

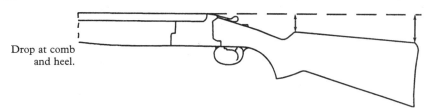

Drop at comb
and heel.

British ones have stocks so crooked that recoil discomfort is guaranteed (not to
mention low shooting).

As far as the vertical eye/rib relationship is concerned, drop is the most
important measurement on a gun. One may adapt to a gun of the wrong length,
or (within reasonable limits) the wrong cast; but it is much harder to adapt to
one with the wrong drop. Drop should be adjusted initially in sporting over-
and-unders so that the pupil of the eye is seen to rest on the rib or breech when
viewed from the muzzle of a proven-empty gun. In side-by-sides, my advice is
to start with the iris' sitting on the rib. All other things being equal, side-by-
sides tend to shoot a little lower than over-and-unders because their barrels,
action bar and grip are subject to more flex on firing. I like to set them up a little higher for this reason and also because a tendency to shoot a little high is an
advantage in a game gun. It equates to a bit of built-in lead and helps to keep
the gun up on the line of high quartering targets.

When tested at the pattern plates, most game shots will be well served by a
pattern distribution, which is about two thirds above and one-third below the
mark. The same distribution may be used for sporting clays or skeet, though
most will prefer a 60:40 or even 50:50 percentage. It all depends on the individual and how he or she sees the target. If you are setting up the gun of a relatively inexperienced shot, encourage a higher fit since it improves target visibility greatly and encourages a good head position. As Chris Cradock would
have pointed out, high stocks are a good habit to get into. Many trap shots (at

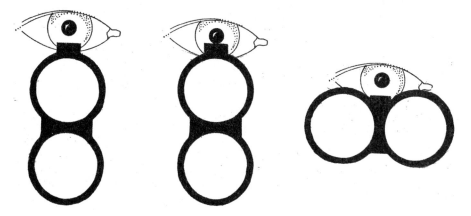

Eye-rib relationship. The first would be a good starting point for a trap gun; the second for a
sporter or skeet gun; the third for a side-by-side game gun.
Remember these are just rough guides.

least those involved in DTL) also prefer higher combed guns because their targets all start on the rise.

Pitch

Once the basic length and drop have been ascertained, one may consider pitch. Usually, the measurements at bump and toe are about 1/8 and 3/8 in. more than the measurement from the trigger to the middle of the butt sole. Most guns have a down pitch in the range 0-3 in. (1 in. or less would be typical on a trap gun, 2 in. on a side-by-side game gun, and 3 in. on an over-and-under sporter); that is, if the butt sole is placed on a true floor and the breech is brought up against a perpendicular wall, the muzzles will project out about 1 - 3in. from the wall.[6] Women and broad-chested men will benefit from a reduced measurement at toe (and from a rounded toe). When fitting for pitch, I watch the gun bedding into the shoulder. If bump or heel come to the shoulder early, something may be wrong. In a gun well fitted for pitch, both bump and toe should arrive at the shoulder at the same time. Moreover, the client should have the impression that he is looking straight along the rib without it appearing to fall or rise excessively. Pitch is useful to keep the gun well supported for high driven shots and also to keep the gun up on line on high crossing and quartering birds.

Cast

As with drop, there are two considerations with cast: eye position relative to the rib, and shoulder position relative to the butt sole. Again, the former is the more important. If the eye of a right dominant, right-handed shot is coming up to one side of the rib – even though the mounting technique is otherwise sound – an alteration to cast or comb may be called for. The same may be said of one-eyed shots. In both cases the eye should be in line with the rib, because that eye is controlling pointing. The plates, and straight-away and driven targets, will reveal other requirements for those two eyed shots with less than absolute eye dominance and who may require extra cast.

The position of the butt at the shoulder in the horizontal plane should be adjusted for the most comfortable and stable shooting position. If the top of butt sole rests against the collar bone, or if the

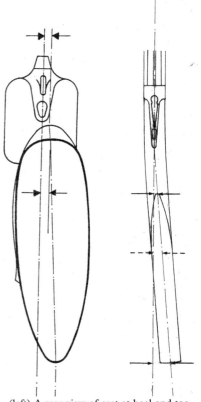

(left) A rear view of cast at heel and toe. Note the cast at toe is greater than the cast at heel. (right) A top view of cast.

bottom of the butt sole is digging into the chest, the shooter is being made unnecessarily uncomfortable. It may be useful to consider three ways in which cast may be built into the stock. It may be angled to one side throughout its length; the comb alone may be offset; or it may be hollowed (swept). Generally speaking, over-and-unders will require less cast than side-by-sides. Indeed, an over-and-under with a lot of cast usually feels 'wrong'.

Grip
The grip or 'hand' is a most important part of the gun stock. The length and width of the grip should suit the hand and should promote a secure grip of the gun in recoil. The grip should not thin excessively to its front (otherwise the hand may slide forward in recoil). The traditional English straight-hand grip is well suited to double triggers (it facilitates the movement of the trigger finger to the rear trigger). The Prince of Wales grip is an elegant alternative for double trigger guns which can offer a bit more muzzle control. Half pistol grips seem to have gone out of fashion but have much to recommend them if well shaped. The full pistol grip seems the most popular with manufacturers of mass produced guns. Acute pistol grips may be suited to those who pull the gun back into the shoulder, but can impede swing (the Etchen grip, which curls back towards the trigger guard, offers an extreme full-pistol design). They may not be well suited to sporting or game shooting, where the better shot tends to push the gun towards the target as the gun is mounted. The ideal full-pistol grip for these applications should not be too sharply angled.

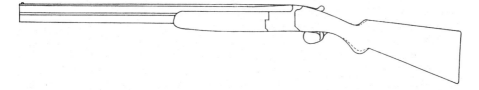

Small modifications to the grip can have very positive benefits. A common problem is that the nose of the cone is too far forward. Full pistol grips may quite easily be made slimmer or converted to semi-pistol or straight-hand types. Wood may be inletted into the comb to create a Monte Carlo effect (a modification often required by people with small heads or long necks).
See page 187

Nose of the comb
The nose of the comb must not prevent the shooter from getting a good grip of the gun (and there are many cases where a slight reduction of the nose of the comb, or where an improvement to the flute that runs alongside it, will improve shooting). These are subtle considerations and every instructor is well advised to strike up a relationship with a good stocker who will not only carry out alterations but will also confirm his diagnosis.

Combs
The comb shape of many guns can be improved. Some English guns have very thin combs (sometimes as a result of refinishing). These may not give the head

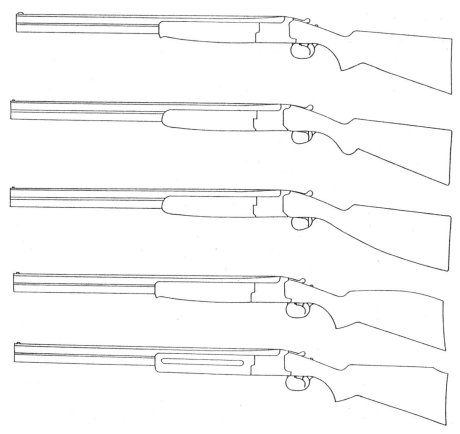

Different types of butt and forend. *Top to bottom*: full pistol grip combined with snabel forend (typical of many sporters); semi-pistol grip and rounded forend (one of my own favourite styles); swan-neck stock combined with rounded forend (as seen on some Browning game guns); a full pistol semi-hogsback (which has the advantage of offering a parallel comb at face) with snabel; and a semi-Monte Carlo combined with beaver-tail forend with finger grooves (as one might use on a trap gun).

adequate support in mounting and may promote an erratic positioning of the head on the comb. On the other hand, too many sporting clay and skeet guns have excessively thick combs originally intended for trap shooting. They may usefully be thinned or reshaped but – be careful: it is easy to go too far. The old adage that one can take wood away but not put it back should always be remembered. Moreover, altering a comb can affect the cast of the gun. This may be useful if deliberate. Comb thinning or 'sweeping' (where only the section of the comb which makes contact with the face is altered) are alternatives or supplements to bending a stock.

Angle of comb and recoil
The angle of the comb is a vital consideration as far as recoil is concerned. A steeply angled comb tends to increase felt recoil because it forces wood into the cheekbone as the gun recoils. When making adjustments in drop, one must pay

particular attention to this. The principle should always be to avoid a steeply sloping comb if you can ($7/8$ in. should be considered a maximum for the difference between the measurements for drop at comb and heel). Sometimes it may be appropriate to bend the stock down to achieve the right location at the shoulder, but it may also be necessary to build the comb up by means of an insert, comb raiser, or adjustable comb to achieve the correct fit at face. One great advantage of Alan Rhone's sophisticated vari-comb conversion is that it allows one to tilt the comb: one may set it at different heights at front and rear to achieve the right drop without excessive incline.

Parallel combs and Monte Carlo stocks

Many shooters will benefit from a parallel or semi-parallel comb because of its felt-recoil-reducing properties and because it promotes consistent gun mounting. Trap shooters may want a Monte Carlo comb (see below). Indeed, any shooter with a long neck and sloping shoulders may benefit from one (because it is deeper than a normal stock). A long neck or sloping shoulders are not auto-

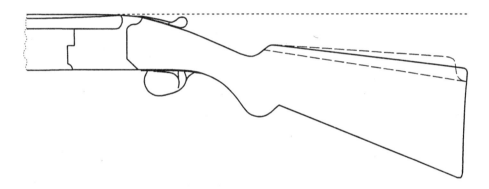

Building up a comb to create a semi or full Monte Carlo stock is one of the most common alterations to guns that I make. The top style is well suited to sporting shooting for those with small heads, the full Monte is usually better suited to dedicated trap guns.

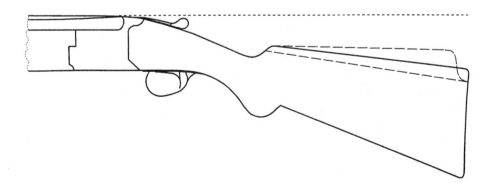

matic indicators that a Monte is required, though. Some shots are in the habit of raising the shoulder to the gun during the mount. Their drop at heel requirements are quite different to those shots who have a more static shoulder. Moreover, some shooters suffer facial bruising from a Monte Carlo style comb (often because the average Monte Carlo stock is thick as well as high, though it does not need to be so).

CASE STUDY Kelly C

Kelly, 32, had been clay shooting for 3 years with moderate success. She was a rather forceful personality and had very strong ideas about everything, not least shooting. A right-hander, with no definite master eye, she was in the habit of shutting an eye before she called for a bird. She had been to another instructor for a lesson and he had advised an enormous comb raiser for her gun. It had been made from wood in crude imitation of a continental style cheek piece which not only raised the top line of the stock excessively (she needed a higher stock, but this one was nearly ½ in. too high), and also created cast-on with its thick side projection (to avoid this, I usually cut in a permanent comb raiser my milling out wood from the top of the comb – this produces an exact wood to wood fit and generally makes a near-invisible job if one takes a little care in selecting timber). The bulbous new comb did not suit her and impeded her gun mount (indeed, the modified butt looked like a club rather than a gun stock). Her pre-shot preparation was poor too (she did not bother to read the birds with anything like sufficient care) and her timing and follow through were erratic. I would like to say that I succeeded with Kelly, but I did not. I was never able to win her confidence. She simply would not believe her gunfit was so wrong having paid several hundred pounds to sort it out. Moreover, she could not clear her mind sufficiently to develop a methodical pre-shot preparation routine. She is still trapped in B class.

Forends

Forend shape is another important variable of gunfit. Forends may be of a huge variety of patterns: the splinter of the traditional English game gun, the slightly fuller Purdey design, the lengthened splinters once popular with pheasant shots, the schnabel of many over-and-under sporters, the tulip schnabel as seen on the Laurona, the beavertail of the trap gun (occasionally seen on side-by-sides) and so on. Some forends may be wide, some will be deep, some will have finger grooves positioned high or low, some will thicken in one direction or the other.

Any forend, like any grip shape, must suit the individual's hand shape and promote consistent mounting. On side-by-sides, I think the Purdey style just about ideal. On over-and-unders – whatever discipline they are intended for – I prefer a parallel-sided and well rounded (in cross section) forend with fine checkering to its entire surface. I find that the tulip forends offered by some manufacturers do not offer the same control, and fail to ensure that the hand is consistently positioned in relation to the bore axis. A very deep forend can raise the point of impact. Generally, forend and grip should be considered together. A very thick forend is rarely suited to a very thin grip. Similarly, if forend and grip put the front and rear hands on very different levels, they may be a hindrance.

Alterations in the field

If one is dealing with the client's gun, one is limited in the alterations one can make in the field. However, it is surprising just how much can be achieved with a penknife, some electrician's tape and some imagination. When you get a stock right, do not touch it but hand it to the stockmaker with all the bits attached, however horrible it may look!

Working at the plates

When testing guns at the pattern plates, the first shots should be taken pre-mounted. Once you are happy that the client is competent, you may decide to let him shoot gun down. In either case, the client should not rush and should maintain focus on an aiming mark, not on the gun. Never make, or suggest final alterations on the basis of just a few shots. Be patient and note any trend. Once a gun seems to be 'on the money', you should move to a variety of targets which will check different aspects of gunfit. The straight, going-away bird is a good test of cast and may also show if a gun is firing too high. A high, overhead shot is a good test for length. A rising target may show up a low shooting gun. Fast crossers will test stock length and show-up glitches (such as those resulting from sticky recoil pads). Harder quartering birds on both sides may be used to check subtleties of cast, drop and pitch.

Regulation

I always check the regulation of client's gun as a matter of principle when he comes for a fitting. It is amazing how many guns do not have two barrels which shoot to the same place. The easiest, but rough way to check regulation is to draw a large cross on a pattern plate or paper and to shoot at it with both barrels. Fire three or four shots from each barrel in rifle style. If you have doubts about your holding ability, sit down and use a table as a rest. If you are concerned by the results, repeat the test with horizontal and vertical lines only. This allows you to put all your effort into checking horizontal and vertical plane regulation separately.

I have found that many cheap guns have less than perfect regulation (I remember one budget over-and-under which threw its top barrel pattern 3 feet high at 20 yards). It is not, however, unusual to find a quality over-and-under which has a top barrel that fires significantly higher than the bottom. This is because the line of recoil is higher for the top tube than for the lower one, causing more rotation at the shoulder. Nevertheless, a high-shooting second barrel is a characteristic which should be regulated out of a quality gun. This should be done at manufacture by a careful consideration of barrel geometry but may be achieved later by placing shims between the barrels or by skilled work on the bores.[7] In trap shooting, it may be worthwhile to consider setting up the bottom (first) barrel to shoot high; and the top (second) barrel to shoot flat. The first shot will be taken at a rising target; the second, typically, at a dropping one. A simple alternative to re-regulation on a trap gun with a high-shooting top barrel, is to use it for the first shot.

CASE STUDY Keith A

Keith, 28, was a pigeon shooter and wildfowler who also enjoyed clays. Though knowledgeable in many respects, he was chronically indecisive and worried about everything to do with his gun and shooting. He changed chokes at every stand and put much thought into whether or not he should use 7½s or 9s. His gun was equipped with an adjustable butt plate and it was set at an outrageous angle. His basic style was rather strained considering how much he shot. As far as sporting clays were concerned, he was lucky if he hit 50%. Keith tested left eye dominant, but preferred to shoot off the right shoulder, closing an eye (a tactic with which I have no problem provided it gets results). His mount looked most odd, though. His gun seemed to fit (bar the outlandish angle of the butt-sole), but it was apparent that something was very wrong. When I made the first test for fit for drop, his pupil appeared to sit on top of the breech. However, it transpired that he was subtly raising his head to compensate for a low comb. He was unaware of this and because he was well practised in the habit, it took me some minutes to spot (the clue, which I should have picked up, was the small size of his head). After applying a little gentle pressure to the pate of his skull with my hand to check his cheek was properly positioned on the comb, I retested for drop and noted that his eye was buried well beneath the breech. With a 3/8 in. comb raiser fitted to the gun, his shooting immediately improved by a factor of 20% (the dramatic rise was due to the fact that his head positioning, though practised, was inconsistent, sometimes he was losing sight of the target and either opening the left eye causing cross firing or raising the head causing misses above and behind). This gave him a significant boost in confidence and led the way to a methodical consideration of the rest of his technique. My gunsmith, meantime, added a piece of wood to his stock to match the rise of the comb raiser. As is my usual practice, I had it mad a little higher than needed so that final adjustment could be made on the field. This is more time consuming – the gun must be returned to the gunsmith for finishing – but it ensures that exactly the right comb height is achieved.

Alterations of stocks by gunsmiths

Unless they have a steel tube strengthening them, gun stocks may generally be bent quite easily, either by heat (steaming, hot oil, or infrared light) or by removing minute slivers of wood at the head of the stock. The latter method has the advantage that it is permanent and does not attack stock finish. That said, the infrared method is also very good. It is rare for a stock bent in this way to return to its old position; nor does infrared heat, when properly applied, damage stock finish.[8]

Conclusions

Be methodical. Be patient. Only manipulate one variable at a time (i.e., length, drop, pitch or cast). If the gun is too long, the client will not be able to mount it easily; if it is too short, it will not control recoil well. If it is too low in the comb – and this is probably the most common problem that will be encountered – it may cause low shooting; but it may also cause head lifting (ironically causing misses above) or it may cause the left eye to take over because the view to the right eye is blocked. When gun fitting (as when instructing) you must think cause and effect. Things are not always what they seem. Make sure that the client is not adapting his body to a fundamentally ill-fitting gun. I have seen dozens of stocks unnecessarily mutilated because an inexperienced or lazy fitter did not spot an eye dominance or head positioning (mounting) problem.

NOTES

1   One might speculate that the conditioning of boys in society through sport and other activities such as the use of tools may affect the development of eye dominance. As sex roles change, the typical pattern of sex-related eye dominance in which most men have one dominant eye and most women do not, may change too.

2   A proprietary product available in the USA consisting of an adhesive, opaque plastic dot, ideally sized and configured for the purpose. They are quite expensive but work extremely well and make a neat and durable job.

3   I have a test report in my own collection concerning a W. & C. Scott pigeon gun which has been compiled by Mr Watts, who was clearly a highly competent professional with a sophisticated understanding of guns and gunfitting. It is notable that he was not a proponent of try-guns in an age when they were most popular. I concur with his view that an experienced instructor does not necessarily need a try-gun to achieve a good gunfit.

4   Greener is often credited with the invention of the Monopeian sight, in fact it was invented by the Rev. E.Elmhurst though they were made by Greener and other gunmakers. The confusion may be explained by the fact that the device, was not patented by Elmhurst. Tozer notes in his work *Practical Hints on Shooting* of 1887 that the sporting victor 'had persistently declined to guard it by Letters Patent, saying that he did not wish to debar any gentleman the privilege of adopting the the system without let or hindrance.' Elmhurst actually wrote a pamphlet The Monopeian Gun but I have never seen a copy.

5   There is one potential advantage to shooting off the opposite shoulder, however, the strong arm is available to direct the barrels.

6   There are more sophisticated systems for measuring pitch by angle. The standing-against-the-wall method is marginally affected by barrel length, but is the one most commonly used in practice. The measurement of pitch is far less important than how the pitch interacts with the user.

7   Most benchmade over-and-unders have spacers placed between the tubes – effectively bending one or both barrels. I would hazard the guess that this is required by the demi-bloc style of construction. A monobloc may be machined with the tube axes perfectly pitched to print where desired. That said, more than a few famous-name, mid-price monobloc over-and-unders print their top barrel high.

8   When stocks are bent by the heat methods, they are generally held in a jig and heated at the grip. When the wood is pliable, the stock is bent over (usually to double the required alteration). The wood is allowed to cool and the modification should be permanent.

CHAPTER 10

Practical Instruction

BEGINNERS

Teaching beginners (if the job is to be done well) is a more complicated task than many might think. A great deal needs to be communicated in a short space of time, and there is little opportunity for the instructor to relax. This should not put you off, but it should make you determined to set about the task in a methodical and responsible manner.

Start with a smile

The first thing that every one of my new clients gets – regardless of age or experience – is a handshake with a smile. I want them to see shooting as a happy, friendly and polite sport. Once ushered into the clubhouse (assuming there is one), the client is offered refreshment. My manner is relaxed and friendly (but not too familiar). I tell the client my Christian name and ask them to call me by it (unless, by instinct, I think this inappropriate). At all times, I am sensitive to the client's mood. I want to put the individual, who may be a little anxious at being in an alien environment, at ease. The client must set the level of interpersonal intimacy. Some clients feel most comfortable with a very business-like approach (at least, initially); others respond best to a warmer style.

A first impression can only be made once. If the clients can relax with you, it will make instruction much easier and more enjoyable for both parties. Conversely, if they tense up or feel threatened, instruction will be much harder. After a little friendly chatting about the journey to the ground, the weather or any other subject as appropriate, ask the client whether or not he (or she) has any previous experience of shooting and the sort of shooting he is primarily interested in (do not force an answer out of someone who has not yet made up his mind). As you talk with the client, you will also get an idea about personality and levels of individual motivation and focus. These will direct your style of presentation and, to some degree, the content of your instruction (to be effective, you must be able to adjust your delivery to suit the individual).

Seven Essentials

Before any instruction with live (lightly-loaded) cartridges can commence, you must ensure that the client has:

1 No physical, mental or visual impediment to safe shooting.
2 An understanding of the potential danger of firearms (with specific mention made of the two Golden Rules and the need to carry a shotgun action open).
3 Been tested for eye dominance and has some idea of its implications, i.e., the requirement to shoot with both eyes open or one eye shut, squinted or blocked.

PLATE 17

Alan Rose in two guises with the same client - gentle guide and sergeant major.

PLATE 18

Classic cross-firing. This left-handed shooter needs to block the vision to the right eye, change shoulders or acquire a cross-over stock.

Many young shots and many women arrive for lessons with guns which are too low in the comb. I had run out of comb raisers on this day, so I built the stock up with a piece of cardboard. This young man went on to break most of his birds.

4   Been briefed on the basic parts of the gun and their function (trigger, safety, top-lever, bead, etc.) and shown how the gun is closed (under control and with the muzzles pointing in a safe direction).
5   An understanding of the required bird/bead relationship (which you should communicate through demonstration or by means of a simple diagram) and the need to focus on the target rather than on the gun, as one would in rifle or pistol shooting. (One of the essential skills in good wingshooting is to learn how to sustain focus on the target whilst maintaining the barrels in peripheral vision.)
6   A gun allocated to him (but kept in your possession) which is a reasonable fit for length and comb height and not too heavy.
7   Ear and eye protection (and an understanding of why they are needed).

Sorting out all the above should take no more than fifteen minutes (it can be done in much less). Do not overload with useless information. Do be methodical. It is all too easy for novice instructors to forget one or the other of the above. Adopt a routine to ensure that you do not leave anything out.

Lead by example
While assessing, briefing and equipping the client you are, in effect, performing. Your own gun-handling must be impeccable. Never be afraid to be a little theatrical in your movements (especially as far as muzzle control is concerned). Indeed, cultivate such a style as makes it more likely that the client will copy you.

Supplements to traditional instruction
Before taking a new client out to the firing point, you might show him a short video about gun safety and proper gun handling (I sometimes do this with groups). You can give students handouts, and use wall charts and demonstration pieces – cut-up cartridges, blown-up guns, boards with different clay targets mounted upon them – to supplement verbal instruction, if kept within reasonable limits. It all helps to make learning more interesting and therefore more effective. Telling someone about the dangers of 20-bore cartridges in 12-bores, for example, is far more memorable when combined with the sight of pair of burst barrels.

Dry practice
When I have the chance, I like to cover the basics of stance and gun mounting before going out to the firing point. This may easily be combined with rudimentary fitting (does the gun need a butt extender or comb raiser?). Do not overdo it. Just show the client the basics of a stance suitable for him, and note the positions required of head (well down on comb) and hands (rear thumb wrapped around grip, front hand midway on forend). Fine tuning comes later.

Gun up or gun down?
Since a low start position complicates the teaching process considerably, the vast majority of *ab initio* students should be taught gun-up to begin with (with

Cleaning Guns

Anyone teaching beginners how to shoot should also teach them how to disassemble and assemble their guns and how to clean it. This is a habit which should be formed early in a shooting career. Many experienced shots allow good guns to be ruined through laziness. Guns should always be cleaned after shooting . The sooner this is done, the better. I keep several rods for cleaning because this speeds up the process considerably. These include one which is no more than a stick to push paper through the bore, a rod with wire brush attached and one with a jag for patches (by means of which one may lubricate the bore). An old tooth brush, a feather or two and some pipe cleaners may also be useful for getting into nooks and crannies. Boiled linseed oil will occasionally be needed for the wood (apply a little to the pad of the finger and rub in small circles), dedicated gun-grease should also be on hand to lubricate the knuckle and hinge pin and oil for the mechanics of the action, the bores and for wiping over before storage. In all cases, oil should be used very sparingly. If guns are over-oiled and left standing with muzzles up and butt down oil can seep into the stock and damage the wood.

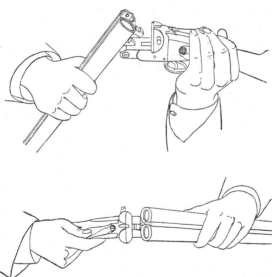

Cleaning should begin (and end) with a safety check – many accidents have occurred while cleaning guns. Make the point to all your clients that not only should they prove a gun empty before cleaning it but that they should only point it towards a wall which would stop a shot charge (i.e. not at a partition wall). The physical process of cleaning should begin with a wipe down and visual inspection. Cleaning is always an opportunity to check the gun over and to note such things as dents, hairline cracks or lost beads. After checking the gun over begin routine disassembly. Do not over do it. If the gun is break action remove barrels and forend. If it is a semi-auto, remove the barrels, forend and bolt assembly as a matter of course (and the trigger lock assembly periodically). If the gun has multi chokes leave them in for the first stage of cleaning. Ejector extractors should occasionally be removed on break action guns, but this should not be required for routine cleaning. Similarly, the bottom plate of boxlock guns may also be removed on rare occasions (for example if the gun gets wet) as may the locks of sidelock guns (provided one has a perfectly fitting turnscrew and the knowledge of how to use it confidently).

Push crumpled newspaper or two sheets of lavatory paper (the ideal size for a 12-bore barrel) through the bore to get rid of the main fowling (make sure that bore is clear and unobstructed after doing this). If required, use a phosphor bronze brush to get rid of leading and plastic residue (which will be at its worst in the forcing cones and choke area). If leading is bad, you may consider using a proprietary bore cleaner such as Parker Hale 009 (use something similar a couple of times a year even if the bore appears OK – you will be amazed at what comes out). If there is surface rusting, it may be removed by wire wool wrapped around a jag. Continue to push through paper plugs until the bore is bright. Remove the multi-chokes if fitted. If you do this routinely at this stage you will not end up with that most tedious of problems – a gun in which the chokes are rusted solid. Clean the surface of the chokes and their threads and apply a little lubricant. Wipe the area inside the muzzles where the chokes locate. Use a wire brush if required. Replace the chokes. Pay attention to the rib and ejectors too (this where the feathers and pipe cleaners come in handy) and, occasionally, remove the ejector extractors to do a thorough job.

Now consider the action. Wipe the face and remove all fouling. Check for debris inside the action walls and remove if necessary using the tooth brush to get it out. Put the barrels back on the action putting a dab of grease (not Vaseline) on cross-pin (or studs) and on the bearing surfaces at the knuckle (to prevent galling and other problems it is advisable to do this every time you clean the gun). Now the forend may be replaced. If the gun has been damp or is to be stored for some time, use a lightly oiled patch to give the bores a protective coating. It always pays to wipe the gun down with a very lightly oiled cloth to complete the basic cleaning process. We are not quite finished. *Prove the gun empty and unobstructed before putting it away* (I have twice seen a cleaning rod fired at a bird!). Avoid stripping a gun unnecessarily for cleaning. Do not start removing screws unless it really is required and only of you have a turn-screw which is precisely the correct size and you feel competent in what you are doing. Guns cabinets maybe equipped with a vapour pack (such as Napier's VP 90) to reduce the risk of condensation leading to rusting. Note that central heating can be bad for guns. They are ideally stored where there is an opportunity for some air to circulate.

Quick clean: Prove empty. Disassemble, push paper through bores until bright (or use a 'Paradox' cleaner), wipe action face, clean and lubricate knuckle and hinge. Remove multichokes and wipe over. Reassemble. Prove empty and unobstructed.

Semi-autos: In gas guns, one must regularly clean the ports in the gas collar; build up of residue here will prevent the gun functioning (and can be a cause of problems in these firearms). A dedicated tool for this job is useful as is a brush or scraper for use inside the gas collar.[1]

gun-down shooting being introduced as soon as practical).[2] Moreover, the instructor will often place the gun butt in the client's shoulder for the first few mounts. This shows exactly where the gun should be positioned and ensures the butt is correctly placed for further instruction.

The procedure for butt location by the instructor is as follows. Ask the client to fold his arms in front of his chest; with the arms still folded, place the gun butt in position. Once it is located ask the student to bring his head onto the comb (at a later stage of instruction, this would not be good advice but there is no option here) and his hands onto the grip and forend. Adjust as necessary.

Key points
- Make sure the client stays muzzle aware.
- Make sure he keeps the head on the stock when the gun is mounted.
- Make sure he keeps his weight on the front foot.[3]
- Do not allow a fundamental error to pass by uncorrected – as many student instructors do – make sure the basics are right before progressing.

- Keep correcting mistakes one at a time, very gently, until the penny drops.
- Do not expect the client to assimilate everything you say immediately.
- Seek feedback to ensure instruction has been understood.

Now we are ready to move to the firing point. As you walk, describe how you are carrying the gun: action open, resting on the forearm (other methods may be mentioned later). Note, in the early stages of training you will be in charge of the gun at all times, except when the student is actually performing a specific exercise under your supervision.

At the firing point: target requirements
The ideal first time target for a right-handed, right master-eyed beginner is the low house bird from station 2 on a skeet layout. The high house bird on station 6 is perfect for left-handers. By starting someone new to shooting on a crossing target, you equip him with the fundamental skill of shotgun marksmanship: learning to shoot ahead of a moving target. Avoid low driven targets because they may shower the client and instructor with bits. If no crosser is available, the next best option is a simple slow going-away bird. (Sometimes, this will be too much to ask and one should set up a slow bird which requires no lead at all. You must use your judgement.)

If the client is a right-hander with a right master eye, you will be standing just to his right rear with the trap release button (if there is one) in your left hand. I would usually say something like this: 'I am going to show you a clay in flight now. It is coming from there [point]. Here it comes [release a bird]. Do you see the opening in the trap house? I want you to watch the next clay very carefully. Look just in front of that opening. The clay is coming *now*! [release another]...Lock your eyes onto it'.

Your immediate tasks are:

1 to emphasise the importance of sustained visual contact;
2 to get the client to relate to a moving target;
3 to communicate the idea that one must shoot in front – into blue sky – to break a crossing bird.

You need to get these ideas across progressively. For this reason, I often get clients to point at a bird with a finger before they move up to a gun with snap caps. It is not always necessary, but it just about guarantees results without a

---

The recoil test

The recoil test is to be used with discretion where you anticipate a problem with recoil. Once the client has acquired an elementary level of competence in stance and gun hold and mount (and progress with dry training until this is accomplished), ask him (or her) to mount the proven-empty gun at a specific spot on the wall or horizon (be specific to avoid confusion). With the gun mounted in a horizontal position, hold the barrels with both hands from the side, and simulate the effect of recoil – a reasonably heavy (but not silly) rearwards shove. Typically, the client will be thrown slightly off balance. This is a simple way to show what recoil does, and how it needs to be controlled by keeping the centre of gravity forward.

lot of fuss (and emphasises the importance of pointing in shooting). We shall proceed on this basis.

Having shown the client a couple of birds, set his stance up towards a realistic killing zone (you may even have foot marks prepared on the firing point). Point the spot out clearly: 'When we shoot, we want to break the clay about there', while pointing at the killing zone. Continue:

'Now, I am going to show you another bird. This time, I want you to point your left-hand index finger [assuming a right-hander who will fire off the right shoulder] at the clay, and keep pointing as it flies. Imagine you are a fighter pilot locking onto an enemy aircraft!'

[Pause]

'O.K. Start with your finger just in front and slightly underneath the trap house opening. Ready... The clay is coming *now*!...Point...Point...eyes locked on the clay.'

Forward allowance and the beginner

Just as most beginners will need to be taught gun up, they will also need to be taught a conscious approach to applying one or other lead technique initially (otherwise the vast majority would end up missing everything behind). My first choice is pull-away for *ab-initio* instruction, although I will use other methods if they are better suited to the individual (the method described below is easily adapted to maintained lead – my second favourite – or swing through).

Assuming you are teaching a version of pull-away, the finger pointing exercise will progress thus: 'You did exactly what I wanted last time – you kept your finger pointing at the clay (if he did not, repeat the basic exercise). When we shoot at a moving target, however, we need to be ahead of it to make up for its forward movement.'

(Pause).

'So this time, I want you to point at the clay as before; but once you are pointing at it, I want you to pull ahead of it and hold a small gap. Don't rush.' If the client asks, 'How big a gap do you want?', say, 'About this much (indicating a reasonable gap with your hands)'.

'Ready. Point your finger just in front of the traphouse opening. The bird is coming *now*...Point. Point...Pull in front, *bang!*'[4] If you use your voice well, you will give the client the required timing.

The next stage is to move on to dry training with the gun and a snap cap (so the action of the trigger comes as no surprise when cartridges are introduced). This should happen as soon as the client has taken on board the idea of forward allowance.[5] When you start this new phase, you may need to locate the butt in the client's shoulder as described earlier (and you should continue with this procedure until the client feels confident to pre-mount the gun himself). Always minimise the time the gun must be held in the shoulder. Speak as little as possible, and be aware that you can support the gun if need be under the forend to reduce the client's muscular effort.

Before allowing the client to 'shoot' with the gun and snap cap, make sure the body weight is forward (applying very gentle pressure with the palm of your

---

Young Shots

With Young Shots who are just starting (or nervous or disco-ordinated adult beginners) I like to begin proceedings after a basic briefing on safety and a simple eye dominance check with a very easy bird which requires little or no lead. The ideal target would be a high angle incomer going slightly to one side – the sort of bird which appears to sit in the air. The angle must be considered with care so that the firing point is not likely to be struck by bits when the clay is broken. Having shown the target and aligned the client to it – take away as many of the decisions as you can – ask the client to point at the bird with extended arm and finger. Once you have ascertained that he or she can do this, introduce the gun (which should be a reasonable fit for height of comb and length), giving help with mounting if appropriate. Have a dry run first: 'Just point the gun at the bird, I'll tell you when to pull the trigger'. If a go or two without cartridges produces a 'kill' by your judgement, load the gun and start shooting in earnest. I do not advise this 'dolly bird' approach with everyone, a simple crosser provides a better grounding in basic technique. The sitting bird scenario is a routine for confidence boosting. Your instinct and experience will tell you when it is required. A slow going away bird may also be used in this context.

---

hand against the back of the client's firing shoulder just before target release can help get the message across). You must also ensure that the head is down on the comb – beginners and novices love to look up (all the more if you have given them a gun with too low a comb). Keep to the same words for the firing sequence:

'The clay is coming *now*. Point... Point... Pull in front. *bang!*' Take charge of the gun between shots. You will have been responsible for loading.

As soon as you judge that a clay would have been broken by a live cartridge, progress to actual live firing. Again, use the same key words. If you use the progressive method as described, most people will break the bird in their first two or three shots. If the student needs to increase his lead dramatically, tell him so, for example, 'Twice as much'. Sometimes, you may need physically to push the gun gently ahead to achieve the forward allowance needed (and often the student will exclaim, 'That much?'). Keep verbal instruction to the barest minimum in the early stages of live firing. Allow the student to concentrate on moving the gun (it is quite enough to worry about). Once a few birds are broken, and the student has the 'feel' of breaking a bird, you can consider finer points of style.

Build technique slowly

When the student is breaking simple clays consistently, get him to call for his own targets. Give him responsibility for closing the gun. Then make him responsible for the safety catch (but note his final thumb position carefully). Allow him to load single cartridges (with you controlling the supply).

Once elementary skills are mastered, change positions to give the client experience of different angles. You may also decide to introduce gun-down shooting. When this happens (and I do not believe it should be delayed too long), get the student to adopt a position with the gun initially just out of the shoulder. As always, be progressive. Once good results are obtained, the heel of the stock may be positioned below the armpit (or under the armpit if you are teaching the Churchill mount). The key to success with gun-down shooting is a sense of rhythm, good use of the front arm, and a good starting position for the muzzles (just below the bird's line of flight in most cases). Get the client to call out the time as he mounts and swings on the bird: *One: Two: Three.* Use your voice first to build up his sense of rhythm.

Preparation

My teaching – at all levels – emphasises the importance of preparation. Whatever method of forward allowance is being used, one should select visual pick-up, holding, and anticipated kill points: 'Where do you think we are going to break it? Where are you going to hold the gun? Where are you going to look?' It will also be useful to get the client to mount the gun on to the anticipated kill point, and wind back to the holding point. Teach the beginner, indeed all students, to be disciplined about preparation. A conscious routine makes clay shooting much more consistent and should be introduced as soon as possible.

As the teaching continues beyond the first lesson, the instructor should familiarise the student with the basic shots. The mid-range right-to-left and left-to-right crosser (start close and move out gradually); the going-away bird; rabbits; straightforward, driven targets at middle height; birds on the quarter; and teal. Simple pairs may be introduced too, both simultaneous release (ideally two floppy going-away birds), and on report. In the latter case, if the birds are coming from the same trap (as they should be at this stage), it is important to get the client to bring the gun back towards the trap after the first shot so as to pick up the second as efficiently as possible. You can introduce a slight delay to help the client. Do not have fixed ideas about when the client should be introduced to certain targets; progress should always relate to individual performance. The client dictates pace.

Conclusions

Remember the essentials and be progressive in your teaching. (Show a clay. Point a finger at it, etc.) Introduce gun-down shooting as soon as practical. Do not be afraid of revision. Try and give the client clear principles that can be taken away from the lesson: muzzle awareness, the gate post concept for the stance (if appropriate), the necessity of sustained visual contact and gun movement. Your goal is simple: to make the client a safe shot and independent of you as soon as possible.

INTERMEDIATE LEVEL INSTRUCTION

Start with the basics. Your job is to find any holes in technique (even the best shots have them). Eyes and gunfit must be carefully checked (and more time should be spent on gunfitting than with the beginner or novice; the intermediate level shooter may well benefit significantly from small changes to his gun's fit and balance). You should check mounting style carefully, and having watched performance on simple targets, you should put the intermediate level shot through his paces on a wide variety of birds to see if any angle or style of presentation is a particular problem. Consider gun movement, centre of gravity, head position on firing, visual contact and timing.

The goal (once any basic flaws in technique and equipment have been eliminated) is to teach intermediate shooters a new discipline and control. The rationale behind this is simple enough: when attending shoots, I am often amazed at the basic errors that experienced shots make. We all lift the head, stop the gun or misread a bird occasionally. But when people who have shot for years, repeatedly begin with their gun or their feet in the wrong place, it is cause for more thought. The reason may appear to be sheer sloppiness, but is perhaps more likely to be simple ignorance of precisely what should be done.

Once I have checked eyes, fit and basic technique, I will introduce the intermediate level sporting, skeet and game shot to a number of exercises which I have devised to increase control and discipline. The importance of good preparation and gathering pre-shot intelligence must be repeatedly emphasised: where is the bird coming from, what type of target is it, where is it first seen, where is it going and what will it pass (branches, leaves, etc., which might be used as aids to rapid visual contact)? Where should the eyes look? Where should the gun wait? Where should the feet point?

I take the client onto a skeet layout (if available), where I get them to experiment with different systems of forward allowance (swing-through, pull-away, Positive Shooting, maintained lead and interception). I also get them to try different stances and start positions and I ask them to kill the bird in different places with different methods. This training will make them much more aware of their stance, timing and gun hold. It will develop finesse and much improve control and understanding the art of shooting.

CASE STUDY David B

David had just taken up shooting but had already acquired 3 guns. An extrovert, he was in a hurry and demanded of himself instant results. His basic technique was surprisingly sound. In his first couple of months he had developed a good stance and a reasonable mount. His basic problem concerned gun movement and forward allowance. His gun fit was not quite right and he fell to bits in front of an audience. He was one of those potentially difficult clients who would do the same thing every time no matter what you told them. On a mid-range crosser he would, typically, be half a yard or so behind on every shot. He just would not risk getting in front. He was still trying to calculate as he pulled the trigger and this was causing him to stop. His upper body rotation and preparation were poor. The only way to solve this was with patience and gentle encouragement. I explained the theoretical lead required (because he was a thinker), suggested a pull-away technique (because it can encourage you to shoot with an accelerating gun) and made him much more aware of pick-up and hold points. We increased range and speed of target progressively. He began to connect. His gun fit problems were aggravated by the fact that he had bought three entirely different guns. I persuaded him to stick to one and have its stock modified to suit him (he had very long arms and needed a 1½ in. extension). The audience problem was due to the fact that he was an extrovert who wanted to be seen to do well by others. Having established this 'ego drive' it was possible to use it as a motivator: 'If you want to do well, you'll have to risk missing in front...'

I will expose the intermediate level shooter to long range (but relatively straightforward) birds to build confidence, and to show him the need for much greater forward allowance in some circumstances. The discovery that some birds may need 10 feet or more of lead can come as a great revelation! I may introduce an element of pressure and competition into training (but not too much). I continually emphasise that vision is a skill and that sustained visual contact is fundamental to success.

Once I have established what method or methods work best for the individual, I will help him to create a training plan that he can implement when I am not there. I will also spend considerable time on dry mounting drills and suggest they be practised at home much like a Karate kata. The key to success in my system of shooting and instruction is self-awareness. Some good shots may insist, 'Well, I shoot O.K. and I don't know or care what I do'. Possibly, but for most people at the intermediate stage, greater self-awareness is essential to progress. Not knowing what one ought to do ensures that on occasion everything will fall to bits for no apparent reason. My task as instructor and coach is to make the reasons for success apparent.

ADVANCED INSTRUCTION

Instructing advanced students always presents a special challenge. However, do not assume that just because someone is a good or very good shot, that he has a perfect technique. Always check eye dominance, gunfit and basic technique as a matter of routine. As with intermediate shots, a slight change in front hand position or centre of gravity may bring good results. Gunfitting will be of special importance to the advanced shot: subtle changes to the stock maybe required. Balance, barrel length, chokes and trigger pulls are also more important to the advanced shot than to others. At this level, the right gun can make a significant difference. Similarly, exercises to improve trigger and muzzle control can be especially beneficial.

The key to advanced instruction, however, is confidence training: the knowledge that one can cope with any target under any circumstances. The Army has a motto: 'Train hard and fight easy'. The advanced shot and his instructor must find the weaknesses in technique and work on them relentlessly. Hidden or occasional faults – head lifting, poor gun movement – must be isolated and eliminated (behaviour is especially hard to modify when it has been much practised – use aids such as video recording and playback to make the client really aware of what is wrong; do not be afraid of extended repetition at this level, and explain to the client just why it is required).

The eyes must be trained to sustain visual contact. You must demonstrate to the advanced shot why this is so important, and what can be achieved by improved visual contact. Tactics for specific situations must be developed. A training plan must be created and goals set. As far as target presentation is concerned, you must be imaginative. Do not try to beat the Gun with range: but get him shooting at targets where the pick-up is especially difficult, or the angle deceptive. Create difficult simultaneous and report pairs. Do not be too clever – you do not want the Gun to lose his rhythm – but keep him under pressure, challenged and interested.

The advanced shot must be trained out of the idea of bad days. Never mind his mood. Never mind fatigue. Never mind the weather (bad weather is a good opportunity for training). The focus must be on the perfection of technique and self trust. With proper training of mind and body there need only be good days and better ones (if you doubt it, look at the scores of current champions). I do a lot of psychological training with my advanced clients, including the application of visual rehearsal and relaxation techniques (see: Psychology chapter). They must learn what stress is and how to use it positively. Fitness training is important at this level too, especially when the breakthrough required may amount to no more than one or two birds per hundred.

Ultimately, the advanced shot must know that he has practised a proven technique so well that he may focus his energy on the bird and nothing but the bird every time. He need have no problem with concentration, because he has worked out exactly what to concentrate upon and when. Before shooting, he sets himself up with discipline; after calling for the target there is only one thing to concentrate upon: the bird. He is totally engaged. At the highest levels of performance, shooting becomes an act of Zen-like meditation. Even at sub-elite levels, competence and confidence combined will bring results. A small set of changes in technique, attitude and equipment can provide the winning edge.

SPECIFIC DISCIPLINES

SKEET SHOOTING

Skeet is a discipline which is predictable. There is little excuse for being caught unawares by a skeet target. You know where is coming from and where it is going. You know what it is, how far away it is, and its approximate speed of travel. Nevertheless, many poorer skeet shots fail to prepare themselves adequately before shooting. The instructor should always be on the lookout for this and develop a precise routine with the client for each station (considering foot position, hold point and point of first visual contact). Make use of the centre peg and other markers, so that the client knows exactly how to stand and hold the gun for each shot. Taking a sporting approach to skeet, I change my foot position for the singles – setting the rear foot at approximately 90 degrees to the killing point – and always advocate setting the stance to favour (or nearly favour) the second target on doubles. (I have tried other systems, such as pointing the belt buckle or navel into the low house trap mouth, but for my style of shooting, the religious adherence to the 90-degree rule brings the best results.) I consider the line of the birds carefully, and note where I will look for them. With the exception of Low 1, I avoid looking into the trap mouth.

Typical problems

A common error at skeet is to shoot over or under High 1 because the gun is

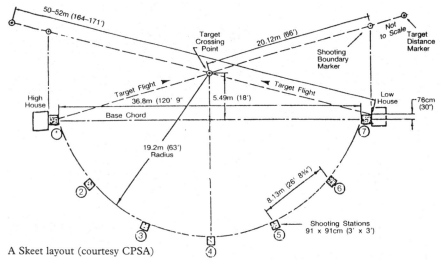

A Skeet layout (courtesy CPSA)

incorrectly positioned. When stepping onto 1 make sure you are positioned immediately below the trap opening. The barrels should be held at about 30 degrees, with the eyes looking a few inches over the muzzles, and the High House target should be shot just over or before the centre post. The motion of the gun involves a slight forward push (almost as if one were trying to bayonet the target). One shoots at or into the bird. Low 1 requires a very slight turn to the left. Experienced shots can miss this bird in front (it only requires the slightest lead); others may miss it behind because of poor rotation or use of the front arm. Once the feet are set up to the killing point, the best advice is usually to 'shoot the front edge'.

On High 2, many shots miss the bird over or in front because they misread it or try and shoot it in the wrong place. The starting point for High 2 should be about halfway from trap mouth to centre peg (where the bird should be shot). Another system is to keep the barrel parallel to the front wall of the trap house. Do not rush it or leave it late. Shoot it decisively 'on the front edge'. The low bird wants about 2 ft if shot deliberately. On the double, the foot position should favour the second (low) target.

Station 3 is relatively straightforward, but it is notable that the lead on Low 3, as on the other mid stations (3, 4 and 5) is appreciably greater. You may be able to see a yard or more.

On Station 4, shooting behind the single targets is common too. However, on the double, many miss the second bird in front and over the top. The required lead for first and second targets is different. The first target is a true crosser, the second is at a quartering angle (unless one is a very quick shooter) and slowing. As a sporting shot, my lead picture for the double is something like 3 feet for the first bird, about half that for the second and slightly underneath (it is still quite possible to miss the bird behind if one checks the swing). It can be helpful to shoot the first bird of the pair with maintained lead to buy time (without rushing) for the second shot.

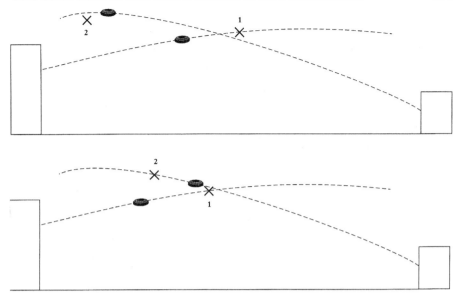

Leads on skeet pairs will depend on how quickly you shoot. If shooting the pair from station 4, the well practised skeet shot may shoot his first bird before in reaches the centre of the field and the second just after it crosses (see diagram immediately above). The more deliberate shot, perhaps more used to sporting, will take the second bird significantly later (top diagram). In this case it may be missed both behind and (more often than you might think) in front and over the top.

On Station 5 High – an apparently easy target – it is easy to ride the bird and miss it as a consequence. On Station 5 Low, one must be careful not to shoot over the top. It is a common mistake to take the gun too far back.

On Station 6, many shots have problems with the low bird, typically misreading the line and shooting in front or over the top. Again, one should not come back too far for this target. The best way to shoot is with confidence 'on the bottom front edge'. On the pair at 6, it is especially important to set the stance up to favour the second target. If one does not do this, it is all too easy to run out of swing and drop off line on the second bird (resulting in a miss low and behind).

On Low 7, note where the low bird is going relative to the centre post (relatively high or low, right or left) before taking up your position. This should be an easy target, but it is possible to be caught out. The good shot will shoot this bird with a minimum of movement because he is set up well. The feet should move for High 7 and the pair.

Windy conditions

Skeet scores sometimes drop very markedly in windy conditions. This is usually because Guns have got into the bad habit of shooting targets in a particular spot, and have got away with being lazy with regard to visual contact. In other words they have learnt to shoot skeet robotically with less than perfect fundamental technique. The wind, which causes birds to fly off normal line – and often at unusual speed – catches them out. On a windy day, good visual contact and disciplined pre-shot preparation with regard to hold and pick-up points (which may have changed significantly) become absolutely essential. The shot who has visual discipline does not need predictable conditions to shoot well, he has a system applicable to all situations and disciplines. He will automatically allow for any unexpected target 'bounce'.

NSSA shooting

The technique is essentially the same a English skeet save for the double on 4 and the two singles on Station 8. The secret to shooting Station 8 is not to overlead the bird. Prepare yourself well. Do not rush. Just take the hands and gun to the bird and pull the trigger. There is a knack to it: once acquired it is a relatively easy shot. Do not let your clients be frightened by Station 8.

SPORTING

As with skeet a great many shots fail to prepare themselves properly when facing sporting targets. However, in sporting there is, arguably, more excuse. Good preparation must be based on good intelligence gathered immediately before shooting (this is also true of skeet – where conditions can vary – but not to the same extent). Every opportunity should be taken to consider the bird/birds before shooting. Once basic flaws in technique have been eliminated, encourage clients to ask questions like:

- Where is the target coming from?
- Where is it going?
- What type of target is it?
- How far away is it?
- How fast is it?
- What is its angle? Is it deceptive?

CASE STUDY Jane B

Jane, 39, was a beginner. Brought up on a farm, she had shot as a girl, but motherhood and an office job had intervened. She had tried skeet on a have-a-go day and was now determined to take it up seriously. We worked together for about half a dozen lessons. She set about the task with method and determination. Her eye dominance was inconsistent, and she tried squinting and a small patch on protective glasses experimentally, settling on the latter as more comfortable. She practised her stance and mount every night according to materials that I provided (a pamphlet and a video). From the start of her shooting career, she was careful about gun hold and visual pick-up. She bought a Beretta 303 skeet gun, but soon traded up for a high-combed ladies model 390 (something made in small numbers for the US market). This gun had a Monte Carlo stock which suited her high cheek bones. It was a significant purchase (she was shooting on a tight budget) but she decided the expense was worth it because it would allow her to progress faster and the multi-choke facility would allow her to shoot sporting too. In many ways, Jane was the ideal client, she did exactly what was asked every time. Moreover, when something did not work her, feedback was clear and immediate. She knew her mind and was determined to learn as fast as possible. Her problems were the usual ones initially: inconsistent visual contact, lack of confidence in shooting in front of moving targets, poor timing and a follow through which needed smoothing out. But the foundations were sound: her pre-shot preparation was always excellent. Within 6 months Jane was shooting 23 consistently and has just shot her first 25 and is determined to shoot 100 soon. I am sure she will.

- Is it rising or dropping?
- Where do I want to shoot it?
- How much lead will it need?
- Where am I going to hold my gun?
- Where am I going to look for the target?
- Is there a tree or a branch or a physical feature in the landscape which might help me?

If there are two targets …

- Which should be shot first?
- Will I have to shoot one in a less than ideal position?
- Will I need to change my foot position?
- Will I have to adopt a compromise position?

This may seem a great deal of effort, but it is well worth it. The difference between the average sporting shot and the expert is the amount of focused effort put into each bird. There are no shortcuts, anyone who wants to put in high sporting scores consistently has to work hard before the shot is fired.

As far as specific targets are concerned I might list some typical errors common to shots of every ability level.

Flat quartering targets like woodcock are often missed in front and over the top (targets quartering away tend to give an illusion of speed if one is positioned close to the trap). When birds are quartering away, one should avoid bringing the muzzles too far back.

Grouse and low driven birds tend to be missed over the top, hence the old phrase, 'Grouse wear spats'.

Rabbits tend to be missed over the top (it is good advice to shoot them on their bottom edge as this allows much more room for error). Fast quartering rabbits are often missed in front (and over too. It is a mistake to take the gun too far back with quartering or indeed crossing rabbits. On all rabbit targets the muzzle should also begin under the line).

Dropping targets are usually missed above. Most Guns do not appreciate the need for under allowance and smooth follow through on these birds. Many times, I have missed a mid-range dropper giving it two or three feet under, when in fact it needed five or six. I have shot droppers which needed as much as eight to ten feet under. Droppers may also be missed behind (their forward motion may be masked by their apparently slow speed).

Long, slow incomers are notoriously difficult and are often missed above and behind (and occasionally in front). There

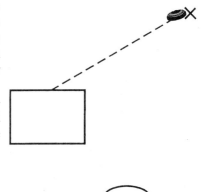

With quartering shots, I often tell clients to shoot them 'on the front edge'. With typical presentations, they can be easily missed both behind (usually because the gun stops) and in front (because they are misread and over-lead).

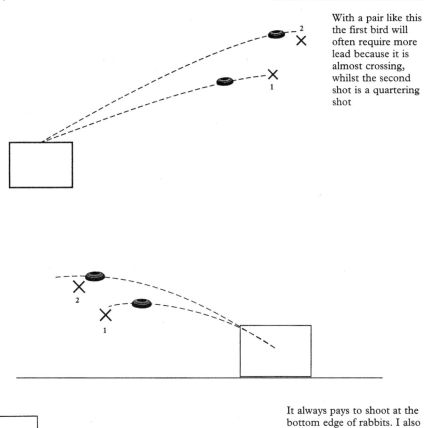

With a pair like this the first bird will often require more lead because it is almost crossing, whilst the second shot is a quartering shot

It always pays to shoot at the bottom edge of rabbits. I also frequently find myself telling clients to shoot 'at them' without hesitation – this simple instruction can solve long-standing bunny phobias.

Droppers not only require an allowance underneath (and it is often more than you think) but an allowance corresponding to the direction in which they are moving. They may appear to be almost stationary in the horizontal place but this is rarely the case. They are frequently missed behind as well as over the top.

are three techniques with these birds which might be tried: leave to the last minute and snap shoot; lock on to the target with the CPSA method and smoothly pull to one side and slightly under; or – often my favourite – 'boxing'. The bird is put in an imaginary box (let us say two foot square). If movement is from the right, the bird is placed in the top right-hand corner and the tip of the gun in the bottom left. The boxing technique works with many other odd targets including: 'chandelle' targets (birds launched side-on in a high parabolic curve) and slower battues. Most battues are missed significantly behind, however. They are deceptively fast (typically requiring as much as fifty per cent more forward allowance than a standard target).

Teal fall into two basic categories: those which go straight up and which are easily missed underneath; and those which quarter away and are easily missed over the top (especially as far as the second bird of a simultaneous pair is concerned). With straightforward, near vertical presentations of teal pairs at moderate range, I often find myself saying to myself or to clients, 'A foot over the first, a foot under the second'. It will not work for every situation but, regardless of the specific measurement stated, it gets the client thinking that the two birds require a different approach.

Long crossers and high driven birds tend, as one would expect, to be missed behind. Orientation to the killing point is critical on a long crosser. On high driven birds one should take the bird a little before it reaches an overhead

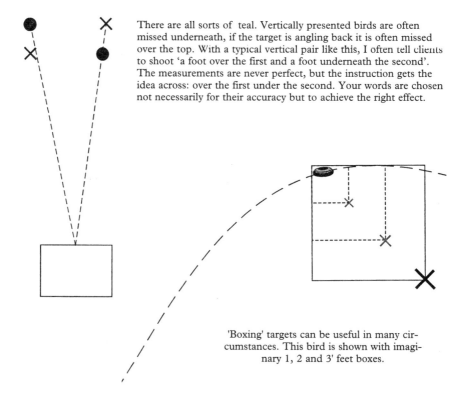

There are all sorts of teal. Vertically presented birds are often missed underneath, if the target is angling back it is often missed over the top. With a typical vertical pair like this, I often tell clients to shoot 'a foot over the first and a foot underneath the second'. The measurements are never perfect, but the instruction gets the idea across: over the first under the second. Your words are chosen not necessarily for their accuracy but to achieve the right effect.

'Boxing' targets can be useful in many circumstances. This bird is shown with imaginary 1, 2 and 3' feet boxes.

PLATE 19

All guns should be tested at a pattern plate for point of impact. This may also give valuable information about choke and quality of pattern.

Cartridge cases on top of the trap house roof indicate basic holding points for the common five-point system. However, the height of the hold may need to vary to suit conditions.

Chris Cradock instructing a left-hander.

PLATE 20

The instructor's hand plays a crucial role. It can be used to subtly apply pressure to keep the shooter's weight forward, or, as here, to make an adjustment to hold position. Never let a basic error slip by uncorrected if you can help it. I will not let the client take the shot unless I am happy with his preparation for it.

position to facilitate follow-through (bending back beyond the vertical tends to be uncomfortable) and to ensure consistent target speed (on many towers birds are running out of pace as they reach the vertical position). This may be used to one's advantage if one has read the bird well, but my usual preference is to take the bird in good style before it reaches the vertical. Long birds may also be missed off line. Indeed, this is almost as common as missing behind. The remedy is to pay particular attention to visual contact and use of the front arm. At range, all errors are compounded. One will not get away with sloppy technique. On any long target, the gun should only start moving once clear visual contact has been established. It should not be mounted prematurely (muzzles and body movement establish the swing before the gun is brought to shoulder and face). A slow start, but decisive finish suits both targets.

Long birds encourage a slow start, while birds (especially quartering targets) from a trap near the shooting position promote a more explosive swing and mount. In both cases though, there is a danger of stopping the gun: in one case because the gun is moving slowly and lacks momentum, and in the other because there is a tendency to rush to stop. In both cases the prescription is to make better use of the front arm (to ensure one pushes through the bird), and, simultaneously to use the body to power the swing, either by bending the back for high driven birds (if using the Stanbury system or something similar) or tank-turret like upper body rotation in the case of crossing and quartering birds. I sometimes use the expression 'Whole Body Shooting' to my students, which implies that when one is shooting well, the whole body is involved.

Birds which are crossing or quartering very low are often missed above because of the psychological barrier of the ground itself. Similarly, birds which are crossing or quartering between trees are often missed behind because the tree tends to make one stop the swing.

Pairs
As far as simultaneous pairs from the same trap are concerned, the best advice is to consider both targets quite separately. As A. J. Smith used to say, 'There is no such thing as a pair'. I am reminded of a pair thrown off a 100-foot tower which fooled me for a long while. The two birds did not appear that far apart (nor that different); but one, in fact, required almost 50% more lead than the other, because it had been launched at a different speed and at a subtly deceptive angle.

Generally, one should shoot the rear bird of a simultaneous pair first so that one may smoothly swing onto the second. There will be exceptions: for example, when the front target is likely to disappear behind cover if not shot first, or when it so dominates one's vision that not shooting it is uncomfortable. Always consider the first target that you will shoot most carefully. If you face a pair of teal, and one is going vertically up and the other angling to one side, shoot the angling bird first. If you do not, it will become a problem later.

Report pairs from a single trap are popular birds. The key to this shot is always to bring the muzzles back swiftly for the second shot (as with following pairs). Average shots often attempt to engage the second bird with a stationary

A brief history of Clay Shooting

Clay target shooting traces its ancestry and much of its terminology to the practice of live pigeon shooting. In this, pigeons (usually Blue-Rocks) were placed in box traps and shot on a field which looked much like a modern trap layout. Gambling was a feature of most live pigeon shoots and the activity acquired a not quite respectable reputation. Nevertheless, great skill was required to do well. Terms like 'Pull', 'Trap' and 'no bird' all stem from box-trap pigeon shooting. Live pigeon shooting reached its zenith in the Victorian era and is still practised in some parts of the world (for example, Spain, Portugal, Texas, Mexico and Egypt). It was finally banned in Britain by the Captive Birds Act of 1921, although earlier Defence of the Realm legislation had prohibited the activity during the WWI because of a fear of carrier pigeons being used by spies to send messages.

As early as the 1860s glass balls began to be used as an alternative to live birds. They achieved considerable popularity and many famous shooting wagers involved glass ball targets with shots like Doc Carver and Capt. Adam Bogardus competing for large stakes. In about 1880 the 'terracotta pigeon' appeared (the invention is usually attributed to George Ligowsky). It was a better target than the glass ball, but the first birds were literally made of clay and baked in ovens. They proved hard to break but fragile when transported. An improved clay, 'the composition target' was introduced in the mid 1880s. These were made of limestone and pitch (although plaster of paris was also used in some targets). The composition birds proved a huge success. By the 1890s American shooters were using millions of targets a year (now the world total is an amazing 2 billion). Trap shooting was the first of the competitive clayshooting disciplines to achieve a wide following. The first national tournament took place at New Orleans in the USA in 1885. In England, where clay shooting had been introduced in 1883, the Inanimate Bird Shooting Association (the forerunner of the CPSA) held its first championship in 1893. Trap shooting became an Olympic event in 1900.

Meantime the new 'shooting schools' of famous English gunmakers began to use clay targets to simulate the flight of live birds. This practise developed into what is known today as 'sporting clays' (although the first English Amateur Sporting Championship was not held until 1925). Skeet, the other popular form of clayshooting, also traces its origins to attempts to simulate game shooting. It was invented by three American bird hunters Charles Davies, his son, Henry and friend William Foster during the First World War era. Originally they had a full circle and one trap and called it "shooting round the clock", the idea was to mimic all the angles one might face in the field. Legend had it that the neighbours complained about the fall-out of shot. The circle was cut in half and another trap added. The modern game was born. The name comes from a Norwegian word for shooting and was suggested by Gurtrude Hurlbutt, a Montana housewife, in a competition arranged by the National Sportsman magazine (to which William Foster was a contributor).

gun, using some sort of unconscious interception method. It rarely works. When facing a report pair from separate traps, one should always move one's feet – if there is time – between shots if it will reduce body tension and promote a smooth swing. Most shots seem very reluctant to move their feet. Yet it can be a great aid to balance and consistent shooting. If there is not time to move the feet, adopt a compromise position or adopt a stance favouring the second or harder target. Most shots seem very reluctant to move their feet. When facing a tough simultaneous pair, the advice is similar. Adopt a compromise on the feet, or favour one target if there is a need.

Birds from behind

Note exactly where the bird is coming from if possible (turn and look). The secret to this shot is to take the eyes well up but not the gun. Early visual contact will make this bird much easier to shoot, especially when a simultaneous pair is presented.

CASE STUDY Alexander H

Alex, 39, was a first class competitive shot, but had not yet won a major championship. He put a great deal of effort into each target, he was good at reading awkward birds. All things considered, his basic style was excellent. He was averaging 90% at sporting. He was not as confident as he might be, however, and as a result, lost the occasional bird from stopping the gun. He also had a long neck which had caused some gun fit problems. He came to me with a brand new 32 in. gun. It was a beautiful thing, constructed to his specification, but he was not connecting with some fairly straightforward birds. The gun was tightly choked, had medium weight 1580 gram barrels and significant cast to compensate for Alex's not-quite-dominant right eye. The gun was also high in the comb and Alex was convinced this was the cause of his difficulties. On measuring the gun carefully and watching Alex shoot, two things became apparent. He was missing down the left hand side of some targets (straightaways and quartering) and he was nearly as frequently behind on mid and long range crossers. He was not missing many birds above, however. Careful examination of the gun revealed the fact that the comb had an unintentional off-set, the heel had right-hand cast-off, but the nose of the comb was slightly off-set left. This was negating the effect of the cast, causing the left shooting. The error behind was caused partly by a longer than ideal stock, partly by an excessively muzzle heavy balance and partly by a lack of confidence compounded by the misses caused by the first two problems. A negative cycle had developed. With the gun fit adjusted and a little weight removed from the barrels by over-boring and a little added to the stock by means of a lead plug, Alex had a gun which did what he wanted it to (it did not prove necessary to reduce choke – he began to enjoy it). We also worked on his use of the front hand. I expect him to make a national squad soon.

TRAP SHOOTING

The first prerequisite of good trap shooting is a well-fitting gun. A less than perfectly fitted gun will be more of a handicap in this group of disciplines than in any other. Trigger pulls, barrel length, choke and barrel weight are also important factors as is the right cartridge. Trap shooting should be an instinctive business and this requires the right equipment. Some have suggested the conscious application of lead on trap targets, I do not favour this. It is unnecessary if one has good technique, good equipment and a confident approach. It is also a very boring way to shoot: one cannot focus all one's energy on the bird.

Stances for trap shooting, especially for the international disciplines, tend to be a little closer footed than those for skeet and sporting. This is because upper body rotation is of paramount importance at trap: one foot position has to suit a variety of target angles. You may adopt a straight front leg stance or slightly bend the front knee. I prefer the latter stance, but it is imperative not to lean too far forward as this may hinder upper body rotation. As far as foot position

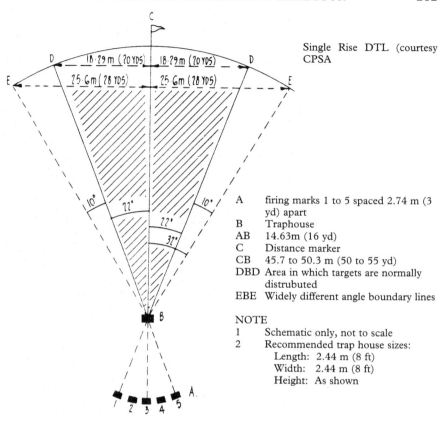

Single Rise DTL (courtesy CPSA

A   firing marks 1 to 5 spaced 2.74 m (3 yd) apart
B   Traphouse
AB   14.63m (16 yd)
C   Distance marker
CB   45.7 to 50.3 m (50 to 55 yd)
DBD Area in which targets are normally distrubuted
EBE Widely different angle boundary lines

NOTE
1   Schematic only, not to scale
2   Recommended trap house sizes:
     Length: 2.44 m (8 ft)
     Width: 2.44 m (8 ft)
     Height: As shown

is concerned, in down the line, you will not go far wrong is you routinely point the front foot towards the central distance marker. If you read books on trap, you find all sorts of advice on where the feet should point. One system, as devised by Lee Braun of Remington, advises that a line drawn across the toes should always be parallel to the extreme left angle bird (the gun hold then favours the right-hand targets). Some suggest positioning the body to favour extreme angles on 1 and 5. Another system is merely to take up a relaxed stance and mount the gun forward (or simply let it 'fall' naturally across the body at an angle of about 45%) to ascertain the point of least lateral tension. One then shuffles the feet around until one's initial gun hold equates to this point of least tension. This ensures maximum unrestricted swing right and left. There are no absolutes My own preference is to keep the left foot pointing at the central dis-tance marker from each position with a slightly bent front knee. Some will want to favour the right hand bird. Each individual must evolve a way of standing which is balanced and which gives them a sense of confidence and control on all the birds.

Gun hold

As with stance, there are different schools of thought on gun hold. Two common systems involve either holding centrally for all shots or splitting the trap house roof in to five segments. There are subtleties which may also be introduced: for example, one may hold slightly in or out from the far corners; one may hold slightly right (or left for left handers) of centre to avoid obscuring the straight away shot from position 3. This also encourages good gun movement. some advise holding in an arc rather than in a straight line.

Kaye Ohye, who has shot 1000 on at least two occasions, suggests a slightly modified five point system: the right-hander on position 1 should hold just inside the left-hand edge of the trap house roof, 'quarter-house' left on 2, centrally on 3, quarter-house right on 4 and, on the edge of the trap house on 5. On the other hand, Frank Little, another trap shooting phenomenon, suggests a central hold on 1 (he notes that holding on the left hand edge creates a blind spot to the right), centrally, or just right of centre on 2, slightly right on 3 (to improve visibility on the straight away and to create good gun movment), slightly further right on 4 and about ¼ right on 5. These positions are intended for ATA trap but might easily be adapted to DTL.

As far as vertical rather than lateral hold is concerned, most would agree that one-eyed shooters are well advised to hold on the level of the front edge of the trap house roof or even lower (holding higher will impede vision of the target). Two-eyed shooters are best advised to hold higher, about 6 in. to 1 ft above the traphouse (and higher still in some cases). Holding too high will cut down gun movement and may lead to 'spot shooting'. Some gun movement – in the vertical plane beyond the holding point – is required for good shooting, but the precise amount of vertical gun movement will vary with individuals and conditions. For example, on a windy day with the wind coming from the rear (and thus forcing the birds down) a low start may be called for.[6] If there is a wind from the front pushing targets up, a higher hold may be needed. If conditions are variable, it is good advice to hold for the low birds. As a two-eyed shooter, my preference is for a simple 5 point hold system slightly above the trap house (assuming normal conditions). This is the system I would first teach a beginning DTL shot.

Pre-shot focus
Use of the eyes before the call is a critical factor in trap shooting. Nearly all authorities agree that the eyes should maintain a soft focus just in front of the

Three of the most common holding systems for trap. The second five-point high hold would only make sense for two-eyed shots.

trap house when calling for the bird (adjusted to position so that one is looking into the zone in which birds will appear). Once the bird appears, one should
focus upon it, and once again, the importance of sustained focus cannot be
overemphasised. It is a mistake to rush the movement of the eyes or to hesitate.
The gun moves decisively once the line of the target is established and focus
secured.

Teaching beginners

Start beginners on Position 3 with a trap locked to provided a going away bird
(you should have previously placed clays on the trap house roof as an aid to gun
hold); in some cases, it may be appropriate to go forward a few yards. Make
sure they are standing well – not too edge-on or with feet too far apart – so that
they know where to look and so that they sustain focus on each bird with the
head well down. Once the straight-away on 3 is mastered, move gradually left
(in increments of a yard or so). Continue the process to Position 2 and all the
way to 1. Once the client can kill the going away bird on 1, move leftwards
stand by stand. Once you have got to 5, angling targets may be introduced.

Beginning trap shooters tend to 'rifle shoot'. They try and aim their guns and
consciously align bead to bird 'riding the target'. This is a grave error.
Moreover, one often sees them with the weight too far back and feet set wide
apart in what looks more like an archery stance. The combination of aiming,
poor visual discipline, poor stance and poor confidence leads them to shoot the
target late at the apex of its flight. The common result is a miss over the top.
Annother common cause of misses over the top is blotting the target out.
Shooters who adopt the longbowman stance may have particular problems
with left hand birds – the stance restricts swing. Head lifting (often a consequence of poor stance) is a common problem at all ability levels, but is typical
of beginners. Moreover, beginners must understand in trap (and indeed in all
shotgunning) that the trigger must not be pulled unless the upper body and

---

The Modern Clay

Clays are usually made with a limestone filler and a binding agent of bitumen - a
petroleum end product - coal tar pitch or petroleum pitch (although clays have been
made from, plaster of paris, metal, plastic and ice amongst other materials). The
standard UIT target which is used in the U.K. for all disciplines is 110mm (4 5/16
in.) in diameter (plus or minus 1 mm) with an overall height between 25 and 26 mm
(about 1 in.). In addition to standard targets, there are midis (90 mm wide and
notable for their speed), minis (60mm in width and notable not only for their small
size but because they slow quickly), battues (which are about 100mm wide, very thin
and cut through the air much faster than a standard target - hence requiring more
lead), rabbits (which are much more solid than a standard clay since they need to
bounce along the ground1) and rocket clays (a thick and heavy battue used in
FITASC competition). Flash targets - birds which have a quantity of coloured powder above or below their dome – are sometimes used to make a more spectacular
and visible break in shoot-offs or for other special occasions. In the United States,
the dimensions of the standard target are different from those in the U.K. The US
bird is narrower (4¼ in.) and marginally higher.

gun are one locked unit. The Pivot point of all movement should be the base of the spine. The upper body moves as one unit once the mount is completed as if one had a ball joint at the base of the spine.

More experienced shots may fall in the habit of shooting too quickly, before they have locked focus onto the bird fully. Another common cause for missed targets is a poor mount. It should not be forgotten that although trap shooting is shot gun-up, there is still a mount involved. Bringing the head down to the stock as some trap shots do is a very poor habit and may well lead to head raising. It is far better to develop a routine for pre-mounting the gun. I prefer to start the process with a mount at about 30° to the horizontal, some prefer a 'flatter' mount. Whatever angle of the barrels is found to be most comfortable (there are no absolute rules save for avoiding extreme positions), it is important that the comb comes to the face well. With the gun mounted, the eyes may consciously check alignment with reference to the centre and frontbead, before consciously shifting focusing forwards (this is by no means mandatory, but explains why some prefer a centre bead on the rib of a trap gun).

Once stance and mount have been mastered, and one knows where to look for the target, good trap shooting technique boils down to consistent, unhurried but absolutely sustained visual contact. This was brought home to me recently when I was shooting a DTL competition in very difficult conditions at a coastal gun club. My first round was disrupted by my attempts to find a technique to suit the stormy and very unpredictable conditions. Nothing worked until I determined to achieve good visual contact (I told myself: 'See those rings!') and forget everything else. I did this, trusted my inner abilities and dropped two more targets out of 75 (which may not sound good, but it was several less than anyone else on the appalling day in question). Regardless of the score, I had learned that if: (1) I relaxed; and (2) I focused on the bird, I would kill it. Doubt had vanished. One hundred straight on another day would have caused me no greater satisfaction. I had become one with the target(!) I had discovered the right way to shoot these targets: do not rush in the wind (in fact, never rush). See the bird. Trust your focus. Let natural hand-to-eye co-ordination do the work.

Any client who has not shot a round relying purely on visual contact should be encouraged to do so. It is a psychological barrier with some, they do not feel they dare let their unconscious self do the shooting for them. It is just too simple. I have advocated a more conscious approach on certain sporting targets, but experiment and observation lead me to conclude that all trap targets may be killed with *subconscious gun movement* provided focus is *consistent* (to achieve this, focus itself should be applied consciously). For this reason, I advocate – once basic technique is mastered and the gun properly set-up – clearing one's mind of all other technical considerations when trap shooting. SEE it: FOCUS: SHOOT. To encourage beginners to shoot without delay, this may be modified to FOCUS: FAST.

Timing: calling for the target

The way one calls for the target will affect one's speed of shooting. The call should be clear and confident, not a scream, squawk or whimper. One should call for the bird as one wants to shoot it – decisively. However, one should call for the target with relatively empty lungs. If the call is powered by full lungs and body moves and preparation is disturbed.

Squad rhythm

Good Trap shots are rather fussy about whom they will shoot with. Most prefer to shoot in a regular squad because they are used to the timing of fellow members and can relax within this context. The phrase 'I lost my rhythm' is often used by trap shooters when something distracts them and they lose their concentration. Training for serious competition should involve deliberate attempts at distraction by the instructor/coach. Generally, trapshooters are well advised to develop a technique and not to deviate from it.

Specific problems

Some Trap shots have difficulty with the straight away shot on Position 3. Overswinging is a common problem because this bird requires a more compact movement than As discussed, some may find that a central gun point interferes with their vision of this bird and may usefully try holding slightly right. Others have difficulty with extreme angles. These require a more flowing motion. Some advocate consciously seeing a lead on these birds, I do not. The important thing is confidence and good visual contact as noted.

CASE STUDY Jimmy G

Jimmy, 47, was a sporting shooter who wanted to take up trap more seriously. His average score at DTL was a low 16 or 17, though he was a reasonable performer at sporting, typically breaking 70% plus. Having gone through the usual initial checks, I picked up multiple small problems with technique, a more serious tendency to rainbow off line and a general lack of method in preparation. I also noted that Jimmy's gun was muzzle heavy and rather low stocked. He had managed to get away with the latter deficiency more-or-less at sporting, but it was the fundamental cause of his poor showing at trap. Rather than build up the stock of his 30 in. sporter, I lent him a dedicated trap gun of the same make and action type and of the same barrel length. It was a fixed choke model (three-quarters and full) allowing for a less muzzle-heavy, balance. The gun also had a comb approximately ¼ in. higher. His average immediately, jumped from 16 up to 22. As with Keith, this provided the boost in confidence required to get down to the less dramatic, but equally important (if more time-consuming) work of sorting out his basic technique. Poor upper body rotation was causing the rainbowing (as it often does). It was further aggravated by a back problem. I retrained Jimmy by getting him to swing on crossing birds whilst I placed a straightened hand beneath each arm-pit from behind to prevent him from dropping either shoulder in the swing. We worked on his use of the front arm (improper use of the front arm is also often linked to rainbowing off line) and on his approach work. A slight alteration to cast was required to compensate for eye dominance which was less than 100% absolute. He has now shot his first 25.

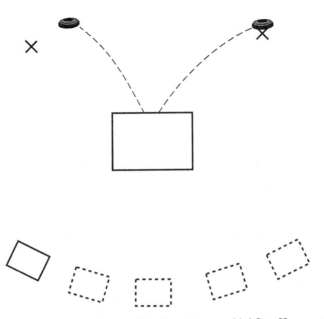

With double rise most instructors advocate taking the going away bird first. Here we are shooting from position 1. The first shot is taken with little or no allowance, the second may require a significant allowance underneath and to one side. I always shoot single trap birds instinctively relying on visual contact and instinctive point ability, but my approach to the second bird in double rise is a little more deliberate.

DOUBLE RISE AND DOUBLE TRAP

These disciplines require a different rhythm which can only be acquired through practice. Most experts shoot the straight-away bird first. Stance should be a compromise between both targets, or should favour the second target. In both Double Rise and Double Trap, the second bird is often missed over the top. In the latter case it may also require a significant allowance to one side – lateral lead – which may not look quite right initially. Once this rather unusual sight picture has been assimilated, one may progress to a more instinctive form of shooting. The best Double Rise and Double Trap shots shoot extremely quickly, but novices should not try to emulate them until they have acquired a real feel for the targets. Of all the many techniques which may be employed, I have found success with two. The first is to spot shoot the first target (one can accept the lack of gun movement in this case because of the fixed trajectory) from a high gun hold. The other technique, which seems to work, well is to start from the outside edge of the straight-away rather than the inside. This encourages an unchecked swing to the second bird.

GAMESHOOTING

There is more to be taught to the novice game shooter than the beginning clay shot. The former must learn safe gun-handling procedures in a variety of circumstances as detailed earlier, he must also learn those practices adopted on the clay shooting field (both because training will begin there and because most shots do some clay shooting these days). The student gameshot will be given very similar basic drills for gun closure, mounting, and swinging as the aspiring clayshot. He or she will learn that good footwork – whatever style of stance is adopted – is one of the keys to effective gameshooting and moving the feet should be introduced at a relatively early stage of training. The importance of balance, rhythm and visual contact will also be stressed.

As far as shooting method is concerned, the most useful technique for *ab initio* instruction will be swing-through, though maintained lead, 'touch and push' (the flowing less deliberate form of pull-away) and snap shooting have their applications too. Once the student has achieved consistent kills on the most basic targets, the instructor must introduce the proper use of the safety catch. After the student has developed a good basic style, and can confidently engage simple driven, going away, crossing, and quartering targets with proper use of the safety catch, an element of target unpredictability may be introduced (but do not introduce this too early).

Start with driven targets presented left or right. Pairs of targets may also be introduced, initially on report, but once these are shot confidently, simultaneous targets may be shown. Before progressing to harder birds make sure that the client is developing a flowing and natural style and is not tempted to be a 'target tracker' (as clay shooting sometimes encourages). An unchecked swing is important in all shooting, but especially important in game shooting where birds are typically accelerating rather than slowing down. The game shot's gun should not dwell in the shoulder.

A stance must be developed which can cope with unpredictable targets. The shooter cannot anticipate in the same way as when clay shooting. Whenever there is time, you should teach the client to step into the line of the bird, the front foot and muzzles moving in harmony both being lifted together. Rhythm is important. 'YOU' as first visual contact is established and as the tip of the muzzles go the bird; 'ARE' as the gun moves ahead and as the the feet move towards the anticipated killing point; 'DEAD' as the gun comes firmly into face and shoulder and as the trigger is pulled. Vision is locked on the head or beak.

The tip of the gun should go to the bird and then smoothly move in front without delay or tracking. The student must maintain focus on the target and keep the gun moving, firing instinctively as the bird is brushed out of the sky. While the rhythm of game shooting is the same as clay shooting gun down – 3 beats – the tempo is different. Game shooting tends to be a faster business than clay shooting. Most shots who are proficient at both game and clays, and who have thought about it, will tell you that their 'timing' is different in the two situations. This has certainly been my own experience. You will find many self-taught game shots develop a 'flick' at the end of their swing to speed themselves up. This is not to be encouraged, rather help the client to build an elegant, decisive, style. Precision without checking.

Further training

Obviously birds should be varied as much as possible and awkward shots

CASE STUDY John N

John, 43, was an occasional game shot. He had inherited a gun – a heavily cast, best quality, side-by-side sidelock – but was disappointed with the way it shot and with its heavy recoil. John's technique, such as it was, was instinctive. He had adopted a very long forward hand position and his feet tended to be wide spaced. A right-hander, he tested fully right eye dominant. On considering the gun it was apparent that it was both overly cast and too short for him. The comb was also a little low. The barrels were only 26 in. long and the overall weight was not much over 6 lb. The gun bore a very famous name, but John did not shoot it as well as his old off-the-peg Webley 700. My advice (given at the end of our first encounter) was to sell the newly acquired gun and buy something more suitable for his 6 ft 1 in. frame or invest the windfall. John's technique required polishing, meantime. His greatest failing was to take his eyes off the bird and bring them back to the gun. He also needed some encouragement to move his feet in anticipation of the bird (to 'step into the line'). His understanding of forward allowance was limited. When I noted he might need to be 8 feet ahead of a bird at 40 yards he was truly amazed ,'I never give them that much', 'Well, try it and see what happens'. The high tower proved the point. He adopted a less exaggerated stance and brought the front hand back to the tip of the forend. We worked on his timing and tempo over several lessons. He developed a more relaxed style. He tried my over and under and liked it during these proceedings, 'it seems a lot more controllable and does not recoil as much'. He is now buying one for himself and pocketing a £10,000 profit on the old sidelock side-by-side.

---

practised. Clays will never be a substitute for live birds. But an imaginative instructor can do much to make training on clays as realistic as possible. The 'walk-up', the 'grouse butts' and the high tower are the student gameshot's best classroom. In the walk-up the student will learn how to walk safely with a loaded gun and how not to be 'caught on the wrong foot'. The grouse butts will develop the confidence to keep cool when things become fast and furious. The tower (if equipped with a variable trap) will teach rapid target assessment and the need for good footwork. Use mini and midi targets. If no tower is available, an angling auto-trap or a conventional trap and trapper may be placed behind a hedge or bank. Sometimes it may be appropriate to put more than two birds in the air. If you present 3 or 4 targets and mix the sizes, you will encourage the client to pick his or her birds and to maintain good visual discipline.

You must also teach the game shot to deal with occasions when the ground is less than ideal, as is often the case in the field. Potential pigeon and duck shooters will want to shoot from simulated hides – both sitting and standing. With beginners you will include things like climbing over the odd fence as progress is made from stand to stand.

Instructing game shooting – other points

Although game shooting requires a faster more instinctive style of shooting than clay shooting, the game shot must not rush. Most game shots are too hurried in their movements, often mounting too early. Another common and related problem is lack of muzzle control. You must get the idea across that the tip of the muzzles may be placed on the bird at an early stage, but that does not mean that tracking of the bird is extended or that the stock is brought to the face and shoulder immediately. This should happen smoothly as the swing and

Shooting behind the line

One important skill for the driven game shot is learning to take a bird 'behind the line' safely. This is the procedure I teach based on a Stanbury style stance:

Keeping an eye out for flankers and pickers up, take your first shot forward in the normal manner with the weight over the left (front) foot.

Mark your second target. If it should not be shot forward, you must decide whether you will turn to the right or the left (the decision is usually made simply on whether the bird is going to the right or left of your position).

Keeping concentration on the line of the second bird, bring the gun into an almost vertical position (if you are wearing a cap the rib of the gun should almost touch the peak - just imagine you're a Guardsman on parade!).

Now one may begin the turn. The left foot leads. A step is taken by the left foot to the right or left (depending on which way you decided to turn) and rearwards. After the left foot initiates the turn, the right (rear) foot rotates rearwards on its ball.

With the feet approximately at 1 o'clock (left) and 3 o'clock (right) to the target, the muzzles come down on to the line of the bird and the shot is taken in the normal manner.

This all sounds fairly complicated because it has been split into stages to make it simpler to explain, in reality it is a continuous and natural motion and precise positions will depend on individual physique. The most important point to emphasise is the need to keep the muzzles well up during the turn.

Double gunning

Game shooters should be taught techniques for rapid reloading (one of the simplest is to use a quilted shooting vest with large open pockets rather than a jacket). Some will want to learn how to handle pairs of guns. This is a skill which requires considerable practice from both Gun and loader to achieve safe control and good timing. Some points to watch here include:

The right handed shot always changes guns to the right side, the left-handed shot to the left.

The safety catch must be applied before passing the gun back.

Assuming a shooter using his right shoulder, the fired gun is handed back with the right hand (the loader taking it with his left), the fresh gun is taken with the extended left arm/hand (the loader standing just to the right and slightly behind the shooter).

Guns must be kept pointing up vertically as they pass from hand to hand.

The shooter keeps looking forward throughout the process.

The loader must make sure that when he is opening the gun, the muzzles are safely pointing into the ground, and not down the line.

When no second target is visible the shooter will pass his gun back even though only a single shot has been fired.

Teaching and learning double gunning is great fun, but one must as always keep an eye on safety. Once the client is competent in the basics, start building up the pressure. Speed up target release so they are forced to take some birds without perfect footwork, and others behind the line.

Wingshooting

Until the mid seventeenth century, birds were shot on the ground or water or while perching. From about the mid seventeenth century the French developed a new method of 'shooting flying'; it was brought to England, together with a new type of light-weight gun, by the courtiers of Charles II (although birds continued to be shot in the old way for generations). The challenging new sport rapidly became popular amongst the landed gentry who had a particular passion for partridge shooting (which harsh Restoration game laws kept a most exclusive quarry). Shooting flying became even more fashionable during the 18th century and was made easier by the rapid development of more efficient firearms. The introduction of the patent breech (late eighteenth century), the percussion system (early nineteenth) and reliable breech-loaders (circa 1850) ensured that wingshooting became a major sport in Victorian and Edwardian England. In the early twenty-first century it is one of the most popular participatory sports with more than 600,000 shotgun certificate holders in England and Wales.

---

mount progress. Encourage your students to take pride in the elegance and rhythm of their shooting. Explain that one does not shoot everything that flies overhead, one picks one's birds. The psychology is one of relaxed control, not frantic slashing and poking. Adrenaline tends to cause technique to break down even in better shots. Good training can do much to prevent this. I have noted in the field that low birds driven straight towards the shooter are easily over-led (much more often than one might think). Mid- and long-range birds are *usually* missed behind but often off-line too. Poor footwork and poor use of the front hand cause many misses as does poor visual contact and poor committment to the shot (hesitation). Eye dominance is a criticial issue for some game shots. Those who need to squint an eye – and in the game shooting context it should not be squinted too early – will usually be able to engage straight driven birds at low to middle heights; beyond this many run into problems (as they lose sight of the bird) and may be best advised to turn and take the bird as a crossover (ensuring, of course, that the muzzles are kept well up at all times).

NOTES

1   Oiling is another issue with semi-automatic shotguns. Some say they should be left dry, other that they should be well lubricated. The best advice is to keep these guns lightly oiled, some designs are certainly more lubrication sensitive than other. Over oiling is always a mistake.

2   I have found that many well co-ordinated clients are capable of being taught gun-down from the start, but I would not suggest novice instructors attempt this.

3   I often use the analogy an imaginary 'gate post' going through the front shoulder, front hip and front knee of my clients – beginners have a tendency to push out their hips to the front and to arch the back to help them support the weight of the gun; not only is their stance incorrect, they fail to use the front arm properly.

4   As teaching progresses, I often find myself using the phrase 'touch [the target] and push [ahead].

5   Finger pointing would not usually continue beyond 4-5 birds in total; if it needs to, something is wrong – probably the client's understanding of the gap required (easily rectified) or your diagnosis of eye dominance (again, easily rectified, but only if you recognise your error).

6   Similarly, if birds are being thrown low for any reason, a low hold may be required.

CHAPTER 11

Gun knowledge

As a shooting instructor, you will be expected to know guns. A working knowledge of the history of sporting guns will be useful – it locates in time and space many technical points and creates a framework for understanding the complexities of gun design. You must have a 'hands-on' familiarity with the classic action types so that you may handle guns confidently and so that you can answer questions about them with authority. You also need to know about cartridges, basic shotgun ballistics and the rules and marks of proof. These subjects need to be researched systematically. There are various things which you can do to accelerate the learning process and which will supplement the information presented here:

1   Handle and, if possible, shoot unfamiliar guns whenever the opportunity arises.

2   Spend time at the pattern plates. If you are interested in comparative shotgun ballistics, you may find a chronograph a worthwhile investment (their prices have dropped a great deal in recent years).

3   Make the effort to read the test reports on new guns and cartridges appearing in the shooting press (and keep records of them for future use).

4   If terms like Purdey bolt, snap action, third bite, doll's head, Greener cross bolt or the Scott spindle are a mystery, make the effort to find out what they are. Similarly, learn the language of the gun trade: lumps, flats, face, bar, wall, fence, strap, knuckle, hook, loop, dogs, bolt, tumbler, striker, bridle, sear, bent, pin, saddle, sideclip, ball and so on. If you do not understand a particular gun's mechanism (or something about the barrels or stock) ask a friendly gunsmith to explain it.

5   Visit (making appointments where good manners dictate) manufacturers, importers, the proof houses, museums, private collections, auction houses, and, not least, trade shows. The annual SHOT Show in the United States is an experience never to be forgotten. Imagine an event on the scale of the Ideal Home Show entirely devoted to guns and shooting and you will have an idea of it.

6   Get wired up and use the Internet – it's an amazing research tool and shooting is particularly well represented.

7   Build up a library of technical books and any other publications which may be used as references, e.g., catalogues, magazines, brochures and auction catalogues.

The shotgun, a simple definition
A shotgun is a smooth bore weapon which fires a cartridge which typically con-

Starting a technical library

Where does one begin? I shall be as pragmatic as possible. W.W. *Greener's The Gun and its Development* should be on top of your shopping list, as should Burrard's 3-volume masterpiece *The Modern Shotgun* (published in facsimile by the Field Press). *The Modern Sportsman's Gun and Rifle* by J.H. Walsh, *Practical Hints on Shooting* by '20-Bore' (rare, but a mine of information), Teasedale Buckell's *Experts on Guns and Shooting*, Lancaster's *Art of Shooting* and Colonel Peter Hawker's *Instructions to Young Sportsmen* should also be high priority items. As far as more recent volumes are concerned, Churchill's *Gameshooting*, Stanbury and Carlisle's *Shotgun Marksmanship*, Fred *Etchen's Common Sense Shotgun Shooting*, Gough Thomas's *Guns and Cartridges for Game and Clays*, *Cradock's Manual of Clayshooting* and Richard Akehurst's *Game Guns and Rifles* are all important references. I also think David Butler's *The American Shotgun* is especially good (one of the clearest and most concise technical works on the shotgun) and Bob Brister's celebrated *Shotgunning: the Art and the Science* is another must along with Michael McIntosh's excellent *Best Guns* and Don Zutz's *The Double Shotgun*.

Geoffrey Boothroyd's *The Shotgun: History and Development* is a readable and reliable historical primer and good place to start before really getting to grips with Greener and Walsh. Much the same might be said of Crudgington and Baker's two volumes on *The British Shotgun*, the first of which covers the period from 1850-1870 and the second, 1871-1890, the era when the English gun as we know it today was perfected (a third volume was promised but has not appeared yet). My little book, *Gunfitting: the Quest for Perfection*, covers that subject in some detail (and also considers the development of the stock in some historical detail). Pollard's *History of Firearms*, edited by Claude Blair, is a useful and wide-ranging general reference, while Richard Beaumont's *Purdey's the Guns and the Family* is a fascinating insight into the British gun trade during its golden age and also contains a lot of useful information on the development of the much copied Purdey gun. *London Gunmakers* by Nigel Brown is also an excellent and informative work filled with valuable information about the gun trade in and around the metropolis.

Be selective when you buy books. Many books, old and new, only regurgitate the same basic information. You do not need to spend a fortune. I buy books to use rather than to collect so a less than perfect copy at a reasonable price is good enough for me. Mine is a working library in which perfect copies would soon get dog-eared. Start with the classics. The books by Greener and Churchill mentioned above would be a good first purchase, together with Gough Thomas's *Shotguns and Cartridges for Game and Clays* and Cradock's *Manual of Clay Shooting*. You should also subscribe to several magazines and make an effort to keep up with new products. I have found it very useful to read periodicals from the United States as well as those from the UK. Generally speaking, the American magazines include more technical information than their British counterparts.

---

tains small spherical shot (although other types of shot are known and some shotguns may fire a single ball or slug). A shotgun is to be distinguished from a rifle which has spiral grooves in the barrel to impart a spin to a single bullet.

Basic mechanics of the shotgun: the side-by-side

Side-by-sides are made both as boxlocks and sidelocks. Boxlocks have simplicity on their side, but sidelocks may be made with finer trigger pulls (down to 2 lb or even less – though such light pulls can hardly be recommended) and provide more space for ornamentation. The Anson and Deeley design (first patented 1875) is almost universal as far as British boxlocks are concerned.

Cocking on opening, it is brilliantly simple and relatively cheap to make (in plainer grades at least). Sidelocks are constructed to a variety of patterns. Most British and foreign guns copy either the Purdey (patented 1880 by Frederick Beesley and sold to Purdey for £55) or, more commonly, the simpler Holland and Holland design. The Purdey is especially ingenious. Unlike the H&H gun, it cocks on closing – so that the leaf mainsprings are not left compressed when the gun is disassembled. Moreover, different limbs of the same spring power both the tumbler and the gun's self-opening feature[1].

Most sidelock shotguns are so called 'bar' actions in that a recess is machined in the wall of the action body (or bar) to accommodate the main-spring. In 'back' actions, seen on some older guns – and also, used for strength, on many double rifles[2] – the spring is positioned to the rear of the lock. One may usually identify a bar action by noting the pin visible at the front of the lock-plate; viewed from the other side, this is the peg upon which the mainspring locates. If no pin is visible there are three possible conclusions, the gun may have a back action, it may have false sideplates disguising a boxlock or it may be a 'pinless' back-action gun – a style of construction favoured in some very high quality guns.

Both boxlocks and sidelocks will have a bolting mechanism to lock the barrels in the closed position. In the vast majority of cases this will operate on the Purdey Double Bite system patented in 1863. It utilises two lugs, properly called 'lumps', positioned beneath the barrels at the breech end. The front one has a circular recess – the 'hook' – which literally hooks on the 'hinge-pin' (also called cross-pin) near the action's front or 'knuckle'. In both lumps a slot or 'bite' is cut. On closing the gun a skeletonised bolt slides forward engaging the bites in each lump and locking the action and barrels together. Some guns will also have a top extension (or in the case of over and unders, top extensions) as part of their bolting mechanism. The idea is to increase strength, but some extensions are more decorative than practical.

Opening in both box and sidelocks will usually be controlled by a Scott-style spindle and top lever (patented 1865). This arrangement, like the Purdey double bite with which it is so often combined, is near universal today. There

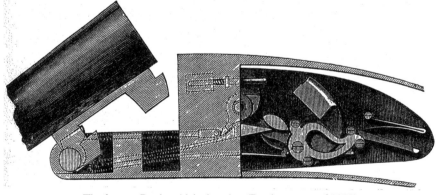

The famous Purdey sidelock action (Beesley patent of 1880)
(from *The Gun and Its Development* by W.W.Greener).

PLATE 21

(above) This is a Beretta 682 used by Chris Cradock for instruction. Chris had several stocks for it to suit both right- and left-handers; note also the adjustable plate. Chris also made much use of a Beretta 303 *(below)* for instructional purposes. It is one of my favourite guns too.

Gunfitting in the Kemen factory in the Basque country of Spain. Providing proper safety checks are made, this sort of dry fitting is useful but it should be combined with observation and test on the range to ensure reliable results.

PLATE 22

(above) I have found the little Webley .410 bolt-action an excellent gun for the instruction of young shots when equipped with a shortened stock and comb raiser. It handles well (unlike many cheap break-action .410s) and recoil is very modest.

(below) The Kennedy Competition (made by Pcrugini and Visini in Italy) is typical of a new generation of competition guns inspired by the Perazzi detachable trigger lock gun with Boss-style bolting.

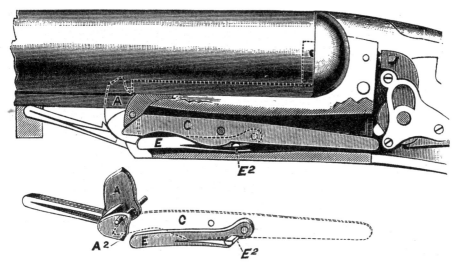

Southgate's famous ejector mechanism (from *The Gun and Its Development* by W.W.Greener).

are, however, a number of other mechanisms seen in old guns. Jones' rotary underlever was common before the Purdey double bite/Scott spindle combination became predominant. The side-lever was once quite popular (Grant were especially famous for them) and has been used more recently on cheap .410 side-by-sides of Spanish origin. Other mechanisms include hingeing under- and top-levers, the former being pushed down, the latter pushed up to open the gun.

Two other hammerless action types are worthy of brief mention, the Darne – in which the barrels do not hinge down but slide forward to allow for loading – and the trigger-plate action in which the lock-work is carried on a plate, the bulk of which is behind the action body. Apart from being used in several high quality Scottish 'round action' guns such as the Dickson, this type of mechanism has also proved popular with mass market manufacturers and is frequently encountered on cheaper Spanish side-by-sides. Hammer guns may also be encountered. These may be made either with bar or back action locks and all the opening mechanisms mentioned (not to mention some other really obscure ones). Early breech-loading hammer guns may have non-rebounding locks and require extra care in handling because of it. Rebounding locks, first patented by Stanton in 1867, kept the hammer slightly raised – so that the striker was not forced forward in its uncocked position – and incorporated a safety lock in the action bar so that an accidental blow could not drive the strik-er into the back of a loaded cartridge.

Over-and-unders
Like side-by-sides, over-and-unders are made as sidelocks, boxlocks and as triggerplate actions (Beretta 68 series). Moreover, many modern over-and-unders, though they may be described as boxlocks, are made in similar style to a trigger plate gun with the bulk of the mechanism contained between top and

bottom straps rather than in the body of the action, as in the true boxlock. Some guns, like the Browning Superposed (the last design of John Moses Browning, first marketed in about 1930) and the Merkel, have a full width hinge pin, others, like the Beretta and Perazzi, utilise stud pins engaging recesses on the side of the barrels. This 'bifurcated lump' system was perfected by Boss and Woodward before the First World War (bifurcate simply means to divide into two branches). Its great advantage is that action height may be minimised, improving the handling qualities of the gun and reducing the effects of recoil on firing the top barrel (the higher it is relative the shoulder, the greater the rotational effect on firing).

Over-and-unders may be bolted in a variety of ways. Boss guns incorporate wedges on the inner walls of the action which bear against the barrel lumps – a system much copied in better quality guns such as those of Perazzi, Kemen and Gamba – as well as having squared bolts emerging from the breech face and engaging bites on either side of the chambers. Woodward guns have a unique tongue and groove system locking barrels and action together on closing as well as squared bolts coming out of the action face and engaging bites on either side of the bottom chamber mouth. (The most copied feature of the Woodward design, however, are the simple but ingenious stud pins at the knuckle of the action).

Berettas have small conical bolts which emerge from the action face and mate with circular bites to either side of the top chamber as well as shoulders on their barrels which engage recesses in the top rear of the action wall. Brownings have a full width bolt which comes out of the bottom of the action face and mates with a slot bite beneath the bottom chamber mouth. This system is much copied. Some over-and-unders also have barrel extensions and cross bolting, although they are hardly necessary in a modern gun and may – if made large (as they are on many German over-and-unders) – impede fast reloading.

Single triggers

These are a feature of most modern over-and-unders (and, of course, some side-by-sides). Basically, there are two types, 'inertia' triggers in which recoil energy is used to operate the mechanism and 'mechanical' triggers which are dependent on trigger pressure alone. Mechanical single triggers are usually made on the 'three-pull' system; which requires that the trigger is pulled three times, not twice, before the second barrel fires. There is because there is an involuntary second pull on firing the gun, without taking it into account in the trigger design, the gun would always 'double'. There is a slight, but significant, advantage in having a single trigger on a competition gun (provided it is reliable). Instructors should be aware that those used to single triggers may experience some difficulty when first exposed to double triggers. This is quickly overcome with practise. My own scores with a double trigger gun are now almost identical to those with a single trigger. On side-by-sides, double triggers are usually preferable because of their reliability.

A number of better quality over-and-unders now incorporate detachable trigger locks. Perazzi are famous for this style of gun, but they are also made by

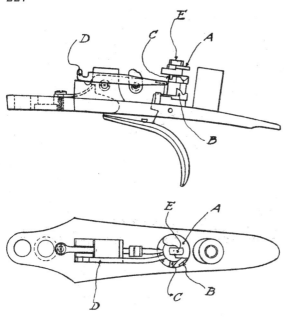

The Boss single trigger mechanism (from *The Gun and Its
Development* by W.W.Greener).

Kemen, Gamba, Rottweil, Holland & Holland and others. The Rottweil guns, unlike the others mentioned,[3] make use of coil springs to power the firing mechanism. One advantage to a detachable trigger is that two trigger mechanisms may be carried (which can provide an instant cure if a trigger problem afflicts a gun in competition). It is also a useful way to disable a gun when travelling. However, one must make sure that the trigger pulls in the spare unit match those in the primary unit otherwise timing may be seriously affected when the mechanisms are exchanged.

Single trigger malfunctions

From time to time, a student will look at you blankly after firing a single shot at a pair of targets and cry, 'It won't go!' while looking befuddled. The second barrel has failed to fire. The first thing to do, in this typically confused situation, is to make sure the muzzles of the gun are immediately controlled (confusion can lead to sudden turning). Once the gun is dealt with safely, one may consider what went wrong. Assuming that it is not a fault in the design or manufacture of the trigger, there are three typical causes of single trigger malfunction: the client may not be letting go of the trigger between shots; he stock may be too long (aggravating the former problem); finally, inertia triggers may fail to operate because the cartridges are too lightly loaded to operate the mechanism. This may be remedied either by changing the trigger spring (Beretta, for example have two strengths for 68 series guns) or by using a more powerful cartridge.

Release triggers

In America many Trap shots – especially those who suffer from flinching – prefer to use release triggers. Disconcerting devices until one is used to them, they allow for or the gun to be fired by an act of muscular relaxation rather than contraction. They may be fitted to either double or single barrel guns (and to semi-automatics). From the point of view of the instructor, the release trigger has evident safety implications. Although these devices tend to be used by experienced shots, anyone specialising in Trap or working in the U.S.A. needs to know how to deal with them. To disarm a single or double gun with an activated release trigger, the simplest method – though it is a little awkward initially and requires the greatest care throughout the procedure – is as follows:

1 Control the muzzles safely downrange and keep controlling them.
2 Now, while maintaining trigger pressure, squeeze the stock under the armpit.
3 From this controlled position, remove the front hand from the fore-end and, bringing it over the top of the barrels and action, operate the top lever.
4 Once the gun is fully open (and you must make sure that it is open to full gape), release trigger pressure and continue or unload as required.

Semi-automatics

There are, essentially, four types of semi-automatic, long-recoil designs (such as the Browning A5[4]), short-recoil guns (such as the Browning 'Double Automatic'[5]), gas-operated weapons (such as the Remington 1100 and Beretta 300 series) and inertia designs (such as the innovative, rotary-bolt, Benelli). The barrel on both long and short recoil designs move – several inches in the case of the former, an inch or so in the case of the short-recoil gun. The essential difference between the two is that in the long-recoil semi-automatic, the barrel and bolt travel rearward, locked together, the full length of the receiver. At the rear of the recoil stroke, the bolt is retained while the barrel returns forward, sliding off the empty cartridge case and then ejecting it. When the barrel is fully forward, the bolt is tripped to spring forward and chamber the next cartridge. With the short recoil system, the barrel travels rearward only far enough to impart energy to the bolt, whereupon the bolt is cammed out of lockup and carries on rearward alone, extracting the empty cartridge case from the chamber of the barrel and ejecting it from the gun.

I am not especially fond of either design, though good in their day they have been superseded by guns which are less cartridge sensitive. Fixed barrel gas guns – which bleed off some of the gases generated by the propellent to cycle the action predominate today. The latest generation – the Beretta 390 and 391, Browning Gold and Remington 11-87 – incorporate a venting mechanism on or near their gas collar, so that excess gas pressure is simply dumped and the action may be set up to function reliably on low powered cartridges without increasing strain on the action unduly when more powerful loads are used. Gas-operated guns are increasingly popular. Because of their low recoil, they can make excellent guns for instruction.

ADVISING CLIENTS ON GUN SELECTION

As a shooting instructor, you will frequently be asked to advise clients on gun selection. This is a complex business and requires considerable study if one is to give useful answers.

THE SIDE-BY-SIDE VERSUS THE OVER-AND-UNDER

Is it possible to say whether the side-by-side or the over-and-under is the better gun? Traditionally, the classic English and Scottish game gun has been a side-by-side 12-bore. In recent years, the over-and-under has become very popular both for clay and game shooting. The truth is, both guns have their strengths. I will place my neck on the block and say that I think the over-and-under is, generally, the better gun. The best game shots I know use them and they are indisputably the gun of choice for most serious clay shooting competition. In the past, all sorts of tosh was written to support the bogus notion that the over-and-under was inferior to the traditional side-by-side[6].What is written here is intended to set the record straight.[7]

Advantages of the over-and-under configuration
Over-and-unders have the advantage of a single sighting plane and tend to control recoil more effectively. Although there is still some lingering prejudice against them in game shooting circles, many of the finest game shots of recent times shots have chosen the over-and-under, Sir Joseph Nickerson immediately springs to mind; he shot a trio of over-and-under Purdey Woodward 28-bores. Moreover, there can be no argument that the over-and-under reigns supreme on the clay shooting circuits. Not since the days of Percy Stanbury has a side-by-side been seen regularly taking the prizes in the big competitions like the British Open.

Disadvantages of the over-and-under
First, it can be more complicated to manufacture than the side-by-side and therefore more expensive in comparable qualities. Another potential – and a particular irritation when one is game shooting – is the gape. Many over-and-unders do not open quite wide enough for really rapid reloading (although the problem is eliminated in the new Holland & Holland guns). Moreover, some over-and-unders are too high in profile (especially those made with a full-width hinge pin) and can be ungainly. The weight of many mass-produced over-and-unders can be a disadvantage as far as the game shooter is concerned (hence, as far as mass produced guns are concerned, the 20-bore over-and-under warrants serious consideration for game shooting).

The over-and-under: a modern invention?
The over-and-under has also been criticised as a modern invention. This argument was put forward by misinformed gameshots, apparently unaware that some of the very earliest double guns were configured with one barrel on top of the other. Sophisticated over-and-under game guns were made in the mid-1600s. Percussion lock over-and-under shotguns were developed in the second quarter of nineteenth century. Greener built an experimental side-opening over-and-under shotgun in the 1870s, Dickson created another, a most elegant side-opener, in 1888 and Boss and Woodward both introduced their famous low profile, drop-action, guns before the First World War.

Conclusions
There are beautiful side-by-sides and horrible over-and-unders. However, the over-and-under offers obvious benefits if well conceived. Those arguing about

the relative merits of side-by-sides and over-and-unders have often failed to note that one cannot compare guns of different weights or guns of different qualities. It is no good making pronouncements on the relative game shooting merits of an eight-plus pound competition over-and-under and a six and half pound side-by-side game gun. My own preference for game shooting is the over-and-under, my tools of choice being a 30 in. fixed choke Beretta 687 20-bore and a 28 in. barrelled 686 multi-choke 12-bore (though I have found one with especially light barrels). Much of my competitive clay shooting has been with a 31½ in. barrelled Perazzi or a 32 in. barrelled Kemen (both fixed choke guns but weighing 8 lb or more). More recently I have tended to favour long-barrelled semi-automatics (most especially by 32 in. Beretta 303).

REPEATERS

As with over-and-unders, there has been a considerable prejudice against repeaters in Britain. Nevertheless, pumps may be used for rough or vermin shooting and in the United States are popular for both clays (though less so than a generation ago) and live quarry shooting. In this country pumps are not as popular and the subject of prejudice, some of it irrational. Self-loading shotguns, however, are becoming more accepted and offer excellent value for money. The most commonly encountered repeaters in the United Kingdom are gas operated semi-automatics like the Beretta 303/390/391, the Browning Gold, and the Remington 1100 and11-87. The simple old 303 is my particular favourite, however, because of its handling qualities and because there is a 32 in. sporting model. (Beretta would be well-advised to produce 32 in. tubes for the 391).

Gas guns – the first of which was the High Standard which appeared in 1956 – can be excellent guns for clay shooting. They are particularly suited to Skeet and Sporting, for instruction and also for some forms of live quarry shooting (pigeon shooting and wildfowling for example). They can be a little awkward on a trap layout, however and they are not accepted on formal game shoots. This is because the gun cannot, immediately, be seen to be clear by companions (a problem which, prejudice apart, might easily be overcome with the use of a breech plug and streamer).

I am a real fan of gas-operated semi-automatics provided they function reliably and are also reasonably well balanced. They were underrated in the United Kingdom for some years, though the swing of fashion has been in their favour again recently (twenty or thirty years ago there was little doubt that Remington 1100 was considered THE Skeet gun). Gas guns may also be much improved by modifications such as trigger tuning and over-boring. Firms like Seminole and Angle Port in the USA make a speciality of this. One simple modification is worth noting: enlargement of the gas port holes[8]. When done by an expert (and no one else should attempt it), this can solve the cycling problems which can beset some gas-operated guns when used with 24 g and lighter loaded 28 g shells.

The Benneli, rotary bolt, inertia action guns are also worth serious consideration. The design, which incorporates twin steel locking lugs, is ingenious and the guns are extremely well made in my experience. It dispenses with the need for gas bleeds, complex linkages and pistons. It is worth noting, however, that older Bennelis were not intended for light loaded cartridges. They can make excellent field guns but can be frustrating if one wants to use cartridges with modest payload and pressure. The latest Bennelis have been adjusted to shoot light-loaded cartridges. As for the old style, recoil-operated semi automatics, though good guns in their day, most are ill balanced (the Browning Double Automatic being a notable exception) and rather awkward in use. Long-recoil guns have a curious 'double-shuffle' when fired. This, of course, is caused by the barrel and bolt moving back together for several inches during the firing cycle. A drawback common to all repeaters, and especially gas operated semi-autos, is that they are tiresome to clean.

So much for barrel configuration and action type, what about bore size?

THE 20-BORE VERSUS THE 12

The 20-bore tends to be made lighter than the 12 and consequently, it tends to swing more quickly. This can be an advantage in a game gun, but it can be a definite disadvantage in a competition clay gun – which is why serious NSSA Skeet shots often make use of special light weight alloy tubes which convert their heavy 12-bore guns into even heavier 20, 28 or .410s as required – and for any shot who has a tendency to rush their shots.

As far as game guns are concerned, the scale of the 20-bore gun and the pro-file of its action are appealing. With most 12-bore over-and-unders (notable exceptions being the Boss and Woodward pattern weapons) one has impres-sion that one is shooting a bulkier gun than a side-by-side of the same bore dimension. Because the action is notably smaller, the stock of the 20-bore gun is often better proportioned, allowing for a more graceful gun. Some of the best proportioned over-and-under guns being massed produced at present are 20s.

We have already noted that 20-bores can swing too quickly. Their light weight can also effect their recoil. Some hold the mistaken belief that the gun with a smaller bore size will automatically recoil less. This is not true, as with any firearm, the key factors are the weight of the gun, the stock shape, the pel-let payload and the powder charge and type. A lightweight 20 firing a heavy load can kick like a mule. Conversely, a medium weight gas-operated 20-bore semi-automatic with a sensibly designed stock can be one of the friendliest guns with which to introduce a young person to shooting. It has the advantage in this teaching context of low recoil, and low weight at the muzzles. As dis-cussed above, light weight guns can over-swing, but for teaching those with under-developed muscles in the weak or front arm, less weight forwards can be a very useful feature.

What about killing power? Is there a disadvantage in the relatively small pay-load cartridge? In the United States $1^{1}/_{8}$ oz and even $1^{1}/_{4}$ magnum loads are common (the latter in 3 in. chamber guns), in the UK normal 20-bore load-ings range from $^{3}/_{4}$ to 1 oz. I have found the 1 oz load extremely effective gameshooting. If one gets really technical about cartridges, a supporter of the 12-bore might note that the shot column in a 20-bore cartridge must be longer for the same weight of shot, and that therefore the pellets in the 20 are more likely to suffer deformation in the bore and to string out as they proceed towards the target[9]. My practical experience is that this is not a significant problem. If one is a fan of lighter loaded cartridges for game shooting, the modern 20-bore would seem the practical equal of the 12-bore in many circumstances. It is certainly a lot of fun to use.

The most significant disadvantage of the 20-bore is that, like all small bores, they tend to be a little harder to shoot. This is not so much because of any significant ballistic inferiority, but rather because the guns tend be light and therefore a little harder to control. It is less of a problem in over-and-unders, and, in all cases, it can be minimised – but not eliminated – by the use of longer barrels (28 or 30 rather than 26 in.). I have shot more cartridges than I care to remember through both 12 and 20s of all possible types. Looking at the easily verifiable statistics obtained on a sporting clays layout, my scores when using a 20 over-and-under are consistently about 5% less than my scores with an over-and-under 12 (similar to my scores with a side-by-side 12). For 16-bore see footnote.[10]

28-BORES AND .410S

Smaller guns are harder still to shoot, both because of their handling qualities and because of a real payload disadvantage as far as cartridges are concerned. It has always seemed strange that we force smallbore guns on ladies and young shots in the mistaken belief that we are automatically making things easier. In truth, shooting a 28-bore well at driven game might be compared to jumping fences at the gallop whilst riding side-saddle. Wonderful to see but not the easiest way to do it! The 28 is useful for walking-up, however, and particularly appealing in longer barrel lengths as far as adult users are concerned.

CONCLUSIONS

The final choice must always rest with the individual. My prejudices are clear: I like the twenty for game shooting, *ab initio* instruction of young people and non-competitive clays. For serious clay shooting and and mid and long range live quarry shooting the twelve still reigns supreme. Over-and-unders are to be generally recommended for game and clays. Gas operated semi-automatics warrant serious consideration for instruction, competitive clays, pigeon shooting and wildfowling and are especially suited to anyone who experiences problems with recoil or who is shooting on a tight budget. Side-by-sides are elegant and offer a special challenge.

SPECIFIC GUNS

Let us now consider some specific shooting disciplines and the guns best suited to them, as if one were going out to make a purchase. We will start with *game shooting*. And, having noted my prejudice in favour of the over-and-under, I will start with side-by-sides as a gesture of appeasement to those traditionalists who prefer that configuration.

If money were no object I would consider the best London makers first. Best guns bought new or second-hand hold their value well (which must be a consideration when paying ten or twenty thousand pounds per gun). If I were looking for a pair of classic side-by-side game guns, therefore, top of my list would be a pair of Purdey, Boss, Woodward, Grant[11] or Hollands. Ideally, they would be 'sleepers' made between 1900 and 1939 which had seen very little use (and this must be confirmed by minute examination by a competent person).

If I wanted to spend less, I would find a similar pair of best quality guns by a less fashionable, but still well recognised maker. There are many wonderful guns available at relatively modest cost because they lack the right London name. One's priority should always be craftsmanship and condition: far better a pristine Evans, Beesley, Watson[12] or Hussey than a tarted up, but essentially knackered Purdey or Holland & Holland. As far as Birmingham is concerned, Powell and Westley Richards made, and still make, guns of the very highest quality (as did W & C Scott – a much under-rated name). If my preference were for something a little unusual, I might opt for a brace of Grant or Atkin sidelever guns, or, if I favoured short barrels for gameshooting, a pair of the celebrated Churchill XXVs. As far as older English sidelocks are concerned, I think many are now overpriced. I would not consider a gun or guns with marginal barrels in respect to wall thickness (yet it is amazing how many are sold and how little it seems to affect price – *Caveat Emptor*).

If I were considering a new single gun (or, indeed, a pair) without consideration of cost, I would probably go for the relatively new Holland & Holland Royal over-and-under 20-bore if my only concern was shooting: I have found it a true delight to use. The Woodward style over and under guns made by Purdey are also magnificent in 20 bore. David McKay Brown's over-and-under has attractive, compact, lines and shoots well. William Evans, Cogswell and Harrison, Wilkes, Holloway and Naughton, Watson and Churchill are all now building best quality over-and-unders.

If I wanted a spectacular work of art to be treasured by future generations, I might consult Peter Nelson, Peter Chapman, Hartmann and Weiss (Hamburg) or John Richardson, all of whom have hard earned reputations for superb quality work. If my pocket were not quite so deep and practical use was the first consideration, I would carefully consider the detachable trigger lock Holland over-and-unders and the first class boxlocks made by Tony White (he is also developing a new trigger plate over and under). The best Italian guns – those made by companies like Abbiatico and Salvinelli, Bosis, Bertuzzi, Desenzani, Fabri, Perugini and Piotti – also warrant very serious consideration[13].

The engraving on high grade Italian guns is especially good. SO Berettas 20-bores can be exquisite in high grades (to my eyes, the 12 looks a little wide in the fences). I might also be tempted by a Perazzi 20 (especially if I could get one with light 32 in. tubes – my own eccentric preference). Coming down a few pegs, the Beretta EELL sideplated over-and-under guns offer especially good value (the limited edition Jubilee model is particularly eye-catching). Paul Roberts imports a range of B. Rizzini 'Artemis' boxlock over-and-unders; the plainer grades come with attractive colour case hardened actions and the top of the range EL is equipped with outstandingly engraved side plates and exceptional wood.

Boxlocks side-by-sides often seem undervalued today, especially when the name is not in vogue. I have always been fond of the better Webleys such as the 701 and 702 – better finished versions of the popular 700. In small gauges these guns are especially desirable. Plain grade side-by-sides (such as the 700) are often a relative bargain in today's inflated market. One must, however, take the greatest care in assessing their condition (particulary with old guns). The cost of working on a quite pedestrian boxlock are similar to those of working on a £20,000 sidelock. If one has any concerns, no risk should be taken – rectification may well cost more than the gun is worth. I would also avoid as a matter of principle any older single trigger side-by-sides (boxlock or sidelock) because reliable, single triggers on English bench-made guns are the exception.

If I were looking for a sound, attractive, game gun at medium cost, I would consider buying a second-hand, but near new AyA No 1 or Model 56 or a Browning Superposed (the Swan neck stock A1 has always appealed to me). If the budget was even more limited, I would consider the AyA No. 2 or a Beretta 686/687 (all of which are excellent workhorses). Recently, I acquired a beautiful, hand made, Vostock over-and-under game gun which is notable not only for its excellent quality, but for a most unusual aluminium action and extra full recess (not retro) chokes (its only drawback is that it is, like most Russian guns, a non-ejector). If I were in the market for a real budget gun I would consider a second-hand AyA boxlock, a Miroku over-and-under or a Winchester 101 Game. For bargain hunters, Spanish non-ejector side-by-sides can be bought in near-new condition these days very cheaply. No one seems to want them. Single barrel guns are often scrapped. Much the same fate befell hammer guns a couple of generations ago. I can remember buying one at Thomas Bland's for £5 as a teenager, Wally Casely, the manager, noting, 'You might as well have it, Michael, otherwise we'll only put a hammer through the barrels.' One wonders how many others suffered that sad fate.

As far as **barrel length** for game shooting is concerned I would advise 28 in. as the norm for 12-bores and 28 or 30 in. for 20-bores. Shorter barrelled 12-bores – 27, 26 and 25 in. guns – can be useful for the occasional shooter (they are more instinctive to use). Short and medium barrel lengths may also be better suited to those of small stature – height is a characteristic which should be taken into consideration when selecting barrels. Long barrels will appeal to the wildfowler (30 in. may be used for most things if required, 32 in. is best restricted to the foreshore). Longer barrels will also be favoured by the shot who wants to shoot clays as well as game. 30 in. barrels are to be preferred if clay shooting is to become the main interest, 28 in. will usually be better if game shooting is the first priority. **Barrel weight** is as important as – and, indeed, directly related to – barrel length. A game gun must not have heavy barrels. Nevertheless, excessive barrel weight is a problem in many mass produced guns marketed for field use (especially those made with thick barrel walls to accommodate multi-chokes). Overall weight in game guns should not be excessive, nor should they be too light or recoil will be a problem. A twelve bore side-by-side should fall between 6¼ and 7 lb, an over-and-under 12-bore between 6½ and 7½ lb. For twenty bores, the figures might be 6 to 6 ½ for a side-by-side and 6 to 7 pounds for an over-and-under (similar to a 12-bore side-by-side). Guns can be made lighter, but their are no benefits to be gained.

Rib type is not that important, my preference is a narrow, 6 mm, flat, file cut rib on an over-and-under intended for game and for a traditional concave rib on a side-by-side game gun. I hold one particular objection, however – raised, ramped, ribs for game shooting, especially when they are attached to side-by-sides. Winchester used to make an excellent gun called the Model 23 which, in my opinion, was spoilt by its raised rib – it hindered natural pointing. I once shot a 23 converted to a flat, file-cut, pigeon-rib, by an English gunmaker and it was completely transformed.

Sensible **chokes** for general game shooting might be improved and quarter or improved and half. My own preference, however, is to combine an open first barrel with a tightly choked second (¾ or full). With this old fashioned combination one may shoot at short to mid ranged birds most effectively to one's front and pick out longer targets in leisurely style when the need or opportunity arises. Finally, when buying guns (as when buying cars and houses), always consider selling them! If you buy a classic gun, in good condition, with normal barrel and stock dimensions, it will be easier to sell in the future than something more unusual.

GUNS FOR CLAYSHOOTING

Cost is not so much of a factor with clay guns. Even Perazzis, Krieghoffs and Kemens are relatively inexpensive in their plainer grades when compared with a new Holland or Purdey. Of those just mentioned, I believe the Perazzi is an especially fine trap gun and the light barrelled Kemen (which is very similar to the Perazzi in most other respects) an excellent sporter. The Krieghoff – an evolution of the old Remington 32 – has many admirers in all disciplines (but most notably in Trap and Skeet), and is remarkably strong and beautifully made. Nearly all Krieghoffs (the exception is the old style Skeet gun with Tula chokes) have an adjustable barrel hanger which allows for adjustment of the point of impact of the bottom tube. The hanger varies in .5 mm increments, roughly equating to 3½ in. at 40 yards.

One does not need to spend a great deal to succeed at clay shooting, however. Many, if not most, competitions have been won with guns in the mid price bracket: Brownings, Berettas, Winchesters, Remingtons and Mirokus. The clay shooting novice is sometimes tempted to buy a new and, apparently, glossy gun by one of the less well known makers. This is usually inadvisable. He will be much better off buying a gun like a Beretta 686/Silver Pigeon, Miroku 3800/38 or Browning 325/425 in good, near-new second-hand condition or a new 'plain Jane' model. These guns hold their value well and, with superior materials and engineering, last longer and give far less trouble than most cheaper guns. Semi-automatics, new or second-hand, also offer exceptional value. A old Beretta 303 or a new 390 or 391 model modified by Seminole or Angleport would be at the top of my list. Another excellent gun for serious competition is a 682

Beretta fitted with lightweight, fixed choke, 32 in. trap barrels (a number have been made up to this specification by GMK most specially choked by Nigel Teague).

For general clay shooting or Sporting Clays specifically, I would usually advise buying a 30 in. gun, unless the client is very small in stature. Shorter barrel guns are less stable in most peoples hands – a more important consideration in clay shooting than game shooting – and do not point quite as well. Really long barrelled guns, 31½s, 32s and the new 34s tend to be tools for the experienced (lead needs to be applied more deliberately with them), they are certainly too much gun for a novice (though, once one is a convert, it is hard to go back to anything else).

Multichokes can be useful on a gun (and may make it easier to sell). But it is notable that more than a few really expert shots prefer the handling qualities of long-barrelled fixed choke guns which have less weight in the muzzles. Any gun can be converted to interchangeable chokes without altering its balance by Nigel Teague or Briley (UK agents, Chris Potter Guns). Many take this route, so that they can combine the handling qualities of fixed choke barrels with the convenience of interchangeable chokes.

SPECIFIC DISCIPLINES

SPORTING

Almost every sort of gun has been used for Sporting clays over the years. I can remember when many shots carried two guns, a Skeet gun for close birds and a trap gun for long targets. Some even burdened themselves with a game gun for the mid range stuff! The multichoke arrived on the scene and changed everything. People carried one gun but changed chokes neurotically from stand to stand. Today, I would advise the average shot (averaging between 65-75%) to stick with one gun, fixed choke or multi, set up with a choking of about quarter and half, or, to keep things really simple, half and half. Changing chokes (save on the occasional abnormally close bird or rabbit) just distracts, half choke will kill any target on a sporting range.

The Beretta 68 series, Browning B25 and derivatives, and the Winchester 101/6500 type guns, in 30 or 32 in. barrel configurations can be ideal sporting guns. The old style, heavy silver-actioned, Beretta 682, the back-bored Miroku MK38 32 in. and 32 in. Browning 208s (the narrow ribbed version of the 208) are certainly clay shooting classics. The Kemen KM4 has also achieved some remarkable victories in recent years. My own competitive shooting improved notably when I started to use one. I put this down to the first class handling qualities of the gun, which has long, light, over-bored (and, typically, very tightly choked) barrels. Unfortunately, some Kemens have had a bit of problem with cracks appearing in the stock at the grip. If buying second-hand keep an eye open for this. It probably relates to the amount of wood that must be removed to accommodate the detachable trigger lock action and might be easily remedied by a slightly increased grip thickness. The problem is rarely

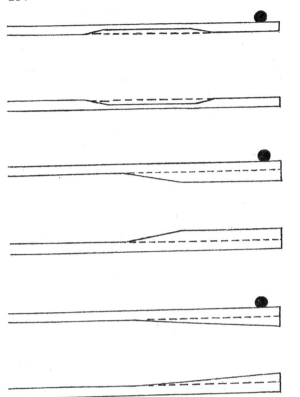

Different systems of choke: recess choking (sometimes seen in older guns and used to introduce choke into barrels which have been shortened), parallel choke (the most common system encountered) and conical choke (as seen in cheaper guns but also in longer form in some high quality choke tubes).

encountered on the similar Gamba (another Perazzi-inspired gun). Moreover, the Gamba in my experience produces less felt recoil.

Beretta have recently brought out two new guns, the 682E and DT10, both of which are offered as sporting or trap guns and both of which feature the new 'optima-bore' back-bored barrel with long (and almost invisible) forcing cone and new, longer chokes. The new 682 has a slightly tapered rib and a lighter than average barrel. The DT10 – which looks much like an ASE but is slightly wider in the action – is notable for its quickly detachable trigger lock.[14] Amongst the semi-autos, I especially like the Beretta 303 and 391 as noted. The Remington 11-87 Light-Contour Sporting Clays model is a good gun and the Browning Gold in its various guises is an ingenious piece of modern engineering. My friend Stuart Clarke was having great problems with his shoulder some time ago. He had achieved many victories over the years with an over-and-under, but pain had almost caused him to stop shooting. On noting his predicament, I suggested he try a gas operated semi-auto again (he had, of course, used them before) and, after some lengthy discussion, lent him my Beretta 303 (the action and barrel of which belonged to a gun handed down to me by Chris Cradock). Stuart tried it with the original 30 in. barrel and a 32 in. I had since acquired from GMK. The former worked best for him. He acquired a similar 30 in. Beretta 390 modified by Angle Port in the United States, further modified the grip and went on to win the British Open.

Sporterising

The practice of 'sporterising' trap guns is common. This may just mean lowering the stock or it might also include choke work too and details such as the removal of a centre bead. As already discussed, fixed choke trap guns may have less weight in the barrels and can seem to handle better, especially as far as long-barrelled sporters are concerned.

Using two guns for sporting

Quite a number of serious sporting shots still favour a two gun battery. For those shooting in the 80 or 90s this can make real sense. The first gun might be any of those described earlier, but the second should be a tightly choked, trappish gun. It can enable a good shot to pick up a few extra birds on the harder stands presenting birds at significant range. Such a gun can be especially useful on teal and long quartering shots. The two guns in a double gun battery can be (indeed, it is best that they should be) of a very similar pattern, save for comb height. This keeps handling differences to a minimum. I sometimes put a skeet gun in the boot for major competitions, just in case any target is put on at ridiculously close range.

TRAP SHOOTING

For Down the Line, the most common form of trap shooting in the United Kingdom, one might begin by using any 30 or 32 in. sporter (even 28 in. guns can be made to work quite well). Traditionally trap guns are fairly heavy (in the region of 8 lb in the case of over and unders), have long barrels, high combs and plenty of choke. One can learn the basics of trap shooting without a dedicated gun. I have seen many good scores put in with sporters (even those with relatively open chokes). The only qualification worth making concerns comb height. It is difficult to do well with a low shooting gun (and I would make the distinction between low shooting and flat shooting), so a rubber comb raiser can be a useful addition in some cases (or, if none is a available, or the rubber raiser creates too high a comb, the comb may be built up by other means such as card or plasticine and vinyl electrician's tape).

The best value Trap gun will be something like a fixed choke Miroku MK60 or MK38 (the latter offering a barrel backed-bored to .739 in.) or indeed a second-hand, fixed choke, Miroku, Winchester or Beretta 68 series. If price is of less concern, one might consider any of the new Beretta or Browning Trap guns or one of the high grade Mirokus (some of which are beautiful guns, with good wood and excellent engraving). I tend to advise fixed choke guns generally for the fast trap disciplines (although heavier multichoke barrels may be no great disadvantage for DTL and may even promote steadiness in some individuals[15]).

Semi-automatics can be acquired very reasonably in Trap configuration, but they are not always popular with other shooters on a Trap field. In this case, I think the prejudice has some justification. Apart from throwing out their cartridge cases, the action type requires a lot of potentially fumblesome handling on a Trap line (the problem is most acute in those disciplines like DTL, ABT and OT which require two cartridges to be loaded).

Many believe the best trap guns made in the world today are those of Perazzi (Perazzi and Beretta seem to split the main medals). The great advantage to any Perazzi gun (and the Kemen copy from Spain) is the superb quality of its trigger pulls. Perazzis also have barrels of the highest quality with great attention paid to straightness and regulation. Unlike most mass produced over-and-unders, most Perazzis are made with leaf mainsprings. The guns may be made to individual specification relatively quickly and with a vast range of barrel, rib and woodwork options. For a serious trap shot they are worth every penny. The Beretta SO and ASE range of sidelocks are also beautiful trap shooting guns with superb trigger pulls and the craftsmanship of the Krieghoff range is first-class too.

When one gets serious about trap shooting one may require different guns for different disciplines. There is little point in discussing this in detail – one must find out through experience and experiment what suits – but I will note that to do my best that I need a gun with a comb about $1/8$ in. higher at ABT than I do at DTL. Moreover, the weight of the barrels is a very important consideration, excessively heavy barrels do not suit the fast Trap sports, they make it harder to react to fast, unpredictable, targets. They may, however, promote steadiness in the slower and more predictable disciplines such as English DTL and ATA trap.

Monte Carlo stock

A feature of many Trap guns is a Monte Carlo stock which has a parallel comb relative to the top surface of the rib. The advantage to a Monte Carlo stock, or any with a parallel comb, is that error in head placement will have less effect on shot placement. A parallel comb also reduces felt recoil. Most trap guns are built to pattern a bit high. It is perhaps worth noting here that the way one uses one's eyes may affect one's needs. A 'one-eyed' shot often prefers a flatter shooting gun – 50:50 or 60:40 pattern distribution – because he tends to be an aimer. The two eyed shot by contrast will probably prefer 60:40 or 70:30 in a trap gun. Some US experts even go to 90:10.

Other typical features of a Trap gun are twin beads (intended as an aid in initial alignment) and a fairly full pistol grip, sometimes equipped with a palm swell. Unlike a Sporter, a Trap gun is usually designed to be pulled back to the shoulder (so that the upper body can lock up as a unit with the gun)[16]; a Sporting or game gun in contrast is pushed towards the target slightly as the gun is mounted. This, one suspects, is why full, acutely angled grips have become the norm for trap. Some Trap guns have a high rib; the advantage to this is that it increases visibility of the target (an especially important consideration for the one eyed shooter). Some shots, however, find a raised rib distracting because there is a subtle change in one's perception of the target relative to the barrel.

ENGLISH SKEET

Although some shots use purpose built Skeet guns many prefer to use 'sporters'. The trend in English Skeet has been towards longer barrels and more choke in recent years. One regular champion I know prefers 30 in. barrels with 8 and 12 points of choke in his Browning B25. The over-and-under is used by most, but the semi-automatic can be a very effective English Skeet gun, both the Beretta 300 series and the Remington 1100/11-87 are worth serious consideration. My tool of choice for English Skeet is a late model (with wider fore-end) Beretta 303, equipped with heavy, 1140 gm 30 in. barrel. Beretta semi-auto barrels come in a variety of weights: I have another ported 30 in. 303 tube weighing 1080 gm. This more lively barrel is well suited to sporting applications. I used to prefer a flat shooting skeet gun; now I find my results have improved with a higher stock set up to throw a 60:40 rather than a 50:50 pattern.

AMERICAN SKEET
As for English Skeet as far as twelve bores are concerned. The guns of preference for 'multi-gauge' shooting will be equipped with alloy tubes such as those made by Briley or Kolar. US experts seem to favour heavier guns such as the Kriekhoff.

OLYMPIC SKEET
Purpose built Olympic Skeet guns are made by several firms including Beretta, Rottweil, Perazzi, IAB and Vostock. The Vostock MU8 and Rottweil Olympia stand out as superb dedicated Olympic Skeet shooting tools, the later designed by Olympic Champion Konrad Wernhier. Olympic Skeet guns are often equipped with special retro or 'Tula'[17] chokes for maximum spread and, so is sometimes incorrectly claimed, increased pellet stringing. Barrels longer than 28 in. are generally considered a disadvantage in this discipline. Olympic Skeet guns are often set up to shoot higher than other skeet guns to compensate for the fast chopping action caused by the low gun start.

WOMEN

Women often get poorly advised about their guns. Like men, they come in all shapes and sizes. Generally, though (and there is no sexism intended) women have a smaller skull size and less arm strength than men. It is also unusual to find a female shooter with one eye which is absolutely dominant. All these factor may affect gun choice. Many (probably most) women can happily use a middle or lighter weight 12, but not all. For general clay shooting, it is often sensible to recommend to female beginners the combination of a lightweight 12 (which may be labelled a game model by the manufacturer) with a light loaded 24 g cartridge such as the Express High Velocity. The gun should be finished off to the correct length, have an adequate comb height and be fitted with a soft and well rounded recoil pad as appropriate. Gas operated semi-automatics can also be excellent guns for lady clayshots.

For either game or clay shooting one may, on occasion, advise a 20-bore. Before doing this though, it is as well to remember that they can be significantly

PLATE 23

(above) One of Alan Rhone's excellent Vari-Combs. They can be a most useful addition to a teaching gun. Note the Rhone conversion allows the comb to be tilted, cast may also be adjusted. *(Picture: Alan Rhone)*

(below) This stock has been altered for a female shot – women and children tend to have smaller skulls than adult males and require a higher than average comb to get an eye looking down the rib as it should – although this has been neatly done, I prefer to see an additional piece of wood blended in it to form a monte carlo or semi-monte carlo style comb. It looks less ungainly and is less likely to cause a glitch in mounting. The only advantages to this style of comb is that it may be added without removing wood (so the gun may be returned to its original dimensions without damage) and in some cases the increase in width may be useful.

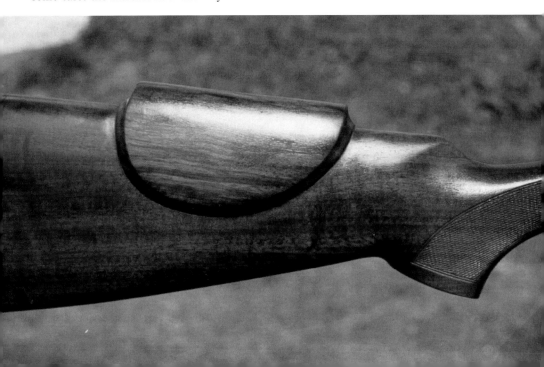

PLATE 24

(above) Note that the instructor
has come down to the boy's level
and note again the positive use of
the hands.

(right) The instructor has clearly
achieved a bridge of
communication with this young
shot. Note the young man's
concentration and the instructor's
gentle care.

harder to shoot. For clay shooting, the 12-bore set-up as mentioned is, in most cases, a better alternative. As far as stock modifications are concerned make sure that if a gun is shortened for a lady client that it is also rebalanced (there may be a need to add weight to the stock). It should also be noted that, as women and young people tend to have smaller heads on average than the typical adult male for whom most guns are made, they require a higher stock because. This is because the distance between the cheek bone and the centre of the eye socket is reduced and without a higher comb they would have to lift the head (a cardinal sin) to see the target. In the United States, I noted recently that the Beretta 390 was being marketed with a shorter, higher, stock especially for ladies. This should become a standard practice. Women may also require a thinner grip to match their hand.

YOUNG SHOTS

The first thing to be said about selecting guns for young people is that parents should resist buying a shotgun for a child too young. I have always felt it better to teach the basics of good gunhandling with an air-rifle (providing it has a reasonable trigger pull). The manner of sighting may be different, but it is a great way to instill good habits young and there is far less problem with weight and recoil. For most kids the earliest one may productively start instruction falls between the ages of ten and twelve (although, I admit, my own children had a few shots with a 9mm rimfire 'garden gun' well before this). Much depends on physical development, this is not just a question of skeletal height but of muscular strength, co-ordination and psychological maturity.

I prefer to give a child a few shots with a bolt action Webley .410 (firing a 2½ in.) cartridge a year or so before serious instruction starts. This serves to wet their appetite. The Webley – equipped with a comb raiser – is an excellent gun for the purpose because it is relatively light AND soft to shoot (at £50 or so, buy any you see). When serious instruction starts on clays (and it should begin no where else) the tool of choice is a gas operated 20-bore semi-automatic or, if the gun is of good shooting quality, a 28 bore (which may have a useful weight and recoil advantage over the 20 and is ballistically far superior to the .410). Both Browning and Beretta make excellent little over-and-unders in 28 bore, and they are ideal – save for their stock dimensions which tend to be too low in the comb and long in the stock – for the initial instruction of youngsters. As with women, young people require a stock which fits them. It needs to be shorter, higher and slimmer in the grip than a stock for an adult.

I am not a great believer in the old, slow, progression from .410 to 28 to 20 to 12. I like to move young shots on to a 12-bore (of suitable dimensions and matched to a suitable cartridge) as soon as possible. Smaller, light guns, are harder to shoot with, their use in instruction is only justified by lack of muscular strength. Once muscles develop there is no good reason to continue with their use. As far as specific guns are concerned I especially favour the Remington 1100 20-bore, the 28 in. Beretta 686/687 boxlocks (28-, 20- or 12-

bore - the latter in narrow rib, game configuration) and as noted above the Browning Elite 28 bore. I see many young people who are given cheaper guns with terrible trigger pulls, their parents would have been much wiser to wait and spend the money in the meantime on instruction. Just about the worst gun you can give any youngster is a cheap, folding, single barrel or over-and-under .410. To discover why this is the case, try shooting one. The last one I shot had 10 lb trigger pulls.

(In the above I have referred to 'giving' guns to young people: it goes without saying that, legal restrictions apart, no young person new to shooting should be given a gun to use unsupervised. Even when the legal age minima are reached, a responsible and knowledgeable person must decide when the young shot is ready to go 'solo'.)

LEFT HANDERS

The adaption of a side-by-side or over-and-under to a left hander is usually fairly straightforward, provided no extreme of cast is required. By combining stock bending with work at the head, a half-inch shift can usually be attained. On double trigger guns, the trigger blades may be bent to suit the southpaw (although this is a refinement which many have managed without). Both Benelli and Remington have made left-handed semi-automatics.

VETERAN SHOTS

Many older sportsmen favour – or are told that they ought to favour – light-weight shorter-barrelled guns (at least as far as game shooting is concerned). Though light guns can be a help to some people, extremes of weight and barrel length are best avoided with advancing years. A lightweight gun is certainly no guarantee of success and may hinder shooting and shooting comfort very significantly. Many shots, and especially many older shots, mistakenly believe that they are not moving their guns quickly enough, when, in fact, they may be moving too quickly to achieve consistent results. A light-weight gun can exacerbate the problem: the best prescription for any veteran shot having problems is an eye-test, a check gun-fit, a lively, medium weight gun, a sensibly loaded cartridge and plenty of regular practice.

DISABLED SHOTS

Shots who are confined to wheel chairs are well advised to use guns which do not recoil excessively – the body cannot roll with the punches – and which are not excessively long in the stock (sitting makes it hard to swing). Gas-operated semi-automatics are ideal. Good recoil pads, muzzle porting and even shock absorbing telescopic stock conversions should be considered. Stocks for disabled shooters should not be too long (if they are swing will be impeded) and extremes of barrel length and gun weight should be avoided. Fore-end and grip design are especially important as the hands will do more work when body rotation is limited.

Gun Weight: general comments

Novice shots often buy lighter guns than they should, and end up being unnecessarily punished by recoil. My own preference is for heavier guns with lively barrels. (Purdey have often made their guns heavier than those of less celebrated makers). Greener used to suggest that the right weight for a game gun was 96 times the shot charge. Thus a gun firing the standard $1^1/_{16}$ oz game load should be just under 6½ lb and a gun firing $1^1/_8$ oz, 6¾ lb. This remains a good rule of thumb for a 12-bore side-by-side (much less than 6¼ is unnecessarily punishing). My preference in a 28 in. barrelled 12-bore side-by-side game gun is about 6½ lb. I might say the same for a 30 in. 20-bore over-and-under game gun. A 12-bore over-and-under for live quarry shooting wants to weigh about half a pound more.[18]

Guns for clay shooting should be significantly heavier: as far as over-and-unders are concerned, never much less than 7½ lb (for adult males). In the United States, some competitors use very heavy guns for ATA Trap (I used several guns which weighed between 9 and 10 lb on a recent trip). Heavy guns may also suit DTL (but not the faster international trap disciplines). Many attempts have been made over the years to produce superlight guns – Turner's Featherweight gun, the Lancaster 12-20 and the Baby Bretton – but usually such creations are more fun to carry than they are to shoot. A recent trend among manufacturers of over-and-unders is to offer lighter weight models with alloy actions for game shots. Some of these guns – which are not excessively light – may also suit women and young shots for clay shooting provided a suitable low-payload, medium velocity cartridge is selected.

Balance

Best quality guns are often said to be beautifully balanced. Generally, this means that they are neither muzzle nor stock-heavy and that the weight is concentrated primarily in the area between the hands. This is a good prescription for most Sporting and game guns. However, in a Skeet gun, a forward balance with considerable weight in the muzzle is seen as an advantage by some competitors who feel this weight distribution promotes a good follow through. We have noted elsewhere that many Sporting shots using long barrels favour fixed choke models because they are lighter at the muzzles. In international Trap

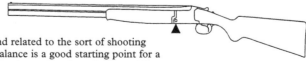

Point of balance is personal and related to the sort of shooting you want to do. A hinge pin balance is a good starting point for a 28 or 30 in. over-and-under sporting gun; a skeet shooter might prefer a muzzle-heavy gun to encourage a smooth follow through.

shooting balance is a critical consideration and it is notable that the best Trap shots are extremely fussy about barrel weight.

Multi-chokes

These can be a bonus provided that the gun barrel weight is not increased excessively to accommodate them. Fixed choke guns are easily converted to thin-wall interchangable chokes by the likes of Nigel Teague and Briley. There has been some argument recently about the relative merits of short and long chokes and those with and without parallel sections internally. My own opinion is that short chokes seem to be as effective as long ones at the plates but may not look quite as 'sexy'. As for taper chokes, traditionalists argue in favour of the parallel choke – a choke in which a forcing cone leads into a parallel section which extends to the muzzles – but many of the world's best shots use taper chokes with the greatest success.[19]

Choke keys

Concealed chokes which require a key can be a nuisance. Anyone using a multi-choke gun is well advised to obtain the style of choke with a protruding knurled section. This allows for chokes to be safely tightened without the need for tools. It is worth making the point here that a surprising number of guns are damaged either because they are fired with loose chokes or because concealed chokes are allowed to rust. Anyone using a multi-choke gun must develop a routine for tightening the chokes and should also get in the habit of removing and cleaning after each shooting session – failure to do either of these things can have costly consequences. A universal choke key – nothing more than a metal cone with cross-bar – is a useful investment for the instructor. Chokes which are stuck should be treated with penetrating oil and left over-night before resorting to a gunsmith. If you do this make sure the barrels are detached from the rest of the gun so that oil does not seep back into the stock.

Regulation and pattern.

My work requires that I test a large number of guns each year. I am often surprised by how poorly some modern guns are regulated. Many double guns have two different points of impact at 40 yards though the patterns should overlap at this distance. I have known some cheap Spanish guns to have pattern centres several feet apart! Mass manufacture is one reason for this, although another is sleeving without check-firing before the job is finished. A skilled barrel maker can alter the point of impact by a number of methods, the choke area of the barrels may be modified, heat may be applied to the barrels by various methods and there are other tricks of the barrel maker's trade. Moreover, Briley offer eccentric boring on chokes to change the point of impact.

Custom work

Many modern guns have wider bores than their predecessors (for example, some Brownings and Mirokus are now made with a bore of .739). In guns with tight bores (.729 or less), 'back-boring' can be a useful modification as it seems

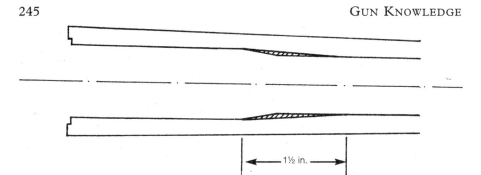

Forcing cone enlargement can be a useful modification, particularly for guns firing steel shot.

to reduce felt recoil in some circumstances and may improve pattern quality. Companies offering this service include Briley, Stan Baker and Seminole in the United States. It can only be undertaken if there is sufficient barrel wall-thickness. If the work is done in the United States one's only guarantee of safety is the reputation of the firm undertaking the work (the firms mentioned are expert), a gun which has been back-bored in the UK will need to be reproofed if the modification has taken it above its original proof size. I have had the best results with back-boring in the moderate range .735 - .740, but take further advice before modifying a gun.

If forcing cones are very short, lengthening to 1½ or 2 in. may be advisable (Seminole take semi-automatic cones out as far as 5 in. and the new Beretta optima bore combines subtle, and much longer than average, forcing cones with a wider than average bore – 18.6 mm). One must be careful, though, with inexpert back-boring and forcing cone modification. If felt wad cartridges are to be used, neither modification may be advisable at its extreme as they can lead to gas escape around the wad which does not expand to the bore dimension in the same way as a plastic one with a skirt.

Trigger work will be required on any gun which has excessively heavy or dangerously light pulls (falling outside the range 3-5 lb) or which suffers from excessive creep. The latter is a particular problem on repeaters. If a recoil pad is required, none performs better than a Kick-Eez. As someone who tends to mount on the shoulder rather than in the shoulder pocket, my preference for Sporting is their concave sole Trap pad (which can be bound with vinyl electrician's tape to prevent snagging in the mount), rather than the flatter so-called sporting type. Pads may also be faced with leather or entirely covered with it to avoid glitches in the mount. Finally, it is worth noting that ribs may be modified or changed. This can transform an old, wide-ribbed, trap gun into a very useful sporter (provided one is careful not to change the point of impact as a result of altering rib height). Chris Symonds is especially well-known for this work in the UK.

CARTRIDGES

Advice on Cartridges

You will often be asked for your opinion on cartridges. I try to keep things simple. I cannot help feeling that a lot of people spend more than they need to on premium cartridges in the mistaken belief that it is going to improve their score or bag. Happily most modern cartridges are excellent – much better (and significantly cheaper) than they were a generation ago. Instructors should become familiar with various types of cartridge case – parallel tube, compression formed, Gorden system, paper and metal and all plastic – and should also note the differences in the various wad types – plastic, fibre and felt – and the permutations and combinations of wad column construction. This subject is considered in detail in a forthcoming book. Here, it is enough to note that there is much, much more to cartridges than meets the eye, every component – case, primer, propellent, wad or wads and shot – has been refined for the best part of two hundred years.

Payload equivalents		UK Shotsize equivalents	
$13/_{16}$ oz	23 g	AAA	5.2mm
$7/_8$	24	BB	4.1
$15/_{16}$	26	1	3.6
1	28	3	3.3
$1^1/_{16}$	30	4	3.1
$1^1/_8$	32	5	2.8
$1^3/_{16}$	34	6	2.6
$1^1/_4$	36	7	2.4
$1^1/_2$	42	$7^1/_2$	2.3
$1^5/_8$	46	8	2.2
$1^3/_4$	50	9	2.0

Cartridges for clayshooting

All the major manufacturers offer excellent 24 and 28-g economy loads which will do the job more than adequately for most people. Apart from price, look for well formed cases with strongly attached rims, acceptable recoil (ultra high velocities and pressures are to be avoided), clean burning and, of course, good patterns (i.e., even patterns without excessive gaps, excessive clustering, balling, or abnormal central concentration.)

Better clay shots may benefit from a better quality cartridge (but premium grade cartridges will only be of significant advantage to top competitors, most notably, those involved in the International Trap disciplines and FITASC Sporting). Plated shot, as used in some of the most expensive cartridges (where plating is combined with hard lead alloy), reduces central concentration and promotes more even patterns (though one suspects this has more to do with the hardness of the shot than the plating process).[20]

Sporting

For Sporting shooting (except for competitors in the top 10% of AA) I advise standardisation on a single pellet size: $7^1/_2$ (2.3 mm) or 8 (2.2 mm). Attempting to match cartridges to targets, like changing chokes from stand to stand, only

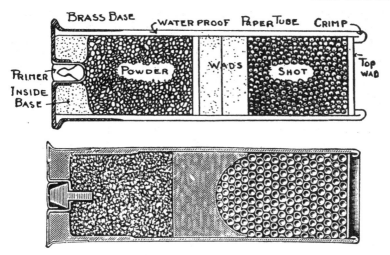

(top) An old style felt wadded cartridge with rolled turnover closure and an over
shot card rather than the modern pie crimp. (below) Greener's Swedish wad
(sometimes made with concavities at both ends) a forerunner of the modern
plastic cup wad.

serves to distract. For those who insist on changing cartridges, 9 (2 mm) shot
may, generally, be selected for close targets and medium range targets where
the belly is presented to the shooter (but avoid it for hard composition birds
such as rabbits or on very windy days because it is more prone to drift). For
everything else, and especially edge-on targets at range, use 7½ shot. As far as
velocity is concerned, I prefer high speed cartridges for Sporting, but not at the
price of recoil. It is a question of experimentation. Every shooter should make
the effort to identify a plastic wadded and a fibre or felt wadded load which
suits his style. He should (without getting too obsessive) check the cartridges
at the plates to see how they perform in his gun. It is a mistake to buy cartridges
at a shoot, the range is limited and the prices usually high. Moreover, one may
be forced into buying a cartridge of which one has no experience.

Skeet
Skeet shooters do not have as many choices to make as other shots. Nearly all
UK shots use no. 9 shot in a 24- or 28-g load, although recent changes in the
rules of English Skeet allow for the use of shot sizes 6 - 9 (Olympic Skeet shots
may only use 24 g loads). I can see no advantage to using smaller or larger shot,
or larger payloads, even if the rules permitted it. Velocity, within reasonable
limits, is not a great concern for Skeet shooting; comfort is of paramount
importance. The two essential qualities in a Skeet cartridge are acceptable
recoil and evenness of pattern.

Trap
As for Trap, some prefer to use no. 8 shot in the first barrel, but use a larger
size, 7½ or 7 (2.4 mm), in the second barrel (the bigger pellet retains kinetic

energy slightly better at range). Most Trap shots, however, use 7 or 7½ in both barrels. My own preference would be for 7½ shot in both barrels in a fast 24-gramme or 28-gramme load (as appropriate to the discipline). Note that not all cartridges are correctly labelled: many cartridges sold as no. 7½ are in fact 7s. If in doubt, carefully cut a cartridge to remove the pellets and use a micrometer to measure their diameter.

Slower velocity cartridges are required in American competitions by the rules of the ATA, which stipulate a maximum 3 dram equivalent load of shot no larger than number 7½ US and a payload no greater than 1¹/8-oz (32 g). This equates to a 1,200 fps velocity limit for a 1¹/8-oz load. Plated shot is also banned from US Trap competition. If one can break 1000 straight with unplated shot being fired at moderate velocities, as a number of top competitors have, one might well ask who needs anything more? As far as ATA and DTL are concerned you probably do not, but high performance loads are useful for the more challenging International trap disciplines.

The principle is always the same. Within the confines of the rules, one chooses the cartridge in which one has most confidence. Trap shooting is all about confidence – it's important in other disciplines but critical here. One must get used to the cartridge – intimately familiar with its feel and performance. Lack of confidence in the cartridge or anything else will destroy one's timing. Some serious competitors will change pellet size or brand to better match the make of target being thrown (some birds being known to be harder than others). If that makes them more confident, fine. But, for most, it would be just one more thing to think about – an unnecessary distraction and a potentially disruptive change in routine. For the great majority, there is more to lose than to gain. The best advice to them is to find a really good cartridge and stick to it.

Cartridges for game shooting

Confidence is critical. In this case I do find myself using and advising the use of premium grade cartridges. They seem to make a real difference. For formal driven shooting, I would recommend 1- or 1¹/16-oz 12-bore loads for pheasant at modest to medium ranges. Ideal shot size would be 6 or 7, although some people feel more confident with no. 5s. For really high birds, such as those sometimes seen in the West Country, I would prefer a slightly heavier payload: 1¹/8oz. or even 1¼ oz. My favourite 20-bore load for pheasant at sensible ranges is 1 oz of no. 6 shot in a 2¾ in. (70 mm) case. Most people find recoil less of a problem when game shooting because of the adrenaline factor and may therefore choose a high performance cartridge without ill effect. They can also boost confidence. However, if recoil is a problem, do not despair. Modern light game loads are very efficient.

Classic English guns

All other proof requirements being satisfied, I believe that it is commonsense that cartridges with low BAR figures should be advised for older game guns. Non-toxic shot should not be used in a classic gun without consulting a gunsmith – in some cases the gun may require modification (see below).

Non-toxic shot

In England and Wales, non-toxic shot is now required for shooting wildfowl and for use in a number of listed sites of special scientific interest. This may well be the thin edge of the wedge. It is certainly an unfortunate state of affairs as the dangers of lead shot have been much exaggerated. Moreover, it is odd that our shooting organisations have not done more to defend us. Nevertheless, non-toxic shot is a fact with which we must now live. Serious alternatives to lead include steel, Tungsten Matrix, Tungsten Iron, Bismuth and tin (although copper, zinc and other substances have been tried). Steel shot cartridges are the cheapest option (but still significantly more expensive than lead). They have certain limitations, however.

Steel, in fact iron, shot is both much harder and lighter than lead. Because it is hard, it requires the use of a protective plastic shot-cup (and chokes of half or less combined with lengthened forcing cones). Because it is light, it lacks kinetic energy and – in normal lengths of cartridge at least – this limits its range. Within 35 yards it works quite well. One is well advised, however, to select a pellet size two sizes larger than lead to achieve a similar killing performance. As far as clay shooting is concerned, I have found steel to be surprisingly effective as a first barrel load for DTL.

Tungsten Matrix shot – Tungsten powder with a plastic polymer – was developed by Royal Ordnance and Eley in the late 1980s (and is now marketed by Gamebore-Kent). It is extremely expensive, but performs well in most respects save for the fact that it is abrasive and requires a special shot-cup. As with steel, choke should not be greater than half and forcing cones may be extended for maximum performance.

Bismuth is my favourite alternative to lead. Early bismuth shot had a tendency to shatter but this has been much improved by increasing the tin content in bismuth shot alloy. Like Tungsten Matrix, Bismuth is horribly expensive, but it performs much like lead, and being very similar in its properties may be used much like it. Bismuth does not, for example, require special wadding, nor is there a need for barrel modification. I have shot thousands of Bismuth cartridges at game and clays and found it hard to tell any difference with conventional loads (except on price, where the difference is profound). The only ballistic qualification is that it makes sense to use shot a pellet one size larger than normal (which is also advisable with Tungsten).

Tin shot is also soft, but it is light and, like steel, lacks kinetic energy at range. Early tin cartridges were driven at high speed to overcome this but the recoil was unacceptable. Tin, like steel, is now much improved, its primary application is as a short and mid-range substitute for lead.

Relative densities

Lead	11.3
Steel	7.8
Tungsten matrix	10.8
Bismuth	9.6
Tin	7.3

Shot size selection

Decoying pigeon: 6 or 7 (7½ trap loads will also do the job)

Snipe: 7, 7½ or 8

Woodcock: 6, 7 or 7½

Partridge: 6, 7 or 7½

Grouse: 6 or 7

Capercaillie: 4 or 5

Pheasant: 5, 6 or 7

Duck (foreshore): 4 or 5 (tungsten matrix or bismuth); 2 or 3 (steel)

Duck (flighting inland): 5 (tungsten matrix or bismuth); 4 (steel)

Geese (foreshore): BB 1or 2 (tungsten matrix or bismuth); BB (steel)

Geese (inland decoying): 2, 3 or 4 (tungsten matrix or bismuth); 1 or 2 (steel)

Rabbits: 5 or 6

Hares: 4 or 5

Magnum loads

'Magnum' usually means heavy load in the shooting context and hence a higher powder charge and – sometimes – proof test. (Always check the proof marks on your gun before contemplating the use of a magnum load.) A magnum shotgun cartridge does not necessarily provide more kinetic energy as far as individual pellets are concerned. As a general principle, encourage your clients to use fieldcraft to reduce range and discourage the use of heavy loads which bruise both shoulder and pocket. Such loads can give a false sense of security and encourage some people to attempt silly shots at extreme range. That said, one, rarely considered, advantage of a heavy payload cartridge is that a killing pattern may be achieved at range without excessive choke. The key benefit of the typical magnum shot shell is a larger number of pellets and hence less gaps in the pattern. Provided one can stand the recoil, there may be a greater margin for error. Magnum loads can improve the killing performance of light non-toxic pellets.

Other specialist cartridges

There are a number of special purpose cartridges worth a brief mention. Subsonic cartridges are often required at grounds which have a noise problem. They are seen by many shooters as a handicap, but I have found the latest subsonics to be excellent loads for the instruction of novices and surprisingly effective generally, though their performance breaks down beyond 35 or 40 yards.

Spreader loads

Loads which offer an especially wide pattern – have been offered by many companies over the years (the Browning Dispersante was especially well known). A spreader load may be created by using unusually shaped shot (square), or by splitting the shot column either by using several wads with the shot load divided in sections between them, or by splitting the shot column with a cruciform divider. Dedicated spreader loads are illegal in most clay disciplines. Nevertheless, by experiment one may quite legitimately find a conventional cartridge which exaggerates or minimises the effect of choke. For those with tight, fixed-choke guns, this can be useful intelligence.

Cartridges for instruction

I favour lightly loaded, low or moderate velocity, cartridges for nearly all instructional situations. Even light-loaded 24-g ($^7/_8$ oz) 12-bore loads will do far more than most shots realise. Shot size might be 7½, 8, or 9. Frankly, it does not make much difference in the context of basic or intermediate level Skeet, Sporting or game instruction (for Trap shooting stick to 7½ or 8). For instructing with 20-bores, I would always choose a sub-1 oz load. On the question of case length, it makes sense to use 2½ in. shells for both 12- and 20-bore. Such cartridges may be used safely in 2½, 2 ¾ or 3 in. chambered guns, simplifying safety. Although the primary need is for an economic and soft-recoiling training load, instructors must always keep a variety of shells on hand. Semi-automatics do not function reliably with many 2½ in. loads, and some clients will want to use full power 2¾ in. cartridges. You will also need some 2½ in. .410, 28 and 16-bore shells to cover all eventualities.

Recommended reading
The American Shotgun by David F. Butler
American Shotgun Design and Performance by L.R. Wallack
Best Guns by Michael McIntosh
Boss & Co. by Donald Dallas
The British Over and Under Shotgun by G. & S. Boothroyd
The British Shotgun Volumes 1 and 2 by Crudgington and Baker
Cogswell & Harrison: Two Centuries of Gunmaking by Graham Cooley and John Newton
Cradock on Shotguns by Chris Cradock
The Double Shotgun by Don Zutz
Game Guns and Rifles by Richard Akehurst
Gameshooting by Robert Churchill
The Greener Story by Graham Greener
The Gun and its Development (9th Edition) by W.W.Greener
Gunfitting: the Quest for Perfection by Michael Yardley
Heyday of the Shotgun by David Baker
Hints on Shooting by '20 bore'
In the Gunroom by Major Sir Gerald Burrand
The Italian Gun by Smith & Morrow
Lock Stock and Barrel by Adams & Braden
London Gunmakers by Nigel Brown
The Modern Shotgun by Major Sir Gerald Burrard
The Modern Sportsman's Gun and Rifle by J.H. Walsh
Positive Shooting by Michael Yardley
Purdey Gun and Rifle Makers by Donald Dallas
Purdey's: The Guns and the Family by Richard Beaumont
The Shotgun by Macdonald Hastings
Shotgunning the Art and the Science by Bob Brister
Shotguns and Cartridges for Game and Clays by Gough Thomas.
Shotguns and Gunsmiths by Geoffrey Boothroyd
Sidelocks and Boxlocks by Geoffrey Boothroyd

NOTES

1 When Holland & Holland guns are made as self-openers, a separate coil spring is used to power the opening mechanism. It is concealed in a tube beneath the barrels and hidden by the forend.

2 Less metal needs to be removed from the body of the action.

3 A few MX 8 Perazzi have been made with coil springs.

4 The first and hugely successful semi-automatic shotgun patented in 1900 by John Moses Browning and still in production (albeit in very limited numbers) at the time of writing.

5 This was designed by John Moses Browning's son, Val.

6 Similar arguments were marshalled against the percussion system, breechloaders and the semi-automatic pistol in their day.

7 Though, dare I admit, that recently I have returned to the side-by-side for much of my competitive sporting clay and skeet shooting! We all need a challenge.

8 On the Beretta 303, for example, an excellent gun as noted, the standard gas bleed holes are tapered measuring 2.9 at their widest, this can be enlarged in cases of persistent malfunctioning with light cartridges with a 2.9 mm drill bit, or, as a last resort, with a 3 mm bit. The work is trickier than it may sound and must be performed by a competent gunsmith.

9 A long shot column causes the bottom pellets in the shot column to be squeezed between the rapidly expanding gasses and the heavy mass of shot above them. Because of the axial squeeze pressure, more pellets are deformed, and these will tend to fly out from the main body of the pattern.

10 There seems to be a recent vogue for the 16-bore. I cannot understand why, unless it is nostalgia. A good 20 will do everything the 16 will and the catridges are much easier to obtain. An English 16 would typically be made at about 6 lb firing a $^{15}/16$ oz load. There is no ballistic or weight advantage compared to the modern 20. No doubt someone will soon write an article favouring the return of the Cogswell & Harrison 14¾-bore. On paper it seems to make some sense, but where do you buy ammunition?

11 Grant became Grant & Joseph Lang in 1925, acquiring Harrison & Hussey in 1932, Charles Lancaster in 1935 and Watson Bros. in 1939. In 1960, the firm acquired Henry Atkin and became Atkin, Grant & Lang. In the 1960's, the firm became associated with Churchill, by then also owned by the colourful American arms dealer, Sam Cummings. In 1971, the firm became Churchill, Atkin, Grant & Lang, Ltd. Nigel Brown notes that this company ceased trading in 1980 but the names Churchill and Atkin, Grant & Lang live on under new ownership.

12 The Watson name has been revived by Michael Loucha in Southwark, London. Mr Loucha is currently working on best quality sidelock over and unders with his own improvements to the self-opening and ejector systems.

13 Tony Kennedy has made a speciality of importing these guns in the U.K.

14 I recently tested this model in 32 in. form and was much impressed by it.

15 If guns are offered with the thin style of multi-choke, such as the Briley, this does not apply. A multichoke may be a convenience worth having provided it does not necessitate thick and lifeless barrels.

16 Although my friend Peter Croft, would note that this is a common error in trap technique. He makes the point very strongly that the shoulder should go to gun in trap shooting as in other disciplines.

17 The Tula choke gets its name from the famous Russian arsenal. A Tula choke incorporates an expansion chamber in the bore, sometimes with a roughened surface, behind a widely flared muzzle.

18 Purdey advise that a 2¾ in. 12-bore side-by-side should be made between 6 lb 12 oz and 6 lb 14 oz, a 2½ in. 12 between 6 lb 8 oz and 6 lb 10 oz, a 2¾ or 2½ in. 20-bore between 6 lb and 6 lb 4 oz. Their advice for a 28-bore is 5 lb 3 oz and between 5 lb and 5 lb 4 oz for a .410. As far as over-and-unders are concerned, the great firm suggest a weight of 7 lb to 7lb 8 oz for a standard 2¾ in. 12, and 6 lb to 6 lb 6 oz for a 20. The advice for 28s (and .410s) is 5 lb 10 oz to 6 lb.

19 My own opinion is that a parallel section can improve patterns. Moreover, without a parallel section, a greater constriction may be required to achieve a desired percentage.

20 Copper and nickel are using for the plating. Antimony is used to harden shot and the percentage varies in modern shot between 1 and 8%. 2% would be typical in shot intended for shooting and 5% in trap loads.

CHAPTER 12

<u>Conclusion</u>

Final Thoughts: the Seven Deadly Sins of shooting

1 Not having a stock which fits.
2 Not having precisely diagnosed eye dominance.
3 Failing to keep the eyes (or eye) on the bird.
4 Stopping the gun during the swing.
5 Being unbalanced in one's shooting stance.
6 Failing to address the target properly.
7 Being inexperienced or mistaken in regard to the required forward or other allowance for a specific target.

I often watch people struggling to shoot with guns which do not fit them. Whilst a good shot can perform reasonably with most guns, nobody shoots really well with a gun which does not fit. The problem, though, is that many people do not realise that their gun does not fit, they may have adapted to its shape, to the extent that the wrong dimensions now feel right to them.

There is a similar situation with regard to eye dominance. Many people do not realise that they have a problem. They assume that because they can see the target that they can point towards it. This may not be case. Happily, though, gun fit and eye dominance are problems which may be easily and more or less permanently eliminated with the right advice. The next 5 'sins' are rather different.

Keeping the eyes on the bird. It is easy to say that one should always keep the eyes on the bird, it is very hard to do every time – when we are tired, when we are cold and when we are not quite as motivated as we should be. Nevertheless, if there is one golden rule of shooting beyond those concerned with shooting safety, this is it (and I make no apologies for repeating the point yet again). When clay shooting you should always look for the *precise shape* of the target, when game shooting, focus on the *head or beak* of the bird. **Sustain focus and have faith in your eyes**. In the context of shooting, vision is a *skill*. Locking hard focus on to a moving object more than momentarily is not instinctive. The shooters who is disciplined about sustaining visual contact with the target will apply lead subconsciously far more accurately than if he tried to measure it out deliberately every time. One has to to learn to trust the process and it is much easier said than done.

Don't check! Stopping the gun – failing to follow through after one has pulled the trigger – is one of the most common faults in wingshooting. It may be due to simple ignorance of the importance of follow-through. It may be due to a poor mount. It might be because the gun is too long or because it recoils too much. It might be because the shooter has not learnt how to use his forward hand to direct the gun or it might be because he is lifting his head to look at the target. Whatever the reason, stopping leads to misses behind. The first part of the cure is to become aware of the problem and to concentrate on a smooth follow-through with every shot. Often people stop their swing simply because their body is pointing in the wrong direction which bring be to sins 5 and 6.

One cannot shoot properly if one is in an unbalanced position or if one is not addressing the target correctly (for example, if one's body is pointing in the wrong direction, one will run out of swing which will cause the gun to stop). Everyone must find the way of standing which suits them best; there should be little tension and a feeling of stability.

As far as address is concerned, one must – when the opportunity is there – set up the stance towards the KILLING POINT of the target (not towards the area where the target is coming from). Moreover, the gun barrels should await the target on or beneath its line of flight (assuming a crossing bird), never above it.

Experience of different targets may seem obvious, but many people have difficulty with some birds simply because they simply have no idea of how much lead they need to apply to achieve a kill. Many are reluctant to shoot into space. Nevertheless, it is one of the key skills of shotgunning. As Ed Scherer used to say: If you are shooting and want to do the biz, shoot where the bird is going and not where it is'.

Twelve qualities of a shooting instructor

There are certain qualities which all shooting instructors must possess or develop which go beyond the immediately obvious need for technical competence. These include:

1 *Dedication*
2 *Integrity*
3 *Enthusiasm*
4 *Authority*
5 The ability to *communicate*
6 *Selflessness*
7 *Flexibility*
8 *Patience*
9 A sense of *humour*
10 *Tact*
11 A willingness to accept *responsibility*.
12 The ability to *empathise* with the student.

None of these should need that much explaining. A shooting instructor must be dedicated because shooting instruction is a complex activity which requires the greatest effort to master. Integrity is essential, because of the trust every client places in you – without integrity that trust could easily be abused. Enthusiasm is needed because the enemy of learning is boredom, and, moreover, enthusiasm is infectious. Authority is required because the pupil must have complete confidence in the instructor in order to achieve his or her best. Authority is a presence born of true confidence based on the knowledge that one 'knows one's stuff'.

The ability to communicate is important, because even with great depth of knowledge, you will be a useless teacher if you cannot get it across to your pupil. It is a two-way process. It is not just about talking at someone, it also involves listening and establishing the clients needs. Selflessness is on the list because the ability to instruct well requires the suppression of ego (rather too many instructors bully their students unnecessarily).

Flexibility is about keeping an open mind and not forcing your prejudices down the student's throat: to be a flexible instructor requires more intellectual and physical effort than to be a dogmatic one, but it is far more satisfying in the long run. Patience is a virtue and it will, on occasion, be sorely tested when instructing. You must be able to cope with such stresses, because a shooting instructor *never* loses his temper.

A sense of humour is critical because it is no pleasure to be taught by someone without one. It also fulfils a similar function to ear protection – it prevents your being damaged by your work. It does not mean that you constantly bombard the client with risqué stories but there are some otherwise very good instructors who do not achieve as much as they might because they appear cold and distant. Tact is required because it is good manners and because it sweetens the bitter pill of criticism.

The need for an instructor to accept responsibility should need little elucidation: the potential dangers of shooting are self-evident. There is another aspect to the acceptance of responsibility however: the instructor must accept responsibility for his own teaching and be ready to admit his own mistakes. As one very experienced instructor once told me: 'If the client misses the target it's your fault not theirs.'

Finally, a good instructor must have the ability to empathise with the client. This goes beyond the suppression of self, it is the ability to put oneself in the shoes of the person being instructed, to feel what they are feeling, to understand what is happening from their perspective. The teacher who can empathise, who has this sensitivity – for that is what it amounts to – will achieve results far faster than one who cannot.

Appendices

APPENDIX 1

A Father's Advice (written by the late Commander Mark Beaufoy M.P. for his son on reaching his thirteenth birthday in 1908).

If a sportsman true you'd be
Listen carefully to me.
Never, never let your gun
Pointed be at anyone;
That it may unloaded be
Matters not the least to me.
When a hedge or fence you cross
Though of time it cause a loss,
From your gun the cartridges take
For the greater safety sake.
If 'twixt you and neighbouring gun
Bird may fly or beast may run,

Let this maxim e'er be thine;
"Follow not across the line."
Stops and beaters, oft unseen,
Lurk behind some leafy screen;
Calm and steady always be;
"Never shoot where you can't see."
Don't be greedy, better spared
Is a pheasant, than one shared.
You may kill, or you may miss,
But at all times think of this -
"All the pheasants ever bred
Won't repay one man dead."

APPENDIX 2
Useful Addresses

MAJOR CLAY SHOOTING ORGANISATIONS

The British International Clay Target Shooting Federation (BICTSF - formerly the International Board)
Roger Peace
11 Beech Crescent
Darrington
Pontefract
West Yorkshire WF8 3AD
01977 791242
Email: bictsf@globalnet.co.uk

Clay Pigeon Shooting Association (CPSA)
Bisley Camp
Brookwood
Woking
Surrey GU24 0NP
Tel. 01483 485400 Fax 01483 485410
www.cpsa.co.uk

The Irish ICPSA (J.M.O'Reilly)
Kilsallagh
65 Glendoher Drive
Rathfarnham
Dublin 16, Eire
Tel: 003531 4931484

Ulster CPSA
Jim Dowie
31 Ranfarly Crescent
Dungannon
County Tyrone BT71 6PH
Tel: 02887 727435

The Welsh CTSA (Secretary John Osborne)
45 Picton Road
Hakin
Milford Haven
Dyfed SA73 3DY
Tel: 01646 693076

The Scottish Clay Target Association
Box 400
24 Station Square, Inverness IV1 1LD
Tel: apply English CPSA for new number

The Manx CPSA
Mrs Lushington
Tel: 01624 880744

The Jersey Clay Target Shooting Association
Mr Mo Gotel
Tel: 01534 876588

Amateur Trap Shooting Association (ATA)
601 W. National Road
Vandalia
Ohio 45377
U.S.A.
Tel: 001937 8984638 Fax: 8985472
www.shoot.ata.com

National Skeet Shooting Association (NSSA)
5931 Roft Road
San Antonio
Texas 78253
U.S.A.
Tel: 001210 6883371 Fax: 6883014
www.nssa-nsca.com

National Sporting Clays Association (NSCA)
Details as NSSA above

National Rifle Association (NRA)
11250 Waples Mill Road
Fairfax
Virginia 22030
U.S.A.
Tel: 001703 2671000
www.nra.org   www.nrahq.org

ISSF (formerly UIT)
Bavariering 21
D-80336 Munich 1
Germany
Tel. 004989 5443550 Fax. 5435544

FITASC (Federation Internationale de Tir aux Armes Sportives de Chasse)
10, rue de Lisbonne
Paris 75008
France
Tel: 00421 934053 Fax 935822

Federation Francaise de Balle Trap (FFBT)
20 Rue Thiers
92100 Boulonge Billancourt
France
Tel: 0033 141410505
www.ffbt.assoc.fr

U.S.A. Shooting
Olympic Training Center
One Olympic Plaza
Colorado Springs
Colorado 80909-5762
U.S.A.
Tel: 001719 5784883

Another generally useful website is
www.shotgunsports.com which is full of useful information and links to others organisations.

OTHER SHOOTING AND TRADE ORGANISATIONS

Sport England (Sports Council)
16 Upper Woburn Place
London WC1H OQP
Tel: 020 7273 1500
www.english.sports.gov.uk

National Coaching Foundation
114 Cardigan Road
Headingley
Leeds LS6 3BJ
Tel: 0113 274 4802
www.ncf.org.uk

The Sportsman's Association
Address and telephone changing at time of writing
www.sportsmans-association.org

The British Association for Shooting & Conservation
Marford Mill
Rossett
Wrexham LL12 0HL
Tel: 01244 573000
www.basc.org.uk

Countryside Alliance
367 Kennington Road
London SE11 4PT
Tel: 020 7582 5432
www.countryside-alliance.org

Campaign for Shooting (as above)

The Gun Trade Association
PO Box 47
Pershore
Worcs WR10 2YP
Tel: 01386 861430
www.brucepub.com/gta

The Game Conservancy Trust
Fordingbridge
Hampshire SP6 1EF
Tel: 01425 652381
www.game-conservancy.org.uk

The Muzzle Loaders' Association of Great Britain
PO Box 339
Saint Helier
Channel Islands
Jersey JE4 9YQ
Tel: 01534 733194 Fax: 01534 733194
www.mlagb.com

The National Rifle Association (UK)
Bisley Camp
Woking
Brookwood
Surrey GU24 0PB
Tel: 01483 797777
www.nra.org.uk

The Sports Council
16 Upper Woburn Place
London WC1H OQP
Tel: 020 7388 1277

PROOF HOUSES

The Worshipful Gunmakers' Company
48 Commercial Road
London EC1 1LP
Tel: O20 7481 2695
Guardians of the Birmingham Proof House
Gun Barrel Proof House
Banbury Street
Birmingham B5 5RH
Tel: 0121 643 3860

GUN IMPORTERS

Browning Sports UK Ltd. (Browning and Winchester products)
37D Milton Park
Milton, Abingdon
Oxfordshire OX14 4RT
Tel: 01235 444100   www.browning.com

Alan Rhone (Krieghoff)
PO Box K80
Wrexham
Clwyd LL13 0ZH
Tel: 01978 780390 email: Alan@Krieghoff.co.uk
www.Krieghoff.co.uk

Gunmark Ltd (Beretta and Lanber)
Carlo Beretta House
11 Brunel Way
Fareham
Hampshire PO15 5TX
Tel: 01489 579999   www.gmk.co.uk

ASI/AYA
Alliance House
Snape Maltings
Saxmundham
Suffolk
Tel: 01728 688555

Viking Arms Ltd (Ruger and Merkel)
Summerbridge
Harrogate
North Yorkshire HG3 4BW
Tel: 01423 780810   www.vikingarms.co.uk

Sportsmarketing (Rizzini)
Commerce Way
Whitehall Road
Colchester
Essex CO2 8HH
Tel: 01206 795333

Beechwood Equipment (Benelli)
PO Box 162
Weybridge
Surrey KT13 9PJ
Tel: 01932 847365
Email: sales@beechwoodequioment.com

Dynamit Nobel (RWS U.K. Ltd.) - (Perazzi and
Rottweil)
Upton Cross
Liskeard
Cornwall PL14 5BQ
Tel: 01579 362319
(parent company website: www.dynamitnobel.com
& Perazzi: www.Perazzi.com)

Kennedy Gunmakers (Laurona, Krieghoff,
Fabarm, Fabri, Piotti etc.)
The Old Armoury
Bisley Camp
Brookwood
Woking GU24 0NY
Tel: 01483 486500
www.kennedyguns.demon.co.uk

BRITISH GUNSHOPS

Litt's
Unit 3
Maesglas Retail Estate
Newport
Gwent NP9 2XF
Tel: 01633 250025/843252 www.litts.co.uk

Richardsons of Halesworth
32 Quay Street
Halesworth
Suffolk 1P19 8ER
Tel: 01986 872520

Elderkin & Son (Gunmakers) Ltd.
Spalding
Lincolnshire PE11 1TG
Tel: 01775 722919/724621   www.elderkin.co.uk

Chris Potter Guns (U.K importers of Briley)
2-6 Grover Street
Tunbridge Wells
Kent TN1 2QB
Tel: 01892 522208
www.gun.co.uk

Garlands
Raddle Farm
Edingale
Tamworth
Staffordshire
Tel: 01827 383300
www.birmingham.co.uk/garlands

James Purdey & Co. Ltd.
South Audley Street
London W1
Tel: 020 7499 1801
www.purdey.com

J.Roberts & Son
66 Great Suffolk Street
London SE1 0BU
Tel: 020 7734 7611
www.jroberts-gunmakers.co.uk

Holland & Holland
33 Bruton Street
London W1
Tel: 0207-499-4411
www.hollandandholland.com

William Evans
67 St. James Street
SWI A 1PH
Tel: 020 7493 0415
www.williamevans.com

CARTRIDGE MANUFACTURERS

Lyalvale Express Ltd.
Express Estate
Fisherwick
Nr Lichfield
Staffordshire WS13 8XA
Tel: 01543 434400
www.lyalvaleexpress.com

Hull Cartridge Company Ltd
Bontoft Avenue
National Avenue
Hull
Humberside HU5 4HZ
Tel: 01482 342571
www.hullcartridge.co.uk

Eley Hawk Ltd.
PO Box 707
Witton
Birmingham
West Midlands B6 7UT
Tel: 0121 356 8899   www.eley.co.uk

Gamebore Cartridge Company (Gamebore and
Kent cartridges)
Great Union Street
Hull
Humberside HU9 1AR
Tel: 01482 223707   www.gamebore.com

AUTOMATIC CLAY TRAPS

CCI
Priors Haw Road
Corby
Northamptonshire NN17 5JG
Tel: 01536 260933 www.cci-international.com

Laporte
Unit 9, Ellesmere Business Park
Swingbridge Road
Grantham
Lincolnshire NG31 7XT
Tel: 01476 577011
(parent company, Laporte France) www.laporte-shooting.com

Farey
Gull Road
Guyhirn
Wisbech
Cambridgeshire PE13 4ER
Tel: 01945 450273 www.fareyclaypigeontraps.co.uk

Promatic
Station works
Hooton Road
Hooton
South Wirral CH66 7NF
Tel: 0151 327 2220 www.promatic.co.uk

Anglian Auto Traps
9 Southcliff
Walton-on-the-Naze
Essex CO14 8EJ
Tel: 01255 673146

MANUAL TRAPS

W.J. Bowman Ltd.
East Markham
Newark
Nottinghamshire
Tel: 01777 870243
www.courtfield.co.uk/wjbowman

Stuart Clay Traps Ltd.
PO Box 14
Woodbridge
Suffolk IP12 1DG
Tel: 01394 385567 www.stuartsgunsandtackle.co.uk

John Lee
Juba Traps
Horsehaven
Rackenford
Tiverton
Devon EX16 8EL
Tel: 01884 881236

CLAY MANUFACTURERS

CCI (see under Automatic Clay Traps)

Laporte (see under Automatic Clay Traps)

Clay Pigeon Company
Sherwood House
Normanton Lane
Bottesford
Nottinghamshire NG13 0EN
Tel: 01949 843777 Email:linda@claypigeon.co.uk

SUPPLIERS OF TOOLS

Helston Gunsmiths (Bend sticks, length of pull gauges, measuring cradles):
Water-ma-Trout,
Helston,
Cornwall TR13 0LW.
Tel: 01326 573385
www.helstongunsmiths.com

ADJUSTABLE STOCK CONVERSIONS

Alan Rhone
PO Box K80
Wrexham
Clwyd LL13 0ZH
Tel: 01978 780390
email: Alan@Krieghoff.co.uk
www.Krieghoff.co.uk

INTERCHANGEABLE CHOKE SPECIALISTS

Nigel Teague (Precision Chokes)
Larkspur Cottage
Old Court
Tortworth
Wotton-U-Edge, Gloucestershire
Tel: 01454 260226
www.teaguechoke.co.uk (for information on replacement chokes)
www.precisionchokes.co.uk (for information on custom choke conversions)

Chris Potter Guns (Briley Chokes in UK)
(see above under Gunshops)

West Country Guns (Rhino chokes in UK)
The Square
Wiveliscombe
Somerset TA4 2JT
Tel: 01984 623829

Briley (USA)
1230 Lumpkin
Houston, Texas 77043, USA
Tel: (001713 932 6995
www.briley.com/mfg

Seminole (USA)
3049 US 1
Mims, Florida, USA
Tel: 001407 383 8556
www.seminolegun.com

CUSTOM RIBS

Chris Symonds (also sleeving, rebarrelling and general repairs)
8 Sheppard Close, Clacton-on-Sea
Essex CO16 8YA
Tel: 01255 435797

CLOTHING

Farlows of Pall Mall
5 Pall Mall, London SW1 5NP
Tel: 020 7839 2423 www.farlows.co.uk

Holland and Holland see above

Purdey see above

Bob Allen Sportswear
214 Jackson
PO Box 477
Des Moines, Iowa
USA
Tel: 001515-283-2191

Cabela's (excellent US outfitter
Tel: 001800-237-444 www.cabelas.com

David Ripper and Sons Ltd.
The Old Corn Mill
Congleton Road
Sidlington
Macclesfield SK11 9JR
Tel: 01260-224406

EAR PROTECTION
Custom Made Ear Protection
Antone Spiroc-tica
PO Box 3432
Poole BH15 1BQ
Tel: 01202 668762
(*Antone offers a variety of custom made plugs including
an excellent 'filtered noise plug' which incorporates a
non-electrical attenuator. Normal speech may be heard
easily as well as traps and game. These plugs are used by
many instructors.*)

MODERN BOOK SUPPLIERS
Tideline books
PO Box 4
Rhyl
Clwyd LL18 1AG
Tel: 01745 354919 www.tidelinebooks.co.uk

Coch-y-Bonddu Books (Paul Morgan)
Machynlleth
Powys SY20 8DJ
Tel: 01654 702837
www.fishing.org/bonddu/

Holland & Holland Ltd see above
James Purdey and Sons see above

SPECIALIST BOOK DEALERS
Gunnerman Books
PO Box 214292
Auburn Hills
Michigan 48321, USA
Tel: 001810 879 2779/9226

David A.H. Grayling
Verdun House
Shap
Penrith, Cumbria CA10 3NG
Tel: 01931 716746

Hereward Books
17 High Street
Haddenham, Ely
Cambridgeshire CB6 3XA
Tel: 01353 740821; Fax 741721
www.hereward.books@dial.pipex.com

John Scott (Sporting Books)
The Beeches
Wynniatts Way
Abberley, Worcester WR6 6BZ
Tel: 01299 896779

PERIODICALS
Shooting Times
IPC Magazines Ltd.
King's Reach Tower
Stamford Street
London SE1 9LS
Tel: 020 7261 5000

Sporting Gun as above

Clayshooting
4 Fordbrook Business Centre
Marlborough Road
Pewsey
Wiltshire SN9 5NU
Tel: 01672 64299
www.clubclayshooting.com

Shotgun Sports (USA)
PO Box 6810, Auburn
California 95604
USA
Tel: 001916 889 2220
www.shotgunsportsmagazine.com

Sporting Clays (USA)
5211 South Washington Avenue
Titusville
Florida 32780
USA
Tel: 001407 268 5010

SHOOTING CONSULTANCY
Michael Yardley
The Old Bakehouse
Brightlingsea
Colchester
CO7 0BG
Tel: 01206 306740 Mobile: 07860 401068
e-mail: yardleypen@aol

VIDEO SUPPLIERS
Video Excel Productions (for my *Positive Shooting*
video)
5 Parson's Hill
Colchester
Essex CO3 4DT
Tel: 01206 564144

FIRST AID COURSES
St John's Ambulance National Headquarters
1 Grosvenor Crescent
London SW1X 7EF
020 7235 5231

The British Red Cross
9 Grosvenor Crescent
London SW1X 7EJ
020 7235-5454

Bibliography

Adams, Cyril, and Bradon, Robert, *Lock, Stock and Barrel*, Safari Press, Longbeach, CA, 1996. The Sportman's Press, London.

Akehurst, R., *Game Guns and Rifles*, 1969. The Sportsman's Press, London, 1992.

Andersson, Stellan & Akerman, Jan, *The Practical Gun*, Queen Anne Press London, 1986.

Anon., *An Essay on Shooting*, Grueber & McAllister, Dublin 1789, facsimile edn, intro by W.S.Curtis, Richmond Publishing Co. Ltd., Richmond, Surrey, 1975.

Anon., *Notes on Shooting*, 9th edition, Curtis's & Harvey Ltd, London, 1915.

Arnold, Richard, *The Shooters Handbook*, revised edn, Nicholas Kaye Ltd, London, 1965.

Automatic and Repeating Shotguns, revised edn, Kaye & Ward Ltd, London, 1976.

Pigeon Shooting, revised edn, Kaye & Ward Ltd, London, 1979.

Clay Pigeon Shooting, Kaye & Ward Ltd, London, 1973.

Arthur, R., *The Shotgun Stock*, A.S.Barnes & Co., New York, 1971.

Askins, Col Charles Sen., *Wing and Trapshooting*, Outdoor Life, New York, 1922.

Askins, Maj.Charles, *Wing and Trapshooting*, Macmillan, New York, 1948.

Askins, Col Charles Jnr, *The Shotgunners Book*, Stackpole and Company, New York 1958.

Askins, Charles, *The American Shotgun*, 1910, facsimile edn, Wolfe Publishing Inc., Prescott, AR, 1987.

Association of Clay Target Shooting Grounds, *Clay Target Shooting: An Introductory Guide*, Brunton Business Publications, Andover, Hampshire, c.1997.

Atwill, Lionel, *Sporting Clays*, An Orvis Guide, The Atlantic Monthly Press, New York, 1990.

Austyn, Christopher, *Modern Sporting Guns*, The Sportsman's Press, London 1994.

Badminton Magazine, The, edited by Alfred E. T. Watson, vol.3 (July-Dec.1896), Longmans, Green & Co., London, 1896.

Baekland, George, *Gunner's Guide*, The MacMillan Co., New York, 1948.

Barclay, Edgar Norman, *Shooting for Beginners*, The Shooting Times Library no.3, Percival Marshall & Co., London, 1963.

Barker, A.J., *Shotguns and Shooting*, Paladin Press, Boulder, Colorado, 1973.

Barnes, Frank C., *Cartridges of the World*, 5th revised edn, DBI Books Inc., Northbrook, IL, 1985.

Cartridges of the World, 7th revised and expanded edn, DBI Books Inc., Northbrook, IL, 1993.

Barnes, Mike, *The Game Shot*, The Crowood Press, Marlborough, Wiltshire, 1993, (first published 1988.

Barnes, Mike, compiler, *The Complete Clayshot*, David & Charles, Newton Abbot, Devon, 1993.

BASC (British Association for Shooting & Conservation), *Handbook of Shooting: The Sporting Shotgun*, revised edn, Pelham Books, London, 1989.

Batley, John, *The Pigeon Shooter: A Complete Guide to Modern Pigeon Shooting*, Swan Hill Press, Shrewsbury, 1996.

Beaumont, Richard, *Purdey's: The Guns and the Family*, David & Charles, Newton Abbot, 1984.

Bentley, Paul, *Clay Target Shooting*, A. & C. Black Ltd, London, 1987.

Competitive Clay Target Shooting, A. & C. Black Ltd, London, 1991.

Clay Shooting with The Experts, B.T. Batsford Ltd, London, 1994.

Bidwell, John, and Robin Scott, *Move: Mount: Shoot*, The Crowood Press, Marlborough, Wiltshire, 1990.

'Blagdon', *Shooting*, Cogswell & Harrison, London, 1900.

Blaines, *Rural Sports*, third edition, Longman, London, 1858.

Blair, Claude, *Pollard's History of Firearms*, Country Life Books, London, 1983.

Blatt, Art, *The Gun Digest Book of Trap & Skeet Shooting*, DBI Books Inc., Northfield IL, 1984.

The Gun Digest Book of Trap & Skeet Shooting, second edition, DBI Books Inc., Northbrook [sic], IL, 1989.

Bogardus, Adam H., *Field Cover and Trap Shooting*, Orange Judd Co., New York, 1879.

Field Cover and Trap Shooting, New York, 1879; facsimile edition, Wolfe Publishing Co. Inc., Prescott, AR, 1987.

Boothroyd, Geoffrey, *The Shotgun: History and Development*, A.& C.Black, London, 1985.

Shotguns and Gunsmiths: the Vintage Years, A. & C. Black Publishers Ltd, London, 1986.

Sidelocks and Boxlocks: The Classic British Shotguns, Sandlake Press, Amity, OR, 1991. Safari Press, Longbeach, CA and The Sportsman's Press, London, 1998.

Boothroyd, Geoffrey, and Susan Boothroyd, *Boothroyds' Revised Directory of British Gunmakers*, Sandlake Press, Amity, OR, 1997. Safari Press, Longbeach CA and The Sportsman's Press, London 1999..

The British Over-and-Under Shotgun, The Sportsman's Press, London, 1996.

Bowen, Bruce, *The Orvis Wing-Shooting Handbook*, Lyons & Burford, New York, 1985.

Brander, Michael, *The Game Shot's Vade Mecum*, Adam & Charles Black, London, 1965.

A Concise Guide to Game Shooting, revised edn, The Sportsman's Press, London) 1988, originally published as *The Game Shot's Vade Mecum*.

Brander, Michael, ed, *The International Encyclopedia of Shooting*, Pelham Books Ltd, London, 1972.

Braun, Lee D., *Trap Shooting*, second printing, Benjamin Company, 1975

Skeet Shooting, third printing, Benjamin Company, 1979

Brindle, J., *Shotguns and Shooting*, Nimrod Book Services, 1984.

Brister, Bob, *Shotgunning: The Art and the Science*, Winchester Press, Tulsa OK, 1976.

British Proof Authorities, *Notes on the Proof of Shotguns & Other Small Arms*, 5th edn, London and Birmingham, November 1993.

British Shooting Sports Council (BSSC), *Shotgun Shooting*, Know The Game (KTG) Series, 5th edn, E.P. Publishing Ltd, Wakefield, Yorkshire, 1978.

Shotgun Shooting, Know the Game (KTG) Series, 6th edition, A. & C. Black Ltd, London, 1987.

Brown, Nigel, *London Gunmakers*, Christie, Manson & Woods Ltd, London, 1998.

Browne, Bellmore H., *Guns and Gunning*, J.Stevens Arms and Tool Co., Chicopee Falls, Mass., 1908

Browning, John, and Curt Gentry, *J.M.Browning: American Gunmaker*, Browning, Ogden, Utah, 1982.

Broomfield, B., & C. Cradock, *Shotguns on Test*, 1980.

Burrard, Maj. Sir Gerald, Bt., *In the Gunroom*, Herbert Jenkins, London, 1930.

The Modern Shotgun: Volume II The Cartridge, 3rd edn, facsimile edn, 3 vols, Ashford Press Publishing, Southampton, Hampshire, 1985.

The Identification of Firearms and Forensic Ballistics, 3rd edn, Herbert Jenkins Ltd, London, 1956.

Butler, David F., *The American Shotgun*, Lyman Publications, Middlefield, CT, 1973.

The American Shotgun, Galahad Books, New York, 1973.

Buxton, Aubrey, *The King in His Country*, Longmans, Green & Co. Ltd, London, 1955.

Cadman, A., *Shouldergunning for Duck*, The Shooting Times Library no.6, Percival Marshall & Co., London, 1963.

Campbell, Robert (ed), *Trap Shooting*, Rutledge Books and the Benjamin Co. Inc., New York, 1975.

Trapshooting with D.Lee Braun, Remington Sportsmen's Library, The Benjamin Co. Inc., New York, 1969.

Skeet Shooting with D.Lee Braun and The Remington Pros, Remington Sportsmen's Library, The Benjamin Co. Inc. , New York, 1974.

Carlisle, Dan, and, Dolph Adams, *Taking More Birds: A Practical Guide to Greater Success at Sporting Clays and Wing Shooting*, Lyons & Burford, New York, 1993.

Carlisle, G.L., *Grouse and Gun*, Stanley Paul & Co. Ltd, London, 1983.

Casin, Jean-Francois, *La nouvelle reglementation des armes*, Les Armes en France Series, Gerfaut, Paris, 1995.

Chalmers, Patrick, *The Shooting-Man's England*, The English Scene Series, vol. I, Seeley Service & Co. Ltd, London, 1936.

Chapel, Charles Edward, *Field, Skeet and Trap Shooting*, revised edn, A.S. Barnes & Co. Inc., New York, 1962.

Chapel, Charles Edward, *Field, Skeet and Trap Shooting*, Chapman & Hall Ltd, London, 1950.

Chenevix Trench, Charles, *The Poacher and The Squire*, Longmans, Green & Co. Ltd, London, 1967.

A History of Marksmanship, Longman, London, 1972.

The Shooter and His Gun, Countrywise Books, London, 1969.

Christian, Chris, *The Gun Digest Book of Trap & Skeet Shooting*, third edition, DBI Books Inc, Northbrook IL, MCMXCIV.

Churchill Ltd, E.J., *Some Notes on Churchill Best Guns*, London, 1922.

Churchill, Robert, *How to Shoot: Some Lessons in the Science of Shot Gun Shooting*, Geoffrey Bles, London, 1925.

How to Shoot: Some Lessons in the Science of Shot Gun Shooting, 4th edn, Geoffrey Bles. London, 1932.

How to Shoot: Some Lessons in the Science of Shot Gun Shooting, The Sportsman's Press, London, 1988.

Game Shooting, Michael Joseph Ltd, London, 1955.

Game Shooting, 5th edition by MacDonald Hastings, Michael Joseph Ltd, London, 1963.

Clay Pigeon Shooting Association, *Safety Officers Manual*, CPSA, Corby, Northamptonshire, c.1998

Senior Coaches Handbook, CPSA Buckhurst Hill, Essex, 1990.

Come Clay Pigeon Shooting with the CPSA, no.1, issue 5, CPSA, Buckhurst Hill, Essex, 1989; March 1999.

How to Run Small Shoots, no.2, issue 1, CPSA, Corby, Northants, reprint Feb 1999.

How to Form a Clay Pigeon Shooting Club, no.3, issue 2, CPSA, Corby, Northants, reprint April 1999.

The CPSA Safety Guide, no.4, issue 9, CPSA, Buckhurst Hill, Essex, January 1994; and April 1999.

CPSA General Rules and Regulations, no.5, issue 2, CPSA, Corby, Northants, May 1999.

Shotguns and the Law, no.6., issue 4, CPSA, Corby, Northants., March 1994; and issue 5, reprint April 1999.

Rules and Regulations for Down The Line, no.8, issue 3, CPSA, Corby, Northants, reprint May 1999.

Rules and Regulations for English Skeet and Skeet Doubles, no.9, CPSA, Buckhurst Hill, Essex, August 1994.

Rules and Regulations For Sporting, no.10, issue 7, CPSA, Buckhurst Hill, Essex, 1993.

Rules and Regulations: Automatic Ball Trap, no.11, issue 5, CPSA, Corby, Northamptonshire, reprint March 1999.

Rules and Regulations for Universal Trench, no.14, CPSA, Buckhurst Hill, Essex, c.1997.

Coats, Archie, *Pigeon Shooting*, 2nd edn, André Deutsch Ltd, London, 1986.

Coles, Charles, ed, *Shooting and Stalking*, Stanley Paul, London, 1983.

Cooley, Graham and John Newton, *Cogswell & Harrison: Two Centuries of Gunmaking*, Sportsman's Press, London, 2000.

Conley, Frank F., *The American Single Barrel Shotgun*, Frank F. Conley, Carmel Valley, CA, 1989.

Cox, Nicholas, *The Gentlemen's Recreation*, J.C., London, 1677; facsimile edn, E.P. Publishing Ltd, Wakefield, Yorkshire, 1973.

Cradock, Chris, *Cradock on Shotguns*, B.T.Batsford Ltd, London, 1989.
A Manual of Clayshooting, revised edn, B.T.Batsford Ltd, London, 1988.

Croft, Peter, *Clay Shooting*, Ward Lock, London 1991.

Curtis, Capt. Paul A., *Guns and Gunning*, Alfred A. Knopf, New York, 1946.

Crudgington, I.M and D.J. Baker, *The British Shotgun, vol.1 (1850-1870)*, Barrie & Jenkins Ltd, London, 1979.
The British Shotgun, vol.2 (1871-1890), Ashford Buchan & Enright, Leatherhead, Surrey, 1992.

Dallas, Donald, *Boss & Co.: Builders of Best Guns Only*, Quiller Press, London, 1995.
Purdey Gun and Rifle Makers: The Definitive History, Quiller, London, 2000.

Davies, Ken, *The Better Shot*, Quiller Press, London, 1992.

Dawson, Maj. Kenneth, *Son of a Gun*, Country Life Ltd, London, 1929.

Digweed, George and Richard Rawlingson, *It's Got to Be Perfect: the George Digweed Story*, Brunton Business Publications Ltd, Andover, Hampshire, 1996.

Dobson, W., *Kunopaedia. The Art of Shooting Flying*, 1817.

Dougall, James Dalziel, *Shooting Simplified*, second edition, Robert Hardwicke, London, MDC-CCLXV.

Downing, Graham, *Shooting for Beginners: An Introduction to the Sport*, Swan Hill Press, Shrewsbury, 1996.

Drought, Capt. J.B., *A Shot in the Making*, Herbert Jenkins Ltd, London, 1937.

'East Sussex', *The Shotgun and its Uses*, Simpkin, Marshall, Hamilton, Kent & Co. Ltd, London, 1914.

Eley, *Layouts for Clay Target Shooting*, 1971.
Sporting Clays, 1964.

Eley and M. Rose, *Shooting Technique*, 1978.

Elliot, A. & G., *Gun Fun and Hints*, 1946.

'Emjy', *The American Gunmaker: John M. Browning*, Fabrique Nationale, Herstal, Belgium, 1978.

Etchen, Fred, *Commonsense Shotgun Shooting*, Standard Publications Inc., Huntington, West Virginia, 1946.

Eton, D.H., *Trap Shooting: The Patriotic Sport*, revised edn, Sportsman's Review Publishing Co., Cincinnati, 1920.

Expert, *Notes on Shooting*, 1915.

Fletcher, Henry, *Come and Shoot: An Introduction to British Game Bird Shooting*, The Sporting Scene Series, Museum Press Ltd, London, 1951.

Fletcher, John and Philip Upton, *Shooting Magazine: Introduction to Clay Shooting*, Argus Books, London, 1987

Forehand, Ray, *Advanced Competition Shooting*, ReadMe Publications, Dallas, 2000

Francotte, Auguste and Claude Gaier, *FN-Browning 100 Years of Sport and Military Firearms*, Didier Hatier, Brussels, 1989.

Frankland, Sir Thomas, Bt., *Cautions to Young Sportsmen*, 2nd edn, James Robson, London, 1801.

Frost, David, *Sporting Firearms and The Law*, 4th edn, British Field Sports Society, London, 1995.

Garnam, Peter, *Shotguns*, Field Sports Hand Books, Vista Books, London, 1963.

Garner, P., *Shotguns*, 1963.

Garnier Ruffer, Jonathan, *The Big Shots: Edwardian Shooting Parties*, Debrett's Peerage Ltd, Tisbury, Wiltshire, c.1977.

George, J.M., *English Guns and Rifles*, Small-Arms Technical Publishing Co., Plantersville, South Carolina, 1947.

George, Mike, *Gun Safety*, Sporting Gun/EMAP Pursuit Publishing Ltd, Peterborough, 1988.

'Gough Thomas' (G.T.Garwood), *Gun Book*, A. & C. Black, London, 1969.
Shooting Facts and Fancies, Adam and Charles Black, London, 1978.
Shotguns and Cartridges, The Shooting Times Library no.1Percival Marshall & Co., London, 1963.
Shotguns and Cartridges for Game and Clays, Adam and Charles Black, London, 1970.
Shotguns and Cartridges for Game and Clays, 5th edn, edited by Nigel Brown, Adam and Charles Black, London, 1990.

Govett, L.A., *The King's Book of Sports*, Elliot Stock, London, 1890.

Greener, Graham, *The Greener Story*, Quiller, London, 2000.

Greener, W. W., *Sharpshooting for Sport and War*, R. A. Everett & Co., London, 1900.
Modern Breech-Loaders 1871, Cassell, Petter & Galpin, London; facsimile edn, Greenhill Books, Lionel Leventhal Ltd, London, 1985.
The Breechloader and How to Use it, 1892; and 1905.
The Gun and its Development, 5th edn, Cassell & Company Ltd, London 1892; 9th edn 1910.
Choke-Bore Guns, Cassell, Peter and Galpin, London

Grennell, Dean A., *The ABC's of Reloading*, second edition, DBI Book, Northfield, ILL.

Gunmakers Company, The, and the Guardians of the Birmingham Proof House, *Rules of Proof*, 1954.

Gunmakers of the City of London, the Joint Authority of the Worshipful Company of, and the Guardians of the Birmingham Proof House, *Notes on the Proof of Shotguns and Other Small Arms*, 1960; 1976; 1981.

Gunmark Ltd, *A Guide to Good Shooting*, Fareham, Hampshire, c.1990.

Hammond, S.T., *Hitting vs. Missing*, 2nd edn, Forest and Stream Publishing Co., New York, 1900.

Harris, Clive, ed, *The History of the Birmingham Gun-Barrel Proof House*, 2nd edn, Guardians of the Birmingham Proof House, Birmingham, 1949.

Harrison, E., *A Dissertation Upon Guns and Shooting*, Cogswell & Harrison, London, 1906.

Hartman, Barney, *Hartman on Skeet*, McClelland & Stewart Ltd, Toronto, 1973.

Hastings, MacDonald, *The Other Mr. Churchill*, Harrap, London, l963.

English Sporting Guns and Accessories, Ward Lock & Co. Ltd, London, 1969.

Churchill's Game Shooting, 5h revised edn, Michael Joseph Ltd, London, 1975.

The Shotgun, David & Charles, Newton Abbot, Devon, 1981.

Shooting - Why We Miss, Pelham Books, London 1976.

Hawker, Lt Col Peter, *Instructions to Young Sportsmen*, 8th edn, Longman, Orme, Green & Longmans, London, 1838.

Instructions to Young Sportsmen, Herbert Jenkins Ltd, London, 1922.

Instructions to Young Sportsmen, facsimile edition, The Field Library, Ashford Press Publishing, Southampton, Hampshire, 1986.

Hawker, Col P., *The Diary of Col.Peter Hawker 1802-1853*, Richmond Publishing Company, 1975 (reprint of 1893 edn).

Hearne, A., *Shooting and Gunfitting*, Herbert Jenkins, London, 1946.

Hinman, Bob, *The Golden Age of Shotgunning*, Wolfe Publishing Co., Prescott, Arizona, 1982. (Cradock used 1971 edn)

Hoare, Tony, *Successful Clay Pigeon Shooting*, The Crowood Press Marlborough, Wiltshire, 1991.

Hobson, J.C. Jeremy, *What Every Gun Should Know*, David & Charles plc, Newton Abbot, Devon

Hughes, Steven Dodd, *Fine Gunmaking: Double Shotguns*, Krause Publications, Iola, WI, 1998.

Hutchinson, Horace G., ed, *Shooting*, The *Country Life* Library of Sport, vol.1, George Newnes Ltd for *Country Life*), MCMIII.

ICI, *The Stringing of shot*, 1926.

Skeet, 1934.

Irvine Robinson, John, *Random Shots: An Anthology from the First 50 Years of the Shooting Times*, Pelham Books/Stephen Green Press, London, 1990.

Jackson, Anthony, *So You Want To Go Shooting*, Arlington Books Ltd, London, 1974.

Jackson, Tony, *Classic Game Shooting*, Ashford, Southampton, Hampshire, 1990.

Jarett, Alan, *Shooting at Clays*, Stanley Paul, London, 1991.

Jennings, Mike, *Instinct Shooting*, Dodd Mead & Co., New York, 1959.

Johnson, Derek, *Victorian Shooting Days*, Boydell Press, Woodbridge, Suffolk, 1981.

Johnson, L.W. 'Bill', *et al.*, *Outdoor Tips*, A Remington Sportsmen's Library Book, The Benjamin Co.Inc./Rutledge Books Inc., New York, 1972.

Jones, Owen, *The Sport of Shooting*, 2nd edn, Edward Arnold & Co., London, 1928.

Keith, Elmer, *Shotguns*, Stackpole Co, Harrisburg, PA, 1950; facsimile edn, Wolfe Publishing Co.Inc., Prescott, AR, 1988.

Keith, Elmer, *Shotguns*, Stackpole Co., Harrisburg, PA, 1950.

Kemp, Martin, *Shooting Game*, A. & C. Black Ltd, London, 1972

Kennedy, Monty, *Checkering and Carving Gunstocks*, 2nd edn, ed Thomas G. Samworth, The Stackpole Co., Harrisburg PA, 1977.

King, John, *Clay Pigeon Shooting*, The Sportsman's Press, London, 1991.

King, Peter, *The Shooting Field: One Hundred and Fifty Years with Holland & Holland*, Quiller Press Ltd, London, MCMLXXXV.

Knight, Richard Alden, *Mastering the Shotgun*, revised edn, ed by Bob Bell, E.P. Dutton & Co. Inc., New York, 1975.

Kynoch Ltd., *Shooting Notes and Comments*, Birmingham, 1910.

Labisky, Wallace, ed, *Shotguns and Ballistics*, premier issue no.1, Clearview Products Inc, Oklahoma City, OK, c.1995.

Lancaster, Charles (A.A. Thorn), *The Art of Shooting*, 1889, 14th facsimile edition, with preface by Fred Butler,The Field Library, Ashford Press Publishing, Shedfield, Hampshire, 1985.

The Art of Shooting, 13th edition, McCorquodale & Co. Ltd, London, 1962.

Laycock, George, *The Shotgunner's Bible*, revised edition, Doubleday, New York, 1987.

Leffingwell, William Bruce, *The Art of Wing Shooting*, Rand, McNally & Co., Chicago 1895.

Lewis, Jack, and Steve Comus, *The Gun Digest Book of Sporting Clays*, DBI Books Inc, Northbrook, IL, MCMXCI.

Lewis, Jack, *Gun Digest Book of Modern Gun Values*, 4th edition, DBI Books Inc., Northfield, IL, MCMLXXXIII.

Lind, E., *Complete Book of Trick and Fancy Shooting*, Winchester Press, 1972

Linn, John R. and Stephen A. Blumenthal, *Finding the Extra Target*, Shotgun Sports Magazine Book, Shotgun Sports Inc., Auburn, CA, 1989.

Lippard, Karl C., *Perazzi Shotguns*, Vietnam Marine Publications, Colorado Springs, CO, 1994.

Little, Crawford, *Pheasant Shooting*, Unwin Hyman Ltd, London, 1989.

Little, Frank, *The Little Trapshooting Book*, Shooting Sports Magazine Book, Further Adventures Inc., Auburn CA, 1994.

Long, W.H.T. ('Scolopax'), *The Gun in the Field*, Robert Hale Ltd, London, 1948.

Lonsdale Library, *Shooting*, 1929.

McIntosh, Michael, *Best Guns*, Countrysport Press, New Albany, OH, 1989.

McFarland, F.M., *Clay Pigeon Shooting*, The Shooting Times Library no.16, Percival Marshall & Co., London, 1964.

Madis, George, *Browning: Date of Manufacture*, Browning, Brownsboro, TX, 1988.

Marchington, J., *The Complete Shot*, 1981.

Marchington, John, *The History of Wildfowling*, A. & C. Black, London, 1980.

Shooting: a Complete Guide for Beginners, Faber & Faber Ltd, London, 1982.

Marshall-Ball, Robin, *Sporting Shotgun*, Saiga Publishing Co. Ltd, Hindhead, Surrey, 1981.

The Encyclopaedia of Sporting Shooting, B.T. Batsford Ltd, London, 1992.

'Marksman', *The Dead Shot*, 4th edition, Longmans Green & Co., London, 1866.

The Dead Shot, 7th edition, Longmans Green & Co., London, 1896.

Meyer, Jerry, *The Sporting Clays Handbook*, Lyons & Burford, New York, 1990.

Migdalski, E., *Clay Target Games*, 1978.

Migdalski, Tom, *The Complete Book of Shotgunning Games*, Masters Press, Indianapolis, IN, 1997.

Mills, Desmond and Mike Barnes, *Amateur Gunsmithing*, Boydell Press, Woodbridge, Suffolk, 1986.

Missildine, Fred with Nick Karas, *Score Better at Trap*, Winchester Press, New York, 1971.

Score Better at Skeet, Winchester Press, New York, 1972.

Score Better at Trap and Skeet, Winchester Press, New York, 1971.

Montague, A., *Successful Shotgun Shooting*, Winchester Press, New York, 1971.

Moreton, Dave, ed, *Gun Talk: Practical Advice about every Aspect of the Shooting Sports from America's Greatest Gun Writers*, Winchester Press, New York, 1973.

Morin, Marco and Robert Held, *Beretta*, Acquafresca Editrice, Chiasso, Switzerland, 1980.

National Skeet Shooting Association, *BB Fliers: BB Gun Moving Target Program*, NSSA/National Sporting Clays Association, San Antonio, TX, 1993.

Nicholls, Bob, *Skeet and How to Shoot It*, Putnams, New York, 1947.

The Shotgunner, GP Putnams Sons, New York, 1949.

Nichols, J.C.M., *Shooting Ways and Shooting Days*, Herbert Jenkins, London, 1944

Nickerson, Joseph, *A Shooting Man's Creed*, Sidgwick & Jackson Ltd, London, 1989.

Nobel Industries, *The Versatile Clay Bird*, 1921.

Nobel Industries Ltd, *The Handbook of Clay Target Shooting*, Nobel Industries Ltd, London, 1927.

Oberfell, George G. and Charles E. Thompson, *The Mysteries of Shotgun Patterns*, Oklahoma State University Press, Stillwater OK, 1957.

O'Connor, Jack, *Complete Book of Shooting*, Outdoor Life, New York, 1965.

The Shotgun Book, Alfred A. Knopf, New York, 1973.

The Shotgun Book, 2nd revised edn, Alfred A. Knopf Inc., New York, 1978,

Ohye, Kay, *You and The Target*, 2nd edn, The Scattergun Press, Austin TX, 1987.

Page, Thomas, *The Art of Shooting Flying*, fourth edition, Scotcherd and Whitaker Norwich, 1785 (1st edn 1766).

Parker, Eric *et al.*, *Shooting by Moor, Field and Shore*, Seeley, Service & Co. Ltd, London, 1929.

Parker, Eric, *Elements of Shooting*, The Field Press Ltd, London, 1924.

Payne-Gallwey, R. and A.J. Stuart-Wortley, *Shooting*, Badminton Library, London, 1885.

Payne-Gallwey, R., *The Holland and Holland Shooting School*, Badminton Magazine, London, 1896.

High Pheasants in Theory and Practice, Longmans Green & Co., London, 1913; also facsimile edns: The Richmond Publishing Co.Ltd, Richmond, Surrey, 1970, 1972, 1976; Nimrod Press, 1985; and Sporting Books Specialists, new foreword by John Richards, 1996.

Letters to Young Shooters, Longmans Green & Co., London,1895.

Peterson, Harold L., ed, *Encyclopaedia of Firearms*, The Connoisseur, London, 1964.

The Book of the Gun, The Hamlyn Publishing Group Ltd, London, 1968.

Pollard, Maj. Hugh B.C., *Shotguns*, Sir Isaac Pitman & Sons Ltd, London, 1923.

Powell, R.F. and M.R. Forrest, *Noise in the Military Environment*, Brassey's Defence Publishers, London, 1988.

Purdey, James, & Sons Ltd, *Purdey Guns, Instructions*, limited edition, London, 1929.

Purdey, T.D.S. and Capt. J.A. Purdey, *The Shot Gun*, The Sportsman's Library, Adam & Charles Black, London, 1938.

'Purple Heather', *Something about Guns and Shooting*, Alexander & Shepherd, London, 1891.

Raymont, Michael and Colin Jones, *Modern Clay Pigeon Shooting*, Chancery House Publishing Co., London, 1974.

Remington, *Illustrated Skeet Fundamentals*, USA, c.1951.

Remington Arms Co., *How to Start a Shooting Sports Program*, Outdoor Empire Publishing, Seattle, WA, 1977.

Reynolds, Mike with Mike Barnes, *Shooting Made Easy*, The Crowood Press, Marlborough, Wiltshire, 1989.

Roads, Christopher, *The Gun*, BBC, London, 1978.

Rose, Michael, *Guncraft: Clay and Game Shooting*, Chancerel Publishers Ltd, London, 1978.

The Eley Book of Shooting Technique, Chancerel Publishers Ltd, London, 1978.

Rose, R.N, *The Field 1853-1953*, Michael Joseph, London, 1953.

Ruffer, John Edward Maurice, *Good Shooting*, David & Charles, Newton Abbot, Devon, 1986, based on *The Art of Good Shooting*, 2nd edn, 1976.

Ruffer, Maj. J.E.M., *The Art of Good Shooting*, David & Charles Publishers Ltd, Newton Abbot, Devon 1972.

Russell, James, *Trap Shooting Secrets*, James Russell, Eugene Oregon, 1997.

Precision Shooting, James Russell, Eugene Oregon, 1997.

Rutterford, K, *Collecting Shotgun Cartridges*, Stanley Paul, London, 1987.

Scherer, Ed, *Scherer on Skeet II*, Ed Scherer, Waukesha ,WIS 1991.

Schwing, Ned, *The Browning Superposed: John M. Browning's Last Legacy*, Krause Publications, Iola, WI, 1996.

Scott, Robert F., ed, *Shooter's Bible*, no.72, 1981 edn, Stoeger Publishing Co., South Hackensack, NJ, 1980.

Sedgwick, Noel M., *The Young Shot*, The Young Sportsman's Library, 2nd edn, A. & C. Black Ltd, London, 1961.

By Covert, Field and Marsh, Herbert Jenkins Ltd, London, c.1940.

Sell, Francis E., *Sure-hit Shotgun Ways*, Stackpole Books, Harrisburg, PA, 1967.

Service, Douglas, *Introduction to Shooting*, The Beaufort Library vol.8, Seeley Service & Co. Ltd, London, 1957.

Sharp, R., *Modern Sporting Gunnery*, Simpkin, Marshall, Hamilton etc., London, 1906.

The Shooting Times Anthology, Percival Marshall & Co., London, 1963.

Shooting Sports Trust, *Buying a Shotgun*, 1981.

Smith, A.J., *Sporting Clays*, Argus Books, Hemel Hempstead, 1989.

Smith, A.J. and Tony Hoare, *A.J. Smith's Sporting Clays Masterclass*, Argus Books, Hemel Hempstead, 1991.

Smith, Lawrence B., *Modern Shotgun Shooting*, Charles Scribner's Sons, New York, 1935.

Better Trap Shooting, E.P. Dutton Inc., New York, 1931.

Shotgun Psychology, Charles Scribner's Sons, New York, 1938.

Smith, Steve and Laurie Morrow, *The Italian Gun*, Wilderness Adventures Press, Gallatin, MT, 1997.

Spearing, G.W., *The Craft of the Gunsmith*, Javelin Books, London, 1988.

The Craft of the Gunsmith, Blandford Press, Poole, Dorset, 1986.

Sporting Arms, *Handbook on Shotgun Shooting*, 1940.

Sprake, Leslie ('Middle Wallop'), *The Art of Shooting and Rough Shoot Management*, H.F.& G.Witherby, London, 1930.

Stack, R., *The Shotgun Digest*, Follet Publishing Co., Northfield IL,1974.

Stadt, Ronald W., *Winchester: Shotguns and Shotshells*, Armory Publications, Tacoma, WA, 1984.

Stanbury, Percy and G.L. Carlisle, *Shotgun Marksmanship*, 4th edn, Stanley Paul & Co. Ltd, London, 1986.

Clay Pigeon Marksmanship, 3rd edn, Herbert Jenkins Ltd, London, 1978.

Clay Pigeon Marksmanship, 3d edn, Barrie & Jenkins Ltd, London, 1982 (with some updating).

Shotgun and Shooter, Barrie & Jenkins Ltd, London, 1970.

Stevenson, Jan and Michael Yardley, eds, *The Firearms (Amendment) Bill: A Research Report*, 2nd edn, Piedmont Publishing Ltd, London, 1988.

Stevenson, Jan (chief author), *Modern Sporting Guns*, Salamander Books Ltd, London 1988.

Stewart, Jackie with Mike Barnes, *The Jackie Stewart Book of Shooting*, Harper Collins Publishers, London, 1991.

'Stonehenge', *The Shot-Gun and Sporting Rifle*, Routledge, Warne & Routledge, London, 1859, revised facsimile edn, The Border Press, Brecon, Powys, 1994.

Teach Yourself Shooting, London (Cogswell & Harrison Ltd.), 1970.

Teasdale-Buckell, G.T., *Experts on Guns and Shooting*, 1900, facsimile edn, Ashford Press Publishing, Hants, 1986.

The Complete Shot, second edition, Methuen & Co., London, 1907.

Tennyson, Julian, ed by Peter H. Whitaker, *Rough Shooting From Month to Month*, A & C Black Ltd, London, 1965.

Thomas, B., *The Shooter's Guide*, Gale and Fenner, London, 1816; facsimile edn, The Richmond Publishing Co., Richmond, Surrey, 1971.

Thorp, Raymond W., *Doc Carver*, W. Foulsham & Co., London, 1957.

Tickner, John, *Tickner's Rough Shooting*, The Standfast Press, Saul, Gloucestershire, 1976

Tubby, Pamela, ed, *The Book of Shooting for Sport and Skill*, Frederick Muller Ltd, London, 1980.

'Twenty-Bore'('20-Bore'), *Practical Hints on Shooting*, Kegan Paul Trench & Co., London, 1887.

Venner, Dominique, *Le Livre des Armes: Carabines et Fusils de Chasse*, Jacques Grancher, Paris, 1973.

Wallack, Louis Robert, *American Shotgun Design and Performance*, Winchester Press, New York, 1977.

Walsh, J.H., ('Stonehenge'), *The Modern Sportsman's Gun and Rifle, vol.1: Game and Wildfowl Guns*, Horace Cox, London, 1882; facsimile edn, W.S. Curtis Ltd, Newport Pagnell, Buckinghamshire, 1988.

Walsingham, Lord and Ralph Payne-Gallwey, *Shooting Field and Covert*, 2nd edn, Longmans Green and Co., London, 1887.

Shooting (Moor and Marsh), Longmans, London, 1893.

Walshingham, Lord, *Hit and Miss: A Book of Shooting Memories*, Philip Allan & Co. Ltd, London, 1927.

Wentworth-Day, J., *The Modern Shooter*, Herbert Jenkins Ltd, London, 1952.

Westley Richards, *British and Best*, Westley Richards, Birmingham, c.1995.

Guns and Rifles: a Century of Gun and Rifle Manufacture 1812-1912, Birmingham, 1912; facsimile edn, Armory Publications, Oceanside, CA, 1988.

Whitaker, Peter H., *Approach to Shooting*, Burlington Publishing Co. Ltd, London, 1942.

Wilkinson, Frederick, *Small Arms*, revised edn, Ward Lock & Co. Ltd, London, 1967.

Guns, Hamlyn Publishing Group Ltd, London, 1970.

Willett, Roderick, *Gun Safety*, Arlington Books, London, 1967.

Willett, Roderick Fraser, *Modern Gameshooting*, Lonsdale Library, London, 1975.

The Good Shot, Moonraker Press, Bradford-on-Avon, 1979.

Willock, Colin, *Duck Shooting*, revised edn, André Deutsch Ltd, London, 1981.

Willock, Colin, ed, *The Farmer's Book of Field Sports*, Vista Books, London 1961.

The ABC of Shooting, London (André Deutsch Ltd.), 1975.

The New ABC of Shooting, André Deutsch Ltd, London, 1994.

Winsberger, G., *The Standard Directory of Proofmarks*, Plainsman Publishing - Canada, 1975.

Worshipful Company of Gunmakers, *A Short Account of the Worshipful Company of Gunmakers 1637-1979*, London, 1979.

Worshipful Company of Gunmakers & the Guardians of Birmingham Proof House, *Notes on the Proof of Gun Barrels*, London, 1952.

Notes on the Proof of Shotguns and Other Small Arms, London, 1981.

Yardley, Michael, *Gunfitting: The Quest for Perfection*, The Sportsman's Press, London, 1993.

Positive Shooting, The Crowood Press, Marlborough, Wiltshire, 1994.

Zutz, Don, *Modern Waterfowling Guns and Gunning*, Stoeger Publishing Co., South Hackensack, NJ, 1985.

The Double Shotgun, revised edn, Winchester Press, New York, 1985.

Shotgunning: Trend in Transition, Wolfe Publishing Co. Inc., Prescott, AR, 1989.

Shotgun Stuff, Shotgun Sports Inc., Auburn, CA, 1991.

Others

Churchill, R, *'Flicker' No.XXV* [flicker book], E.J.Churchill, London, 1930.

Eley, *A Guide to Proof Marks and Eley Cartridges*, Eley, Birmingham, c.1972.

Reloading Eley Shotgun Cartridges, no.80 Series powders, c.1975.

The Shooter's Diary, 1989-1999.

Sheffield, Jim, *Clay Coaching*, Shooting Magazine Supplement, c.1990.

Shooting Magazine, Clay Coaching, c.1990.

Yardley, Michael, *Positive Shooting, Sporting Gun Supplement*, EMAP Pursuit Publishing Ltd., Peterborough, 1992.

The Browning British Field Sports Society Good Shooting Guide, Shooting Times, London, 1995.

Psychology And Sports Science

Bassham, Lanny, *With Winning in Mind*, Xpress Publications, San Antonio, TX, 1988.

Bates, W.H., *Better Eyesight Without Glasses*, Thorsons, London, 1995.

Bull, Stephen, John Albinson, and Christopher Shambrook, *The Mental Game Plan*, Sports Dynamics, Eastbourne, 1996.

Butt, Dorcas Susan, *Psychology of Sport*, Van Nostrand Reinhold Co., New York, 1976.

Decot, Robert 'Bud', *Writings*, Decot Hy-Wyd, Phoenix, Arizona, 1996.

Edwards, Sally, *The Heart Rate Monitor Book*, Fleet Feet Press Sacramento, CA, 1994.

Gallwey, W. Timothy, *The Inner Game of Tennis*, Pan Books, London, 1975.

The Inner Game of Golf, Pan Books, London, 1981.

Geddes and Grosset, *Guide to Natural Healing*, New Lanark, Scotland, 1997

Gross, Richard D., *Psychology:The Science of Mind and Behaviour*, second revised editionHodder & Stoughton Educational, London, 1992.

Hawley, John and Louise Burke, *Peak Performance*, Allen and Unwin, St Leonards, NSW, 1998.

Jackson, Susan and Mihaly Csikszentmihalyi, *Flow in Sports*, Human Kinetics, Champaign, Illinois, 1999.

Jarvis, Martin, *Sport Psychology*, Routledge Modular Psychology Series, Routledge, London, 1999.

Kayes, Michael, *Mental Training for the Shotgun Sports*, Shotgun Sports, Auburn, California.

Liberman, Jacob, *Take Off Your Glasses and See*, Thorsons, London, 1995.

Martin, Dr Wayne F., *An Insight to Sports: Featuring Trap Shooting and Golf*, third edition, SportsVision Inc., Seattle, WA, 1987.

Natural Eyes, *Vision Training.*

Paish, Wilf, *The Complete Manual of Sports Science*, A. & C. Black Ltd, London, 1988.

Parish, Vera, *Stress Management*, Thorsons Principles of Series, Thorsons, London, 1996.

Smith, Lawrence B. 'Lon', *Shotgun Psychology*, Charles Scribner's Sons Ltd, London, 1938.

Taylor, Mark H, *Clay Target Shooting: the Mental Game*, STP Books, Touson Arizona, 1997.

Woods, Barbara, *Applying Psychology to Sport*, Hodder & Stoughton Educational, London, 1998.

Videos

Bidwell, John, *Break A Clay: An Introduction To Clay Shooting*, Sporting Scene in Association with Browning, Gerrards Cross, Berkshire, 1991.

Introduction to Shooting Sporting Clay, Sporting Scene in Association with Browning and Winchester, Gerrards Cross, Berkshire, 1993.

Brammer, Rod and Liam Dale, *Clay Coach Rive: Looper and Finale*, W.A.M. Productions, Gloucester.

Charlton, Jackie, with Major Archie Coates, *Pigeon Shooting Over Decoys*, Yorkshire Television, 1987.

Davies, Ken, *Game Shooting*, Prospectus for Holland & Holland Ltd. and *Shooting Times.*

Denny, Steve, *Shooting French Partridge*, Sporting Scene in Association with Browning at West Wycombe Shooting Ground, Gerrards Cross, Berkshire, 1991.

Instruction for the Novice Shooter, Sporting Scene in Association with Browning at West Wycombe Shooting Ground, Gerrards Cross, Berkshire, 1991.

Woodcock Shooting, Sporting Scene in Association with Browning at West Wycombe Shooting Ground, Gerrards Cross, Berkshire, 1991.

Gambore, *White Gold Final*, 1997.

White Gold & International Cup, 1996.

Gardner, Vic, *Shotgun Safety*, Apollo Films, Yelverton, Devon, 1992.

Holland & Holland, *Since 1835: The Art of Gunmaking*,

Little, Frank, *Trap Shooting Tips*, Frank Little, 1985.

Ohye, Kay, *Trap Shooting - Instructional Tape 1*, Kaye Ohye Video Productions, North Brunswick, 1985.

Trap Shooting: Instructional Tape 2, Kaye Ohye Video Productions, North Brunswick, 1985.

Simpson, Barry and Brian Hebditch, *Sporting Clays*, Gunmark Ltd, Fareham, Hampshire

W.A.M. Productions, *The Game Shoot: Driven Pheasant on a Devon Estate*, Hyperactive Films Ltd.

Yardley, Michael, *Positive Shooting*, Video Excel, Colchester, Essex, 1993.

Safe Shooting, Hyperactive Films Ltd. in Association with the British Field Sports Society and Browning, Lydney, Gloucestershire, 1994.

Start Shooting, Hyperactive Films Ltd, Lydney, Gloucestershire, 1994.

Shooting: the Sport, the Facts, Video Excel, Colchester, Essex, 1996.

Index